Palms
IN AUSTRALIA

Front cover illustrations:
Top: *Veitchia joannis* fruit
Left: Fan Palm *Licuala grandis*
Top right: Chilean Wine Palm *Jubaea chilensis*
Bottom right: Date Palm *Phoenix dactylifera*
Back cover:
Blue Hesper Palm *Brahea armata*
Royal Botanic Gardens, Melbourne.

First published 1984
REED BOOKS PTY LTD
2 Aquatic Drive Frenchs Forest NSW 2086

Text copyright David Jones
Photographs copyright Bruce Gray and David Jones

National Library of Australia
Cataloguing-in-Publication data

Jones, D. L. (David Lloyd), 1944-
Palms in Australia.
Bibliography.
Includes index.
ISBN 0 7301 0007 3.
1. Palms – Australia. I. Gray, B. (Bruce).
II. Title.
584'.5'0994

Edited by Jutta Sieverding
Designed by Warren Penney
Set by Walter Deblaere & Associates
Printed and bound in Hong Kong

Palms
IN AUSTRALIA

David Jones

photography Bruce Gray and David Jones

REED

FOREWORD

There has been a great increase in popular interest in palms in the tropics and subtropics in recent years. Much of this increase can be attributed to the activities of the international, American-based Palm Society. Through the Society's Seed Bank, seeds of often rare, little-known or new palms have been dispersed to Botanic Gardens and private collections throughout the warmer parts of the world. Nowhere is the increase in popularity greater than in Australia. Unfortunately few books are available that give cultural information on palms, especially on recent introductions. David Jones's *Palms in Australia* provides a wealth of cultural detail for palms, presented with a background of basic palm natural history in a form likely to be of great value to the amateur grower. This is a very welcome addition to the small library of books for amateur palm enthusiasts – a work which should also be of interest to growers outside Australia.

John Dransfield
Royal Botanic Gardens
Kew,
United Kingdom

DEDICATION

To Barbara Jones and Joy Gray for their help and understanding, also to our children Sandra and Timothy Jones and Lynette, Caren and Narelle Gray.

Contents

ACKNOWLEDGEMENTS

A book of this size would not be possible without the help of many people and to them we would like to extend our sincere thanks.

Firstly we would like to thank Barbara Jones for competently handling the onerous and finicky chore of typing the manuscript. Without her cheerful help the project would not have gone ahead.

In particular, we would like to thank Tony Irvine from Division of Forest Research, CSIRO, Atherton, for tremendous assistance with the Australian native palms. He read that section of the manuscript and provided much information on rare and unusual species. We are also very grateful to Dr. John Dransfield of Kew Gardens, England for writing the foreword, critically reading the text and also for providing many excellent black and white photographs.

Clyde Dunlop helped with much useful material on palms of the Northern Territory and Kimberley region of Western Australia.

Special mention must be made of John Bolger, who together with John Leaver, painstakingly checked through the manuscript and as well introduced us to a number of palm enthusiasts and their collections.

Many palm growers offered tremendous encouragement for the project. To these people we say thanks and hope that the final product is up to their expectations. They include Bill Snewyn, Dennis Hundscheidt, Stan and Jane Walkley, Rolf Kyburz, Len Butt, Vince Winkle, George Brown, Dusan Bulint and Bernard Trefau.

Peter Hind introduced us to the palm collection of the Royal Botanic Gardens, Sydney and critically read the first draft of the manuscript, offering many corrections and adjustment.

Peter Jones provided practical information on the cultivation of palms in subtropical regions.

Jim Hutchinson helped with useful material on the tissue culture of palms and David Beardsell assisted with scientific material. Thanks are due to Ted Fenner for permission to use his published work on Palm Leaf Beetle and for commenting on that part of the manuscript.

Additional colour photographs for the book were provided by Dennis Hundscheidt, Rolf Kyburz, Chris Goudey, Trevor Blake, Clyde Dunlop, Jim Willis, Tony Irvine and David Beardsell. Some black and white photographs were also provided by *Your Garden* magazine.

For the list of palms growing in various botanical and municipal gardens we thank the directors, town clerks and superintendents involved.

Preface

The initial idea of writing a book on palms revolved around a simple picture production which would enable people to identify these majestic plants more readily. Hours of searching in bookshops and book lists however revealed to me the dearth of horticultural literature on this group of plants and convinced me that an autoritative publication was called for. I hope that need is satisfied by this book.

Palms are currently undergoing a world-wide popularity boom that is being fanned by an ever-increasing group of enthusiasts continually on the lookout for promising new species. This activity is obvious in Australia and to a lesser extent New Zealand, and is particularly evident in the tropics and subtropics but should also be encouraged in temperate zones where there are many suitable species awaiting introduction.

Information on Australian native palms has been difficult to obtain since no popular publication is available and one must search through old or scant scientific texts. This book fills the long-standing gap since all of the native species are included. Their coverage has been more comprehensive and detailed than for the exotic species.

As well as native palms the book discusses all popular exotic species that are grown in Australia and many that at this stage are only to be found in the collections of enthusiasts. There are many more which could be introduced and details of some of these have been included in the hope that this may encourage their introduction. This book is not exhaustive and some species will have been omitted. I welcome information on these so that they can be incorporated into future revisions.

In compiling this book I have made every effort to keep up-to-date with palm nomenclature. This is not always easy and name changes following botanical research must be expected in palms as in any group of plants. Some of the names used in this book may have changed by the time it is published. A detailed list of the synonyms of Australian and New Zealand palms and common synonyms of exotic palms is included in Appendix IX. In the botanical research of palms the lifetime's work of the late H.E. Moore of the L.H. Bailey Hortorium, Cornell University, Ithaca, New York is singularly outstanding.

Palms are a complex group of plants that are poorly understood by the average gardener and this is a constraint on their wider use in the community. This book is designed to promote the cultivation of palms and stimulate interest in them as a group. An alphabetical layout has been used and there has been no attempt at taxonomic grouping. The use of botanical terms has been kept to a minimum and they have been explained where they are first used. A detailed glossary is included and appendixes provide detailed lists not included in the text. Common names are included only where they are well known.

The book is illustrated by 200 colour plates as well as black and white photos. Line drawings are also included to illustrate important structural features. The majority of colour photographs were taken by Bruce Gray and myself but a number were contributed to the project by other people. These photographs are credited in the front of the book. Black and white photographs were provided by Dr John Dransfield and Your Garden magazine.

David L. Jones
Currumbin Valley

PALM SOCIETIES

Anyone interested in furthering their knowledge of palms should join a Palm Society. They are non-profit organisations formed to study palms and foster interest in their culture and conservation and disseminate knowledge about them. Societies are of interest to botanists, nurserymen and enthusiasts whether they be ardent palm devotees or people with a casual interest. The international Palm Society is based in the USA and produces a quarterly journal, *Principes,* which is an excellent, informative publication. Membership of the society is open to any interested person and an Australian Chapter has been established in Sydney. Another active society has been formed in Australia and is based in Brisbane. The relevant addresses are:

The Palm Society Inc
P.O. Box 368
Lawrence
Kansas
USA 66044

Australian Chapter
Mr Nicholas Heath
8 Malory Ave
West Pymble
NSW 2073

Queensland Society
Australian Palm & Cycad Society
C/o Robin MacLeod
P.O. Box 68
Everton Park
Qld 4053

CHAPTER 1
Introduction to Palms

PALMS are woody monocotyledons of the family Arecaceae (earlier name Palmae) which is placed in the order Arecales. They are a natural group of plants with a characteristic appearance that enables most people to recognise them without great difficulty, although unrelated plants with a similar general appearance (such as Cycads, Cyclanths, Pandans, Cordylines) are often included with them by the inexperienced (see also Appendix 8).

Although palms possess some features in common with the families Cyclanthaceae, Pandanaceae and even Araceae, these relationships are really only superficial and the palms stand out as an isolated and distinct group.

Palms are an ancient life form with fossil records from the Eocene period. Being composed largely of non-durable materials, palms do not leave good fossil records and probably existed before this time. Changes have certainly occurred since those days because the pollen of the Mangrove Palm (*Nypa fruticans*), which today is only found in the tropics, has been recovered from sediments near London.

Palms are regarded as being 'Princes' among plants and indeed were labelled such (as 'Principes') by none other than the great Swedish botanist Carl von Linnaeus, the founder of the modern binominal system of plant nomenclature. He recognised palms as a distinct group of plants and described several species. Today Principes is the name of the quarterly journal of the Palm Society which was established in Florida.

NUMBER OF SPECIES

In the literature the estimate of the number of species of palms varies from 2500 to 3500 in 210 to 236 genera. A more accurate modern estimation is probably about 2800 species in 212 genera. More species await discovery and description. Variations in the tallies basically arises because of disagreements between botanists on the deliminations of species and genera. Whatever the number of species, palms are a highly significant group and rank fourth or fifth in size in the monocotyledons.

PALM CLASSIFICATION

Man likes to categorise the species around him and palms are no exception. Those plants with a common set of characters which sets them apart from another group of closely related plants are known as species while a whole group of closely related species comprises a genus. Related genera are then grouped into families, in the case of palms this is Arecaceae.

Palms are a fairly complex group of plants with numerous variations around a basic theme. Although there have been numerous attempts to classify them most have been unsatisfactory and have caused unnecessary confusion. Fortunately over recent years there has been an intensive study of palms carried out by various researchers both in the laboratory and in the field. Chief among these researchers was the late Dr H.E. Moore Jr of the L.H. Bailey Hortorium at Cornell University, New York. Dr Moore devoted his life to the study of the palms and has presented a classification (Moore 1973) which is reproduced here in part.

TABLE 1
Palm Classification according to Moore

Group	Leaf folding	Leaf shape	Number genus/ species	Distribution	Example
Coryphoid	induplicate	costa palmate	32/322	Pantropical	*Corypha, Sabal, Thrinax*
Phoenicoid	induplicate	pinnate	1/17	Africa – Indo-China	*Phoenix*
Borassoid	induplicate	palmate	6/56	Africa – New Guinea	*Borassus*
Caryotoid	induplicate	bipinnate	3/35	Asia	*Caryota*
Nypoid	reduplicate	pinnate	1/1	Ceylon – New Guinea	*Nypa*
Lepidocaryoid	reduplicate	pinnate (rarely palmate)	22/664	Pantropical	*Metroxylon Calamus*
Pseudophoenicoid	reduplicate	pinnate	1/4	Caribbean	*Pseudophoenix*
Ceroxyloid	reduplicate	pinnate	4/30	South America	*Ceroxylon*
Chamaedoroid	reduplicate	pinnate	6/146	Macarenes and South America	*Chamaedorea*
Iriarteoid	reduplicate	pinnate	8/52	South America	*Iriartea Socratea*
Podococcoid	reduplicate	pinnate	1/2	West Africa	*Podococcus*
Arecoid	reduplicate	pinnate	88/760	Pantropical	*Areca, Linospadix, Cocos, Butia*
Cocosoid	reduplicate	pinnate	28/583	South America	*Syagrus*
Geonomoid	reduplicate	pinnate	6/92	South America	*Geonoma*
Phytelephantoid	reduplicate	pinnate	4/15	South America	*Phytelephas*

GROWTH FEATURES

Palms are basically woody plants with a distinctive crown of leaves. Most species have a prominent trunk but a few have underground trunks and some are trunkless. A few are climbers with slender stems produced at intervals from an underground rhizome. While most palms have a solitary trunk, a very significant group produces multiple trunks by suckering from the base. The individual growth habit is usually characteristic but some species may be either solitary or suckering (e.g. *Laccospadix, Ptychosperma, Nengella*).

Palm leaves are very prominent and with a characteristic shape. Most species are either palmate or pinnate but other variations are known. Each species usually carries a characteristic number of leaves in its crown.

Palms flower when they are mature. In some species this may occur after three to five years while others may take more than forty years to mature. Some palms flower only once in their lifetime and die but the majority have regular flowerings throughout their life. A few species flower down the stem from each leaf axil and the whole plant or stem dies when the lowermost bunch of fruit ripens.

Palm flowers are generally small and not showy by comparison with many garden flowers. They are however often borne in profusion and may be quite colourful and are sometimes fragrant. Early literature records that most palms are wind pollinated but today it is known that many species are pollinated by insects such as beetles, flies and bees. Palm flowers may be unisexual or bisexual and it is not uncommon for unisexual flowers of either sex to be distributed on the same inflorescence, often in close proximity to each other.

Palm fruits may be small and borne in profusion or large and carried in small numbers. Frequently they are very colourful and are an additional decorative feature. Some are fleshy and are fed on by animals and birds. The fruits contain one to three seeds which generally have a hard or fibrous covering.

Further details on palm structure can be found in the following chapter.

DISTRIBUTION

Palms are widely distributed in the well-watered zones of the world but are absent or rare in very dry or very cold regions. They are uncommon in the temperate zones but proliferate in the tropics. Not only do the vast majority of species occur here but palms are also a commonly encountered and sometimes dominant component of the vegetation. In the tropics they can be found from the sea shore to inland districts and even to altitudes above 2000 m.

Despite the wide distribution and frequency of palms in the world's tropics there are very few large and widespread genera. In fact, most palm genera contain five or less species and monotypic genera are common. The climbing genus *Calamus* is the largest with 370 species with a pantropical distribution. Many small genera have a worldwide distribution (e.g. *Borassus*, *Phoenix* and *Raphia*) while some larger genera have proliferated in relatively restricted areas. For example, *Licuala* and *Pinanga*, each containing more than 100 species, are largely found between Malaysia and New Guinea while the 133 species of *Chamaedora* are restricted to Central and South America. As a general rule there are more differences than similarities between palms of the Old and New Worlds.

Many palm genera are localised in relatively small areas and there is considerable development of small and monotypic genera endemic to islands. This indicates the ability of palms to evolve and make use of specific niches in the environment. On Lord Howe Island for example there are four species of palms in three genera, all endemic. Two species are common on the coast and extend some way up the mountains, the third is found at intermediate altitudes and the fourth is restricted to the mountain tops. Fiji has about thirty-six species of palm in about thirteen genera. More than ninety per cent of the species are endemic while about half of the genera are not found elsewhere.

The proliferation of palms on some islands can be demonstrated by comparing Australia with the nearby islands of New Caledonia and New Guinea. Australia, with its large but dry land mass, is poor in palms with about twenty-two genera and fifty-seven species. Of these five genera and thirty-six species are endemic (seventy-nine per cent). By contrast New Caledonia, which is small by comparison, has about thirty species of palm in about twenty genera, the vast majority of which are endemic. To the north of Australia, New Guinea has about thirty genera and 270 species, ninety-five per cent of which are endemic. A similar situation applies to the African continent when it is compared with the nearby island of Madagascar.

HABITAT

It has been estimated that more than two thirds of the world's palm species grow in rainforests. Here they may be emergent plants with their crowns well clear of the forest canopy or of intermediate size reaching up among the trees but not emerging or growing as small plants in the generally shady, dull conditions of the rainforest floor. Climbing palms are also common in rainforests and while these have their roots anchored in the soil of the forest floor their uppermost leaves mingle with the outer foliage of the canopy.

Palms that grow in open areas tend to favour wet sites such as marshes and swamps, or the margins of permanent streams, lakes or lagoons. Even sites subject to periodic inundation can support palms because their deep roots can tap ground water during the dry times. Although they may have excellent water-conserving devices, palms are absent from very dry habitats. Even those found in the desert (such as the Date Palm), will only survive where their roots can tap permanent underground water supplies.

A characteristic of palms growing in open sites is that they are frequently found in extensive colonies, usually of a single species (e.g. *Borassus, Livistona, Phoenix, Raphia*). By contrast palms found in rainforest are not often in colonies and many species may exist together in a small area.

A few palms have adapted to specialised habitats where they can compete successfully with other plants. The Coconut Palm (*Cocos nucifera*) is a striking example, growing as it does in colonies around the fringe of tropical beaches. The Mangrove Palm (*Nypa fruticans*) favours the mud of brackish inlets, estuaries and large tidal rivers of the tropics. Here it flourishes and may form colonies which dominate the vegetation. Few palms will tolerate snow but *Nannorrhops ritchiana* from the mountains of Afghanistan and species of *Trachycarpus* from the Himalayas are covered with snow regularly each winter.

HORTICULTURAL APPEAL

Palms are becoming increasingly popular subjects for cultivation in streets, parks and gardens and as indoor and container plants. Because their shapes are more predictable than other trees they can be used as lawn specimens, street trees and for avenues. They are particularly popular in tropical and subtropical areas.

Because of the constant demand for them, palms are now an integral part of the nursery scene, with many nurseries specialising in their production. Some slower-growing species may take many years to become a saleable plant and are quite expensive. Only a few species are regularly stocked by nurseries, but new palms are constantly being introduced from overseas by enthusiasts. As these prove themselves under various conditions, they may be taken up by the nursery trade and produced in quantity. There are many small-growing palms with tremendous horticultural potential that are hardly known because of the lack of propagating material.

PALM HYBRIDS

Like many other groups of plants palms can and do hybridise. In some genera such as *Phoenix* and *Chamaedorea*, hybrids are common and it is unwise to collect seed from plantings of mixed species. In many other genera hybrids are virtually unknown. Hybrids occur in nature and more frequently in horticulture. Within an outcrossing genus even dissimilar species such as *Phoenix reclinata* and *P. roebelensii* may hybridise. As well as hybrids between species, hybrids between genera (e.g. *Arecastrum* x *Butia, Butia* x *Syagrus* and *Butia* x *Jubaea*) are also known, although they occur much less commonly.

PALM ODDITIES

As a group, palms contain some very unusual and interesting plants. It is perhaps not widely known that the largest seed and the longest leaf in the plant kingdom are produced by palms. The seed is that of the Double Coconut (*Lodoicea maldivica*) of the Seychelles Islands. Individual seeds of this palm may weigh up to 20 kg and early this century were prized as a collector's item. Today live nuts of this species are sold to palm enthusiasts and dead nuts to tourists. The longest leaf is produced by the Madagascan Raffia Palm (*Raphia farinifera*), individual leaves of which may be over 20 m in length.

Extremes in height in the palm family are provided by comparing the diminutive Lilliput Palm (*Syagrus lilliputiana*) from Paraguay which is 10 cm to 15 cm tall at maturity with the lofty *Bismarckia nobilis* from Madagascar and the Wax Palm of the Andes (*Ceroxylon alpinum*) both of which rise to more than 60 m from the ground.

CHAPTER 2
The Structure of Palms

PALMS are woody monocotyledons with a distinctive appearance. While they do have basic similarities to other plants, having roots, trunk(s), leaves, flowers and fruit, these organs may be quite different in appearance and structure and some explanation is necessary to aid in an understanding of the group. Not all specialised palm structures are included in this chapter and those not mentioned may be referred to in the glossary.

ROOTS

The roots of palms originate from the base of the trunk and as in other plants perform the essential functions of anchorage and the uptake of nutrients and water. Palm roots are produced from one of two different systems but essentially their functions, irrespective of their origin, are the same. The primary or seminal root system of a seedling is very important for early anchorage and initial uptake of nutrients and water, but is essentially short-lived.

A secondary root system is also produced and this is the most important one to the palm. This system arises from the base of the trunk just near the soil surface and is known as an adventitious root system. This is present in all palms but in clumping palms a new adventitious root system is produced at the base of each new trunk. The accessory or supplementary roots of an adventitious root system may be crowded or sparse, short and stubby or may wander for considerable distances. In some palms (eg *Phoenix* spp. and *Archontophoenix cunninghamiana*) these supplementary roots may be visible at the base of the trunk above the soil surface. Here they arise in a basal swelling and break through the outer bark in clusters. In some palms the roots creep over the soil surface (*Aiphanes caryotifolia*, *Gaussia* spp., *Manicaria saccifera*). *Raphia* species have specialised upright roots similar to the pneumatophores of mangroves. The roots of most palms are thick and tough but some are slender and wiry. The surface of the roots is generally smooth but those of *Clinostigma exorrhizum* and *Socratea exorrhiza* bear numerous spines.

A very few palms produce aerial roots (eg *Cryosophila warscewiczii*, *Clinostigma exorrhizum*) and in even fewer species these develop into prop or stilt roots (*Iriartea ventricosa*, *Verschaffeltia splendida*, *Socratea exorrhiza*, *S. durissima*). In these palms the bottom of the trunk may wither away leaving the aerial parts completely supported by the prop roots (see Fig 2).

TRUNKS

Palms have a woody stem or trunk which gets taller as the plant gets older. The trunk is terminated by the apical meristem or growing apex. This vital organ is protected by the developing leaves and their sheathing bases and is buried well within the trunk. A young palm plant does not start developing a trunk until its apical bud has reached a certain critical size. This is the reason for the slow initial spreading development that occurs in many young palms before they make their trunk.

Palms have no bark as such, although the epidermis is hardened to form a protective layer. Thus they have no secondary thickening as in dicotyledons and once the trunk is formed it can only increase in diameter to a limited extent. Most species attain their maximum girth before the trunk grows upwards. Any thickening that does occur after the trunk develops is due to the swelling of cells with supplementary thickening in their walls. In the Bottle Palm (*Hyophorbe lagenicaulis*) the basal half of the trunk swells grotesquely. A number of palms have unusual swellings near the centre of the trunk and these are due to the localised swelling of cells which expand by the uptake of water, for example the Spindle Palm (*Hyophorbe verschaffeltii*), Pot-bellied Palm (*Colpothrinax wrightii*) and the Cherry Palm (*Pseudophoenix vinifera*). Variations in the thickness of individual palm trunks are believed to be caused by dry and wet years with the terminal bud tending to swell more in the good seasons. The swelling at the base of some palm trunks is for support and is mainly caused by the development of accessory roots.

Palm trunks are remarkably strong and the slender ones very resilient, withstanding the tremendous bending stresses exerted by high winds, cyclones, etc. The strength is obtained from a peripheral ring of fibre bundles which become lignified while the flexibility is achieved because this surrounds a central soft cortex.

The shape of the trunk is characteristic with the majority of palms having a trunk of nearly uniform width throughout, although a few such as *Gaussia princeps* are tapered. Most are straight but that of the Coconut is curved, probably as a result of a response to light. Some are very slender and may resemble bamboo (*Bactris guineensis*, *Chamaedorea* spp., *Dypsis* spp.,

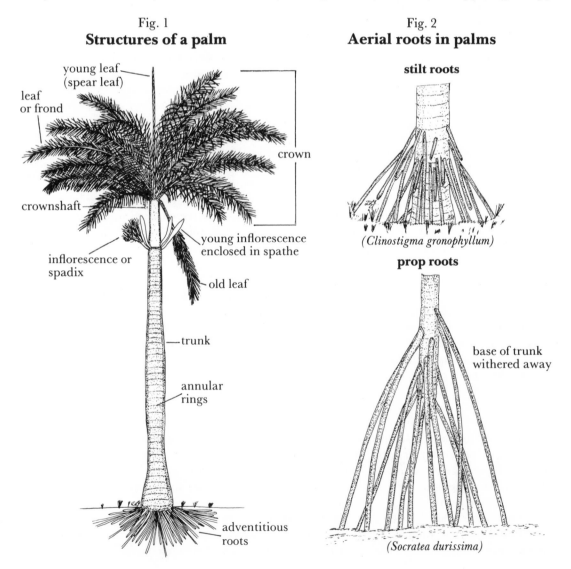

Fig. 1
Structures of a palm

young leaf
(spear leaf)

leaf
or frond

crown

crownshaft

young inflorescence
enclosed in spathe

inflorescence or
spadix

old leaf

trunk

annular
rings

adventitious
roots

Fig. 2
Aerial roots in palms

stilt roots

(*Clinostigma gronophyllum*)

prop roots

base of trunk
withered away

(*Socratea durissima*)

Oenocarpus panamanus), others are slender and woody (*Opsiandra maya, Microcoelum insigne*) and then there is a tremendous range of stoutness (*Sabal* spp.) up to the massive trunks of *Jubaea chilensis* and *Sabal princeps*.

The surface of the palm trunk may be naked (*Jubaea chilensis, Sabal causiarum*), adorned with spines (*Aiphanes caryotifolia, Astrocaryum aculeatum, Bactris plumeriana, Verschaffeltia splendida*) or covered with the persistent bases of leaves which may themselves be adorned with hooks (*Washingtonia* spp.), woolly hairs (*Coccothrinax crinita*), stout interlaced fibres (*Trachycarpus fortunei*), fibres and spines (*Arenga pinnata, Zombia antillarum*) or spines (*Gastrococos crispa, Aiphanes caryotifolia*). In a number of palms the dead fronds persist and hang as a curtain covering much of the trunk (*Copernicia macroglossa, Washingtonia filifera*). In species with naked trunks the degree of smoothness, the colour, the presence of vertical fissures (*Dictyosperma* spp., *Sabal* spp.) or horizontal steps left by the fallen leaf bases (*Archontophoenix alexandrae, Caryota cumingii*) are all useful diagnostic features (see Fig 3).

Scars representing the point of attachment of fallen leaves may be prominent on some palms as a ring on the trunk. These are known as annular rings and their distance apart is a reflection of the vigour of the palms and their number can be used as a guide to the palm's age. The point on a trunk where the leaf arises is known as the node and the area in between as the internode. Small internodes or closely spaced annular rings indicate slow growth while widely spaced rings indicate rapid growth.

The basal part of the trunk of the unique, slow-growing Seychelles palm known as the Double Coconut (*Lodoicea maldivica*) is bulbous and fits into a large wooden socket produced by the plant. This socket is very durable and lasts in the ground long after the palm has died. The base of the trunk of *Butia capitata* has a swollen knob from which the roots emerge. A few remarkable palms have stilt or prop roots which emerge from the base of the trunk (see previous heading).

Crownshaft

In some palms such as *Archontophoenix* spp., *Rhopalostylis* spp. and *Roystonea* spp., the top of the trunk is crowned with a cylinder called the crownshaft. This is formed from the tightly packed tubular leaf bases and is important as a protective measure for the meristem. Its presence provides a useful diagnostic feature. In most palms the crownshaft is bright green but in the colourful Sealing Wax Palm (*Cyrtostachys renda*) the crownshaft is tinged with pink or waxy red to scarlet and is a striking ornamental feature. In some species of *Pinanga* it is yellow. The crownshafts of most species are smooth and glabrous but some are spiny or hairy.

DIAGNOSTIC FEATURES

The trunk is a very important feature in the identification of palms for it divides them into convenient groups. In all there are five groups of palms which can be recognised depending on their trunk, but of these two are of major significance and accommodate the majority of species. These are palms with a solitary trunk or those which produce multiple trunks and have a clumping habit. The other groups are palms with branching trunks, those which are trunkless or with subterranean trunks and those which are climbers. Because climbing palms have many modifications they will be dealt with separately at the end of this chapter.

Solitary Palms

As the name suggests these palms have a single trunk. They are a very common group within the palms and include many familiar, cultivated species. The trunks of these palms are variable between different species or even between forms within a species but are generally fairly constant in their principal characters within a species or form. Thus these characters have diagnostic significance and can be used as an aid to identification. Most have erect trunks but in some species they may be subterranean (*Sabal etonia*). In a couple of unusual species the trunk may creep over the surface of the ground before turning and growing upright (*Elaeis oleifera, Phytelephas macrocarpa*).

Fig. 3
Palm Trunks

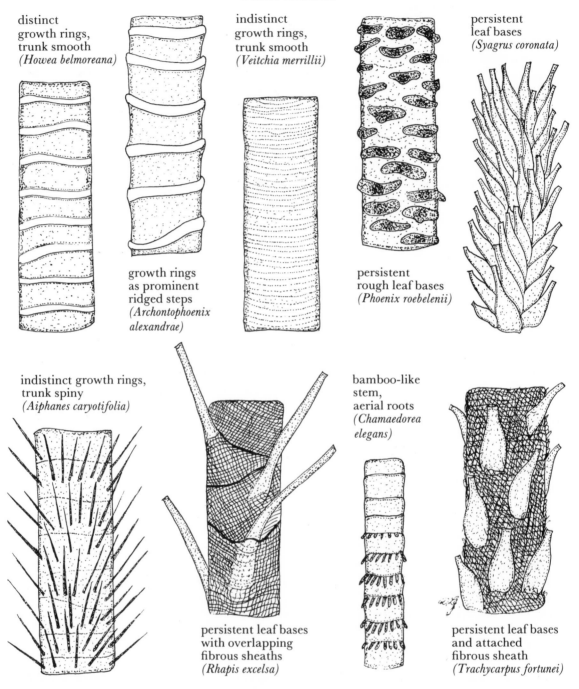

distinct
growth rings,
trunk smooth
(*Howea belmoreana*)

growth rings
as prominent
ridged steps
(*Archontophoenix
alexandrae*)

indistinct
growth rings,
trunk smooth
(*Veitchia merrillii*)

persistent
rough leaf bases
(*Phoenix roebelenii*)

persistent
leaf bases
(*Syagrus coronata*)

indistinct growth rings,
trunk spiny
(*Aiphanes caryotifolia*)

persistent leaf bases
with overlapping
fibrous sheaths
(*Rhapis excelsa*)

bamboo-like
stem,
aerial roots
(*Chamaedorea
elegans*)

persistent leaf bases
and attached
fibrous sheath
(*Trachycarpus fortunei*)

Clumping Palms

These palms produce basal offsets or suckers from at or below ground level and are therefore multiple trunked. Occasionally some suckers are produced on the trunk (e.g. *Chrysalidocarpus lutescens, Phoenix dactylifera*) but this is uncommon.

Within clumping palms some distinctions based on growth habit can be made. In the majority the suckers are produced on the perimeter of the clump as it spreads and they grow normally

Stilt roots of *Areca vestiaria*, north Celebes
(photo John Dransfield)

Spines on *Plectocomiopsis mira*, Sarawak
(photo John Dransfield)

without any restriction on their development. In these types the oldest and tallest growths are found at the centre of the clump and grade down in height to the newest on the outside. Not infrequently the oldest stems appear to slow in their growth rate so that the adjacent but younger stems are not of a greatly different height. Examples of this growth habit are *Chrysalidocarpus lutescens, Chamaedorea microspadix, C. costaricana* and *Phoenix reclinata*. Some species tend to form sparse clumps (*Phoenix reclinata*) while in others the stems are crowded close together (*Chamaedorea erumpens, C. siefrizii, Rhapis humilis* and *Cyrtostachys renda*).

In a few clumping palms a different growth habit is noticeable. One or two stems develop rapidly and dominate the clump while the remaining suckers develop slowly or reach a stationary phase. These do not develop any further unless a mature stem dies or is badly damaged. Thus the clump consists of the mature stem or a couple of stems surrounded by a rosette of undeveloped suckers. This growth habit can be seen in *Hydriastele wendlandiana, Linospadix minor, Laccospadix australasica, Phoenix dactylifera* and *Ptychosperma macarthurii*.

In the clumping palms so far discussed, new shoots or suckers are produced on the periphery of the clumps. An interesting clumping habit is to be found in the very attractive, verdant palm from Mexico, *Chamaedorea cataractarum*. In this species branching occurs by an equal division of the growing apex of a stem. This division takes place deep in the stem and the first sign of a change is an apparent split and pairing of the very young leaves. This split eventually becomes obvious and the two stems gradually grow away from each other until they are quite separate individuals.

Branching Palms

Natural aerial branching in palms is rare and restricted to two genera although branching may occur in many other species following partial damage to the growing apex (see next heading). Branching is slightly more widespread in species with underground trunks although sometimes it is difficult to distinguish this growth habit from the typical clumping palm.

17

Fig. 4
Growth habit of palms

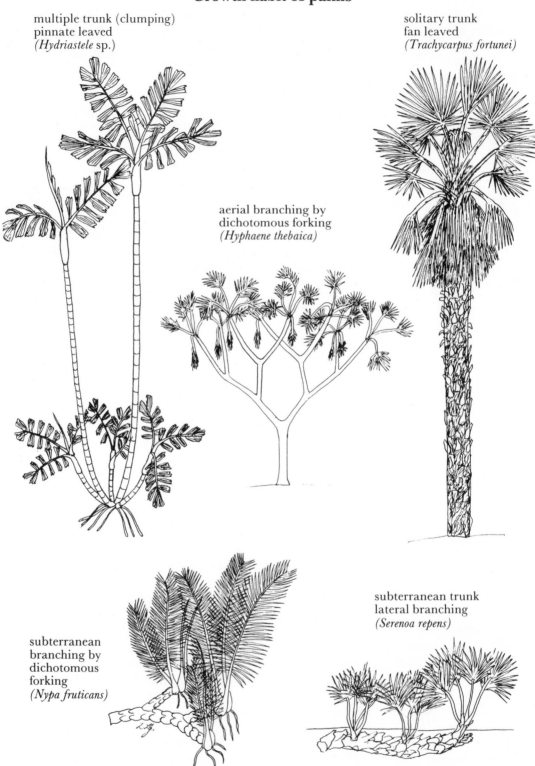

multiple trunk (clumping)
pinnate leaved
(Hydriastele sp.)

solitary trunk
fan leaved
(Trachycarpus fortunei)

aerial branching by
dichotomous forking
(Hyphaene thebaica)

subterranean
branching by
dichotomous
forking
(Nypa fruticans)

subterranean trunk
lateral branching
(Serenoa repens)

Branching in palms occurs in two distinct ways, either forking at the growth apex or lateral branching (see Fig 4).

Forking takes place at the actual growth apex which divides equally into two parts. These develop into branches and the dichotomy can be easily seen if the branching system is studied. This type of branching occurs aerially in the trunks of species of *Hyphaene* and *Vonitra* and in the subterranean trunks of *Nypa fruticans*. Not all species of *Hyphaene* and *Vonitra* fork and within those that do so there is considerable variation in the degree of branching.

Lateral branching takes place in some species with subterranean trunks such as *Allagoptera arenaria*, *Serenoa repens* and *Salacca* spp. This type of branching is similar to that which occurs in trees and the branches arise from the activity of lateral meristems. Branching of this type does not occur in aerial palm trunks.

Abnormal Branching in Palms

Aerial branching in solitary palms is not as uncommon as is believed. It arises as the direct result of sublethal damage to the growth apex and is not to be confused with the dichotomous branching that occurs naturally in some palms such as *Hyphaene* spp.

Following damage, the growing apex may proliferate in different directions which eventually grow out and become branches. Two to many branches may occur and these usually survive and grow, although frequently one will dominate. As an example, several branching specimens of *Archontophoenix alexandrae* exist in Cairns gardens.

Trunkless Palms

Trunkless palms or those with a very much reduced trunk are called acaulescent. Such palms usually do in fact have a trunk although it is very greatly reduced and is subterranean. These species are generally small palms that have become adapted to a specialised environment. Very few palms are acaulescent and they are rarely encountered in cultivation. Examples are *Acrocomia emensis*, *Syagrus campylospatha*, *S. lilliputiana* and *S. amadelpha*. *Chamaedorea radicalis* is one which is fairly commonly grown.

Some palms which have a solitary subterranean trunk may also be described as being acaulescent, however this is not strictly correct as the trunk is merely hidden from view. One example is *Sabal etonia*. Some palms have trunks which may be subterranean or emergent (*Sabal minor*, *Serenoa repens*).

LEAVES

Palm leaves (often called fronds) may be scattered along the upper part of the trunk (e.g. *Chamaedorea*, *Pinanga* and *Rhapis* spp.) or more commonly borne at the top in a crown. Those of palms with subterranean trunks may be described as being radical or basal but they are in fact terminal on the underground trunk. The leaves of palms are not remarkably different from other plants, having the same basic structure. However they are a large, spectacular feature of the plant and do possess a few unique characters. Young leaves emerge vertically or nearly so (at this stage they are often called spear leaves) and thus reduce exposure to radiation and water loss by transpiration. Some palms are quite tolerant of dry conditions and have water-conserving devices including glossy or waxy leaf surfaces with a thick cuticle, a covering of wool or scales, corrugations and folding to reduce exposed leaf area, a high angle of the fronds, twisting of the fronds and variable angles of the leaflets to reduce their angle of incidence to the rays of the sun.

The basal woody structure that extends from the trunk to the first leaflet or segment is known as the petiole. This is usually grooved on the upper surface and may be smooth or the margins of the grooves adorned with teeth or hooks or the whole surface covered in spines or a mixture of spines and fibres or wool. The basal part of the petiole is expanded and clasps the trunk, often for a significant length. This part is variously known as the sheathing base, leaf base or leaf sheath. This sheathing base is entire and undivided in most species but in a few interesting ones is split at the base, for example *Thrinax* spp., *Hyphaene* spp., *Schippia concolor*. It persists on the trunk of some species long after the fronds have been shed (*Phoenix* spp., *Sabal mexicana*, *Trithrinax acanthocoma*) while in others the sheathing base is shed along with the frond, leaving a clean trunk (*Archontophoenix* spp., *Jubaea chilensis*, *Sabal causiarum*) in others the whole leaf may persist (*Copernicia torreana*, *Washingtonia filifera*). The sheathing bases may be naked or variously adorned with hairs, coarse fibres, spines, hooks or teeth. In a very few palms there is an appendage at the upper part of the leaf sheath that is known as the ochrea. This is well developed in species of the climbing genus *Korthalsia*.

The most prominent portion of the leaf is the lamina or blade. This is the green part where photosynthesis occurs and may be entire or variously divided into segments or leaflets. Palms may be grouped according to frond types and this is a major diagnostic feature (see Fig 6).

Feather-leaved Palms

The leaves of these palms are pinnately divided, that is, the frond is segmented by divisions which reach to the stem. Such pinnate leaves have a distinctive appearance and after some observation palms of this group can be readily discerned. As a further aid to identification the fronds often have an appearance resembling a feather or the backbone and ribs of a fish.

In a pinnate leaf the segments are called pinnae or leaflets and the continuation of the petiole to which they are attached is the rhachis. The rhachis is usually straight but occasionally it is

Fig. 5
Palm Leaf Sheaths

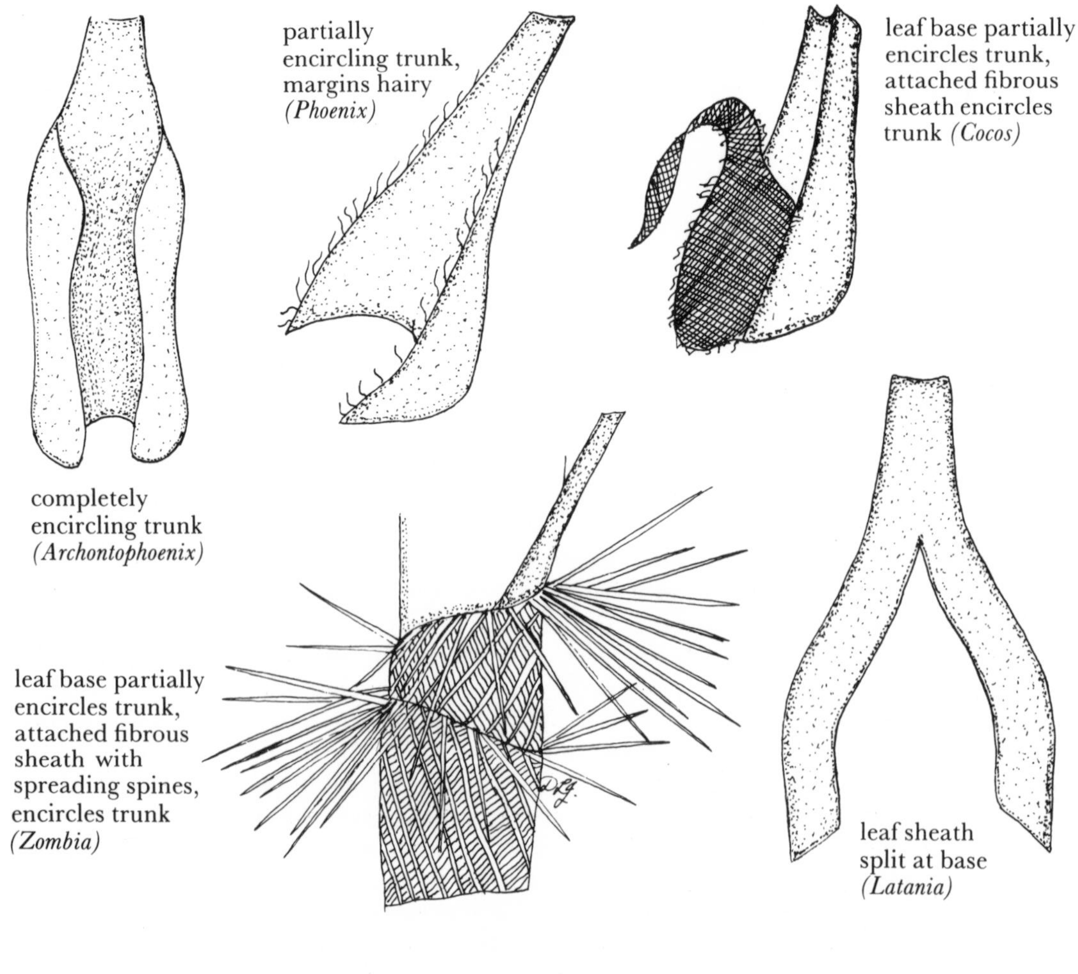

partially
encircling trunk,
margins hairy
(*Phoenix*)

leaf base partially
encircles trunk,
attached fibrous
sheath encircles
trunk (*Cocos*)

completely
encircling trunk
(*Archontophoenix*)

leaf base partially
encircles trunk,
attached fibrous
sheath with
spreading spines,
encircles trunk
(*Zombia*)

leaf sheath
split at base
(*Latania*)

curved and imparts a distinctive appearance to the crown (*Hedyscepe canterburyana, Howea belmoreana, Hyophorbe lagenicaulis*). Leaflets vary greatly in their shape, from long and slender (*Phoenix roebelenii*) to broad and uneven (*Aiphanes caryotifolia*). They may be arranged oppositely or alternately on the rhachis or irregularly in bundles (*Hydriastele*) and may all be in one plane (*Archontophoenix* spp.) or arranged in two or more ranks to give a layered or feathery appearance (*Arecastrum romanzoffianum, Normanbya normanbyi, Roystonea* spp.) which is described as plumose. The leaflets may be stiff (*Phoenix canariensis*) or lax and drooping (*Gulubia costata, Howea forsteriana*). In some species the basal leaflets are reduced to stiff, sharp spines (*Phoenix* spp.). In many others the terminal leaflets are united and may resemble a fishes tail (*Pinanga disticha, Ptychosperma elegans*). Leaflet tips may be entire and pointed or appearing as if they have been bitten off or irregularly chewed (erose or praemorse as in *Ptychosperma elegans*). In most palms the edges of the leaflets turn down and are described as being reduplicate (**∧** in section). In a few genera of which *Phoenix* is a common example, the leaflets are folded upwards and are described as being induplicate (**V** in section). In some feather-leaved palms the tips of the leaflets of new fronds are bound together by a fibrous material (*Dictyosperma, Neodypsis*) and this breaks away as the leaflets expand. Strips of this binding material may hang off young fronds and are termed reins.

Fig. 6
Major types of palm leaves and their structure

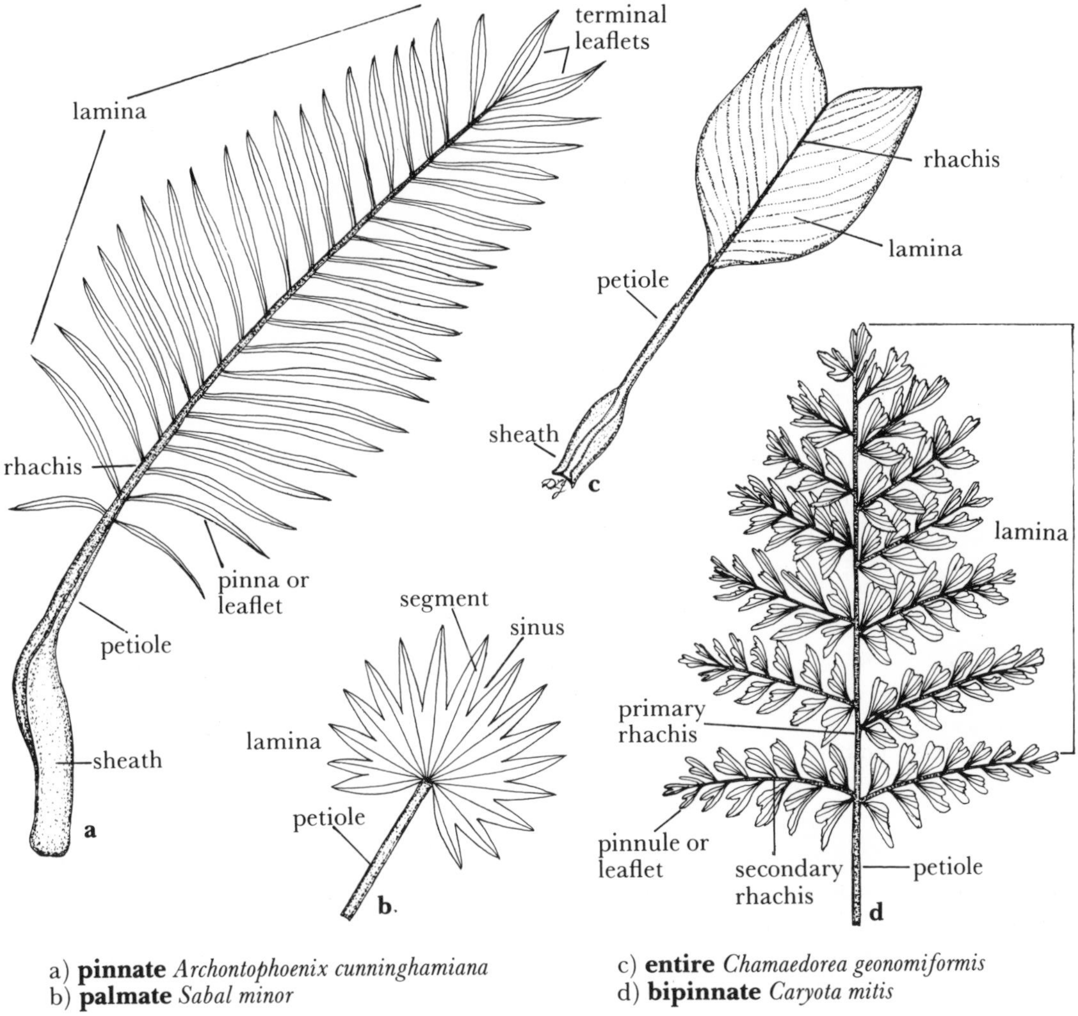

a) **pinnate** *Archontophoenix cunninghamiana*
b) **palmate** *Sabal minor*
c) **entire** *Chamaedorea geonomiformis*
d) **bipinnate** *Caryota mitis*

Fig. 7
Arrangement of pinnae on pinnate-leaved palms

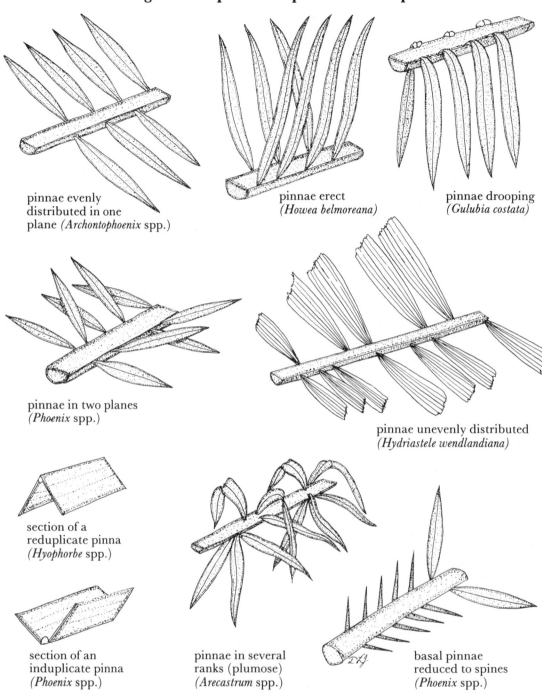

pinnae evenly
distributed in one
plane *(Archontophoenix* spp.)

pinnae erect
(Howea belmoreana)

pinnae drooping
(Gulubia costata)

pinnae in two planes
(Phoenix spp.)

pinnae unevenly distributed
(Hydriastele wendlandiana)

section of a
reduplicate pinna
(Hyophorbe spp.)

section of an
induplicate pinna
(Phoenix spp.)

pinnae in several
ranks (plumose)
(Arecastrum spp.)

basal pinnae
reduced to spines
(Phoenix spp.)

Fan-leaved Palms

The lamina of the leaves of these palms are half-rounded or rounded and divided into many segments. The whole shape resembles a partly or fully open fan and this type of division is called palmate if the segments are divided to the base or palmatifid if they are only divided part way. Palms of this group have a very distinctive appearance (see Fig 9).

The leaf divisions of this group are known as segments and the petiole may either stop abruptly where the segments join or continue as an extension into the lamina (*Borassus flabellifer*, *Sabal palmetto*). This latter type of frond is referred to as being costapalmate and the extension from the petiole is called a rib. In a few fan-leaved palms a small projection juts out at right angles to the end of the petiole. This is referred to by some botanists as the ligule because of its similar position to that organ in grasses, but is more correctly referred to as a hastula. This growth may be small and barely noticeable (*Thrinax parviflora*, *Trachycarpus fortunei*) or up to 30 cm long and prominent as in *Copernicia rigida*.

The lamina of fan-leaved palms may be variously divided with some species being entire and barely notched around the margins (*Licuala grandis*) while others are divided for more than two-thirds of their length (*Licuala spinosa*, *Rhapis excelsa*). In the Australian Fan Palm (*Licuala ramsayi*) the juvenile fronds are deeply divided with widely separated segments while the mature

Fig. 8
Shapes of palm leaflets

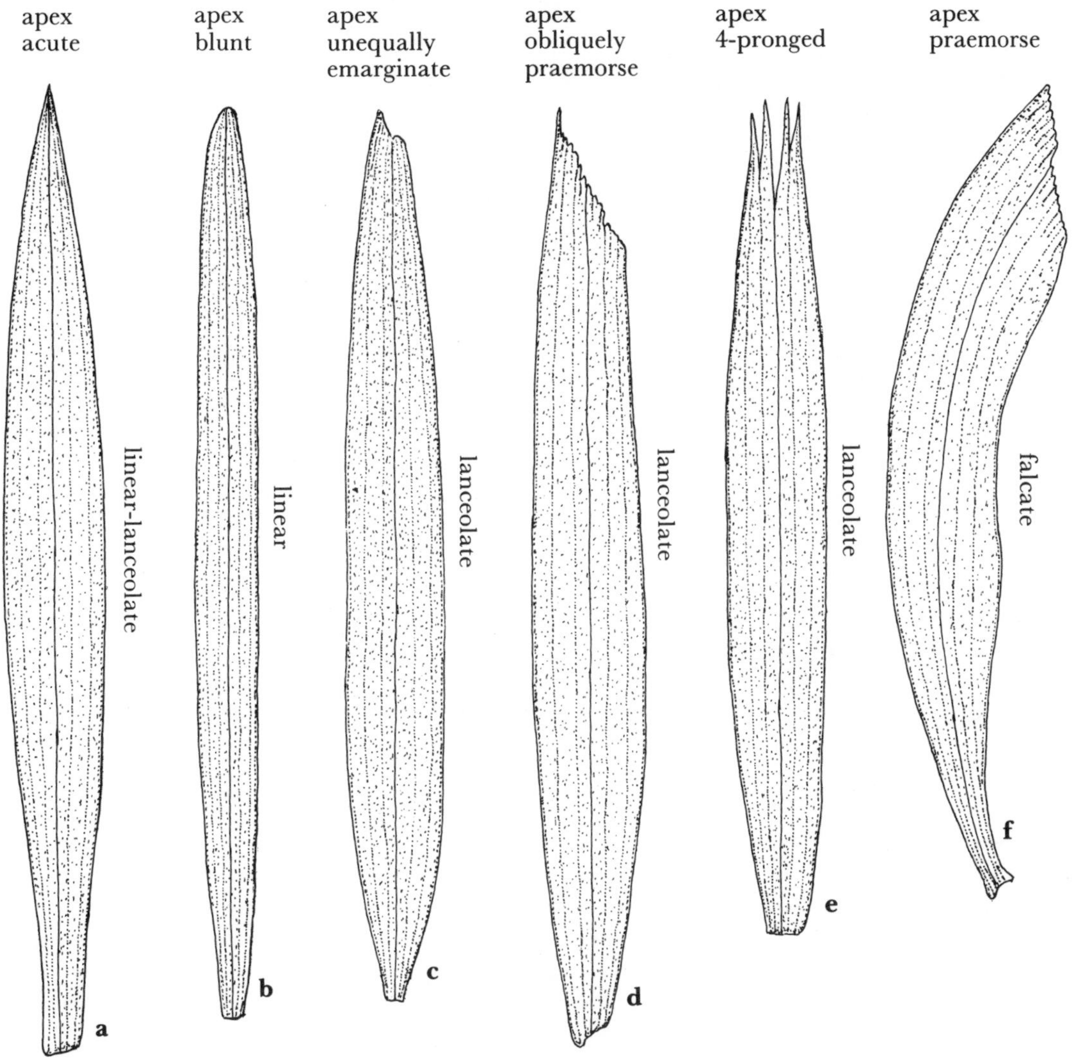

apex acute — linear-lanceolate
apex blunt — linear
apex unequally emarginate — lanceolate
apex obliquely praemorse — lanceolate
apex 4-pronged — lanceolate
apex praemorse — falcate

a) *Archontophoenix cunninghamiana*
b) *Chamaedorea seifrizii*
c) *Veitchia montgomeryana*
d) *Ptychosperma elegans*
e) *Carpentaria acuminata*
f) *Hydriastele wendlandiana*

Shapes of palm leaflets (continued)

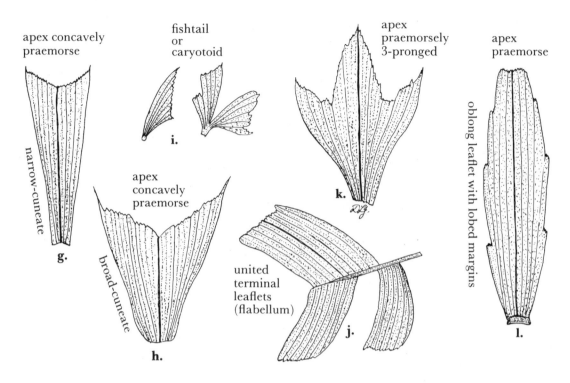

apex concavely praemorse

narrow-cuneate

g.

fishtail or caryotoid

i.

apex concavely praemorse

broad-cuneate

h.

apex praemorsely 3-pronged

k.

united terminal leaflets (flabellum)

j.

apex praemorse

oblong leaflet with lobed margins

l.

g) *Drymophloeus* sp.	i) *Caryota* sp.	k) *Brassiophoenix drymophloeoides*
h) *Drymophloeus* sp.	j) *Hydriastele wendlandiana*	l) *Arenga engleri*

fronds are circular with the segments deeply divided but closely crowded together to impart an almost continuous circular or falsely peltate appearance.

The segments of fan-leaved palms may be stiff or somewhat lax, and often the tips may be drooping (*Livistona chinensis, L. decipiens*). The tips themselves may be entire, long and pointed or even thread-like (*Livistona chinensis*), emarginate (*Licuala grandis*), deeply divided (*Brahea brandegeei, Washingtonia filifera*), or erose (*Rhapis excelsa*) (see Fig 9).

A few fan-leaved palms produce long, cottony threads which arise at the junctions of the segments and along the margins. These palms are frequently referred to as cotton palms and the threads may be more prominent on juvenile fronds than on mature fronds. *Washingtonia filifera* is frequently called the Cotton Palm because of an abundance of these threads on the leaves.

Bipinnate or Fish-tail Palms

The leaves of these palms are twice divided or bipinnate. Though this type of frond division is prominent in ferns it is rather rare in palms and seems to be restricted to the Fish-tail Palms which are members of the genus *Caryota*. The term fish-tail does not actually refer to the method of division but rather to the characteristic shape of the leaflets. This shape is not confined to leaflets of the genus *Caryota* as a few pinnate palms have a similar shape (*Aiphanes caryotifolia, Wallichia caryotifolia*). The terminal leaflets of many other palms may be united and are also shaped like a fish's tail (*Hydriastele wendlandiana, Ptychosperma elegans*).

The ultimate leaf divisions of palms with bipinnate leaves are strictly called pinnules (but they are generally referred to as leaflets) while the primary divisions are pinnae. As in feather-leaved palms the continuation of the petiole to which the pinnae are attached is called the rhachis.

Entire-leaved Palms

The leaves of these palms are simple and undivided in their mature state although they may be damaged by the wind and then may have a pinnate appearance. Very few palms belong to this group but a few examples are *Chamaedorea geonomiformis, Geonoma decurrens, Manicaria saccifera, Johannesteijsmannia altifrons* and *Phoenicophorium borsigianum*. Many other species have similar entire fronds while in their juvenile stages of development (*Verschaffeltia splendida*). Palms with entire leaves may in fact be primitive relics and the leaves only survive intact in very sheltered environments. It is interesting to observe that when the fronds of some of these palms shred they seem to tear at pre-determined points after which they resemble a member of the feather-leaved group. The structure of the fronds of these palms is basically similar to those of the feather-leaved group, being divided into petiole, rhachis and lamina although in this case the latter portion is entire.

Fig. 9

Features of palmate palm leaves

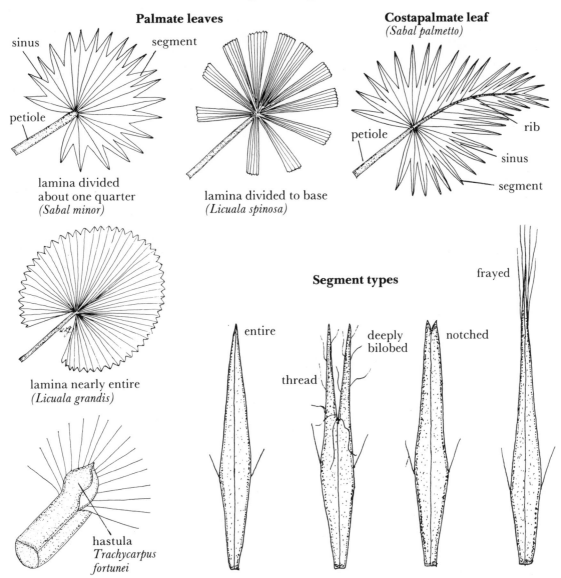

Palmate leaves

sinus
segment
petiole

lamina divided about one quarter
(*Sabal minor*)

lamina divided to base
(*Licuala spinosa*)

Costapalmate leaf
(*Sabal palmetto*)

petiole
rib
sinus
segment

lamina nearly entire
(*Licuala grandis*)

hastula
Trachycarpus fortunei

Segment types

entire
thread
deeply bilobed
notched
frayed

Net-like ochrea of *Korthalsia jala*, Sarawak
(photo John Dransfield)

The distinctively shaped leaflets of *Wallichia
densiflora* (photo David Jones)

THE INFLORESCENCE

Palms flower when mature but the length of time before they flower varies greatly with the species. Some dwarf palms such as the Window Pane Palm (*Reinhardtia gracilis*) and the Parlour Palm (*Chamaedorea elegans*) may flower when three to six years old while at the other end of the scale the Double Coconut (*Lodoicea maldivica*) and the Talipot Palm (*Corypha umbraculifera*) may not flower until they are thirty to eighty years of age.

A number of interesting palms produce one or several inflorescences from a stem which then dies. Such plants are described as being hapaxanthic. If the stem is solitary then the whole plant dies and such palms may be further termed monocarpic. In species of *Corypha* vegetative growth continues for many years and culminates in the production of a massive terminal inflorescence which flowers and fruits before the plant dies. In the Solitary Fish-tail Palm (*Caryota urens*) and the Sugar Palm (*Arenga pinnata*) the plant beings flowering from among the topmost leaves when it has reached maturity. Flowering continues progressively down the trunk and when the lowermost inflorescence has matured its fruit the plant dies. If the palm is a clustering species like *Caryota mitis, Metroxylon sagu* and *Raphia farinifera,* then the life of each plant is prolonged by suckers even though individual stems will die. Hapaxanthic palms are a minority within the group and most palms continue to produce flowers annually when conditions are favourable for them.

The vast majority of palms bear an axillary inflorescence. The position of this inflorescence on the palm is useful in grouping them. Many species, especially those with a crownshaft, carry their inflorescences below the crown and this condition is described as being subfoliar or infrafoliar (*Archontophoenix* spp., *Rhopalostylis* spp.). When the inflorescence arises among the leaves it is referred to as being interfoliar (*Phoenix* spp., *Sabal* spp., *Washingtonia* spp.) and in the rare cases in which it is carried above the leaves it is superior or suprafoliar (*Corypha* spp., *Metroxylon sagu*). In these latter types the inflorescence is not axillary but terminal on the main growing axis. A few small palms produce inflorescences which arise at or below ground level and are described as being radical (*Chamaedorea radicalis, Geonoma procumbens*). Some palms only produce a single inflorescence each year but most produce three to five. In *Opsiandra maya* up to fifteen inflorescences at various stages of development may be present on the trunk at the same time. The length of the inflorescence is often of significance in taxonomy and in palms of the interfoliar type it is useful to note whether the inflorescence exceeds the length of the leaves or is encompassed by them (see Fig 13).

The palm inflorescence is fairly complex and contains many important diagnostic features for taxonomy. The whole inflorescence is called a spadix and when young is completely enclosed in one or more sheathing bracts which are called spathes. These are actually modified leaves and their number and arrangement (which can be very complex) are important diagnostic features. The spathes may be large or small and may be persistent or deciduous, falling as the inflorescence emerges. The large basal spathe which encloses all of the young inflorescence is termed a prophyll. Those spathes which cover the main stalk supporting the inflorescence are called sterile spathes, while fertile spathes are those which enclose an inflorescence branch (see Fig 10).

The main stalk of the inflorescence is known as the peduncle and it may be woody, thick and fleshy or thin and fairly wiry. In most palms the inflorescence is a much branched structure called a panicle and the secondary and higher order branches are referred to as rhachillae. The branching varies from sparse and simple (*Chamaedorea, Rhapisa, Reinhardtia*) to complex (*Brahea, Corypha*). Rarely is the inflorescence an unbranched solitary spike (*Calyptrocalyx spicatus, Howea belmoreana*) (see Fig 15). The curious inflorescence of *Raphia* spp. is an unbranched spike up to 4 m long and 15 cm thick that has variously been likened to a sausage or stuffed stocking.

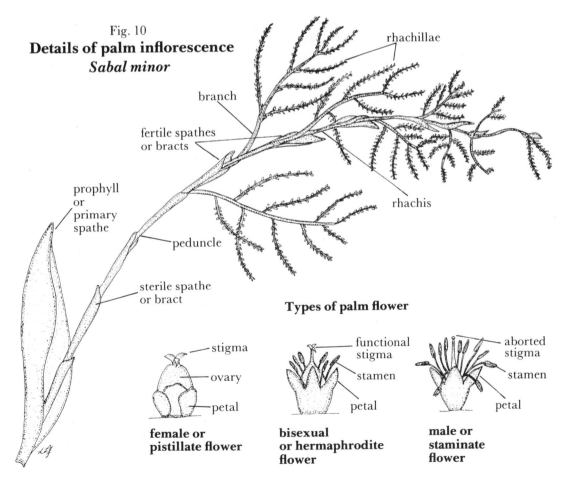

Fig. 10
Details of palm inflorescence
Sabal minor

rhachillae

branch

fertile spathes
or bracts

rhachis

prophyll
or
primary
spathe

peduncle

sterile spathe
or bract

Types of palm flower

stigma

ovary

petal

**female or
pistillate flower**

functional
stigma

stamen

petal

**bisexual
or hermaphrodite
flower**

aborted
stigma

stamen

petal

**male or
staminate
flower**

Fig. 11
Monocarpic growth sequence of *Corypha elata*

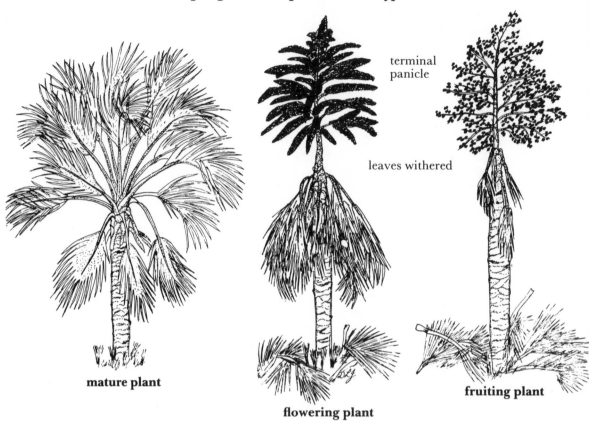

terminal
panicle

leaves withered

mature plant

flowering plant

fruiting plant

Fig. 12
Inflorescence development in *Hyophorbe verschaffeltii*

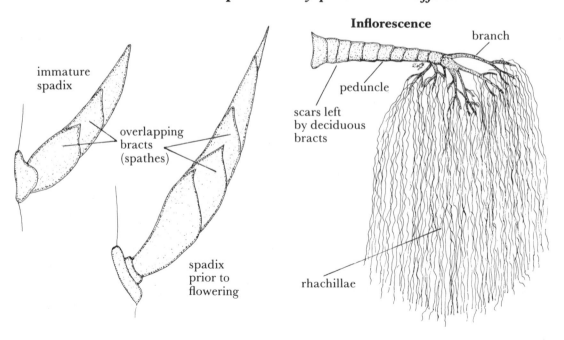

immature
spadix

overlapping
bracts
(spathes)

spadix
prior to
flowering

Inflorescence

branch

peduncle

scars left
by deciduous
bracts

rhachillae

Fig. 13
Arrangement of inflorescences in palms

terminal or suprafoliar
(Metroxylon salomonense)

axillary, interfoliar inflorescence short
(Pritchardia pacifica)

axillary,
subfoliar or
infrafoliar
(Archontophoenix)

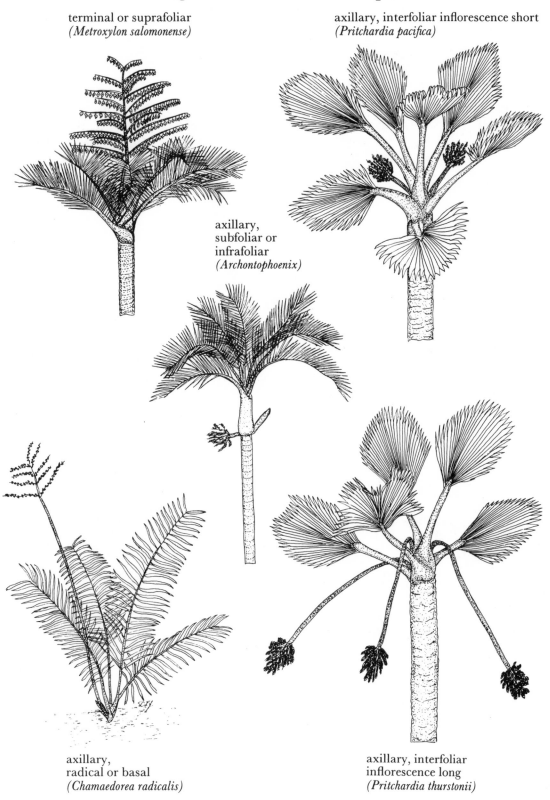

axillary,
radical or basal
(Chamaedorea radicalis)

axillary, interfoliar
inflorescence long
(Pritchardia thurstonii)

Fig. 14
The unusual inflorescence of
Nypa fruticans

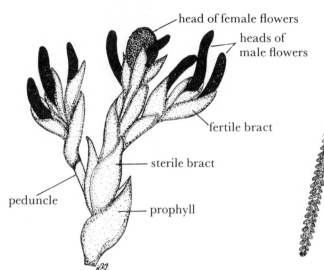

head of female flowers

heads of
male flowers

fertile bract

sterile bract

peduncle

prophyll

Fig. 15
**The simple spicate
inflorescence of
*Howea belmoreana***

Fig. 16
**Sexual dimorphism in
*Chamaedorea geonomiformis***

Male

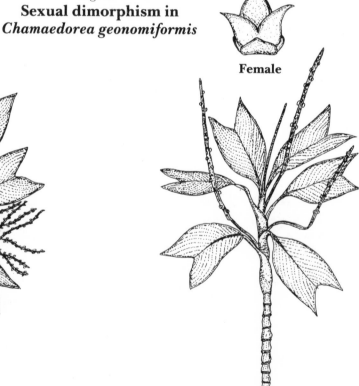

Female

FLOWERS

Individual palm flowers are small and fairly inconspicuous but are carried in profusion along the rhachillae and may be stalked or sessile or often embedded in the tissue of the rhachilla itself. One enterprising worker has even estimated that a single inflorescence of *Corypha* may contain 250,000 to several million individual flowers. Palm flowers vary in colour but those of most species are greenish to creamy-white. Those of *Archontophoenix cunninghamiana* are lilac-mauve, while some species are bright yellow (*Nypa fruticans, Polyandrococos caudescens*), orange (*Arenga engleri*) or reddish (*Acanthophoenix rubra*). The flowers are often strongly fragrant (*Areca cathecu, Coccothrinax fragrans, Hyophorbe verschaffeltii, Microcoelum insigne*) and some may even have an unpleasant scent (*Arenga pinnata*). Many palms are wind pollinated (*Phoenix* spp.) while others attract insects such as beetles (*Salacca zalacca*) or flies and honey bees (*Cocos nucifera*) to carry out the necessary cross-pollination. Palm flowers are generally short-lived, seldom lasting more than one day and often less.

Individual palm flowers may be bisexual (or hermaphrodite) — having both male and female sexual parts present — or unisexual — having only one sexual part functional. Unisexual flowers will be male if they have functional stamens and aborted ovary and stigma and female if they have aborted stamens and a functional ovary and stigma. The distribution of each flower type may be uniform with the whole inflorescence consisting of the one type, or there may be various combinations on the inflorescence. Unisexual flowers may be arranged separately on special parts of the inflorescence or on separate inflorescences on the same plant. Frequently unisexual flowers are arranged on an inflorescence in groups of three (one female between two males). When the unisexual flowers are separate on the one plant, this type of plant is described as being monoecious, and if the unisexual flowers are carried on separate plants they are described as being dioecious. Some species of palm have both unisexual and bisexual flowers present on the same plant and are described as being polygamous.

Palm flowers are made up of a perianth of three sepals and three petals either of which may be free or joined in the basal half. In unisexual flowers the petals of the females tend to overlap and remain partially closed while in the male flowers they become widely separated with the stamens obvious. Bisexual flowers generally open widely. The stamens are borne in whorls and vary in number from six to more than fifty (*Veitchia*). The ovary is trilocular and superior and each locule contains one to three ovules. Unisexual male flowers retain a rudimentary but non-functional ovary (see Fig 10).

FRUITS AND SEEDS

Palm fruits, which are botanically either a drupe, such as *Borassus* and *Sabal* or single-seeded berries as in *Metroxylon* and *Phoenix,* are often a very decorative feature of the plants. They may be conspicuous because of their size (*Borassus, Cocos*), their bright colours (orange — *Polyandrococos;* white — *Thrinax;* blue — *Trachycarpus;* black — *Livistona;* red — *Archontophoenix*), or their production in huge quantities (*Arecastrum romanzoffianum, Phoenix* spp.). The surface may be smooth or delicately patterned with symmetrical or geometrical scales (*Calamus* spp., *Mauritia setigera*) a roughened, compound clump (*Nypa fruticans*) or spiny (*Astrocaryum mexicanum*). The lobed fruit of *Manicaria* are covered with large tubercles.

Fruits of some maritime palms have a built-in flotation system and are distributed by the currents of the oceans. Chief among these is the Coconut, but others that may be distributed by this means are *Borassus flabellifer, Manicaria saccifera* and the Mangrove Palm (*Nypa fruticans*). Infertile fruits of the Double Coconut (*Lodoicea maldivica*) float, but the fertile ones sink and hence the sea is not important for the distribution of this palm.

Many palm fruits are succulent and edible (see Edible Palm Products section) but a number contain toxic materials. Some fruits contain caustic material (Calcium oxalate) in the skin and pulp which causes severe burning or irritation if eaten or handled. These needle-like, stinging crystals are known as raphides. Examples are *Arenga engleri, A. pinnata, Caryota mitis, C. rumphiana, C. urens* and *Opsiandra maya.*

Fig. 17
Shapes of palm fruits (not to scale)

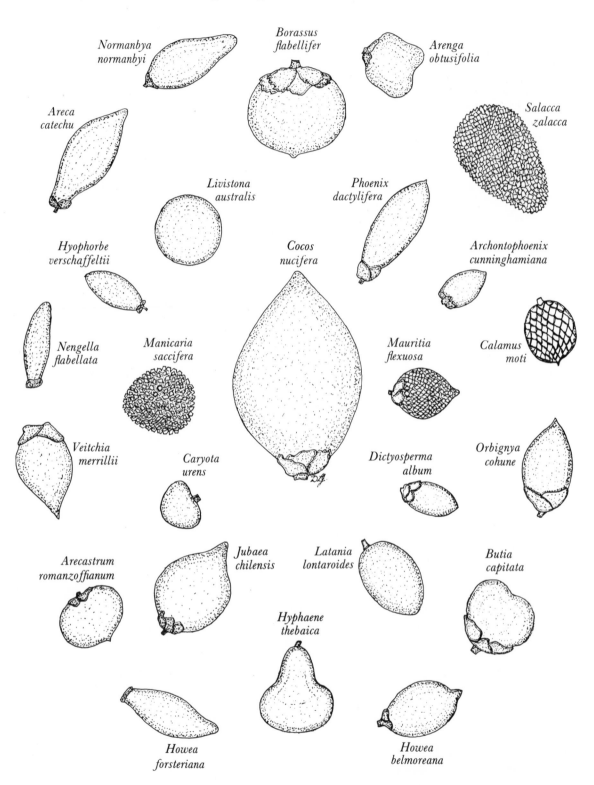

*Normanbya
normanbyi*

*Borassus
flabellifer*

*Arenga
obtusifolia*

*Areca
catechu*

*Salacca
zalacca*

*Livistona
australis*

*Phoenix
dactylifera*

*Hyophorbe
verschaffeltii*

*Cocos
nucifera*

*Archontophoenix
cunninghamiana*

*Nengella
flabellata*

*Manicaria
saccifera*

*Mauritia
flexuosa*

*Calamus
moti*

*Veitchia
merrillii*

*Caryota
urens*

*Dictyosperma
album*

*Orbignya
cohune*

*Arecastrum
romanzoffianum*

*Jubaea
chilensis*

*Latania
lontaroides*

*Butia
capitata*

*Hyphaene
thebaica*

*Howea
forsteriana*

*Howea
belmoreana*

Fig. 18
Palm fruit in section

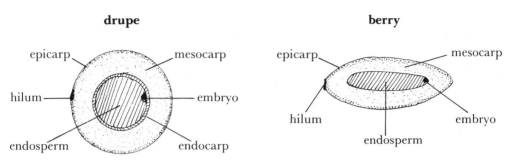

drupe

epicarp — mesocarp

hilum — — embryo

endosperm — endocarp

berry

epicarp — mesocarp

hilum — embryo

endosperm

Extremes in size in the fruits of palms can be illustrated by comparing those of the Double Coconut (*Lodoicea maldivica*) which may weight up to 20 kg with those of a *Chamaedorea* which may weigh but a few grams. Many palm fruits are rounded (*Sabal* spp.) but some are ovoid (*Archontophoenix*), pear shaped (*Cryosophila warscewiczii*) or even sickle-shaped (*Chamaedorea falcifera*). Most contain only one seed but some species may have up to three seeds in a fruit (*Arenga, Borassus, Manicaria, Orania*).

Fruit and Seed Structure

Botanically the drupe (which is the fruit of most palms) consists of a thin outer shell known as the epicarp, a fleshy layer of variable thickness known as the mesocarp and an inner hard layer which is attached to the seed known as the endocarp. Most of the seed consists of endosperm which is a cellulose, non-nitrogenous storage material, sometimes referred to as albumen. The embryo is embedded in the cellulose usually at one end. A berry is a similar fruit but lacks an endocarp (see Fig 18).

Seed Germination

Germination of palm seeds occurs when the enzymes mobilise the food resources in the endosperm. Palm seedlings are characteristically slow to appear above ground but below-ground activity can occur quite rapidly. Palms have a single cotyledon but this structure and others in palm seedlings is very different to comparable structures in commonly grown monocotyledons.

The cotyledon of palms is tubular and remains buried. Part of it closest to the endosperm expands into a structure known as a haustorium. This releases enzymes into the endosperm and absorbs the materials needed for growth. At the other end the cotyledon elongates into a tubular structure known as the cotyledonary sheath. The first green leaf which expands into sight is known as the eophyll and this grows through the tubular cotyledon. Between the eophyll and the cotyledon are one to three scale-like or bract-like structures which are in fact modified plumules or primary shoots. The upper part of the cotyledonary sheath is sometimes called the ligule.

The primary root or radicle is the first root to appear on the seedling. It is usually thick, fleshy, white, and very prominent. Appearances are deceptive however, as the primary root is incapable of increasing in thickness and is therefore very short-lived in monocotyledons. A few lateral roots may grow from the radicle and these are of importance in aiding the early establishment of the seedling. Adventitious roots arise from the base of the cotyledonary sheath and quickly replace the radicle root system in importance.

The above notes on germination are basic to most palms, but some groups have variations on this theme. The basic types are illustrated in the accompanying drawing (Fig 19). One interesting feature to note is the presence of an extension between the haustorium and the cotyledonary sheath that is known as the seed petiole.

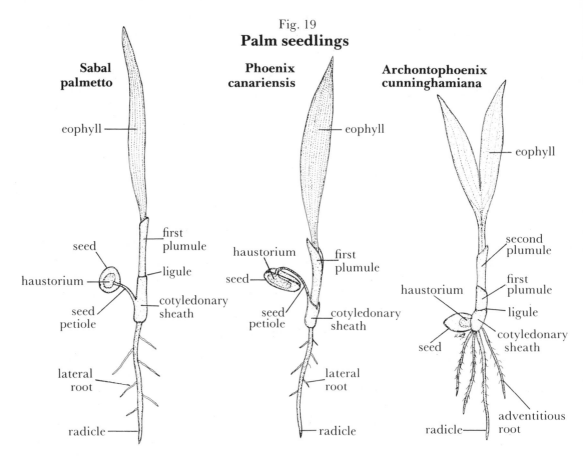

Fig. 19
Palm seedlings

Sabal palmetto — eophyll, first plumule, seed, ligule, haustorium, cotyledonary sheath, seed petiole, lateral root, radicle

Phoenix canariensis — eophyll, haustorium, first plumule, seed, cotyledonary sheath, seed petiole, lateral root, radicle

Archontophoenix cunninghamiana — eophyll, second plumule, first plumule, haustorium, ligule, cotyledonary sheath, seed, radicle, adventitious root

CLIMBING PALMS

A specialised group of palms have adopted the climbing mode of growth. In so doing they have not only occupied an important ecological niche but have also introduced some adaptive modifications to their habit of growth. As there are about 620 species of climbing palms (including about 370 in the genus *Calamus*) they are obviously a very important group and worthy of separate consideration. The main climbing genera are listed in the accompanying table but this is not complete since some groups have the odd climbing species, for example *Chamaedorea elatior*.

Climbing palms basically grow in clumps with new growths being produced at intervals from a basal rhizome. Their slender stems, which are more frequently termed canes, are erect at first but may wander over the rainforest floor until they find some suitable support on which to climb. These canes have very long internodes, are of uniform width, and are very hard like bamboo. When young they are protected by the sheathing bases of the leaves, but these are shed on old stems to expose smooth lengths of cane (rattan).

Nearly all climbing palms are ferociously armed with recurved hooks or whorls of spreading spines, these being liberally distributed on the leaf sheaths, petioles, rhachises and along the inflorescence. These unfriendly projections help the stems to climb into the surrounding forest and discourage grazing by herbivores. Further specialised aids are provided in the form of long filamentous extensions which are liberally armed with recurved hooks. These blow about in the wind and catch in surrounding vegetation. The extensions are of two types depending on their origin. Those projecting from the apex of the leaf rhachis are called cirri while flagella are sterile inflorescence developments that arise in the axils of the leaves. The inflorescences of climbing palms also frequently act as climbing aids, since they are long, pendulous, sparsely branched and are armed with recurved hooks.

Stems of most climbing palms seem almost capable of indeterminate growth and individual stem lengths of over 200 m have been recorded. In many countries these stems are harvested as rattan, the tough, pliant material valued for furniture construction (see section headed Furniture page 54). Climbing palms of the genus *Plectocomia* and *Plectocomiopsis* are hapaxanthic, the plants or individual stems dying completely after fruiting. These climbing palms may have a synchronous gregarious flowering habit with all plants in one area flowering (and therefore dying) simultaneously.

Fig. 20
Habit of climbing palm
Calamus sp.

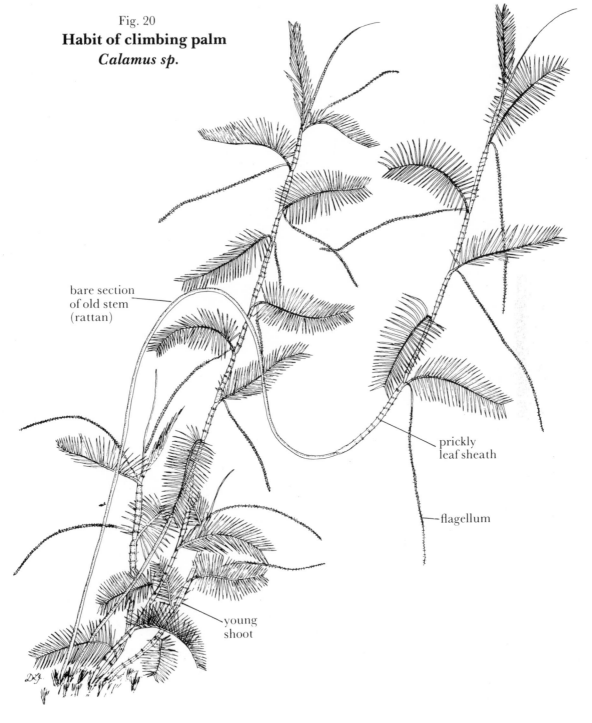

bare section
of old stem
(rattan)

prickly
leaf sheath

flagellum

young
shoot

Fig. 21
Features of some climbing palms

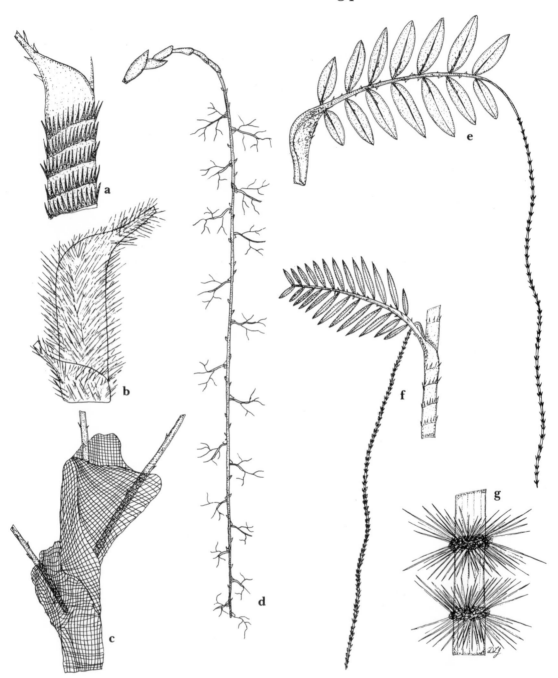

a) whorls of bayonet-like thorns on leaf sheath *(Calamus moti)*
b) numerous spines on stems, sheaths and petioles *(Calamus radicalis)*
c) net-like ochrea on leaf sheath *(Korthalsia jala)*
d) elongated narrow pendulous panicle armed with thorns *(Calamus spp.)*
e) whip-like rhachis extension called a cirrus *(Calamus hollrungii)*
f) whip-like sterile inflorescence called a flagellum *(Calamus australis)*
g) whorls of long spines which may be ant-inhabited *(Daemonorops formicaria)*

TABLE 2

Palm Genera with a Climbing Growth Habit

Genus	Number of Species	Area or Country
Calamus	370	Pantropical
Calospatha	1	Malaysia
Ceratolobus	6	Malaysia
Daemonorops	115	India – Malaysia
Desmoncus	65	South America
Eremospatha	12	Tropical Africa
Korthalsia	26	India – Malaysia
Laccosperma	6	Tropical Africa
Myrialepis	1	Vietnam, Malaysia,
Oncocalamus	6	Tropical Africa
Plectocomia	3	India, China, Malaysia, Indonesia
Plectocomiopsis	6	Indonesia, Malaysia
Pogonotium	3	Indonesia, Malaysia
Retispatha	1	Malaysia
Zalacella	1	Indochina

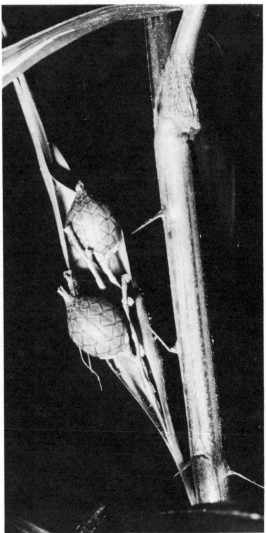

Fruit of *Ceratolobus subangulatus*, Sarawak (photo John Dransfield)

CHAPTER 3
The Economic Importance of Palms

T O THE western person, palms are an ornamental plant most familiar in tropical countries and elsewhere popular for indoor decoration. These same plants however may contribute significantly to the economies of some countries and are of prime importance in the daily lives of millions of people. The contributions these plants make to the world's economy and life style is quite amazing and appreciated by very few people.

A surprisingly large number of products can be obtained from palms. For instance, the various parts of the widespread Coconut Palm can be used in more than 1000 ways and the Palmyra Palm in over 800 ways. The Date Palm is not such a prolific relative by comparison and yet this species helps to keep millions of people alive by its tremendous production of dates in a climate where little else will grow. Numerous other species of palm are also of economic significance. In primitive societies they may provide shelter, food and drink, clothing, fuel, fibre and medicine. A sample of these uses is presented in the following pages.

The unfortunate aspect of man's use of plants such as palms is that it frequently leads to exploitation of wild populations. Many observers have noted the absence or rarity of certain palms around native villages in various parts of the world. Who knows what damage the continuous collection of fruit, palm cabbage or leaves will have on wild populations. Only in very few countries are cultivated plantations established to ease the pressure on the wild.

THREE FAMOUS PALMS
The Coconut Palm

The Coconut Palm (*Cocos nucifera*) has been cultivated for thousands of years and has been so widely distributed by man that today its centre of origin is mere speculation. The nuts, which are an excellent source of food and drink, must have been prized by the early travellers since they are a self-contained unit that does not leak, dry out or become tainted with salt water. These travellers must have not only spread the word about such a useful fruit but also have helped to establish it in new areas with a suitable climate.

Although its centre of origin is believed to have been the Islands of the Pacific or Indian Ocean (some people believe it was around Samoa or New Zealand), the coconut itself is not the type of plant to remain static as it is a coloniser. The nuts float for long distances on ocean currents and if they are washed ashore on a beach with a suitable climate will quickly colonise the area. The original coconut is believed to be the tall-growing variety with a thick husk. Superior varieties with larger fruit, a larger quantity of water and a dwarf growth habit are the result of selection by man. The coconut is found on many beaches of northern Australia but it is believed to have been introduced there by the Torres Strait islanders long before the advent of white men.

The coconut is regarded as the jewel of the tropics and it is undoubtedly the most economically important palm (more than 13 million people are directly or indirectly involved with coconut products) and coconuts are now widely grown in the tropical regions of the world. They are an important economic crop for many small countries, particularly in the Pacific region. In the South Pacific for example it is estimated that about 400 000 people depend entirely on the coconut for their livelihood. About a quarter of the export earnings of the Philippines are derived from the coconut and its products. World production of coconuts is more than 3000 million nuts annually and these are produced from groves totalling more than four million hectares. The major producers are the Philippines, India and Indonesia.

Coconut palms are very easy to grow but need a specific regime for successful fruit production. They are essentially tropical in their requirements and need a fairly uniform temperature range throughout the year and a good, regular, annual rainfall (mean approximately 20°C and 1000 mm rainfall per annum). Coconuts will grow in colder areas but rarely fruit and may be killed by sudden cold snaps. They are widely planted on Queensland's subtropical Gold Coast, but many plants die and very few ever fruit.

Coconuts need well-drained soil but will really thrive if their roots can tap ground water. This is especially applicable in coastal districts where the soils are usually deep and sandy and dry out between periods of rain. Coconuts will grow in other well-drained soils and contrary to popular belief do not have to be planted 'within sight of the sea'. If the climate is suitable and they are not crowded by other plants they will grow and fruit some considerable distance inland, again especially if their roots can tap ground water.

Because of their importance to man and because they have been grown for such a long period, numerous horticultural cultivars have been selected and propagated by seed. On the island of Fiji there are no less than seven different tall cultivars and a further three that are regarded as dwarf-growing cultivars. Within each group the cultivars are mainly distinguished on nut size and colour when ripe. Some produce very large nuts but their total yield is not as heavy as other smaller-fruited cultivars. Estimates of individual yields vary somewhat from 75 to 350 nuts per annum.

The range of uses to which various parts of the coconut palm can be put is truly amazing. Every part is used in some way and even when the trees are blown over or felled for some reason the trunk, the fibrous pith and the apical bud (cabbage) are all used. The meat can be cooked in more than a hundred different dishes or eaten raw or shredded, dried and exported as desiccated coconut; the water, especially that of a green coconut, makes a refreshing drink or it can be blended with the meat to make coconut milk, cream or jam; the shell can be burnt, made into charcoal, used as bowls, scoops or cups; the fibre can be made into mats or woven into string and ropes (see Palm Fibres heading); the leaves used for thatching and the leaflets for weaving; the wood for building; the flowers for palm honey and the sap of the inflorescence for palm sugar, alcohol and the potent drink arrack (see Palm Beverages heading); oil can be extracted from the kernels and the dried kernels (copra) are an important component of this process as they can be stored and transported (see Palm Oils heading); after oil extraction the remaining meaty material can be pressed into a cake suitable for animal feed; coconuts are sold to tourists either whole or with designs carved into the husk; the water of green coconuts has growth-regulatory properties and is added to the growing media used in tissue culture and for raising orchid seedlings.

The Date Palm

The fruit of the date palm (*Phoenix dactylifera*) is of singular importance since it is a staple part of the diet of millions of people. Dates are very low in proteins and fats but are energy rich with some cultivars having a sugar (sucrose) content of up to sixty per cent. As well as being eaten fresh they can be successfully dried and in this state can be stored for considerable periods. Dried dates are the principal agricultural export of many middle-eastern countries. Iraq, Iran and Egypt produce more than half of the world's crop of about two million tonnes and dates are also grown commercially in the Canary Islands, India, Pakistan and in two states of the USA — Arizona and California.

Date palms can be successfully grown in many areas of the world from temperate to tropical regions, but the climatic zones where they will successfully fruit are much more restricted. They need sunny, warm, dry climates (low rainfall, low humidity) and the centres of commercial production are restricted to the areas between the latitudes 15° and 30°N. The hotter and drier the climate the higher the yield and the better the quality. Date palms grown well outside these zones may never flower, let alone produce fruit. In many subtropical regions the flowering and fruiting is upset by high humidity or rainfall.

Date palms thrive best where there is ground water and where this is lacking they respond to irrigation. Propagation is by removing suckers from established plants. The plants themselves are dioecious and so both male and female suckers must be established. Pollen transference is achieved by wind with huge quantities of pollen being released early in the day. This pollen can be collected and will retain its viability for up to twelve months if stored properly. The female flowers can be hand pollinated using collected pollen and this greatly increases the percentage of female trees which can be established in a plantation and thus the yield. Normally one to five per cent of the trees must be males to ensure cross pollination.

Dates are an extremely ancient crop, having been cultivated for over 5000 years. The species is unknown in the wild but is believed to have originated in north Africa. Hundreds of different cultivars are known, these being suited to different situations, soil types, microclimates or the production of fruit of different size, colour and flavour. The plants themselves are very long-lived and are known to bear annually for well over 100 years. At each crop they may bear bunches of fruit weighing about fifty kilogrammes and containing 3000-5000 individual fruits. The bunches are cut when a reasonable percentage of the fruits are ripe and the remainder will continue to ripen. Quality dates to be eaten fresh are selected and picked by hand.

Date palms are widely grown in Australia and are a familiar sight in tropical as well as temperate regions. They grow equally as well in dry inland areas as in coastal districts where they will withstand considerable exposure to salt spray. Date palms do not flower in temperate Australia but will flower and fruit in dry northern inland areas. There was some interest in commercial production in north-western NSW and central and south-western Qld but difficulties were experienced in handling and processing the product.

The Palmyra Palm

The Palmyra Palm (*Borassus flabellifer*) from India and Malaysia is widely cultivated in tropical parts of Africa and Asia for the numerous uses to which it can be put. In fact it is second only to the coconut in the number of plants in the world. As many of its products are important articles of diet in countries where food is scarce, this adds further to its reputation and importance.

Palmyra palms are tall, very stately plants which usually grow in large colonies. The plants themselves have stout leaves which can be used in many different ways for shelter and weaving and the petiole for the production of fibre. The trunk provides heavy, strong timber, sago and cabbage; the fruit and seeds are edible (the pulp of juvenile fruits is a delicacy) and the inflorescence can be tapped for sap which can be used for sugar, wine, alcohol or vinegar. Even the swollen roots can be eaten in times of famine. The plant also has an appealing appearance and is widely grown for its ornamental features.

The fruit of the Palmyra Palm is produced in abundance (200 to 300 per tree each year) and is of considerable significance as a potential source of starch. While the pulpy orange flesh of just-ripe fruit can be eaten raw or cooked or made into jam the flesh of very ripe fruit loses its consistency and becomes dry and hard. The seeds are collected, grown on specially prepared mounds of soil and harvested when the sinker (actually the first bladeless juvenile leaf) becomes fleshy and tuberous. This sinker is regarded as a delicacy and is very nutritious, being rich in starch. Because of their prolific fruit production Palmyra Palms are obviously an underexploited source of starch. It has been estimated that a hectare of mature palms (2500 trees) could produce up to 750 000 fruit per annum. If these were converted into edible sinkers the yield of

Bucket made from leaf of *Borassus flabellifer*, Madura, Indonesia (photo John Dransfield)

nutritious starch would be quite considerable. These yields are hypothetical and to date need to be proved as heavy planting of other crop palms usually results in a drastic reduction of the yield per tree.

EDIBLE PALM PRODUCTS

Sago

Sago is an edible, starchy material obtained from the central pith of the trunks of many species of palm. Starch is a storage reserve of the plant and is laid down in good seasons or during certain growth cycles and is drawn on by the plant in times of energy need such as during growth or flowering. Sago varies tremendously in its consistency depending on the species of palm, from an almost floury substance to a coarse, granular material. It is frequently found embedded among fibres and must be scraped clean or freed by water. In all cases the collection of sago is from the trunk and involves the complete destruction of the palm.

Sago yields may be quite substantial (more than 600 kg from a trunk) and the material is a primary source of carbohydrate for millions of people in Asia. It is also a minor revenue earner because high-quality sago is exported to Europe by a number of countries, but mainly Indonesia and Malaysia. Sago can be cooked into various dishes such as meals, gruels or puddings and made into bread. Sago is low in protein and is usually supplemented with food such as meat or fish. In Indonesia and in the Amazon region of South America Sago Palms and others may be deliberately killed and left to decay. The rotting pith makes an ideal food source for the larvae of moths and beetles and when these grubs are large enough they are collected and eaten, providing a useful source of protein.

The most important commercial source of sago is from the various species and cultivars of Sago Palms belonging to the genus *Metroxylon*. One species is of particular importance and it is

41

scattered from New Guinea to Malaysia and is widely planted further afield. All species of this genus are large, handsome, pinnate palms.

Cultivars of the Sago Palm (*M. sagu*) produce most of the best commercial sago. *M. vitiense* from Fiji also produces sago but is mainly of local importance. Spineless cultivars of *M. sagu* were previously known as *M. laeve* and the spiny forms as *M. rumphii*. All species commonly form colonies in marshy, sometimes-brackish ground and have stout trunks 5 m to 10 m tall. At maturity (fifteen to thirty years of age) a huge terminal panicle 4 m to 5 m long is produced. The palm then flowers and dies after producing the ripe fruit. The best sago is obtained if the tree is felled just as the inflorescence begins to emerge. The trunk is then split or cut into sections and the pith removed and pounded in water until the starch separates. This starch can be used in liquid form or dried into a flour or granular sago. Yields are somewhat variable but one palm may contain as much as 600 kg of sago in its trunk.

Two genera of monocarpic palms other than *Metroxylon* are also important in the production of sago, although these are primarily of local significance. The trunks of various species of *Caryota* (commonly called Fish-tail Palms) contain edible starchy pith. That of *Caryota urens* from India and Malaysia is of very high quality, while the sago of *Caryota obtusa*, also from India, is of lesser quality and is used mainly for bread and gruel. The trunk of the Talipot Palm (*Corypha umbraculifera*) from Sri Lanka and India also yields a sago-like starch which is called Talipot. This palm is now widely cultivated in tropical countries but for uses other than sago. *Corypha utan* from Malaysia also yields a kind of sago that is used locally. Species of *Eugeissona* may be locally important, especially in Borneo.

Many other palms also contain sago which may be harvested as food, but often is used only in times of scarcity. The Mangrove Palm *Nypa fruticans* is one such example as are also *Borassus flabellifer*, the Palmyra Palm, *Roystonea oleracea*, the Feathery Cabbage Palm, and *Sabal adansonii* of some southern states of the USA. The Gomuti or Sugar Palm of Malaysia (*Arenga pinnata*) produces a sago with an unusual or even peculiar flavour that may be an acquired taste. A couple of palms produce a very floury sago which may be baked into a bread-like substance. *Phoenix pusilla* from India and Sri Lanka is sometimes called the Flour Palm for this reason. The Ita Palm, *Mauritia flexuosa*, from South America also has a very similar, floury pith. The sago of *Syagrus coronata* from Brazil is first ground to flour and then made into bread.

Palm Sugar

Palm sugar is known as Jaggery and it is a coarse, dark sugar crystallised from the sap of many species of palms. This product is of tremendous importance to the people of Asia particularly India, Thailand and Burma. Most of the sugar used in these countries comes from palms (some 100 000 tonnes produced and consumed locally each year) and so productive are they that there is no need to grow the more conventional sugar cane or sugar beet. Palm sugar is consumed locally and not exported.

The sap of the palm is usually tapped by cutting off a flower stalk but sometimes the whole tree is felled. Once cut the collection of the sap is carried out daily or weekly for many months. The sugar content of the sap varies but may be up to sixteen per cent. After collection the sap is boiled to form molasses and if boiled further the sugar crystallises and can be stored after drying.

Large quantities of sugar are made from the sap of the Palmyra Palm (*Borassus flabellifer*) which is native to India and Malaysia. This palm grows in large colonies and is dioecious. The inflorescence is cut off the male palm and the liquid is collected daily. Up to 2 L of sap per day may be obtained from a single palm and this flow may continue for three to five months. About 1.5 kg of sugar can be made from 10 L of this sap. This sugar is mainly saccharose. The African species, *B. aethiopum*, is also used for sugar production in a similar way.

Arenga pinnata is known as the Sugar Palm because of the large quantities of sugar that are obtained from its sap (often called arenga sugar). This palm is widely distributed from India to

Cakes of sugar made from *Borassus flabellifer* sap and moulded in baskets made from leaves of the same species, Madura, Indonesia (photo John Dransfield)

the Philippines and is widely cultivated elsewhere. The plants are monocarpic and die once the fruit matures on the inflorescence arising from the lowest leaf axil. The sap is collected by removal of the inflorescences early in their development and the palms produce prodigious quantities of this syrupy material. Sugar is produced in a similar manner from the sap of cut flower stems of the Coconut Palm (*Cocos nucifera*). Its sap contains sixteen per cent sucrose. The sap of the stout trunk of the Chilean Wine Palm (*Jubaea chilensis*) can also be crystallised into sugar, but this is more often used to produce wine or the delicacy called palm honey. In this case the whole tree is cut down.

The best tasting jaggery is made from the sap of the Fishtail Palm (*Caryota urens*) which is widespread in India and Malaysia. The developing inflorescences are cut off and up to 50 L of sap may be collected per day for a few months. The Mangrove Palm (*Nypa fruticans*) is harvested in a similar way. In some areas these palms grow in huge colonies and it has been estimated that about 350 000 L of sap could be obtained from 1 ha of these palms. This sap is very sweet and syrupy.

Date sugar is the term used for the sugar produced from various species of the Date Palm genus *Phoenix*. The Date Palm (*P. dactylifera*) itself can be tapped for the syrupy sap but this is usually considered a waste since the inflorescence must be removed when the flower clusters are just expanding. Poor cultivars or excess male trees however may be tapped for this material. The wild date of India (*Phoenix sylvestris*) is tapped for its sweet juice, much of which is refined into date sugar. In fact, this species is a major source of date sugar and is frequently cultivated for this purpose in India and to a lesser extent in other countries such as Indonesia. The very widely cultivated Canary Island Date Palm (*Phoenix canariensis*) and *P. reclinata* from tropical Africa can also be used for sugar production.

Palm Beverages

Drinks can be concocted from the sap obtained from various parts of some palms and, as well as being thirst quenching, they may be nutritious or energy rich since many have a high sugar content. The beverages can be drunk fresh or allowed to ferment for various periods to produce wines and even distilled further to produce spirits. Palm wine is generally referred to as Toddy. Palm spirits may be generally referred to as 'Arrack' although it is more usual to restrict this term to the spirit obtained from the sap of the Coconut Palm (*Cocos nucifera*).

The sap of the Coconut is tapped by cutting off the inflorescence when it is expanding. It is fermented to form wine which can be drunk or distilled to further increase the alcohol content and form the potent spirit known as Arrack. The Polynesias also prepare an intoxicating drink from fermented coconut milk and the roots of *Piper methystichum*. This is known as Kava-Kava.

A number of other prominent and also less well known palms yield beverages. In all of these the sap is collected as described in the section on Palm Sugar and then fermented to form wine, although in some cases the sap is drunk without fermenting. The sap of the Palmyra Palm is one such example providing the pleasant drink known as sura. Saguir is the fresh drink made from the sap of *Arenga pinnata*.

Examples of palms used in various parts of the world for the production of palm wine are given in the accompanying table.

TABLE 3
Palms yielding sap used for wine production

Species	Country	Species	Country
Arenga pinnata	India, Malaysia	*Mauritia vinifera*	South America
Borassus aethiopum	Africa	*Nypa fruticans*	Philippines
Borassus flabellifer	India	*Phoenix dactylifera*	North Africa
Borassus madagascariensis	Madagascar	*Phoenix reclinata*	Africa
Borassus sundaicus	Timor	*Phoenix sylvestris*	India
Caryota urens	India	*Raphia taedigera*	South America
Cocos nucifera	Polynesia	*Raphia vinifera*	Nigeria
Elaeis guineensis	Africa	*Sabal palmetto*	USA
Mauritia flexuosa	South America		

In certain palms the sweet sap is stored within the trunk itself and its recovery requires procedures much more drastic than the simple removal of an inflorescence. The stout trunks of the Chilean Wine Palm (*Jubaea chilensis*) yield up to 400 L of sugary sap which can be fermented into wine, but the stately palms must first be felled. The crown is removed and the sap may flow for several months. Unfortunately *Jubaea chilensis* is now a rare and endangered palm in its natural state because of over-exploitation for its sugary sap. Another wine palm of South America, *Scheelea butyracea*, is also cut down and a cavity excavated in the trunk. This fills with a creamy or yellowish, sweet syrup which can be drunk fresh or fermented. The sweet sap from the Cherry Palm of Cuba, Haiti and San Domingo (*Pseudophoenix vinifera*) is removed by tapping the conspicuous bulge in the trunk, and fermented to make wine. This method does not completely destroy the plant.

Fruit pulp which is fleshy and sugary can be allowed to ferment to make wine. Palms frequently produce prodigious quantities of fruit and wine making is an ideal way to use this bounty. Those of the Bacaba Wine Palm (*Oenocarpus distichus*) from South America are very pulpy and sweet and are used in this way. Other species of *Oenocarpus* are also reported as being suitable. *Cryosophila nana* from Mexico produces abundant sweet fruit which are made into wine and the species has been planted in Trinidad for this purpose. The succulent, purple, plum-like fruits of three species of *Bactris* from South America are made into wine. These are *B. maraja*, *B. major* and *B. guineensis*. The large purple fruits of the Brazilian Assai Palm (*Euterpe oleracea*) are used to make a popular thick liquid which may be either drunk fresh or fermented. The thin flesh of the fruits of *Leopoldinia piassaba* is agitated with water to make a popular drink in the area of Brazil where it grows.

Alcohol is an important fuel in this energy-conscious world and from palms it can be produced by distillation of the fermented sap. It should be noted in passing that some species of palms are capable of contributing very large quantities of sap e.g. *Nypa fruticans*, and many of these grow in less privileged countries. They are generally easy to grow, can be closely planted (up to 2500/ha) and will frequently grow on poor soils. If modern technology can prove alcohol an economically viable energy source then these plants could well prove to be significant in the future economy of the country where they grow.

Fruits

Edible fruits are not predominant among the palms. Of the 2800 or so species it would appear that less than 100 are recorded as having edible fruit and of these most are only of significance to the people who live where they grow naturally and some are only eaten in times of hardship and shortage. However, the three most important palms viz. Coconut, Date Palm and the Palmyra Palm each have edible fruits and between them help to feed millions of people.

The meat of the Coconut can be eaten raw or cooked in various ways and added to numerous dishes. Its milk provides a refreshing drink and before the shell hardens the young nuts contain a jelly-like material which is both delicious and highly nutritious. A peculiar nut appears occasionally on certain varieties of Coconut Palm in the Philippines and is known locally as the macapuno. This is an abnormal nut and is considered to be a great delicacy since the entire cavity is filled with a soft, sweet, gelatinous, white curd which is chewy and can be eaten fresh or cut into strips and preserved in syrup.

The fruit of the Date Palm is an energy rich and important article in the diet of millions of people. The fruit can be eaten fresh or when dried and stored properly will keep for many years. Other *Phoenix* species have edible fruit but are of much less significance than the Date. The fruit of *P. loureirii* from India is reddish purple when ripe and has a sweet, edible pulp surrounding the hard seed. That of *P. pusilla* from south-east Asia and southern China is a shiny black berry with a dry but sweet pulp. In Africa the fruit of *P. reclinata* are relished by the local inhabitants. Those of *P. acaulis* from south-east Asia are recorded as being edible but astringent.

Both the fruits and seeds of the Palmyra Palm (*Borassus flabellifer*) can be eaten. The flesh of recently mature fruit is bright orange and quite refreshing but is detracted from somewhat by its rather fibrous texture. It can be eaten raw or roasted or made into preserves. In young fruits it is jelly-like and is then highly prized. The kernel of the seed is also edible either immature or mature but is often left to germinate and the sinker, prized for its delicate flavour, harvested. *Hyphaene* species can also be used in a similar manner.

Salacca zalacca is a handsome, clumping palm native to Indonesia and south-east Asia. It has pinnate, erect fronds that arise from a subterranean trunk which usually grows in marshy ground. Everything is liberally covered with long, black, sharp spines. Small clusters of fruit are carried between the leaves and these fruit are highly prized for their edible flesh. They are 4 cm to 8 cm long, pear-shaped and covered with overlapping dull orange scales. The yellowish-cream flesh is sweet and juicy. The fruit are commonly sold in Asian markets and are a popular item. Each fruit contains three seeds and these are also reportedly edible. The fruit of two other species of *Salacca* viz. *S. affinis* and the closely related *Eleiodoxa conferta* are also edible.

A number of other palms produce edible fruit but these are principally of local interest. *Hyphaene thebaica*, the African Doum Palm, is also frequently called the Gingerbread Palm because of the unusual flavour of its fruits which are mainly eaten in times of shortage. Some tribes of American Indians eat the fruits of the Cabbage Palmetto (*Sabal palmetto*), the Cotton Palm (*Washingtonia filifera*) and Saw Palmetto (*Serenoa repens*). Each of these palms only produces small fruits but in large quantities and the plants themselves grow in extensive colonies. The Guadalupe Palm (*Brahea edulis*), which is also found in southern California, produces prodigious quantities of small, black fruit with an edible flesh that is variously described as sweet or dull and insipid. *Brahea dulcis*, the Rock Palm of Mexico, produces long hanging clusters of succulent yellow fruit about 1 cm long. Another Mexican palm, *Cryosophila nana*, has a white shiny fruit with a spongy sweet pulp. It is a prolific bearer and has been planted in Trinidad specifically for its fruit. On Robinson Crusoe's island of Juan Fernandez is the palm *Juania australis* which has edible fruit. The fruit of the Fijian palm *Neoveitchia storckii* are eaten before they reach maturity and in Hawaii the immature fruits of *Pritchardia* were prized by the natives. These palms even had steps cut into the trunks to facilitate fruit collection. In *Calamus rotang* the round fruit have a thirst-quenching, acid flesh. These are sold in local markets and may be either eaten fresh or after pickling. This palm, which is a climber, is one important producer of Rattan Cane used for furniture and weaving. A Borneo palm, *Daemonorops lasiospatha*, has a thick layer of sweet flesh in the fruit. In some areas the prickly *Aiphanes caryotifolia* is cultivated for its edible fruits.

Palms are prominent in South American jungles and quite a few with edible fruit were probably of significance in the diet of the natives. The most widely known of these is undoubtedly *Butia capitata*, the Jelly Palm. This handsome palm is widely grown for its arching crown of bluish green fronds and few people realise that its fruits are quite tasty. They are rounded, about 2.5 cm across and when ripe are yellow suffused with red. They are borne in large clusters and have a fibrous, tasty flesh somewhat reminiscent of apricots. Another species, *B. yatay*, has edible fruit up to 5 cm in diameter. *Allagoptera arenaria* is a trunkless maritime palm colonising the coastal sand dunes of Brazil. Its fruit is green to yellowish when ripe and has a fibrous, somewhat acid flesh. The deep-orange fruits of *Polyandrococos caudescens*, also from Brazil, are globular and with a succulent orange flesh. *Syagrus coronata* is a tall palm with prominent, adhering leaf bases which ascend the trunk in a spiral pattern. It is native to Brazil and also produces fleshy, orange fruit that are edible. The palm *Maximiliana martiana* bears a yellow fruit with a sweet, pleasant, juicy pulp while the fruit of the Mucuja Palm (*Acrocomia lasiospatha*) have a thin layer of firm orange flesh and are eaten by the natives of the Guianas. The Urucuri Palm (*Scheelea martiana*) of the Amazon is a prolific bearer carrying clusters of fruit with a pleasant pulp of similar taste to the Date. This palm is cultivated in Trinidad for its fruit. The fruit of *Orbignya spectabilis* are eaten raw by various Amazon tribes.

Three species of palm in each of the genera *Astrocaryum* and *Bactris* produce edible fruit of good quality. Those of *Astrocaryum murumuru* from Brazil have a juicy, somewhat aromatic flavour while the yellowish fruit of *A. tucuma* are fibrous and fleshy but very rich in Vitamin A. The third species is *A. acaule* also of Brazil. *Bactris gasipaes* is known as the Peach Palm because of the appearance of its fruit which are 5 cm to 8 cm across. They are yellowish when ripe with a dry, mealy flesh and may be eaten fresh or are more usually boiled in salt water. It is interesting to note that this palm produces two crops a year and seedless strains are known, indicating selection and domestication by man. This palm is widely cultivated in South America for its fruit and is virtually unknown in the wild. The Maraja Palm (*Bactris maraja*) has a somewhat acid fruit while those of *B. guineensis*, popularly known as the Tobago Cane, are dark purple and about the size of cherries. The Colombian palm (*B. major*) also produces clusters of egg-shaped, purple fruit that are edible.

Species of *Mauritia* also produce edible and nutritious fruit. *M. flexuosa* (known as the Ita

Palm) is most familiar producing a red fruit with yellow flesh that tastes like an apple but may require cooking first. The oily pulp of the fruit of *M. vinifera* can also be eaten after boiling. Fruit of the related *Mauritia aculeata* can also be eaten. Even the very oily yellow drupe of the African Oil Palm (*Elaeis guineensis*) can be eaten in times of scarcity but may produce nausea.

A few palms have a very thin layer of edible flesh around the seed and while this may provide a tasty morsel when out walking, they are generally not worth the effort of serious collection. The scaly fruits of some species of the large genus of climbing palms, *Calamus,* are white when ripe and have just such a layer of edible flesh. Similar remarks apply to the small, dark fruit of the Dwarf Date Palm (*Phoenix roebelenii*). The Walking Stick Palm (*Linospadix monstachya*) of moist gullies in the Australian bush produces long strings of waxy red, ovoid fruit. These are quite pleasant to chew while walking through the bush but are merely a tasty morsel. The fruits of this little palm achieved fame when they helped sustain the survivors of a plane crash on the Lamington Plateau of south-eastern Qld in 1927. The glossy blue fruits of the Himalayan palm *Trachycarpus martianus* also have a thin layer of edible but rather insipid flesh.

Seeds

Undoubtedly the most famous palm seed that is prized for its edible qualities is that of the Betel Nut Palm (*Areca catechu*). A concoction made from the prepared nut, rolled in a fresh Betel Pepper leaf (*Piper betle*) together with some slaked lime (or a pellet of dried lime) derived from burnt shells and a little tobacco or plant extract is chewed or sucked for about thirty minutes at a time. This preparation promotes salivation and is a mild stimulant. It is also claimed to have other beneficial side effects such as aiding digestion and controlling dysentry and internal parasites such as worms. A deleterious effect is the intensive red staining on the gums, lips and tongues of habitual betel chewers. The practice is very popular and widely spread, being adopted throughout Asia, Polynesia and parts of Africa. The palm itself is native to either Malaysia or the Philippines but is now widely grown throughout Asia.

The preparation and sale of Betel Nut is a very big industry. The egg-shaped fruits are harvested just before they are ripe (when they are colouring but not yet a deep orange or scarlet). The outer fibrous husk is cut off and the reddish-yellow, mottled seed is removed. This is then softened by boiling, sliced and dried in the sun until it is a dark brown colour and is then ready for use. Sometimes the seeds may be roasted before drying. Betel nut palms live for about thirty years and produce fruit for about twenty-five years.

Seeds of many other palm species are chewed in a similar manner to Betel Nut and may be used as a substitute for it. In Sri Lanka the seeds of *Loxococcus rupicola* are prepared and chewed like Betel Nut and sometimes with it. In the Andaman Islands the seeds of *Areca laxa* are chewed in this way while in some of the Indonesian islands it is the seed of *Pinanga dicksonii* which is favoured. In New Guinea and the Solomon Islands *Areca macrocalyx* and *A. guppyana* are used in the same way. In the Philippines Betel substitutes include *Areca caliso, A. ipot, Heterospathe elata, Oncosperma* spp., *Pinanga* spp., and *Veitchia merrillii.*

A few other palms have edible seeds but these are rather insignificant compared with the very large industry surrounding the Betel Nut Palm. The kernel of the Mexican and Central American palm *Astrocaryum mexicanum* is edible and is reported to have a flavour similar to the coconut. Its fruits, which are about 3.5 cm across, are spiny and borne in large clusters. Another with a coconut-like flavour (but more oily) is that of *Orbignya cohune* from Honduras. The seeds as well as the fruits of *Salacca zalacca* are edible, each fruit containing two to three yellow kernels. A similar situation exists for *Borassus flabellifer*. The South American Ivory Nut Palms (*Phytelephas macrocarpa* and *P. microcarpa*) have strangely shaped aggregated fruits, each of which contains up to four large seeds about the size of a hens egg. When immature and soft these can be eaten and are reported to have a nutty flavour. The very cold-tolerant *Nannorrhops ritchiana* from the mountains of Afghanistan has an edible seed which is harvested locally. The seeds of the Brazilian *Syagrus ventricosa* and the West Indian *Bactris major* are sold on local markets. The kernel of the Mucuja Palm, *Acrocomia aculeata,* from South America is reported to be sweet while that of *Jubaea chilensis,* commonly known as the Chilean Wine Palm, is nutty. Those of *Veitchia joannis* are somewhat astringent but are eaten in Fiji, especially by children.

Some kernels may require preparation before they are edible. In India and south-east Asia, the immature seeds of the Sugar Palm, *Arenga pinnata,* are preserved in sugar and sold as a delicacy known as palm nuts. Young seeds of the Mangrove Palm, *Nypa fruticans,* may be treated in a similar way. Those of the African Oil Palm, *Elaeis guineensis,* are roasted and are reported to taste like mutton. A coffee substitute can be made from the roasted seeds of *Phoenix reclinata,* the Senegal Date Palm.

Palm Cabbage

The apical bud of a palm is central in the upper part of the trunk and is surrounded by the undeveloped leaf bases and leaves. In a number of palms, this apical bud together with the very young leaf sheaths and leaves that immediately surround it are edible and highly prized by primitive native tribes and western gourmets alike. This cabbage may be cooked or eaten raw in salads and usually has an appealing nutty flavour. In some countries such as Brazil, Paraguay and Venezuala these apical buds are canned and exported as 'Palm Hearts' or Palmito, although they may be more generally referred to as 'Palm Cabbage'.

The collection of Palm Cabbage relies on the destruction of the palm, for the tree must be felled and all of the surrounding tissue removed in order to reach the delicacy. For this reason dishes containing this material may be referred to as 'millionaires salads' although this term is generally confined to the cabbage obtained from the versatile and important Coconut Palm (*Cocos nucifera*). As well as being of a pleasant taste, Palm Cabbage is very nutritious and must have been (and perhaps still is) an important article of diet to many tribes and races of man.

Nutritional and culinary aspects aside, the harvesting of palm cabbage is a tremendously wasteful process. The vast majority of palms harvested are cut from wild populations and in certain areas this exploitation has reached such a degree that the forest ecology is being changed. It has been estimated that each year in Brazil and Paraguay more than six million palms are destroyed just for the export trade. In the Dominican Republic (a former exporter) the situation became so bad that a permit system was introduced. The exploitation for Palm Cabbage has directly threatened a number of species and has caused them to become rare or endangered in their natural habitat. Examples of this are *Acanthophoenix rubra, Hyophorbe* spp., and *Pritchardiopsis jennencyi.* Not only are mature palms harvested but when young plants reach about 4 cm in diameter they are susceptible to destruction for a mere handful of cabbage and without the opportunity to reproduce.

Palm hearts may well be referred to as millionaires salad if their production is to result in extinction of species and cause a change in the forest ecology. Either western gourmets should stop creating the demand for this product or plantations could be established to grow palms for harvesting. In western Costa Rica an experimental station is examining the possiblities of close planting the very fast-growing Peach Palm (*Bactris gasipaes*) for cabbage. Results show that these palms yield about 1.5 kg of cabbage after about four years and are faster growing and higher yielding than local palms. Peach palms also sucker and therefore the harvested stem is automatically replaced.

A few palms which are called Cabbage Palms probably derived this vernacular from their edible apical bud. Perhaps the best known of these is the Feathery Cabbage Palm or Iraiba Palm (*Roystonea oleracea*) from South America. About 5 kg of the white delicacy called cabbage can be obtained from a mature tree and it can be eaten either raw, cooked or pickled and is sometimes canned for export. The related species *R. elata* from Florida, and *R. boriqueana* from Puerto Rico, also yield a similar cabbage. The Cabbage Palmetto from Florida (*Sabal palmetto*) similarly yields an excellent cabbage and was widely eaten by the Indians of the area. In Australia a number of species of the genus *Livistona* are known as Cabbage Palms. Many of these contain

TABLE 4

Some Palms with Edible Cabbage

Species	Origin	Species	Origin
Acanthophoenix rubra	Mascarene Islands	*Hyophorbe lagenicaulis*	Mascarene Islands
Archontophoenix alexandrae	Australia	*Hyophorbe verschaffeltii*	Mascarene Islands
Archontophoenix cunninghamiana	Australia	*Jessenia bataua*	Brazil
		Juania australis	Juan Fernandez
Areca catechu	Asia	*Licuala paludosa*	Malaysia, Thailand
Arecastrum romanzoffianum	South America	*Linospadix monostachya*	Australia
Arenga ambong	Philippines	*Livistona australis*	Australia
Arenga listeri	Christmas Island	*Livistona benthamii*	Australia
Arenga pinnata	Indonesia	*Livistona humilis*	Australia
Astrocaryum murumuru	Brazil	*Livistona rotundifolia*	Malaysia, Philippines
Astrocaryum tucuma	Brazil		
Bactris gasipaes	South America (cult.)	*Livistona speciosa*	India, Burma, Malaysia
Borassodendron machodonis	Malaysia	*Lodoicea maldivica*	Maldive Islands
Brahea brandeegei	Mexico	*Maxmiliana martiana*	Brazil
Carpentaria acuminata	Australia	*Metroxylon sagu*	Melanesia
Caryota urens	India, Malaysia	*Normanbya normanbyi*	Australia
Cocos nucifera	Pacific region	*Oenocarpus bacaba*	Brazil
Corypha elata	Asia	*Oncosperma horridum*	Malaysia, Indonesia
Deckenia nobilis	Seychelles	*Oncosperma tigillarium*	Malaysia
Euterpe edulis	Brazil	*Pritchardiopsis jennencyi*	New Caledonia
Euterpe macrospadix	Costa Rica, British Honduras, Panama	*Ravenea madagascariensis*	Madagascar
		Rhopalostylis sapida	New Zealand
Euterpe oleracea	Brazil	*Roystonea borinquena*	Puerto Rico
Euterpe precatoria	Brazil, Bolivia, Peru, Colombia	*Roystonea elata*	Florida, USA
		Roystonea oleracea	Cuba, West Indies
Gronophyllum ramsayi	Australia	*Sabal palmetto*	USA
Gulubia palauensis	Palau Island, Carolinas	*Satakentia liukiuensis*	Ryukyu Islands
Heterospathe elata	Amboina	*Scheelea martiana*	Brazil

cabbage and were probably harvested by the Aborigines. For example, *L. benthamii* and *L. humilis* were eaten in the Northern Territory. The most widely spread species is *L. australis* and it became a popular article of diet with the early settlers.

The apical buds of some other palms can be eaten. That of the Inaja Palm (*Maximiliana martiana*) from Brazil and the Nibung Palm (*Oncosperma tigillarium*) from Malaysia are described as being excellent with a very nutty flavour. The major species harvested and exported from South American countries appear to be *Euterpe edulis* and *E. oleracea*. A list, although by no means comprehensive, of palms with edible cabbage is presented in Table 4.

Young developing parts (other than the cabbage) of some palms are eaten, usually after cooking. The very young leaves of *Acrocomia aculeata, Coccothrinax argentea* and *Nannorhops* make an excellent vegetable either raw or cooked. In Italy the young suckers of *Chamaerops humilis* are eaten after cooking while in parts of Asia the young suckers of various *Calamus* species are used in a similar way. In some countries young palm inflorescences may be collected and eaten after cooking e.g. *Chamaedorea elegans* and *C. tepejilote* from Mexico and South America, *Rhopalostylis sapida* from New Zealand and *Trachycarpus fortunei* from China.

Palm Honey

Relatively few palm flowers are attractive to bees but those species which the bees do visit produce a honey that is highly esteemed. Coconut honey is perhaps the best known in this regard. That from the Saw Palmetto (*Serenoa repens*) and *Borassus flabellifer* are also prized.

In Chile 'Palm Honey' refers to an entirely different product although it also is highly esteemed and very popular. The sap obtained from the trunk of *Jubaea chilensis*, popularly termed the Chilean Wine Palm, is boiled to a treacle-like consistency and is sold as Palm Honey.

OTHER MATERIALS
Palm Fibres

A number of important fibres are obtained from palms and even in this modern age of synthetics many of these still retain their place because of certain unique properties. Fibres are obtained from various parts of the palm and are prepared in some way before use.

Perhaps one of the most well-known fibres comes from one of the most familiar palms, the Coconut (*Cocos nucifera*). This is the fibre known as coir and it is obtained from the fibrous husk which surrounds the nut. Coconut fibres may be up to 30 cm long and are used to produce various types of mats, brushes and brooms, carpets, filling, or twisted to form strings and ropes. The individual fibres are light because they are hollow. Coir fibre ropes are still of major importance today because not only are they strong but they are also durable and resistant to sea water and bacterial action. Coir is commonly a by-product of the Copra industry, but another type of fibre is from nuts that are not fully ripe, and these nuts may be harvested for the fibre alone. This fibre is difficult to obtain and may require soaking for up to six months before it can be separated.

Coir is stripped from the copra husks after they have been soaked for up to six weeks. After soaking the fibres are teased, beaten to remove rubbish and dried in the sun. This may be carried out by hand but today it is more commonly done by machine. Long bristle fibres suitable for brushes, brooms and such are separated from short fine fibres which can be used for fillings in mattresses, filters or compressed into panels. The long fibres obtained from green coconuts are spun into yarn which is then used for carpets, mats and ropes. It is not often realised that long fibres are also found on the petioles of coconut leaves and these are twisted into strong string by the Polynesians.

Piassaba or piassava fibre is a group name for a series of important palm fibres produced in South America and Africa. The name is mainly associated with the Brazilian palm, *Leopoldinia piassaba,* but has been attached to fibres from other palms as a matter of convenience. In South America two species of palms are used viz. Para Piassaba (*Leopoldinia piassaba*) from the Brazilian state of Para and Bahia Piassaba (*Attalea funifera*) from the state of Bahia. West African Piassaba is obtained from the petioles and rhachises of the long pinnate leaves of *Raphia* species (*R. hookeri*, *R. palmapinus* and *R. vinifera*).

The fibres from all of the palms mentioned above are collected from natural stands and either exported or used in local industries. Those of the Brazilian palms arise from the leaf bases and cover the trunk. They are untangled and straightened on the trees before cutting. Only flexible fibres less than five years old are cut and these may be up to 1.5 m long. After cutting these fibres are tied together in bunches and a number of bunches are securely tied to form a cone-shaped bundle which is exported. The fibres are used to produce heavy brooms and industrial brushes as well as cords and ropes. The ropes are excellent for marine purposes since besides their resistance to salt water they will not sink.

The West African Piassaba fibre is rather pale and brittle by comparison with the fibre from Brazil. It is also more difficult to obtain since the leaves must be cut and the petioles and rhachises soaked in water for about two months before the fibre can be separated by pounding and beating. It is principally produced and exported from Sierra Leone. It is generally used in the production of brooms and brushes and may be strengthened by mixing with Brazilian Piassaba fibre.

Other species of *Raphia* produce a different fibre known as raffia. This is harvested from the Madagascan palm *Raphia farinifera* and *R. taedigera* from the Amazon basin. These are short-stemmed palms, the former species having exceptionally long leaves (in fact, the longest leaves in the plant kingdom). The fibre is obtained by stripping the surface from young leaflets which may be up to 2 m long. Raffia fibre was widely used in plaiting, basket work and as tying material but has now largely been replaced by synthetic materials.

Palmyra fibre from the Palmyra Palm (*Borassus flabellifer*) is used in brooms, scrubbing brushes and in the manufacture of carpets, twine and rope. It is obtained from the petioles and leaf sheaths which are beaten to separate the fibres. The fibres themselves are wiry and not elastic. They are widely used locally and are also exported from India. Tucuma fibre is harvested from the pinnate leaves of the Brazilian palm *Astrocaryum tucuma* and is useful for marine ropes and fishing nets.

Valuable fibres are obtained from the petioles and leaf bases of the Fishtail Palm (*Caryota urens*) of India and Malaysia. These black, bristly fibres are known as Kittul and are used to produce ropes, brooms, paintbrushes and specialised brushes for raising the pile on fabrics such as velvet. Fibres from the Nipa Palm (*Nypa fruticans*) are also known as Kittul. The Sugar Palm, *Arenga pinnata*, is also known as the Gomuti Palm because of the production of fibres of that name from the leaves. These coarse, black fibres are very resistant to dampness and are used in various types of filters, for caulking boats and in the production of ropes to be used in salt water.

Miscellaneous fibres of small scale or local interest are produced by a number of palms. Buriti and Muriti are two fibres obtained from the petioles of the Chilean palm (*Mauritia vinifera*). Vegetable Horse-hair or African hair used as a substitute for horsehair in upholstery, is obtained from the black leaf fibres of the European Fan Palm (*Chamaerops humilis*) which is widespread from the Mediterranean coast of Europe to Africa. Fibres from the unopened leaves of a species of *Corypha* are used in the Philippines to make fine hats while those from the grossly hairy trunks of the Cuban palms *Coccothrinax crinita* and *C. miraguama* are collected and woven for various purposes. The lattice fibre from the trunk of the Chinese Windmill Palm (*Trachycarpus fortunei*) and that of the Chinese Fan Palm (*Livistona chinensis*) is very useful in nurseries for lining hanging baskets. Fibres from the petioles of the Ita Palm (*Mauritia flexuosa*) of South America are woven into threads.

Palm Oils and Waxes

The fruit and seeds of a number of palms contain oils which have been found to be very useful for cooking and for the manufacture of margarine and lubricants and in the production of many other materials.

The most famous of these palms is again undoubtedly the Coconut (*Cocos nucifera*) the oil of which makes up about twenty per cent of all vegetable oils used in the world. The oil is extracted from the copra which is the flesh of the coconut dried in the sun. The expressed oil is used in the production of dressings and margarines, soap, shampoos and so on. The waste material is pressed and used for animal feed.

The most important palm grown solely for oil is the African Oil Palm (*Elaeis guineensis*) which is native to West and Central Africa. This handsome and very hardy palm is grown in plantations in various parts of the world such as Indonesia, Malaysia, Nigeria, New Guinea, and Central and South America. Oil palm plantings were also tried in parts of northern Australia but the production was found to be uneconomic. One problem was the slow growth of the plants in their early years of establishment.

Mature plants of the African Oil Palm produce three to six dense clusters of fruits annually and each contains about 4000 individual fruit. The fruit vary in size from 3-6 cm long and are black when ripe. The flesh contains thirty to seventy per cent oil which is extracted by a fermentation process and is known as palm pulp oil. It is very similar in its makeup to olive oil and is used in the manufacture of cosmetics, margarines and dressings and in fuels and lubricants. The seed kernels also contain about fifty per cent useful oil and this is extracted after crushing and is known as palm kernel oil. It is less valuable than the pulp oil and is used for the manufacture of soap and glycerine. A selection programme has produced horticultural cultivars which have small seeds and therefore give a greater yield of the more valuable pulp oil. These superior forms are now propagated by tissue culture.

Other species of palms produce useful oils but these are of less importance than the African Oil Palm and may only be of local interest. The American Oil Palm (*Elaeis oleifera*) from South America produces large clusters of fruit similar to the African Oil Palm and also with an oily

A house made from the leaves of *Salacca wallichiana*, south Thailand (photo John Dransfield)

flesh. The oil has been extracted experimentally and was used by the local tribes and early settlers. A valuable oil is also extracted from the seeds of the Cohune Palm (*Orbignya cohune*) which is native to Honduras, but details of its uses are lacking. Two other species of *Orbignya* from Brazil produce fruits that are rich in oils. These are harvested from the wild and are known as Barbassu Palms (*O. martiana* and *O. oleifera*). The oil is used in margarine, soap, for cooking and in lubricants. The fruits of two species (*Oenocarpus bacaba* and *Jessenia bataua*) from the Amazon region give a colourless, sweet oil which can be used for cooking. Two other South American Palms provide useful oils, *Acrocomia sclerocarpa* from the husks of the fruit and *Syagrus coronata* from the seeds.

Many palms have waxy coatings which act as water-conserving mechanism for the plant. These waxes may be found on leaves, petioles and trunks and have some properties useful to man. The most important wax is obtained from the Wax Palm (*Copernicia prunifera*) and is known as Carnauba Wax. This material covers the upper surface of the leaves and is the hardest of all commercial waxes with a very high melting point. Commercially, mature leaves are collected from both wild palms and those in cultivated plantations, allowed to dry and the wax is then collected by flailing these leaves mechanically. The wax flakes off freely and is termed caducous. It is used for a variety of purposes including candles, lipsticks and other cosmetics, records, shoe polish, car polish and floor wax. This wax is exported from Brazil where the palms are grown in plantations. More than 20 000 tonnes a year is produced. Breeding and selection programmes are being carried out to produce high-yielding cultivars.

Other, less-important waxes are present on various palms. The trunks and underside of the leaflets of *Ceroxylon quindiuense* from the northern Andes of Colombia bear a wax which has been harvested. A wax is also harvested from *Syagrus coronata* in Brazil but it is not caducous and must be scraped from the leaves. Several other palms such as *Serenoa repens* have waxy layers but these are not harvested commercially.

PALMS IN CONSTRUCTION
Housing

Various palms contribute to the housing and shelter of people in many countries of the world. In Polynesia huts may be built entirely from parts of the Coconut palm while in Panama, huts also made entirely from palm products may be built around the still-living trunks of a local species of *Astrocaryum*. In Thailand huts may be composed entirely of local palms (*Salacca wallichiana* and *Nypa fruticans*). The Nipa huts of the Philippines are also constructed largely or entirely of palm products as are huts in the lowlands of New Guinea and the Amazon region of South America.

Lumber for the supporting posts and main structural timbers can be supplied from the trunks either sawn into sections or split lengthwise (*Borassus flabellifer, Cocos nucifera, Neoveitchia storckii, Socratea exhorrhiza* and *Astrocaryum* species). Palm trunks are not readily sawn into planks. Minor structural support can be obtained from the petioles (*Cocos nucifera*) and the floor can be formed from split and polished trunks (*Astrocaryum* spp., *Cocos nucifera*).

The leaves thatched on the roof form an excellent waterproof covering and internal partitions can be woven from the leaflets. Internal decorations and utensils can also originate from palms and a notched trunk can form a ladder if one is needed. Such houses are excellent for tropical climates maintaining coolness, dryness and air movement. Magnificent examples can be seen in Fiji.

Thatching of roofs is quite an art and around the world the leaves of numerous species of palms are used for this purpose. Many pinnate-leaved palms are used (*Astrocaryum* spp., *Metroxylon vitiense, Nypa fruticans, Geonoma baculifera*) but some species of fan palms are also suitable (*Coccothrinax argentea, Corypha umbraculifera, Borassus flabellifer, Lodoicea maldivica* and *Livistona benthamii*). Some palms are commonly known as Thatch Palms because of this use. In coastal districts of the tropics the leaf of the Coconut is widely used. Leaves of the South American Monkey Cap Palm (*Manicaria saccifera*) have proved to be a very long-lasting thatch.

Panel made from woven leaflets of *Salacca wallichiana*, south Thailand (photo John Dransfield)

Partition made from petioles of *Salacca wallichiana*, south Thailand (photo John Dransfield)

Furniture

The harvesting of rattan cane is an important industry in south-east Asian countries such as Indonesia, the Philippines and Malaysia. The cane is actually the stems of several species of climbing palms in the genus *Calamus* and a few other genera and it may be exported in bundles or made into various items of cane furniture. *C. rotang* is strictly known as the Rattan Cane but many other species are also harvested including *C. caesius, C. rudentum, C. scipionum, C. trachycoleus, C. manan, C. verus* and *C. tenuis*. The vast majority of rattan is harvested from natural stands, but there is considerable interest in its cultivation and successful plantations have been established in Malaysia and Borneo where *C. trachycoleus* has proved superior.

Rattan stems are usually smooth and naked in the older sections but in the young regions are covered by spiny leaf sheaths which are an aid to climbing. When being harvested the stems are cut near ground level and dragged out of the forest canopy. They are commonly from 50 m to 100 m long but may occasionally reach as much as 160 m. The leaves, cirri and inflorescences are trimmed off and the leaf sheaths removed by dragging through closely spaced pairs of pegs. This leaves the supple stems smooth and these are cut into manageable lengths and left to dry in the sun for at least a month. They may be used whole or split and can be manufactured into an amazing range of furniture items, baskets, bins and so on.

OTHER USES

Horticulture

Palms are a very important component of the nursery industry and each year in Australia and many other countries, hundreds of thousands are grown and sold solely for their ornamental appeal. This results in the direct employment of many thousands of people engaged in their propagation and growth. It also creates demand for seeds and thus provides employment in this area. As an example, palm seed collecting was a major industry on Lord Howe Island and in 1975 produced a gross return to the island of $A100 000. They now export germinated seed.

Fans, Hats and Weaving

Not surprisingly the leaves of various species of fan palms are used to produce fans and sun shelters. The fans may be crudely cut from the leaves or carefully processed into decorative as well as useful implements. Fans may be made from a range of palms but species of *Sabal*, *Livistona*, *Pritchardia* and *Corypha* are prominent in this use. Primitive but effective shelters from the sun and the rain may be made from various species. It is claimed that the large leaves of *Corypha umbraculifera* may shelter from ten to fifteen people at once. The undivided leaves of various species of *Johannesteijsmannia* provide a refuge from sudden storms in the jungles of Malaysia.

Many species of fan palms are used to produce light fibre hats that provide excellent protection in the tropics. The most famous, the Panama Hat, is mainly produced from a palm relative, the Panama Hat Plant (*Carludovica palmata*). Similar-looking hats are made from palms in the same area, such as *Sabal causiarum* which may be known as the Puerto Rican Hat Palm. The leaves of this (and other *Sabal* species) are collected at a certain stage of development, soaked in boiling water and the fibrous leaf segments separated and dried before plaiting into hats. The segments of many others are used in a similar way including *Corypha*, *Coccothrinax*, *Borassus*, *Livistona*, *Lodoicea* and *Pritchardia*. Those of *Livistona jenkinsiana* are used to make a curiously shaped hat worn by the local people in India. In Australia several species of *Livistona* were used to make Cabbage Tree Hats which were very popular with the early settlers. Their preparation was similar to that for the *Sabal*.

Buntal is a fine fibre removed from the unexpanded leaves of *Corypha umbraculifera*. It is used in the Philippines to make quality hats. A curious cap known as the Temiche Cap is made from the pouch-like spathes of the Monkey Cap Palm, *Manicaria saccifera,* which is native to parts of South America. The cap is cut by the local Indians before the spathe is ruptured and is worn as protection from the sun.

Leaflets lend themselves well to various forms of plaiting and thatching and can be used for a large range of articles including internal house partitions, hammocks, mats, baskets and a range of containers used for carrying.

Walking Sticks

Palms have traditionally produced the best walking sticks possibly because the trunks of some species are about the right thickness, are usually very straight and are tough enough for the job. Also they generally polish very well and present a good appearance.

Walking sticks may be made from a number of palms which have thick, straight trunks. These are split and suitable pieces may be turned or sanded and polished. The hard, mottled, porcupine wood of the coconut is very suitable as is also the very straight trunk of the Fijian palm *Balaka seemannii*.

The stems or canes of many of the smaller palms such as *Rhopaloblaste singaporensis* may also be used. Malacca canes are highly prized for the job. These are straight, stout sections of rattan obtained from the climbing palms of the genus *Calamus* (in particular *C. scipionum*). Their only drawback is their pale colouration and they are generally stained or darkened with smoke before sale. Malacca cane is the traditional cane used for officers batons and for punishment in school.

In Australia *Linospadix monostachya* is commonly known as the Walking Stick Palm because of its suitability for this use. This little palm is widespread throughout the moist forests of southern Qld and north-eastern NSW and has a solitary, tough, slender stem which has a curious swelling just below ground level. This swelling provides a convenient hand grip and thousands of these palms were harvested and turned into walking sticks for use by wounded servicemen returning from the First World War. This little palm is also known by the curious vernacular of 'Midgin-ball'. Walking sticks have also been manufactured in Australia from the hard, dark trunks of the Black Palm (*Normanbya normanbyi*).

Vegetable Ivory and other Carvings

Many fine ornaments are carved from the large seeds of some species of palms, the endosperm of which is hard and similar to the texture of animal horn. This material has a remarkable similarity to that of ivory and for this reason is called vegetable ivory. In the past this material was widely used for the production of buttons, billiard balls, dice and such but has been replaced in this use by synthetic plastics and is now mainly used for decorative carving. *Phytelephas macrocarpa* from Columbia and Ecuador is known as the Ivory Nut Palm, the name arising from the usefulness.of its seeds which are about the size of a hens egg. These are collected and exported in large quantities. The related species *P. microcarpa* from northern South America can also be used in a similar way. *Metroxylon amicarum* from the Carolina Islands also produces vegetable ivory and is perhaps not surprisingly known as the Carolina Ivory Nut Palm. A number of other *Metroxylon* species produce vegetable ivory including the Sago Palm (*M. sagu*).

The hard shells of the fruits of certain palms can be used for carvings. Probably the best known of these is the coconut which may be carved while still in the husk or the polished shell may be used. Both types are widely sold to tourists in various parts of Polynesia and the Pacific region. The shells of species of *Hyphaene* from Africa are used to produce animal replicas which are sold locally.

Minor Uses

The number of other uses to which palms can be put is almost beyond recording and only a few will be presented here.

The material known as Olla is used as a substitute for writing paper in India. It is made from the dried and flattened sections of the leaves of *Corypha elata* and *C. umbraculifera* and when finished is parchment like and will take ink. This material has been used for centuries and samples more than 1000 years old are preserved in museums. In Java and parts of south-east Asia *Borassus flabellifer* was a very important source of writing material. An interesting resourcefulness is shown by the Warao Indians of the Orinoco Delta in Venezuala who use the large, entire leaves of *Manicaria saccifera* as sails for their canoes.

Coconut fibre or coir can be used to produce a peat substitute which can be used in nursery potting mixtures to grow plants. The dust and rubbish left over from coir production can be used for this purpose or coir itself can be hammer-milled to produce a higher-quality product.

Coconut shells can be used for such purposes as a fuel for fire, for producing a very high-quality charcoal and for eating and drinking vessels. Drinking water can be obtained from the stems of some climbing palms in the genera *Calamus* and *Daemonorops*.

A red resin is obtained from the fruit of the Indonesian climbing palm *Daemonorops draco* and related species. Dyes can also be obtained from fruit. *Jessenia batua* which gives a dark blue dye is one example.

Palms contribute to warfare and hunting. The strong, straight trunks of the Fijian palm, *Balaka seemannii,* were much in demand for spear shafts. In the Philippines the various species of *Livistona, Oncosperma* and *Pinanga* were used. In Brazil the trunks of *Iriartella setigera* and in Colombia those of *Morenia montana* are hollowed and polished to make blowguns and the 30 cm to 90 cm long black spines from the trunk of *Jessenia bataua* are used for the darts. Similar spines from the trunk of the Malaysian *Arenga pinnata* were used by natives to make arrows. In the Amazon region bows may be fashioned from the trunks of *Jessenia bataua* and *Oenocarpus bacaba* while brittle arrow tips are made from many other palm species. In New Guinea the stems of *Ptychococcus lepidotus* are used to make bows and arrowheads while in the Philippines they were manufactured from *Livistona rotundifolia*. Arrow poisons have been concocted in Malaysia and the Philippines from the very poisonous fruit of some species of *Orania*. Excellent clubs can be made from the very heavy, dense wood of the trunks of some palms such as *Jessenia bataua* from the Amazon region.

CHAPTER 4
The Cultivation of Palms

SOME species of palm can be grown in almost any garden in most urban areas of Australia and much of the North Island of New Zealand. Although the majority of palms are of tropical origin there is quite a range that can be grown in temperate regions and even a few that are very cold tolerant and will still survive in areas with a cold winter climate. A number of species thrive in inland areas and a few extremely tough ones will even tolerate arid conditions. In fact, given water, a good range of palms can be grown in inland towns and can significantly add to the atmosphere of such places.

Palms are very easy plants to grow given the basic requirements of good soil, plenty of water and protection from hot sun at least while they are young. When mature most palms are sun-loving plants and must have full sunshine to achieve maximum growth. This is of special significance in temperate regions where the winter sun is weak and is often obscured by clouds. Within the group there are however shade-loving plants which will not tolerate hot sun without bleaching or burning (see Dwarf to Small Palms page 257).

Any garden can support a palm or a selection of palms. The more hardy sun-lovers need an open position while the smaller types generally need more protection and can be successfully mixed with shrubs. Houses with large areas of protected garden can grow a good selection of palms and these can be complemented with plants such as Cordylines, Dracaenas, Cycads and large ferns. With the exception of very bulky palms, such as *Phoenix canariensis,* most species do not take up a great deal of room in a garden. This is especially true once a trunk is formed and grass, shrubs or annuals can be grown right up to the base of the trunk if this is desired. Palms like company and look good when planted in groups. A collection of mixed species in a suitable situation in the garden will always be a source of interest and conversation.

LANDSCAPING WITH PALMS

The advantage palms have over other plants used in landscaping is that their growth habit and dimensions are entirely predictable. Thus a palm can be chosen to fill a particular niche and the landscaper can be certain, given suitable conditions of soil and growth, that the palm will grow as predicted. Few other plants can be chosen accordingly.

Palms are well suited to planting as specimens in lawns or in groups provided that they are spaced so a mower can be used between them. The palms impart an interesting appearance to a lawn planted in this way and do not interfere with the growth of the grass. Grass, provided that it is regularly watered and fertilised, will grow right up to the base of a palm trunk. Mowing in these circumstances is no major problem, since a palm tree cannot be ringbarked and the mower can be run close to the trunk without damage. If long grass continually grows too close to the trunk and is unsightly a small garden bed can be dug around the trunk.

Palms that produce suckers may be a problem if planted in lawns because the suckers appear at various distances from the trunk. These can be controlled by regular close mowing or else digging out the lawn and creating a circular garden bed around the palm.

Tall, noble palms such as *Arecastrum romanzoffianum* and *Roystonea regia* make excellent specimen plants and a well-grown subject is always a source of admiration. Careful placement of such plants will ensure that the maximum benefit is received from their stateliness. Placed as a lawn specimen which can be viewed from windows or terraces, or framing stairways and balconies is very effective.

Tall palms can also be planted in pairs or groups of the one species or mixed with other palms or other plants. Tall palms look especially effective when planted close together in pairs. If planted side by side and at a slight angle away from each other their trunks tend to curve apart and add an interesting aspect to the garden. Tall palms also look good beside driveways and paths and may be spaced regularly to form impressive avenues (see Palms for Avenue Planting page 259).

Palms, especially the smaller to medium growing types, prefer company and are best planted in groups or mingled with other plants. The grouping helps create a congenial atmosphere and produces a better overall effect. The small shade-loving palms such as *Chamaedorea, Laccospadix, Linospadix* and *Reinhardtia* mix very well with ferns. As with ferns these plants help create an atmosphere of coolness and are a welcome retreat on hot summer days.

Palms provide excellent shade despite the deceptive open appearance of their crowns. A palm grove provides a welcome retreat on a hot day and if combined with water such as in a pond or a pool the atmosphere is further enhanced. An oasis, after all, is a shady retreat in the desert where water comes to the surface and the shade is, of course, provided by palms. Because of their umbrella-like structure and predictable growth, palms can be strategically sited to provide shade for outdoor living areas, barbecues and swimming pools. In hot, dry, inland areas the shade provided by hardy palms such as *Phoenix canariensis* and *P. dactylifera* is greatly appreciated. With their generally slender trunks, palms have the added advantage of not hindering air movement or breeze while still providing the shade.

When planning to landscape with palms numerous factors should be considered in selecting a suitable species. One factor which is often neglected is the debris created by the palm. Fruits of some species are messy and are generally borne in profusion. Coconuts are heavy objects and these palms should not be planted where their fruit can create a hazard. Some palms retain their fronds when dead and this may be regarded as an untidy habit. *Arecastrum romanzoffianum* is a good example. *Roystonea regia* is of similar appearance but with a tidier habit because its fronds are self-shedding when dead.

Palms with spiny trunks should not be planted beside paths or where children run or play as the long spines can easily damage sensitive areas, especially the eyes. The basal pinnae of *Phoenix* species are modified into stiff, sharp spines. Although commonly planted in parks and along streets they are usually severely trimmed to keep the spines out of reach.

ASPECT AND CLIMATIC CONSIDERATIONS

Many factors are involved in the choice of a site suitable for palms. These include aspect, slope, soil type and drainage, exposure to frost, wind and sun and competition from neighbouring trees. The species of palm and its tolerance of climatic conditions also significantly influences the decision.

The aspect selected for palms will be influenced by the conditions existing in the area. In temperate Australia a southerly aspect is generally unsuitable since such an area receives little or no winter sunshine but any other aspect can be suitable. The aspect is generally unimportant in inland regions since only hardy palms can be grown in such areas and these are tolerant of hot sunshine even when quite small. In tropical and subtropical areas many species of palms thrive in full sun, especially if watered heavily during dry periods. This is because most palms are of tropical origin and have generally adapted to the humid atmospheres that exist in the hot seasons. Exposure to full sun, while tolerated by the palm, may be to the detriment of the plants, appearance and the same plants may look lusher and less tattered if grown in partial shade.

Shade can be of special significance in subtropical and tropical regions since sensitive species burn very quickly when exposed. Sun filtered through the canopy of established trees is excellent for shade-loving palms provided that the plants are not exposed to long periods of hot sun through breaks in the canopy. Many tropical trees shed their leaves rapidly during dry periods in the summer, often just prior to flowering. This must be considered when planting shade-loving palms since irreparable damage can be done during a comparatively short period of exposure. Palms, especially some of the smaller types, can be grown under deciduous trees in temperate regions. Here the exposure to winter sun is greatly beneficial as is the annual mulch of leaves. Shade-loving palms will also tolerate exposure to full sun for short periods during the day provided that the sun is not too hot at the time. Morning sun or late afternoon sun is most suitable.

Palms grown under established trees suffer from root competition for nutrients and water and must often be fertilized, watered and mulched at regular intervals if they are to flourish. If the palms were planted at the same time as or soon after the trees then the competition is of less significance since the palm's root system can become established before competition is severe. Once established, small-growing palms appear to cope very well with root competition.

Palms are generally quite tolerant of winds and some species such as the Coconut are renowned for their resistance. Physical damage such as shredding of the leaves of fan palms, or the tips of leaflets of feather palms occurs with mild to strong winds while gales or cyclones may tear the plants out of the ground or break the trunk. Such damage is obvious but insidious effects such as reduced vigour and stunting may accompany cold winds and draughts such as often occur around buildings. Hot, drying winds, especially on hot summer days, may cause desiccation of small plants and sensitive species. Salt-laden onshore winds may similarly damage species in coastal districts. Some wind protection can be achieved by establishing windbreaks or planting in the lee of buildings or existing shrubs and trees.

Frost greatly limits the range of palms that can be grown and most tropical species collapse after exposure to it. Even moderately hardy palms may suffer damage to young and developing leaves, especially if the frosts are heavy or prolonged or the plants are in active growth. Some frost protection can be obtained by planting on slopes where air circulation is unimpeded, near buildings or under established trees.

Soil

Palms are not exacting in their soil requirements and will grow in a tremendous range of soil types. In fact, some palm or other will probably grow in all but the very worst types of soil. Most garden soils in Australia are reasonably well structured and fairly well drained and will support a range of palms. The better the soil type the better the growth of individual palms and the greater the variety that can be grown.

A good guide to the palms that will succeed in an area can be obtained by looking around the region especially in municipal parks and gardens and old established gardens for palms were very popular early this century. When looking at existing palms however and the soils and conditions where they grow, be aware that an established palm is tremendously tolerant of neglect and the present conditions may not reflect the nurturing necessary in their establishment phases.

Most palms seem to prefer an acid soil with a pH of between 6 and 6.5. Where soils are more acid than these levels some correction with dolomite or ground limestone may be necessary. Palms may grow equally well in light sandy soils as in heavier types but the techniques of soil preparation, planting, watering and mulching may differ. Red soils, whether they be well-structured mountain soils, heavier basalt soils or laterites have proved to be ideal for the growth of a range of palms. Those derived from granite and other grey soils can also be good if plenty of organic material is dug in before planting.

Clay Soils Heavy subsoil or clay will support hardy palms but their establishment will be fraught with difficulty and better results will be obtained if the clay is first worked to the stage where it is friable. Clay is difficult to cultivate whether it is wet or dry but can be improved by adding a soil conditioner such as gypsum, organic matter and/or topsoil. This mixture should be gradually worked into the clay until the friability is improved. The more effort that is put into working up such heavy clay soils the better will be the results. Regular applications of organic matter will not only improve the friability but will prevent surface compaction, cracking and drying out. Also, as palms like soils rich in organic matter it will greatly aid the establishment of young plants. If the clay soils are excessively wet, surface or underground drains may be needed to remove the water. For planting technique in clay soils (see Fig 23).

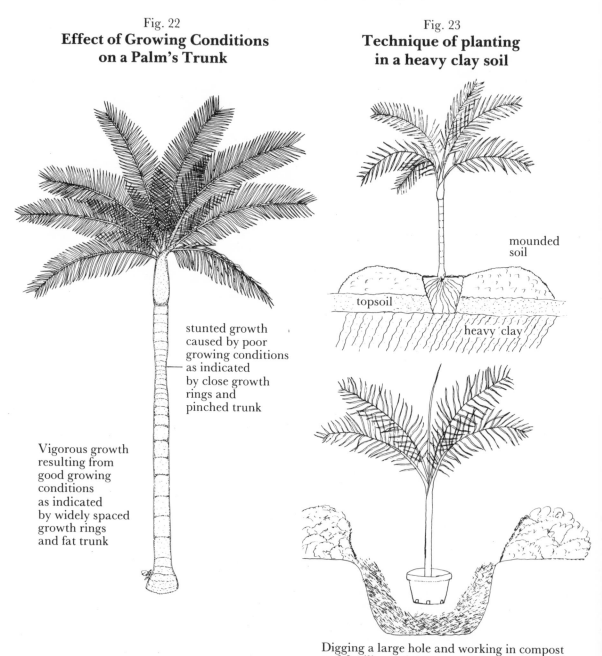

Fig. 22
Effect of Growing Conditions on a Palm's Trunk

stunted growth caused by poor growing conditions as indicated by close growth rings and pinched trunk

Vigorous growth resulting from good growing conditions as indicated by widely spaced growth rings and fat trunk

Fig. 23
Technique of planting in a heavy clay soil

mounded soil

topsoil

heavy clay

Digging a large hole and working in compost and fertiliser prior to planting promotes excellent growth.

Light, Sandy Soils Palms thrive in light, sandy soils because they are usually warmer than heavy soils (and this may be important in winter), are very well drained and aerated and are often quite deep. Such soils are often poor nutritionally however and are usually deficient in organic matter. When very deficient in the latter and when very dry (especially if they are fine sands the granules of which pack together) they may become water repellent and difficult to wet. Heavy mulching with organic materials will help prevent this and greatly aid the establishment and growth of young palms. As sandy soils tend to dry out rather rapidly, regular watering will be necessary, especially in the establishment phases.

Alkaline Soils Alkaline or calcareous soils have an excess of calcium salts in the soil and this creates nutritional problems with elements such as zinc, iron, magnesium and manganese. Such soil types are not uncommon in inland areas. Hardy palms such as *Arecastrum romanzoffianum*, *Brahea armata*, *Butia capitata*, *Chamaerops humilis*, *Livistona mariae*, *Phoenix canariensis*, *Phoenix dactylifera* and *Sabal* and *Washingtonia* spp., can be established quite readily in such soils however the range of suitable species is not as great as in an acid soil. Sometimes the palms may grow although suffering a nutritional problem and then their appearance is not good.

The range of palms and their growth can be increased by adding large quantities of organic matter to the surface and acidifying with sulphur.

Waterlogged Soils Many palms grow naturally in wet or swampy conditions and most of these can be established in well-drained garden soils if they are watered regularly. Palms are rather difficult to establish in waterlogged conditions and the small plants tend to linger and appear unthrifty or die. Such soils can be improved by drainage. *Salacca zalacca* will grow in wet conditions but is tropical in its requirements. *Livistona australis* can be established around the margins of wet or boggy areas and is adaptable to a range of climates. While most palms do not like stagnant water many will happily tolerate wet spots where water is moving such as soaks or springs in the hillside. Palms grown in such sites will be much more tolerant of exposure to hot sunshine. For a list of palms tolerant of wet soils see Appendix 5.

Saline Soils Salted or saline soils have generally lost their structure and the excess of minerals in their profile makes the establishment of palms very difficult. Some hardy palms such as *Phoenix dactylifera* and *P. canariensis* will continue to grow in salted soils after they have established themselves but seedlings will not grow in such situations. Saline soils must be drained so that the salt can be leached through the profile and removed in the drainage water.

Planting

The technique of planting palms is not significantly different from any other type of plant although the correct procedure will greatly aid the establishment of the young palm.

The palms should be thoroughly soaked in their containers before planting and this is best achieved by immersion of the container in water. This pre-soaking is especially important if planting in dry times or in dry areas. The planting hole should then be dug and this should be amply wide and deep to accommodate the root system. Palm enthusiasts advocate the digging of a hole much bigger than the root system, a concept described by one professional horticulturist as a $5 hole for a $1 plant. Not only is the soil broken and loosened to aid root penetration but compost, organic matter and fertilisers may also be mixed into the soil. This work certainly results in rapid establishment and healthy growth but it is a question of labour and time.

If the soil in the planting hole is dry it should be filled with water and allowed to drain before planting. Some fertiliser (either inorganic, organic or slow-release) should be thoroughly worked into the bottom of the hole before planting. About a handful is usually adequate. Some growers advocate working rotted manure and compost into the soil surrounding the hole and this technique definitely aids establishment and is of particular value in sandy soils. If planting into clay soil avoid forming a sump by digging too far into the clay (see Fig 23).

Once the planting hole is ready, the palm should be removed from its container and dead or badly coiled roots trimmed back or straightened out. The plant should be placed in position with the top of the container soil just below that of the garden soil and the soil firmed around the roots and watered thoroughly (5 L to 10 L per plant). The area around the plant should then be mulched (see Mulching page 63).

Watering

Many palms are extremely drought resistant but all look and grow better with supplementary watering during dry periods. Generally the type of area palms come from is a good guide to their draught tolerance. Shade-loving palms are generally rather sensitive to dryness and quickly wilt and look tatty if allowed to become very dry. Similarly dwarf or small palms have few reserves to cope with dryness and are best if watered regularly. It is important to recognise the water needs of a palm before planting and also it is most convenient to grow species with similar moisture requirements together. The shade and moisture loving species prefer plenty of water and it is very difficult to overwater them especially in dry times.

Established palms have a large root system which ramifies a considerable distance through the surrounding soil. This is true of even small-growing palms and it means that the plants are able to tap a vast reserve of soil for their nutrient and water requirements. It also means that water should not be applied only to the soil immediately near the base of the plant but rather should be more widely distributed. If the soil where the roots are growing is well soaked at each watering the plants can last for long intervals without water.

Water is best applied during cool periods or in the evening or early morning. The best technique is to thoroughly soak the root area so that the maximum amount of water becomes available to the plant. The method of water application (i.e. whether it be by hose, sprinkler or drip irrigation) depends on availability and is not of major significance to palms. Sometimes with dwarf palms it is handy to have overhead sprinklers installed as these can be used for both watering and cooling and humidifying the area on hot, dry days. Mulches greatly improve the efficiency of watering and their application is strongly recommended (see Mulching page 63).

Fertilisers

Palms are strong-growing plants and once established are very responsive to fertilisers and manures. Large palms such as *Arecastrum romanzoffianum*, *Phoenix canariensis* and *Roystonia regia* are gross feeders and their growth rate can be increased very significantly by heavy applications of fertilisers. Such rates would be 3 kg to 5 kg applied each time per tree in two to three dressings per year. For the medium and smaller species light dressings of fertiliser at regular intervals are beneficial to their growth and appearance. Fertilisers are best applied during the warm months when the plants are in active growth. This is particularly true of temperate regions where the plants must become hardened in the autumn in order to endure the cold winter. Fertilisers are best applied to moist soil and if watering is not possible they should be applied just before, during or after rain. They should be scattered over the surface of the ground within the drip line of the canopy.

Many growers advocate the use of organic fertilisers such as blood and bone, bone meal or hoof and horn. Animal manures are also very valuable but should not be applied when too fresh. These materials release a steady supply of nutrients for growth and as well are very beneficial to the soil. They are excellent for small-growing palms. They are however quite expensive and may be difficult to obtain. Inorganic fertilisers are cheaper and more readily available and, despite claims to the contrary, are an excellent means of promoting growth. Most inorganic fertilisers are readily soluble and supply nutrients quickly to the plants. A balanced complete fertiliser should be applied annually. The benefit can be maximised if they are applied in conjunction with organic mulches.

Palms seem to require high levels of nitrogen and two supplementary dressings with nitrogenous fertilisers each year promote growth and improve their general appearance. Suitable materials include urea (46% N), ammonium nitrate (35% N), ammonium sulphate (20% N) and calcium nitrate (15% N). Nitrogenous fertilisers are best watered in soon after application. Coconut palms are particularly responsive to applications of nitrogenous fertilisers.

Slow-release fertilisers applied at planting will aid in the establishment and early development of a palm. A handful of such fertiliser well dispersed through the soil in the planting hole is all that is necessary.

Pruning

Pruning in palms is generally limited to the removal of unwanted or unsightly material such as suckers, clusters of fruit or dead fronds. In a number of species the dead fronds are retained for many years and hang as a brown skirt against the trunk. Although regarded as unsightly by some people this feature can add interest to a palm. Good examples are *Washingtonia filifera*, *W. robusta* and *Sabal* spp. This feature, despite being natural, does have some drawbacks such as providing shelter for vermin like rats, sparrows, starlings and mynahs as well as leaving the plants susceptible to fire.

Palms growing in public areas, particularly those planted near paths, must be observed regularly. Many species have large thorns on their petioles and in species of *Phoenix* the basal pinnae are modified into stiff, sharp spines. In these circumstances fronds must be removed when hazardous. Similarly, in public areas the spiny trunks of some palms such as *Aiphanes caryotifolia* can be kept smooth to a height of about 2 m to avoid injury. Climbing palms such as species of *Calamus* with hooked cirri or flagella are best planted away from public areas or else the trailing cirri/flagella should be trimmed out of reach.

Suckers can be a nuisance in gardens, especially if the palms are planted in lawns. This is frequently the case with *Phoenix dactylifera* and *P. reclinata*. Large suckers can be removed by digging and severing the rhizome below ground. Small suckers can be kept under control by regular close mowing.

Fruits are quite a decorative feature of many palms, especially when carried en masse on the tree. On the ground however they are often regarded as being unsightly and in some species may even be soft and messy. If this is a problem the inflorescences are best cut off early in their development.

In a similar manner hanging dead fronds may be unsightly and a cause of concern. The fronds can be cut off regularly as they age and burnt or shredded for garden mulch. This maintenance becomes a problem, especially as the palms grow taller. Species such as *Archontophoenix* and *Roystonea* are self-shedding while in others the fronds hang for a considerable time before falling. This is one of the more significant disadvantages of the popular Queen Palm (*Arecastrum romanzoffianum*). The Royal Palm (*Roystonea regia*) is basically very similar in general appearance to the Queen Palm and would be a better choice if maintenance is seen to be a major problem.

Some people believe that the trunks of tall palms can be cut off at a manageable height and the trunk will resprout below the cut. This is entirely erroneous and any such attempt will result in the death of the plant or, if it is a suckering palm, the death of the stem which is cut. Palms have no capacity to survive once the growing apex is damaged beyond repair and while the fronds can be trimmed back or removed entirely on no account should the crown be touched.

Mulching

Mulching around palms, especially those which have been recently planted, will aid significantly in their successful establishment. Palms are by their nature shallow-rooting plants with a large percentage of the roots being found near the soil surface. The mulch keeps the roots cool and the soil sufficiently moist to encourage new root growth. Its presence on the soil surface greatly reduces the stresses which plants experience during hot, dry weather. As a bonus the mulch also reduces the development of weeds which compete with the plant for nutrients and moisture. It also aids in water penetration.

Mulches should be applied thickly as soon as possible after planting to minimise drying of the soil surface and weed germination. After application the mulch should be watered heavily to compact the surface and reduce dispersal by wind. Although palms are fairly tough once established the mulch should be maintained at least in the early years after planting.

A range of materials that can be used as mulches for palms is available, but some only on a localised basis. These include inorganic materials such as gravels, screenings and water-worn pebbles as well as such organic by-products as bark, wood chips, shavings, sawdust, peanut shells, grass hay and so on. A layer of black polythene sheeting covered with water-worn pebbles is frequently used in tropical regions. Extra fertiliser must be applied to palms mulched with organic materials because these substances will use plant nutrients from the soil as they are broken down, thus depriving the plants of these materials for growth. The fertilisers can be applied annually to the surface of the mulch or the soil.

PESTS AND DISEASES

Pests

In general palms are not bothered by a great number of pests although some may be very damaging at certain times of the year or during seasons which favour their buildup. The following notes may help in their identification and control.

Fig. 24
Palm Beetles

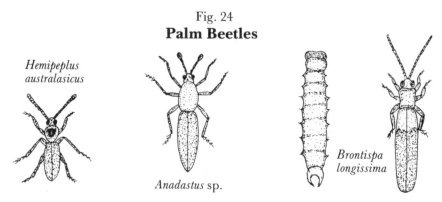

Hemipeplus australasicus

Anadastus sp.

Brontispa longissima

Palm Leaf Beetle *(Brontispa longissima)* An introduced beetle that is potentially a serious threat to some palms in tropical areas of Australia. It is known from Torres Strait Islands and Cooktown on eastern Cape York Peninsula and has recently become established in Darwin. Details of its life cycle and habit have been studied by research workers of the Northern Territory Department of Primary Production and have been published as an *Agnote* written by T. L. Fenner (Ref. 81/13, May 1981). Details of the pest are reprinted here with their permission.

The adult beetle is about 1 cm long, narrow, flat and is orange and black. Its larva is plump and cream with a series of spines down each side and a pair of curved hooks at its rear which resemble those of an earwig. The adult beetles are sluggish during the day and move at night. They have shown the ability to increase in numbers very quickly and to become entrenched rapidly once in a new area. It is quite conceivable that the pest will spread further in tropical Australia and any new infestations should be reported immediately so that control measures can be initiated. Under no circumstances should palms be taken from infected areas.

Palm Leaf Beetle attacks only the very young leaves before they have unfolded. Both adults and larvae shelter within the folds and chew large areas of the surface of the young leaflets. The eaten area turns brown and as the leaves expand takes on a scorched appearance. Once the leaflets expand the pests move to a new unexpanded leaf.

Attacks by this pest are not only unsightly but if they persist can reduce the palm's vigour and in extreme cases result in death. Palm Leaf Beetle favours as its main host the Coconut but attacks have also been recorded on Royal Palms *(Roystonea* spp.), *Carpentaria acuminata, Ptycho-*

sperma macarthurii, Archontophoenix alexandrae and one specimen each of a *Caryota*, a *Phoenix*, a *Washingtonia* and *Arecastrum romanzoffianum*.

Control of Palm Leaf Beetle is by spraying the unfolded leaves with a contact and residual insecticide such as carbaryl. A thorough penetration of the spray is essential and a second spray about seven days later is recommended.

Native Palm Beetles A couple of native beetles feed on the leaves of palms, attacking both natural populations and garden-grown plants.

In Darwin palms may be damaged by a species of beetle in the genus *Anadastus*. The adults are slender, about 1 cm long and are of orange and black colouration. They can be distinguished from the introduced Palm Leaf Beetle by the conspicuous knobs on the end of the antennae. They feed on developing fronds and also recently expanded leaves, damaging the leaf surface.

Fig. 25
Some Common Palm Pests

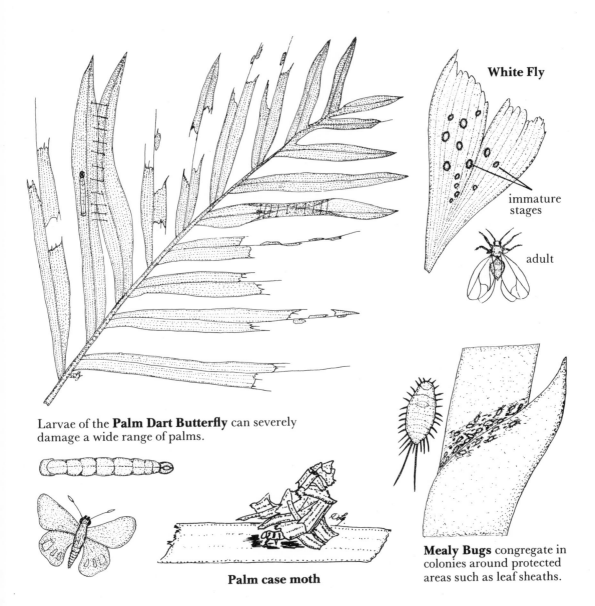

White Fly

immature stages

adult

Larvae of the **Palm Dart Butterfly** can severely damage a wide range of palms.

Palm case moth

Mealy Bugs congregate in colonies around protected areas such as leaf sheaths.

Another beetle (*Hemipeplus australasicus*) feeds on the leaves of some palms in tropical areas of Australia. It is a small, somewhat-elongated beetle about 4 mm long which is pale yellow with a reddish brown spot on the thorax. It chews the surface of the leaf, leaving brown, sunken areas.

Both native beetles are mainly minor pests but if outbreaks become severe they can be controlled by spraying with endosulfon.

Palm Dart Butterflies A destructive pest which severely damages the leaves of a number of palms including *Archontophoenix alexandrae*, *A. cunninghamiana*, *Chrysalidocarpus lutescens*, *Arecastrum romanzoffianum* and *Cocos nucifera*. The caterpillars are slender, translucent and greenish-grey or brownish in colour depending on the species. They have a prominent, striped head and wriggle actively when disturbed. They feed within the protection of a shelter which they make by sewing the edges of leaflets together. Usually the damage is confined to the outer half of a frond and the distal half of the leaflets and severely eaten fronds present a very ragged appearance. Usually the midrib of the leaflet is left projecting from the eaten part.

The adults are small, fairly colourful skipper or dart butterflies that are active on sunny days. Two species are known to damage palms. The yellow palm Dart (*Cephrenes trichopepla*) is widespread across the top of tropical Australia and the Torres Strait Islands extending as far down the east coast as Rockhampton. Its larvae feed on a variety of palms and the species is commercially significant because of its damage to young leaves of sprouting Coconuts. The Orange Palm Dart (*Cephrenes augiades*) is distributed from the Torres Strait Islands down the east coast of Australia to Sydney. Its larvae feed on a wide range of native and exotic palms.

Control is readily achieved by the application of a stomach poison such as carbaryl or the spores of *Bacillus thuringiensis* applied as recommended by the manufacturer. Regular spraying is necessary throughout the summer months.

Palm Moth *(Agonoxena phoenicia)* A relatively minor pest of Alexandra Palm, the larvae feed on the underside of the leaves, while hidden beneath a flimsy silken web. The adults are a small, grey moth with hairy, fringed, slender wings the upper one of which has a longitudinal dark band. It seems to be confined to north-eastern Qld and can be readily controlled by spraying with carbaryl.

Palm Butterfly *(Elymnias agondas)* Palms on Cape York Peninsula are eaten by the larvae of this butterfly which is especially fond of species of *Calamus*. The caterpillars are green with paler stripes and an unusual forked tail. The butterflies are quite handsome having dull brown and white wings with two or three prominent eyes on the hindwing. This insect is of interest but as a pest it is insignificant.

Palm Case Moth This is a very minor pest of palms, the caterpillars of which feed on the leaflets of such species as *Archontophoenix cunninghamiana* and *Dictyosperma album*. The caterpillar itself grows to about 2.5 cm long and is pale coloured with orange or dark red bands. It constructs a silken bag in which it lives and this is decorated on the outside with pieces of palm fronds. The pieces used increase in size as the caterpillar grows and they provide an effective camouflage. Apart from chopping off pieces of leaflets to adorn its case, the caterpillar feeds by grazing the surface tissue of the palm fronds. Damaged sections eventually turn brown. Damage to a palm is usually minimal and populations of the pest can be controlled by hand picking and squashing. Should spraying be necessary carbaryl or pyrethrum are effective.

Other Caterpillars A few caterpillars can be troublesome on palms, especially in the late summer and autumn months. Sections are usually eaten from the leaflets or fronds while they are young and these symptoms are quite obvious.

The Light Brown Apple Moth is a particularly insidious pest because the larvae shelter in the developing frond and join adjacent leaflets together by silk strands. They feed on very young fronds and the damage is obvious only when they expand.

The Painted Apple Moth has a conspicuous hairy caterpillar which can be recognised by the tufts of hairs on its back. It feeds on palm fronds while the tissues are soft. Other hairy caterpillars, which coil when disturbed, are also occasionally troublesome. Control of these pests is the same as outlined for Palm Dart Butterfly.

White Fly (*Family Aleyrodidae*) A species of white fly attacks palms, sometimes quite severely. The adults are small flies and hardly noticeable but the juvenile stages are quite conspicuous and are often mistaken for scale insects. They are generally 2 mm to 3 mm long, oval in shape and black with a conspicuous white fringe of waxy segments. Like scales, they cluster under leaf sheaths, etc and suck the palm's sap. Their activities are followed by sooty mould which develops on their exudates. White flies are a sporadic problem being severe in some years and absent in others. They can be somewhat difficult to control and systemic sprays such as dimethoate may be needed to clean up persistent attacks. Small outbreaks can be dispersed by hosing.

Mealy Bugs (*Pseudococcus* sp) A sucking insect usually readily distinguished by its covering of waxy white secretions and filaments which impart a mealy or powdery appearance. The insects are plump and soft and feed by sucking the plant's sap. They tend to congregate in dry, protected areas such as under leaf sheaths, in spathes and in the developing crown. As their numbers build up the damage they cause can be quite significant and may weaken the plant. Developing fronds in particular may be distorted and misshapen from attacks which occurred while they were still folded in the crown. Weakened plants such as those grown in very dry situations or those held in pots for too long may be subject to very severe infestations.

Mealy bugs are not easy to control. Small infestations can be eradicated by dabbing with methylated spirits but this is impractical on large plants. Systemic sprays such as dimethoate provide the answer but they must be used carefully. A better starting point is to keep the plants healthy and hope that the mealy bugs will be controlled naturally by their predators. The removal of leaf sheaths and other materials that cover infestations of the pest exposes them to the elements and the predators.

Red Spider Mite (*Tetranychus urticae*) Red spider mite, also called two spotted mite, is a major pest of palms and other plants. It is a tiny eight-legged animal that clusters on the underside of leaves and feeds by sucking the sap. The animals usually live in colonies and spin a protective webbing above where they feed. They relish dry conditions and can build up in numbers extremely rapidly. Affected leaves lose their lustre and take on a dry appearance. If feeding continues the leaves yellow and may drop prematurely. Mites may be particularly severe on weakened palms planted in a dry situation or on neglected indoor palms in a dry atmosphere. Regular syringing or hosing of their leaves will help reduce build-up of numbers but spraying is usually necessary for their control. Sprays such as difocol or dimethoate are usually suitable.

Grasshoppers and Locusts Palms, particularly those grown in the tropics, may be literally decimated by large grasshoppers or locusts. Such ravages not only impart an unsightly appearance to the plants but they may also retard or stunt their growth, particularly if the attacks are maintained, and may even result in the death of young plants.

The symptoms of damage are obvious from the tattered leaves. Huge chunks of the leaflets are eaten at random and the midribs are left to impart a skeletonised appearance. In severe attacks all the leaflets are eaten and the palms look very sad indeed.

Control of grasshoppers and locusts is a major problem since they are generally nomadic and are such ravenous feeders that much damage is done before insecticides can work. Squashing is effective on small palms but requires regular observation. A continual cover of a stomach poison such as carbaryl may be necessary during times of severe infestation. Attacks on large palms are difficult to remedy and all that can be really done is to ensure that the plant is sufficiently health to recover from them.

Borers These pests bore holes into the trunk and crown shafts of some palms. Their incidence is generally minor and the scattered holes do not appear to cause any major damage or reduce the structural strength of the trunks. The holes are frequently visible in the older parts of the trunk but these are the vestiges of borers long gone.

The borer that most commonly attacks palms seems to be a species of longicorn beetle. Its larvae bore shallow tunnels usually in the softer upper part of the trunk (where it exudes sawdust) or sometimes in the crown and crownshaft (where it exudes a white waxy sap that resembles toothpaste).

Healthy palms are normally able to tolerate borer attack without any setback but unthrifty palms may be weakened further. Control can be achieved by probing the holes with soft, pliable wire or by injecting them with solutions of a contact insecticide.

Palm Seed Borers Various species of insect feed on the fleshy tissue of palm seeds rendering them incapable of germination. Indicators which can be used to tell affected seeds include a marked reduction in weight and a tell-tale exit hole (although sometimes it may be covered with a flap of tissue). Seeds of native species of *Calamus* are frequently subject to attack with a high percentage being eaten.

Most damage is done by small weevils of the families Bruchidae, Platypodinae and Scolytinae. The presence of a fat, white, legless larva in the seed is usually their hallmark. Adults of the first family are unusual curved weevils about 4 mm long with a deflexed head while the others are small cylindrical beetles. Weevils and their larvae will attack palm seed while it is hanging on the tree while the larvae of the moth *Blastobasis sarcophaga* feed on fallen palm fruits. The adults of this species are a small, dull-grey moth with hairy, fringed wings. On Cape York Peninsula the fruit of *Caryota rumphiana* are frequently eaten out by the larvae of a butterfly known as the Cornelian (*Deudorix epijarbas dido*). The butterflies are fairly small, the males having dull orange markings on the wings and the females being brown.

Control of seed-eating pests is usually impractical although if it is suspected that a batch of seed is contaminated it can be soaked in a solution of maldison before sowing.

Pink Wax Scale (*Ceroplastes rubens*) This scale is very common in tropical and subtropical regions and attacks a wide variety of plants including some palms. The adults are usually 3 mm to 4 mm across, round in shape with irregular margins and a dull waxy red in colour. They are gregarious and congregate around the crown of the palm. The young scales attack the developing leaves but are not obvious until they are adults and the leaves are mature. They are frequently guarded by ants which feed on their exudates.

Healthy palms are not worried by the attacks of this scale but unthrifty palms may be weakened further. Some yellowing of the leaflets is associated with these attacks and black smut or sooty mould may develop on the sugary exudates of the scale. Infestations of this scale should be controlled by applications of white oil.

Palm Scale (*Parlatoria proteus*) This common pest of palms belongs to the group of armoured scales, so called because of the very hard, conical shells which cover each feeding insect. In this case the adult scales are white, about 3 mm across and have a couple of concentric rings near the top. They usually cluster on protected green parts of the palm such as under leaf sheaths, in rhachis grooves or in folded leaflets. The scales are generally well hidden in early stages of infestations but as the attacks become more severe the scales spread to open areas and become obvious. If leaf sheaths or the protective coverings are removed a mass of scales in all stages of development will frequently be exposed. Heavy infestations of palm scale can be quite debilitating and the pest should be controlled as soon as noticed.

Premature yellowing of leaves and the presence of sooty mould around the leaves are sure indications of infestation. When infestations spread onto the undersides of leaves they cause small yellow patches in the area of the leaf around which they feed. Small infestations may be cleared up by dabbing with methylated spirits (one part to four parts water), or sponging with soapy water but severe outbreaks must be sprayed with a material such as maldison, methidathion, or dimethoate. Plants should also be fertilised to help restore their vigour.

Circular Black Scale *(Chrysomphalus aonidum)* This scale is a pest of palms in parts of Qld. The covering is deep, purple-black, circular, and grows to about 2 mm across. It is one of the armoured scales with a raised central point which is of a lighter, brownish colour than the rest of the covering. This scale is found in clusters on the upper and lower surfaces of the leaflets of palm fronds and along the petiole and around the leaf sheaths. Tissue where the pests feed yellows prematurely. Severe infestations of this scale can badly debilitate palms and comments and control as outlined for Palm Scale apply equally to this species.

Cottony Cushion Scale *(Icerya purchasi)* Cottony cushion scale is frequently found on palms especially in subtropical areas. It is a very distinctive large scale readily recognised by its plump, white soft body which can be readily squashed between the fingers. This scale normally feeds in small, crowded clusters and is often to be found on the smaller palms. In *Chamaedorea* species it feeds in places such as the rhachis of the inflorescences and under the upper leaf sheaths. Cottony cushion scale is not a major problem and infestations can frequently be removed by hand. It is generally kept under control by the activities of a predatory native ladybird beetle and its larvae.

Flat Brown Scale *(Eucalymnatus tessellatus)* The young stages of this scale are rather difficult to discern, producing an almost transparent covering which is appressed flat to the leaf. The adult is of similar shape but is easily seen because it is dark brown and about 5 mm long. This scale is a relatively minor pest and usually appears in small numbers. It attacks cycads and some palms such as *Howea forsteriana* and *Chamaedorea elegans* and produces localised leaf yellowing. Control is as for Palm Scale.

Soft Brown Scale *(Coccus hesperidum)* This scale is mainly a pest of young fruit trees but it also attacks palms. Its presence is usually advertised by the masses of secretions and associated Sooty Mould found wherever it feeds. The adults can be readily identified by their soft, waxy coverings, which are brown or of a mottled colouration. These are flat, oval and about 5 mm long. They congregate in dense colonies on the fronds, petioles and leaf sheaths of a variety of palms in temperate and subtropical parts of Australia. Infested palms are very unsightly because of the sticky nature of the secretions of the scale and the heavy growth of Sooty Mould. The appearance of the palms can be improved by regular hosing. Control of the scale is by spraying with white oil.

Fern Scale or Coconut Scale *(Pinnaspis sp)* This scale attacks palms in subtropical and tropical regions and is frequently associated with infestations of the Palm Scale. Colonies of this scale resemble a sprinkling of shredded coconut on the surface where they are feeding. These are the coverings of the male scales and a close inspection shows the dull, inconspicuous female scales scattered among the males. On palms this scale favours sheltered situations such as the folds of leaflets, the junction of stems, under bracts, sheaths etc. It causes yellowing of the tissue where it feeds and generally debilitates the plant. Control can be difficult requiring the use of chemicals such as dimethoate.

Nigra Scale *(Saissetia nigra)* Nigra scale is not a major pest of palms but occasional outbreaks occur. The species can be readily identified by the adults which have a large (4 mm to 6 mm long) shiny-black, raised covering which is usually oval to oblong in shape. Black scale are very fast growing and it is not uncommon to find mature specimens on a recently expanded palm inflorescence. Individuals are easily dislodged from the plant and it is a wise precaution to remove them before they spread. Control is by spraying with white oil.

Termites Termites are a major destroyer of palms in tropical areas. They are communal insects that feed on wood both living and dead and the most destructive species attack from below ground level and work their way up the trunk. The attacks are usually rapid and affected plants quickly decline in health and the leaves lose their lustre, become pale green or yellow and wilt badly even if watered. Once plants exhibit these symptoms there is little that can be done for them and they usually collapse and die.

Termites are extremely difficult to control and regular inspections of palms are necessary in tropical areas. Their feeding lines, which are subterranean, can range a long way and once they establish contact with a tree invasion is rapid. Any obvious colonies in the area should be destroyed along with dead or dying trees, stumps, etc. Colonies can be destroyed with strong contact insecticides applied in solution or as dusts.

Thrips Thrips are a minor problem in palms but in some years they may congregate in considerable numbers and feed on flowers. The resulting damage causes premature browning of the flowers and reduces fruit set. Control is rarely necessary but can be achieved with a contact spray such as pyrethrum.

Rats and Mice At certain times of the year these rodents may become very destructive of young palms by gnawing through the stems. Significant damage may be caused within a short time in nurseries. Control is by baiting.

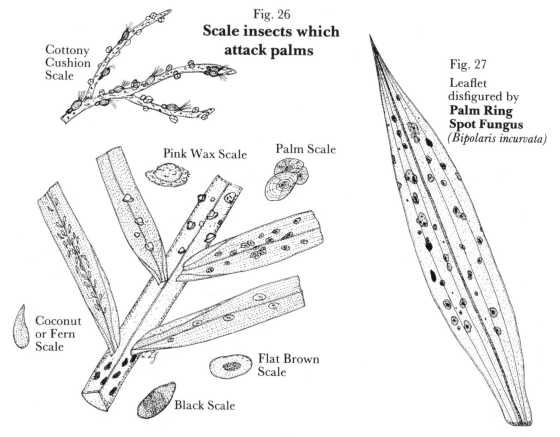

Fig. 26
Scale insects which attack palms

Cottony Cushion Scale

Pink Wax Scale

Palm Scale

Coconut or Fern Scale

Flat Brown Scale

Black Scale

Fig. 27

Leaflet disfigured by **Palm Ring Spot Fungus** (*Bipolaris incurvata*)

Diseases

Few diseases affect palms in Australia and these are mostly of a minor or sporadic nature. The most prominent diseases are dealt with in the following notes.

Cinnamon Fungus (*Phytophthora cinnamomii*) Cinnamon fungus is a vigorous root pathogen that attacks a wide range of plants with devastating effects. Most palms seem to be resistant to its effects but some species are sensitive (*Arecastrum romanzoffianum, Caryota mitis* and *C. urens, Cocos nucifera*) and these only when planted in heavy soils where drainage is poor.

Symptoms of this disease in palms are an unthrifty appearance with a crown mainly of pale or yellowed leaves. In times of sever stress the plants may wilt or even collapse suddenly and die.

Control of affected plants is very difficult and prevention is the best procedure. Sensitive palms should only be planted in well-drained soils. The chemical Ridomil offers considerable scope for the control of this disease once it is present in the plant.

Red Top Red Top is a disease caused by a fungus about which little appears to be known. It attacks the growing apex of the palm and new leaves produced at the time of the attack open out yellow. The centre of the plant eventually collapses and dies and when inspected the tissue is covered with rusty red sporing bodies. Palms known to be attacked include species of *Archontophoenix* and *Howea*. Bordeaux mixture controls this disease but it must be applied thoroughly on all surfaces when symptoms are first noticed.

Core Rot Some palms such as *Livistona australis* and *L. chinensis* are subject to a blackening of the upper part of the trunk in the crown. In severe cases the whole crown rots and becomes a black, soggy mess. This problem is believed to be caused by a fungus but it is not commonly encountered and there are no known control measures.

Palm Rust The leaves of certain species of palms such as *Howea forsteriana, Livistona chinensis, Phoenix dactylifera,* and *Washingtonia filifera* are attacked and disfigured by a rust fungus. These attacks are generally minor and the disfigurement is mostly limited to a peppering of rusty red to orange spots on the leaves. Young or old leaves may be attacked and there is no known means of control although sprays of copper materials such as copper oxychloride may be beneficial.

Palm Leaf Blight (*Gleosporium palmarum*) The leaves of some native palms may be infested with this fungus which causes brown spots and blotches on the pinnae. Sometimes these spots are surrounded by a pale or yellowish area. Attacks are usually of a minor nature and can be controlled with copper sprays. The disease has been noticed on *Archontophoenix cunninghamiana, A. alexandrae* and *Ptychosperma elegans*.

Palm Leaf Spot (*Pestalotiopsis* sp.) This fungus causes small spots on the leaves of some palms such as *Caryota* spp., *Roystonea* spp., and *Arecastrum romanzoffianum*. The fungus is not very aggressive and attacks are usually of a minor nature. The fungus is mainly found on palms in shady positions and is hardly known on plants in the sun. Control is rarely necessary but persistent attacks can be cleaned up with copper sprays such as cuprox.

Palm Ring Spot (*Bipolaris incurvata*) A potentially serious fungal disease which causes leaf spotting often with associated yellowing. It is a problem in tropical areas when humidity is high for long periods and is worse in crowded situations or where air movement is restricted. Copper oxychloride should be used against severe infestations while Mancozeb will give control of lesser outbreaks.

Sooty Mould This widespread and common fungus disease attacks a wide variety of plants. It causes very little damage by itself but it does render the plants very unsightly. Since it grows on the excretions of sucking insects such as scales, white flies and mealy bugs its appearance should be used as an indication of the presence of these pests. Control of sooty mould involves the control of the sucking pests and it usually disappears within a couple of weeks of their removal.

Lethal Yellows Lethal Yellows is a palm disease not present in Australia or the Pacific region. Notes are included here because of the potential danger not only to Australia, where palms are mainly ornamental, but to the various countries of the Pacific which rely on the Coconut and its products. The disease probably originated in the Caribbean region and has spread to Florida and more recently Texas.

Lethal Yellows is a very devastating disease causing rapid death to a wide range of palms (at least twenty-six species) especially the Coconut. It is caused by a mycoplasma-like organism which is related to a virus. Symptoms are yellowing and death of the young fronds in the crown, death of the roots, a change in colour of mature fronds which then droop and become necrotic beginning with the basal ones and moving upwards in the crown. The plant usually dies within three or four months of the attack.

Lethal Yellows is spread by an as yet unknown insect vector (a planthopper is suspected) or by the movement of diseased plants. It is unlikely to enter Australia because of our strict quarantine laws but these notes are included to highlight the potential danger which exists and to discourage anyone from flouting the rules.

Other Damaging Factors

Wind Burn Developing palm fronds may be damaged by hot, dry winds so that when they open they are disfigured by grey or white papery patches. This is usually a minor problem and is only apparent in sensitive species following long periods of such unfavourable conditions.

Frost Burn Very many species of palms, especially those of tropical origin, are sensitive to cold spells and especially frost. Young plants are more susceptible than mature specimens with some height, however there are many recorded cases of frost damage or even death in tall palms following unusual or unseasonable frosts. Roots, especially the growing tips, are very sensitive to freezing and ground temperatures of $-2°C$ may cause considerable damage. A palm has a single growing apex and lacks any secondary measure of survival and once irreparable damage has been done to this apex, death follows. Late spring frosts and black frosts can be particularly damaging. An interesting phenomenon has been noted in palms with a clumping growth habit. Whereas sensitive species with a solitary trunk may be killed, established clumping palms may regrow from the base even though all of the aerial stems have been killed. Such damaged plants may, in a few years time, completely re-establish themselves.

The symptoms of frost damage are the blackening and collapse of developing leaves and brown patches on mature fronds. Sensitive species collapse dramatically, usually going brown or black with the crown becoming a soggy mess. Protection from mild frosts can be obtained by planting close to buildings or large shrubs or under the protective canopies of established trees. In cold areas sensitive species must be grown in glasshouses.

Salt Burn In coastal districts onshore winds deposit salt from sea water on the leaves of nearby plants. This salt is usually damaging to the leaf tissues and only the most resistant plants tolerate it without any damage. Many species of palms suffer this damage which is known as salt burn. However, this generally causes only a minor setback to growth and is mainly a drawback to the plant's appearance. The margins of the leaflets are burnt and become white and papery. There is no means of control except perhaps hosing the plants down thoroughly after onshore gusts. Damage from salt burn has been noticed in *Arecastrum romanzoffianum* (generally tolerant), *Caryota mitis* and *C. urens*, *Chrysalidocarpus lutescens* and *Phoenix rupicola*. Species of *Caryota* seem especially sensitive to salt burn.

Hail Palms, because of their large leaves, are very sensitive to damage by hail. The usual symptoms are for large chunks to be torn out of leaflets, leaf segments, inflorescences and any sensitive areas. The damaged areas may be invaded by secondary fungi such as species of *Alternaria*. A wise precaution is to spray badly damaged palms as soon as possible with a fungicide. An insidious side effect of hail is freezing damage. Hail collects in sunken sites such as the top of the crown and around objects such as the base of trunks and as it thaws the adjacent plant tissue can be damaged. The thick epidermis will protect the base of the trunk from injury except in the case of young palms.

Sun Burn Young plants of almost any but the very hardiest of palms should be protected from direct exposure to hot sun. In fact, most species of palms need to be protected for their firsts two to three years of life and then gradually hardened to the effects of the sun. Shade-loving palms should be protected at all times.

Premature or unexpected exposure to hot sun results in the leaves becoming sunburnt. This shows up as white or brown papery patches in the leaves and in severe cases whole leaves or even the whole plant may die. Sunburnt plants look tatty and unsightly.

Palms should be hardened to the sun before planting out and in very hot conditions should be protected by a surround of leafy branches. Water should not be lacking during such times.

Strong Winds While columnar palm trunks are extremely resistant to strong winds with the long, slender ones even being renowned for their bending and survival ability during cyclones, their leaves suffer greatly by comparison. The leaflets of feather palms and the leaves of fan palms are usually shredded after strong winds and it is not infrequent for the tips to appear as if they have been flayed. Leaves are frequently broken at the petioles but are usually quickly replaced by new ones. Severe wind damage to young palms may result in a setback to their growth and establishment.

Nitrogen Deficiency Palms suffering nitrogen deficiency have a yellowish appearance in the crowns with the older leaves becoming quite yellow or even bleached with necrotic patches on the leaflets. Such afflicted plants stand out quite dramatically, especially if they can be compared with a healthy green specimen. Nitrogen deficiency in palms is particularly common in coastal districts with deep sandy soil. It can be readily corrected by applying fertilisers rich in nitrogen (see Fertilisers section).

Zinc Deficiency Zinc deficiency in plants causes symptoms known as little-leaf because the leaf development is impaired resulting in a reduced, often almost perfect, stunted leaf. Such symptoms have been reported in palms following pot trials (*Principes* 23, 1979, pp 171-2). I have seen garden grown plants with similar symptoms but it is not positive that these are from zinc deficiency. Zinc deficiency can be easily corrected by application of balanced trace element mixtures or zinc sulphate applied to the soil or as a foliar spray (3-5 g/L).

White Oil Damage The practice of polishing the foliage of indoor palms with white oil to create a glossy appearance is a very common one and can lead to patches of dead brown tissue in the leaves. Although it does create an impression of luxuriance in the plants the practice is detrimental and should be abandoned. White oil is frequently associated with plant tissue damage and for scale control should not be used any stronger than a dilution of one part in sixty with water and this can be further reduced to one in eighty during hot weather.

Dryness Like other plants, palms react to dryness by wilting. Palms are generally quite resistant to dry soil but in cases of severe dryness the fronds and leaflets take on a drooping appearance. Frequently also the crown becomes sparser because the leaf sheaths open and the less turgid petioles hang away from the trunk. The leaves or leaflets also characteristically lose any glossy lustre and may fold together or curl inwards. Palms may stay in a wilted state for quite long periods without any obvious detrimental effect although constrictions in the trunk or very short internodes may be the result of such dry periods. Following dryness the tips of the leaflets usually wither and die back.

Twisting Twisting is an unusual condition of palms whereby the crown takes on a distorted or lopsided appearance with most fronds seeming to end up on one side. Frequently the trunk may have a bend or kink below the crown. The causes of this condition are not known but it is suspected that it results from damage caused by wind, hail, tree branches or perhaps pest or disease organisms. The condition is most noticeable in old palms which may be on the decline although sometimes it is seen in younger specimens. It occurs in both species of *Howea* and has also been observed in Bangalow Palm (*Archontophoenix cunninghamiana*).

Transplanting Palms

Advanced specimens of many species of palms can be transplanted quite successfully provided that a significant portion of the root system is removed intact and that correct aftercare is provided.

The amount of the root system to remove varies with the species, its age and size, and the soil type where it is growing. In some cases the position also influences the amount of roots that can be excavated, for example palms that are growing against walls. Some palms such as *Arecastrum romanzoffianum* can be removed with very little of the root system left while others such as *Sabal* spp. need a considerable portion for success. As a general rule a good solid root ball 1 m to 1.5 m across should be removed with any palm 3 m tall or more. Naturally the larger the plant the bigger the root ball that will be necessary for success. For very large palms mechanical equipment such as back-hoes, cranes and low loaders are necessary.

In light sandy soils the soil tends to fall away from the roots in the transplanting process, particularly if it is dry. In such situations the palms may need to be pre-wet or watered regularly during the move. Palms in heavy soils do not have this problem and tend to be slightly more amenable to shifting.

The time of transplanting can be a very significant factor in the success or failure of the project. In temperate regions palms make very slow growth over winter and should not be transplanted during late summer, autumn or winter. The best time in temperate regions is spring or early summer. In subtropical regions the timing is similar except that spring is often dry in such regions and if irrigation is not available then it is best to wait until November or December when regular rains are usual. In tropical regions temperature is not a limiting factor but the plants are best left in the ground during the dry winter months and transplanted during the wet season when conditions are ideal for growth.

Palms transplanted from the wild are generally difficult compared with garden-grown subjects whose roots were probably moulded by the nursery container in which they were originally grown. It has also been noticed that palms grown in large containers transplant much more readily than those which were planted out while quite small. In tree farms where the palms are grown in the ground until they are of a size suitable for transplanting the root system of the palm may be cut regularly every six months to keep it compact and lessen the shock when the plant is finally transplanted.

The transplanting technique for a palm is basically similar to that of any other plant. The roots are severed in a circle around the trunk by cutting with a sharp instrument and a trench is gradually excavated to reach the deep roots. Once the roots are cut right through the root ball can be surrounded by hessian or similar material to hold in the soil and reduce drying of the root system until the plant is repositioned. This material is tied and the plant can then be removed and transported to its new position where it is placed in a well-prepared hole of similar size.

It is essential to realise that the care following transplanting is probably more important to ensure the success of the project than is the actual transplanting. Following planting the soil should be firmed thoroughly around the root ball and a temporary reservoir for the retention of water should be made on the soil surface. The plant should then be thoroughly watered by filling the reservoir several times until the entire profile and root ball is wet. This watering should be undertaken as soon as practical after transplanting. This watering system should be maintained and the reservoir filled at regular intervals during dry periods for two to three months.

During transplanting any damaged fronds should be removed and a few of the others shortened to reduce both transpiration and wind resistance. It is extremely important to stake the palm effectively to prevent movement of the roots in the new soil and this should be done immediately after watering. The most effective system of staking is to use three stakes and guy wires to support the trunk. Further care consists of regular watering, mulching and the control of any pests which may attack the palm in its weakened condition.

As already mentioned some species of palms transplant more readily than others. A generalisation that seems to hold is that those palms with a compact root system transplant better than those with fewer but long-spreading roots. The following observations on the transplantability of different species have been made by Peter Jones, who has transplanted many hundreds of palms while Parks Superintendent with the Gold Coast City Council.

Archontophoenix alexandrae (Alexandra Palm) — moves readily, has a very bunched root system.

Archontophoenix cunninghamiana (Bangalow Palm) — very difficult to move, with a twenty to thirty per cent survival rate. Those from their natural state are extremely difficult whereas those that have been container grown early in their life are somewhat easier.

Arecastrum romanzoffianum (Queen Palm) — very easy to transplant even with seventy five per cent of roots gone, makes new roots readily.

Caryota mitis (Clustered Fish-tail Palm) — transplants readily, needs plenty of water.

Caryota urens (Solitary Fish-tail Palm) — transplants readily, needs plenty of water and very strong staking.

Chamaedorea microspadix (Bamboo Palm) — transplants readily but should be held in a shady position.

Chrysalidocarpus lutescens (Golden Cane Palm) — transplants readily, does not like too much sun or wind.

Cocos nucifera (Coconut) — fairly easy to transplant in early summer before the wet season, trim roots back, new roots appear in the wet, needs a hot position with ground water available.

Howea forsteriana (Kentia Palm) — fairly easy but needs plenty of water and care after transplanting.

Linospadix monostachya (Walking Stick Palm) — easy but should be pre-trenched three to four months before shifting.

Livistona australis (Cabbage Palm) — can be shifted into heavy, wet soils but does not like sandy soil.

Livistona chinensis (Weeping Fan Palm) — easy to shift but likes heavy soils.

Livistona decipiens (Fan Palm) — very easy to transplant, short bunchy roots.

Phoenix canariensis (Canary Island Date Palm) — easy to move but very weighty and needs a strong scaffold to support it for twelve months.

Phoenix dactylifera (Date Palm) — fairly easy to move, has long roots that need to be trimmed back.

Phoenix reclinata (Senegal Date Palm) — moves easily with little setback.

Phoenix roebelenii (Dwarf Date Palm) — does not like root disturbance and is generally difficult to move; needs plenty of aftercare; a little easier if previously grown in a large container.

Phoenix rupicola (Cliff Date Palm) — fairly easy to move.

Ptychosperma elegans (Solitaire Palm) — transplants well.

Rhapis excelsa (Lady Palm) — very easy to transplant, best moved to a shady position.

Rhapis humilis (Slender Lady Palm) — very easy to transplant, best moved to a shady position.

Roystonea regia (Royal Palm) — fairly easy to transplant but very top heavy, strong fibrous root system, does not transplant well if moved from sandy soil to heavy soil.

Sabal palmetto (Cabbage Palmetto) — difficult to transplant; has sparse long roots (forty per cent survival).

Washingtonia filifera (Cotton Palm) — difficult to transplant; has sparse root system of long, spreading roots (forty to sixty per cent survival).

Experience in Darwin has shown that *Carpentaria acuminata* is very difficult to move while *Livistona humilis* is impossible. On the other hand *L. benthamii* has proved quite amenable providing due care is given.

EFFECTS OF RENOVATIONS

Major renovations are not uncommon in gardens especially if the house changes hands or is redeveloped into flats, units etc. It is difficult to start new plants among established ones and because of this garden renovations often consist of building up soil levels to give the new plants a start.

Palms will withstand having a garden bed built up around them provided that the process is fairly gradual. An existing palm will quite happily tolerate an increase in soil height around its trunk of 15 cm to 30 cm but if a metre or more is suddenly applied the results will probably be catastrophic. Palms have the ability to form adventitious roots in the lower part of their trunk and if the filling is applied gradually the new roots can grow into it without harmful effects.

RECLAIMING UNTHRIFTY PALMS

While palms generally tolerate neglect very well, if the growing conditions are unsuitable or severe in the extreme they can become unthrifty and may linger like this for many years. Nitrogen deficiency is a very common cause of this malady but other causes include poor drainage, lack of organic matter and dryness. Unthrifty palms frequently become the target for pests such as mealy bug or scale but these attacks are usually because of the weakened condition and not the cause of it.

Unthrifty palms can be invigorated by studying the cause and correcting it. Nutrition is a frequent cause and a good dose of a balanced fertiliser fortified with extra nitrogen will usually promote a dramatic response. A heavy mulch of some organic material should also be applied and the plants should be regularly watered during dry periods. Dead fronds and leaf sheaths should be removed and burnt. This will expose any pests and these can be killed by spraying or natural predators.

Following these steps will usually be sufficient to promote strong new growth. If strong growth is to be maintained however, it is essential that the fertilisers, mulches and water be applied at regular intervals.

CHAPTER 5
The Propagation of Palms

PALMS can be propagated sexually (from seed) or a asexually (by division, aerial layering or more recently by tissue culture). Most palms are grown from seed and this propagation technique is well within the scope of the average enthusiast. Professional nurserymen each year raise thousands of seedlings of the more popular indoor and outdoor palms as well as lesser quantities of collectors items. Propagation by division and aerial layering is mainly useful to enthusiasts and municipal gardeners and has limited application to nurserymen. Tissue culture is mainly the province of the research worker and for large scale entreprises.

SEED PROPAGATION

Palms are variously described in the literature as being notoriously difficult and slow to germinate or being easy. This variation is probably a reflection of the facilities and expertise of the person involved but it does highlight the variability that a new grower can expect to meet. The following paragraphs explain some of the procedures used and some of the difficulties that may be encountered. It should be realised however that even today there are still considerable gaps in our knowledge of palm propagation.

Seed Collection

The fruit should be collected as soon as it becomes colourful and ripens. The presence of fallen fruit is a good indicator and for many species the whole bunch of fruit may be harvested at this stage. However, the fruit of some palms such as *Borassus* and *Cocos* must be harvested individually as they ripen sporadically throughout the year.

When a whole bunch of fruit is harvested some fruits will be immature and may not germinate. This is especially a problem in species such as *Howea forsteriana*. In this palm it is also very difficult to gauge when the fruit are ripe as they take several years to mature and colour very slowly.

When collecting in the bush or travelling it is often necessary to gather immature fruit or miss out completely. If the fruit have started to colour or even if they are large and plump enough they are worth collecting as some can often be induced to germinate. Immature fruit shrivel very readily and immediately after collection they should be stored in moist peat moss in a plastic bag and sown at the first opportunity.

Germination Requirements

For successful germination palm seeds require prolonged exposure to high temperatures (35°C to 38°C) and high humidity. The high temperatures can be supplied by various methods such as a heated glasshouse, bottom heat cables or simply an enclosed metal shed which the sun will heat rapidly during the day. However, care should be taken as lethal damage may occur to palm seeds of some species exposed to long periods of temperatures above 38°C. The humidity is supplied by watering the mixture containing the seeds and its surroundings.

Palm species vary in the amount of exposure to heat and the temperature they require to induce germination. Thus the Oil Palm, *Elaeis guineensis,* has an effective temperature range of 38°C to 42°C and needs exposure for eighty days. On the other hand the Palmyra Palm, *Borassus flabellifer,* germinates well after thirty-five days at 35°C and *Caryota mitis* after twenty-eight days at 35°C. Temperatures higher than 38°C may be lethal to some palms and useful to others. Response to temperature seems to be cumulative and fluctuations such as occur with overnight cooling are not detrimental, and do not negate the high temperatures of the day.

Moisture is essential for palm seeds to germinate and it has been shown that pre-soaking some species may reduce the period of exposure to high temperature needed before germination can occur. The seeds are simply soaked in water for up to seven days before sowing. It is preferable that the water should be changed daily to remove any inhibitors that are leached out. Some growers use a heated water bath with the temperature held constant and the water circulated around the seeds but this is not essential.

Propagating Mixes

Palm seeds can be sown in a well-structured garden soil and will often germinate satisfactorily and grow quite strongly. Soils however may contain disease organisms or weeds and pests and other materials may be safer, especially if quantities are to be propagated. Nurserymen use materials such as coarse sand, peat moss, vermiculite, perlite, pine bark and sawdust.

Coarse Sand — usually obtained from alluvial deposits. It must be washed thoroughly to remove dirt and weed seeds. Drainage is excellent but it dries out rapidly after watering and is best mixed with a water-retentive organic material.

Peat Moss — rotted organic material which has reached a stable point of decay. It is very acid (pH 4.5), sterile and absorbs many times its volume in water. It has excellent aerating properties and mixes well with other materials. It can be used on its own to germinate palm seeds.

Vermiculite — a naturally occurring mica which is expanded by subjecting to temperatures in excess of 1000°C. It is a very light material with a high water-holding capacity and excellent aeration. It mixes well with other materials but must not be over watered or compacted as it readily becomes cloggy. It is sterile because of the high temperatures used in its production.

Perlite — a naturally occurring silicate material which is treated with temperatures in excess of 700°C. It forms grey, spongy particles which are very light and is best mixed with a water-retentive organic material.

Pine Bark — finely ground pine bark is often called pine peat because of its similarity in appearance and in some properties to peat moss. When fresh it contains toxins and must be stored moist for six to eight weeks before use. It is best mixed with coarse sand or perlite.

Sawdust — like pine bark, fresh sawdust contains plant toxins and hence must be stored moist in a heap for six to eight weeks before use. It mixes well with sand or perlite and has good moisture retention and aeration properties.

Peat moss and vermiculite can be used by themselves as a germination medium for palm seeds but it is more common to use a mixture. Very successful mixtures can be made by combining two parts coarse sand or perlite with one part peat moss, vermiculite, pine bark or sawdust. The mixture must be moistened before sowing as materials such as peat moss and sawdust are difficult to wet when dried out. If weeds, pests or diseases cause problems during germination it may be necessary to sterilise the sowing mixture.

Sowing Techniques

Palm seeds should be sown and covered with 1.5 cm to 3 cm of the propagating media or, as a general rule, covered by at least their own thickness of material. They can be sown quite close together and if potted soon after germination do not suffer through competition. Suitable containers for sowing palm seeds must be fairly deep as the roots appear first and grow rapidly downwards before the first leaves show above ground. Pots are very successful but deep trays can also be useful, especially for large quantities. For optimum rapid germination the seeds should be sown in trays, covered with a plastic bag and held at high temperatures (35°C to 38°C) in a germination cabinet. Few enthusiasts however have the facilities available to produce such conditions and fortunately the palms prove amenable to other conditions although the time taken may be considerably prolonged and the percentage that germinate reduced. Some nurserymen in the tropics sow direct into prepared beds in bush houses or under trees. In these cases the seeds may be sown in a mixture of the above materials or direct into soil. Once the seedlings are large enough they can be dug and potted on. This technique is excellent for easy-to-handle species such as *Sabal* and *Washingtonia* but is not so good with species that resent interference such as *Archontophoenix cunninghamania*.

A few palms, the best known of which is *Borassus flabellifer,* produce a premordial growth known as a sinker. This grows down into the soil for lengths up to a metre before the usual leaf is produced above ground. Palms of this type won't tolerate disturbance even when quite small and for success are best sown direct into a large container and planted in the ground when established. They can also be sown direct into their final position in the ground but are then subject to the ravages of various creatures which find the sinker very tasty. *Lodoicea maldivica* and some species of *Orania* also have this unusual type of germination.

Palm fruits which have only a thin layer of flesh can be sown direct without any prior cleaning but those fruits that are pulpy (e.g. *Butia capitata*) must have the flesh cleaned from the seeds before sowing. If the flesh is not removed fungus disease can rapidly build up, causing the seeds to rot. There is also the strong possibility of germination inhibitors being present in the flesh. The pulp of some fruit can be removed readily (e.g. *Jubaea chilensis*) while others are tenacious and may require fermentation (see next section).

Palms take from one month to two years to germinate depending on the species and the state of the seed when sown. Some species with hard seeds take a long time and the process may be speeded up by first cracking the shell (see Causes of Poor Germination page 80).

Palms with large seeds such as *Borassus* and *Cocos* are best sown direct into a large container. Each container holds a solitary seed which is left half exposed on the top of a good, friable mixture. The containers are then placed in a warm, protected, shady place and kept moist until germination occurs. Once they have germinated the plants can be moved to a suitable growing area until ready for planting out.

Fermentation Technique The pulp of some palm fruits is fibrous and difficult to remove from the seed. Studies have shown that if moistened fruits are hung in a plastic bag for a couple of weeks the pulp ferments and falls away readily from the seed after hosing. This is a very useful technique and results have indicated that subsequent germination of the seed may be improved by the fermentation. Not only is the time for germination reduced but the seedlings appear together rather than over several months. Seeds should not be left to ferment for more than two to four weeks or they may rot, especially if the prevailing temperatures are high.

The Bag Technique An extension of the fermentation technique is to actually germinate the seeds in a plastic bag and not in containers such as pots or trays. The seeds are mixed thoroughly with moist peat moss and the whole lot sealed in a sturdy plastic bag. The bag is then placed in a warm, protected, shady position such as under the bench of a glasshouse or hung from a shady tree. Observations will show when germination takes place and the seedlings can be potted up as needed.

This is a very useful technique for handling large quantities of seed. Little space is taken up and the seedlings can be handled readily without significant damage to the roots although they may become entangled if the plants are left too long after germination or are too crowded in the bag. Germination also seems to be more uniform if this technique is used.

The bags used may be clear or milky white but must be relatively sturdy. They break down if exposed to excessive ultra-violet light and should be examined fairly regularly as the peat and seeds can dry out rapidly if there is a tear in the bag. For this reason the opening of the bag must be well sealed also. It is a wise precaution to include a label with the seeds before sealing the bag.

Bottom Heat Some species of palm germinate very slowly and erratically and in fact in any one batch seeds may germinate over two years or more. Germination of such seeds can be greatly speeded up if they are placed in a bottom heat propagating unit and kept continually warm and moist. The bottom heat unit is set at 25°C to 28°C and the palm seeds are mixed with moist peat and placed just above the heating elements. Exposed seeds are covered with a layer of moist peat and the whole unit is watered daily. Germinated seeds are removed as they reach a certain stage of development and are potted. This technique is especially useful with the Kentia Palm (*Howea forsteriana*) and Curly Palm (*H. belmoreana*) but can be applied to many other species, especially those from the tropics.

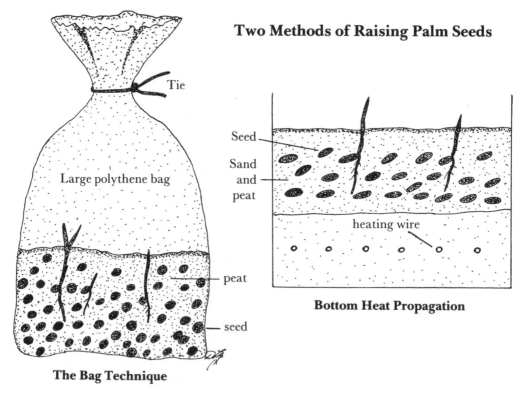

Two Methods of Raising Palm Seeds

Tie

Large polythene bag

peat

seed

The Bag Technique

Seed

Sand and peat

heating wire

Bottom Heat Propagation

Causes of Poor Germination

The most common cause of poor germination in palms is sowing seed that has been harvested while immature, is too old, or has been stored incorrectly. Such seed usually rots fairly quickly after sowing and this in itself is a good indication of the cause. Seeds with a hard shell (e.g. *Butia*) may appear normal while in fact they have rotted on the inside. The rotting will only show up by cracking a sample lot and looking at the contents. The embryos and endosperm of viable seeds fill the cavity and are creamy-white while non-viable seeds are shrunken and discoloured.

The seeds of a number of palms have a hard woody endocarp which is impervious to water and acts as a physical barrier to germination. If the hard endocarp is cracked, sliced open or filed close to the hilum, germination of the seed can begin. These however are arduous techniques for large numbers of seeds and if damage occurs to the endosperm or embryo then the seed can rot. Seeds with hard coats will eventually germinate but these appear very sporadically and may take a long time. Cracking or filing the woody coat has been shown to be beneficial for *Acrocomia* spp., *Arenga engleri* and *Butia capitata*. A technique of using hydrogen peroxide (H_2O_2) has proved useful for seeds of *Licuala grandis* and *Thrinax barbadensis*. The seeds are soaked for seventy-two hours in a six per cent solution before sowing.

The fruit flesh that surrounds the seeds of many plant species contains germination inhibitors and there is no reason to suggest that palms are exceptions. As a consequence it is wise to remove any fleshy pulp that surrounds the seed before it is sown. (For seeds with tenacious flesh see Fermentation Technique page 79.)

Fruits that are fed on by animals may require partial digestion in an animal's gut before germination can be effected. Many colourful palm fruits are readily eaten by animals and birds and although information is scant, some observations suggest that digested palm seeds germinate rapidly and uniformly in the dung. Digestion can result in the breakdown of a woody coat as well as the removal of any inhibitors.

Leaching experiments have shown that inhibitors in parts of the seed other than the flesh (exocarp) may also affect germination. Thus defleshed seeds of such diverse species as *Archontophoenix alexandrae*, *Aiphanes erosa*, *Arenga engleri*, *Chrysalidocarpus lutescens*, *Elaeis guineensis*, *Euterpe edulis*, *Caryota mitis*, *Pinanga* spp. and *Ptychosperma* spp., have responded to pre-soaking in changes of water for up to seven days. The water leaches out soluble inhibitors and swells the embryo. The inhibitors may be present in the woody endocarp or the filmy membrane around the kernel (pellicle).

Potting Seedlings

Palms are ready for potting as soon as the first leaf has expanded. By this stage the root system will be quite long and well branched but not yet tangling with its neighbours. As palms are generally fairly slow growing in their early stages it is best to grow them in pots until they are of a sufficient size to plant out and survive on their own.

A suitable potting mixture must encourage healthy root growth for anchorage as well as strong growth above ground. Potting mixes must be well aerated and hold sufficient nutrients and water for growth without any disease organisms being present. A safe and useful mix can be made up from five parts coarse sand or perlite; four parts peat moss, vermiculite or milled pine bark; three parts friable loam.

Some fertilisers should be added to this mixture to promote growth (see also page 62) and the pH should be adjusted to six using lime or dolomite. Slow-release fertilisers that are available in commercial packs are very useful for supplying nitrogen, phosphorus and potassium. They should be used at the rates recommended on the pack. Trace elements can be added as a prepared mixture if needed. Organic fertilisers such as blood and bone or hoof and horn can also be used at two to four kilogrammes per cubic metre of potting mix.

Young palms are best potted into fairly small but deep containers so that the root system is not too restricted. Plastic growing tubes about 7 cm across are ideal for the first potting and when the palms are well established in these they can be moved into larger containers. Immediately after potting the seedlings should be thoroughly watered to consolidate the soil around the root system. Palms can also be potted into tubs using a similar soil mixture and technique.

After-Potting Care

After potting, the palms must be watered regularly to keep the soil mixture moist and the surroundings humid so as to encourage root and top growth. They should be kept in a shaded position such as in a bush house or under trees where they will receive filtered sun or direct sun for part of the day only. Pests such as slugs and snails, scales and mealy bugs should be controlled when noticed. Fertilising with liquid preparations will encourage growth and these are best applied during the warm months while the plants are in active growth.

Seed Viability

As a general rule palm seeds do not retain their viability for very long and are best sown as soon as possible after collection. There are exceptions of course, such as the Coconut which can germinate after many months at sea. Seeds of *Pseudophoenix* spp. still germinate readily after storage for two years and there is some suggestion that these palms will not germinate if sown fresh. However, for most species it is better to be safe and sow the seeds immediately. For example, species of *Oncosperma* and *Pinanga* may lose their viability within a few days of ripening and this precludes their distribution by post, at least in the dry state. If it is suspected that the fruit of a species may have limited viability then it is wise to mix the fruit with moist peat moss and store in a sealed bottle or plastic bag as soon as possible after collection. The seed will not dehydrate in these conditions and may even begin to germinate in the peat moss.

A useful guide to the viability of various palm species can be obtained by considering the climatic conditions in its place of origin in combination with the thickness of the endocarp. Thus palms from areas with a distinct wet/dry or hot/cold climate and with seeds having a thick endocarp can be expected to retain their viability for longest. Seeds of these palms will last for two to four months without any special storage conditions. On the other hand palms from the hot, wet, humid tropics generally have a thin endocarp and have a very short viability period of

TABLE 5

Viability Guide to Native Palm Seeds. Storage Time (Weeks)

Species	2-4	4-6	8-16	Species	2-4	4-6	8-16
Archontophoenix spp.			X	*Laccospadix australasica*			X
Arenga australasica	X			*Licuala ramsayi*		X	
Calamus aruensis		X		*Linospadix minor*	X		
Calamus australis			X	*Linospadix monostachya*			X
Calamus caryotoides			X	*Livistona australis*			X
Calamus hollrungii		X		*Livistona benthamii*		X	
Calamus moti			X	*Livistona decipiens*		X	
Calamus muelleri			X	*Livistona drudei*		X	
Calamus radicalis		X		*Livistona humilis*			X
Calamus warburgii		X		*Livistona mariae*			X
Carpentaria acuminata		X		*Livistona muelleri*			X
Caryota rumphiana		X		*Normanbya normanbyi*	X		
Corypha elata			X	*Orania appendiculata*		X	
Gronophyllum ramsayi		X		*Ptychosperma elegans*		X	
Gulubia costata	X			*Ptychosperma macarthurii*		X	
Hydriastele wendlandiana	X						

two to six weeks. These must be handled carefully and quickly if they are to be successfully propagated.

The above generalisation holds well for genera with a restricted distribution but considerable variation can be expected in widespread genera where the species occupy a variety of ecological niches. Even for genera restricted to the tropics those species which grow on high peaks can be expected to behave differently from those on the lowlands. Thus these considerations can only be used as a useful guide.

TABLE 6

Viability Guide to Seeds of Some Palm Genera. Storage Time (Weeks)

Genus	2-4	4-6	8-16	Genus	2-4	4-6	8-16
Aiphanes		X		Livistona		X	
Areca	X			Metroxylon	X		
Arecastrum			X	Nengella	X		
Arenga		X		Nypa	X		
Bactris		X		Opsiandra			X
Bentinckia	X			Orania	X		
Borassus			X	Orbignya			X
Brahea			X	Phoenix			X
Caryota		X		Pinanga	X		
Chamaedorea		X		Pritchardia		X	
Chamaerops			X	Ptychosperma		X	
Chrysalidocarpus		X		Raphia	X		
Corypha		X		Reinhardtia		X	
Copernicia			X	Rhapis			X
Cyrtostachys	X			Rhopalostylis		X	
Dictyosperma			X	Roystonea		X	
Elaeis			X	Sabal			X
Euterpe	X			Salacca	X		
Gronophyllum	X			Serenoa			X
Howea			X	Syagrus			X
Hyophorbe			X	Thrinax			X
Hyphaene			X	Trachycarpus			X
Jubaea			X	Trithrinax			X
Latania		X		Veitchia	X		
Licuala		X		Verschaffeltia	X		

Seed Storage

Palm seeds lose their viability by loss of moisture through the endocarp. When a significant amount of moisture is lost the kernel containing the embryo shrinks away from the walls of the endocarp and the surface may take on a shrivelled appearance. If a badly shrivelled seed is cut, the tissue will be discoloured and have a dry texture. Such seeds will not germinate and if sown will rot quickly. The cut-off figure seems to be a moisture loss of more than twenty per cent.

Moisture loss is affected by time, the humidity of the atmosphere surrounding the seed and the temperature. Thus in high temperatures and a dry atmosphere the seeds will lose their viability quite quickly. The embryo of palm seeds can be damaged by exposure to low temperatures and thus a successful method of palm seed storage must reduce water loss but avoid injury from cold. The most successful method seems to be to mix them with fairly dry peat moss, seal in a container such as a plastic bag and store at about 20°C. Some palms will withstand temperatures much lower than this but the very tropical ones will not. Seeds properly stored can be held for periods of six to fifteen months.

The technique employed by some commercial seed firms may or may not be suitable. The seeds are freed of all pulp and air dried for a short period before placing in an aluminium envelope. The air is then evacuated by a suction pump and the envelope is sealed hermetically. Palm seeds will store satisfactorily under these conditions but they are often held at too low temperatures resulting in cold damage to the embryo.

Transport of Seeds

Seed if collected fresh and properly packed will survive air transport to most parts of the world. The seeds should be prepared and packed as outlined in previous paragraphs and despatched by the fastest practical method. As air cargo holds are subject to freezing conditions it is a wise policy to provide some outer insulating cover such as a polystyrene container to prevent cold damage to the embryo. Dry peat moss packing is also a better insulating agent than wet peat moss.

Caustic Fruit

The skin and flesh of some palm fruits contain needle-like crystals of calcium oxalate called raphides which can enter the skin and cause severe irritation or a burning feeling. Handling such fruits is best avoided but if this is not possible then good protective gloves must be worn. The most familiar of the palms with caustic fruit are the various species of *Caryota* but others include *Arenga australasica, A. pinnata, Drymophloeus beguinii* and *Opsiandra maya*. Under no circumstances should such fruit be eaten. Deaths have been reported following ingestion of the fruit of *Caryota urens*.

VEGETATIVE PROPAGATION
Propagation from Basal Offsets

Division is a technique of vegetative propagation and the new plants so produced are identical to the parents. In palms, division can only be carried out on those species that produce basal offsets (usually known as suckers) freely, such as *Chamaedorea costaricana, C. erumpens, C. siefrizii, Chamaerops humilis, Chrysalidocarpus lutescens, Laccospadix australasicus, Phoenix dactylifera, P. reclinata, Ptychosperma macarthurii, Rhapis excelsa* and *R. humilis*.

Division is a simple technique of propagation but if it is to be successful it still requires care both during and after the removal of the sucker. The tools required such as spades, knives and saws must be sharp. The soil should be dug away carefully to expose the base of the sucker. If it has good roots it can be severed with the spade or a saw or a strong, sharp knife. Damage to the tissues should be kept to a minimum and the cut surface can be sealed by rubbing with garden lime. As much as possible of the offset's root system should be removed with it to aid in its establishment.

Often when the sucker is exposed it is found to have few or not roots and this means that it is deriving all its sustenance from the main stems. This is especially a common feature of *Chrysalidocarpus lutescens* and *Phoenix dactylifera*. Such suckers can be transplanted but usually the loss rate is high with the *Chrysalidocarpus* although the technique can be successful with *Phoenix dactylifera*. In fact, in this latter species suckers from the trunk can be removed and successfully established. Existing leaves however must be drastically cut back, and the suckers given plenty of tender loving care.

A rootless sucker can be induced to form roots by a couple of simple techniques. The easiest is to twist or wrench the sucker downwards so that its junction with the parent clump is severely disrupted but not completely broken. The sucker can be reburied in soil and roots should form in about two months. Another technique is to slice or notch the sucker on the lower side near its base. Lime should be rubbed into the cut and the sucker reburied until roots form. Suckers being treated in this way should be kept moist to encourage root development, and may even respond to the application of root stimulants such as Formula 20.

Another very successful technique with suckers employs a plastic bag in a similar manner to the germination process outlined earlier. It is especially successful for establishing divisions of small suckering palms such as *Reinhardtia*. After the division is potted and watered, the entire pot is enclosed in a large clear plastic bag, the top tied and the lot is then placed in a warm, semi-shaded area. After a few months, if the division is growing the bag can be gradually opened for hardening off. At this stage make sure excess water drains away by puncturing or upturning the bag.

Watering is not necessary while the bag is tied but plants may need to be watered during the hardening process. With this method there is no need to remove or cut back the leaves from the division. The technique is also useful for establishing seedlings or small transplanted palms with reduced or damaged root systems.

After separation the sucker with good roots should be planted directly into position or else it can be potted and held in a semi-shaded, protected situation until sufficiently established to plant. The sucker should be planted slightly deeper than in its original soil depth and thoroughly soaked to consolidate the new soil and encourage new root growth. The fronds should be trimmed back by at least one third to a half to reduce transpiration. A mulch applied to the surrounding soil will help the new plant to get established. At no time should it be allowed to dry out.

The optimum time for removing basal offsets from palms is during late spring and early summer when the plants have just started growth or are in active growth. New leaf growth is usually associated with new root growth and if division can coincide with the emergence of new roots then the sucker will establish more easily.

Aerial Layering

Aerial layering, also known as marcotting, is a fairly common technique used to propagate fruit trees and ornamental shrubs and trees that may be difficult from cuttings. It is interesting to note that it can also be used to propagate some specialised palms such as *Chamaedorea* species, some *Pinanga* species and *Rhapis* species and cultivars. This technique is especially useful for *Rhapis* cultivars such as the fine-leaved and variegated-leaved forms. The best time for aerial layering is in the warm growing months.

The technique is fairly straightforward and easily mastered. The stem is cleared of leaf sheaths, fibres etc in the vicinity of a node and the surface of the stem is lightly wounded. A pad of moist to wet sphagnum moss is wrapped around the wounded node and in turn this is wrapped tightly with a piece of polythene film. This whole section must be wrapped thoroughly and tied tightly at each end to seal the bundle and prevent the sphagnum moss from drying out. The plant is then placed in a warm, sheltered environment and kept well watered. After six to twelve weeks roots should show up through the plastic and when a good root system is formed in the sphagnum moss the section can be severed and potted. When potting there is no need to remove the sphagnum moss. After potting the new plant should be provided with plenty of tender loving care until it is well established.

Bulbils in Palms

In palms, bulbil is the term used for vegetative shoots produced on aerial parts of the trunk. Such shoots are rare but are interesting because they are genetically identical to the parent plant and are capable of growth after separation (by a procedure not dissimilar to that for suckering palms). A technique similar to aerial layering can also be used to induce root formation before the bulbil is severed, and thus make separation more reliable.

Bulbils are usually modified inflorescences but may also occur as small growths on the rhachillae. Some plants consistently produce bulbils instead of flowers. In *Arenga pinnata* bulbil formation may occur following damage to the growth apex of the plant. Bulbil formation has been noticed in the coconut, oil palm and other species. Species of *Salacca* have an inflorescence that may trail on the ground. A couple of species (*S. flabellata, S. wallichiana*) form bulbils on the stems of the inflorescence and these come in contact with the ground, form roots and become separate plants.

Tissue Culture

Tissue culture is the propagation of plants from small pieces of tissue which are excised and grown under sterile conditions. The tissue is grown on culture media which contain a balanced supply of plant nutrients and hormones. This propagation technique must essentially be carried out in a laboratory and requires the use of expensive and specialised equipment. By changing the hormone content of the medium the tissue can be induced to multiply or to become organised into plantlets complete with leaves and roots.

The best way to propagate a plant by tissue culture is to remove and grow a bud, either from a shoot tip or a lateral bud in the axil of a leaf. The problem with palms is that each stem contains a single apical bud and therefore the plant must be destroyed if this method is employed. In fact, many plants must be destroyed because of the difficulties of sterilising and establishing a shoot tip in culture. The most common approach for palms therefore is to establish a culture of callus tissue from a developing organ such as a leaf, stem, petiole, inflorescence or root tips. After the callus tissue is growing and multiplying different hormones in the culture medium can be used to generate shoots and roots. The culture of seedling embryos (embryo culture) also has a limited application.

Tissue culture with palms seems to date to be limited to species with commercial significance such as superior specimens of date palms, oil palms and coconuts. In Malaysia tissue cultured oil palms have been successfully planted in the field for evaluation. In fact, only tissue-cultured plants are currently used in propagating this palm. Date palms have also been successfully propagated by tissue culture and planted out on a fairly large scale. Tissue culture of the coconut has proved to be extremely difficult.

There is also interest by nurserymen in tissue culture as a technique for the rapid propagation of uniform, disease-free plants. To date this work is in its infancy and has concentrated on high-value species such as *Howea belmoreana* and *H. forsteriana*. Embryo culture has been carried out on such species as *Caryota urens, Chamaedorea costaricana, Howea forsteriana, Hyophorbe lagenicaulis, H. verschaffeltii, Pritchardia kaalae* and *Veitchia joannis*.

CHAPTER 6
Palms for Containers, Indoors and Out

PALMS AS INDOOR PLANTS

PALMS make excellent indoor plants and have been used in this way for over 100 years. The large, airy rooms and hallways of the stately homes of England have for long been graced by the delicate, drooping fronds of a Kentia or its relative. Today people are well aware of the decorative value of plants in the home and there is a wide range of palms available for selection. Businesses also realise the importance of indoor plants and palms are a significant component of the range used by plant hire firms.

Although palms as a group are generally considered suitable for indoor decoration and are often promoted as such the vast majority of species do not respond favourably to indoor conditions. Practical experience shows that only a limited number of species succeed consistently indoors. More species succeed indoors in tropical regions than in the temperate zones because palms as a group are tropical in origin and therefore the range for selection is greater. Also, indoor plants tend to grow more readily in the tropics because of the open, airy design of houses and the warmer climate. Some modern houses are designed for a more open living style and provide excellent conditions for the growth of plants.

Suitable Species

In general, palms that consistently grow well indoors are those that will tolerate fairly dark positions, a usually dry atmosphere and neglect. The best of these are undoubtedly the two species of *Howea* native to Lord Howe Island, which are generally sold as Kentia palms. These not only look graceful but will grow indoors and tolerate the conditions mentioned previously. When well cared for and in a position which suits them they are a magnificent addition to the indoor decor. Unfortunately they are fairly slow growing and an advanced specimen is very expensive. Some other species can also be very suitable for indoors and these are listed in the accompanying table.

Choice of a Plant

Once the choice of a suitable indoor species is made the next step is to select the plant. As with other plants a good palm should be a sturdy, healthy specimen in active growth. Look for a plant with healthy dark-green leaves. Avoid those with dull leaves that have a dry appearance as they have probably been neglected or held too long in the store or nursery. Plants with very lush, soft growth should also be avoided as they may have just been taken out of a glasshouse and will deteriorate when placed indoors.

Buyers should be especially wary of plants which have pests already established. A few holes in the leaves from caterpillars or grasshoppers is acceptable but colonies of scales, mealy bugs or spider-mites can be expected to proliferate in the indoor environment. These pests are difficult to eradicate once established and it is better to start with clean stock. When checking for mealy bugs or scale it is advisable to look under the leaf sheaths, in the petiole grooves and so on.

TABLE 7

Palms Suitable for Indoors

Species	Light Tolerance	Comments
Aiphanes caryotifolia	Bright	Good, but prickly
Archontophoenix alexandrae	Bright	Not very good
Arecastrum romanzoffianum	Dull-Bright	Good, needs regular spelling
Carpentaria acuminata	Bright	Good, cold sensitive
Caryota mitis	Dull-Bright	Good, needs regular spelling
Caryota urens	Dull-Bright	Good, needs regular spelling
Chamaedorea costaricana	Dull-Bright	Excellent
Chamaedorea elegans	Dull	Excellent
Chamaedorea erumpens	Dull-Bright	Excellent
Chamaedorea geonomiformis	Dull-Bright	Excellent
Chamaedorea microspadix	Dull-Bright	Good
Chamaedorea seifrizii	Dull-Bright	Good, fast growing
Chrysalidocarpus lutescens	Bright	Good
Hedyscepe canterburyana	Dull-Bright	Good, slow growing
Howea belmoreana	Dull	Excellent
Howea forsteriana	Dull	Excellent
Laccospadix australasica	Dull	Excellent
Licuala grandis	Bright	Very tropical
Licuala ramsayi	Bright	Good, cold sensitive
Linospadix minor	Dull	Excellent
Linospadix monostachya	Dull	Excellent
Microcoelum weddellianum	Dull	Excellent
Phoenix roebelenii	Dull	Excellent
Reinhardtia gracilis	Dull	Excellent
Rhapis excelsa	Dull	Excellent
Rhapis humilis	Dull	Excellent

Conditions

Light Palms indoors prefer a position where they receive some light coming in through an archway, window, skylight or doorway. Direct sunlight for part of the day can be tolerated happily by palms provided that it is not long exposure to hot summer sun. Morning sun or sun filtered through shrubs and trees is ideal. Bright light through coloured or frosted glass provides an attractive background for a group of palms and can be quite suitable for their growth. Such glass however may transmit heat and the plants will require more frequent watering and attention to humidity than would be the case in other areas. Solar films applied to windows to reduce heat and glare are very detrimental to indoor palms.

Humidity Indoor atmospheres are generally of low humidity and tend to fluctuate considerably with changes in the outdoor environment as well as heating and air conditioning. Palms generally dislike low humidities although there is a considerable range of response within the group. Species that are intolerant of low and fluctuating humidities lose their lustre and appear dull and are often severely attacked by pests such as spider-mite and mealy bug.

The answer to low humidity is to change the atmosphere around the plants. This does not necessarily mean increased watering although the plants must not be allowed to dry out. Many an indoor palm has been killed by overwatering because its leaves seemingly advertised that it was dry. The dryness is, in fact, caused by the low humidity and cannot be compensated for by increased watering of the potting mixture. Increasing the humidity around the leaves is the most successful solution. This can be achieved by grouping indoor plants so that each contributes to the atmosphere around the other. For the same reason a number of plants in each pot is more successful than just one. Standing the pot in a large saucer of wet, evaporative material such as scoria is also a useful technique to increase the surrounding humidity as is misting the plants at regular intervals with a fine spray.

Temperature The majority of palms are tropical in origin and therefore dislike low temperatures, although some of the successful indoor species grow very well in temperate regions (see Table page 258). Tropical palms in active growth may be damaged by temperatures around 14°C but if they are dormant or are growing slowly they can withstand somewhat lower temperatures. The length of time the plant is exposed to the low temperature also exerts a considerable influence. Low temperatures are not a problem in tropical regions, but in highland districts and temperate zones the winter temperature indoors can drop to a level which can cause damage to sensitive species.

Houses fitted with internal heating avoid the problems of cold damage to indoor palms but the resultant very dry atmospheres may cause excessive water loss. Indoor palms in winter grow slowly not only because of lower temperatures but also through reduced light intensity and short daylight hours.

Care of Indoor Palms

Watering Although watering indoor plants is basic common sense, for various reasons it creates more problems and frustrations than any other aspect of the plant's care. Healthy, actively growing plants need regular watering and the frequency depends upon the prevailing temperatures and humidity. In summer, plants can be safely watered daily whereas in winter their needs are much less. The same parameters as for indoor plants apply — vigorous-growing plants will need more water more frequently than those growing slowly or not at all, plants will need watering more regularly in the summer than in the winter and plants growing in bright light will dry out more quickly than those in dim positions.

Other factors must also be considered such as the type of potting mix, the size of the pot and how full it is of roots and the prevailing temperature and humidity. The potting mixture must drain well but should also retain sufficient water for the plant's growth. Heavy soils that become soggy when watered are useless for palms as they only lead to rotting of the roots and retardation or death of the plant.

Palms that are kept too dry lose the sheen on their leaves, generally look unhealthy and may even wilt. Palms that are too wet suffer damage to the tips of the leaflets which die and become brown. If they have suffered root damage such as rotting of the root tips, waterlogged palms may also wilt because the damaged roots are unable to extract water from the soil. Wilting in palms is not as prominent as in other groups of plants.

The ideal watering regime keeps the potting mixture sufficiently moist to keep adequate oxygen and water available to the roots for growth. Regular topping up can be quite satisfactory but at intervals the potting mixture should be thoroughly soaked so that water flows out the drainage holes. This ensures a thorough wetting of the root system and also leaches out salts which may have accumulated from the breakdown of the fertilisers. This leaching process should be performed out of doors or in a bath or sink.

In any group of indoor plants some specimens are going to require more regular watering than others. It is a temptation to water all of the plants at the same time but this should be avoided and individual needs catered for. For example, if all of the plants are watered each time the most vigorous plant dries out then the least vigorous ones will receive too much.

Recuperation Indoor palms, like any indoor plants, appreciate a 'freshen-up' at intervals. This can consist of a hosing down in the garden to wash the dust off the leaves and refreshen the plants generally. This simple act can also be important in reducing pest build-up and discouraging species such as mites which like dry conditions. It is also a good policy to put palms outside in rainy or drizzly weather but they must not be left out if the sun appears. Such sudden exposure can drastically burn plants that have been shielded from it.

Resting indoor palms by moving them to a shady position in the garden or bush house is very beneficial. Here they are well watered, repotted or fertilised if necessary and generally encouraged to recuperate and put on new growth. Once spelled the plants can then be moved back indoors. With planning a series of palms can by cycled in this way and those indoors can always be at their peak. Palms should be rested outside for two to three weeks after every two-month period indoors.

Fertilisers Indoor palms benefit from the application of fertilisers but these should only be applied during the warm growing months of the year. Fertilisers applied during winter when growth is slow or sudden applications of quick-release fertilisers to starved or debilitated palms may be of no benefit and indeed may even cause severe burning. Fertilisers are best applied in small does at regular intervals and the soil mixture should be watered thoroughly and regularly after their application. Quick-release fertilisers should never be applied to newly potted palms or to those where the root system has been damaged (for example by waterlogging), because the weakened or new roots can be readily burned.

A wide range of commercial products are available to fertilise indoor plants and most of these will be successful with palms. Fertilisers are usually incorporated in the potting mix to encourage initial growth and these may be supplemented with side dressings when it is felt that the growth is in need of a boost. Complete fertiliser mixtures are usually used in the potting mixes and these may be quick or slow releasing. Organic manures and fertilisers can be very beneficial but some such as blood and bone have the drawback of being smelly and attractive to dogs. A suitable potting mixture including fertilisers is presented on page 92.

Supplementary fertilising of palms can be carried out using slow-release fertilisers, plant pills, or liquid preparations. Liquid fertilisers are very beneficial and are usually safe except where the plant is suffering from overwatering. A useful, cheap, nitrogenous preparation can be made by dissolving 1½ teaspoons of urea or ammonium nitrate in a watering can of water. Commercial preparations have the amounts to be applied on the packet and these recommendations should be adhered to. Some nutrients can be applied through the leaves in a process known as foliar feeding. This is generally a much less satisfactory and more expensive way of boosting growth than root applications.

Pests Pests are dealt with in detail on pages 64-70 but it should be mentioned here that container-grown palms may be more susceptible to certain pests than are those palms grown in the garden. The three most serious pests of container-grown palms are mealy bugs, spider-mites and scale insects. Spider-mites revel in dry conditions and are mainly a pest of indoor palms. Their effects can be reduced by frequent misting or hosing. Mealy bugs and scale may be present on any palm but become very severe on those that are weakened or debilitated through neglect. Healthy plants resist pests far better than weakened ones.

PALMS AS OUTDOOR PLANTS

The preceding section deals mainly with palms for indoor decoration. What is not generally realised is that palms also make excellent container plants for outdoor decoration on areas such as terraces, patios, verandahs, around barbecues, pools, to name just a few. Because the plants are outdoors they do not have to tolerate the restricted environment of indoor plants and a much wider range of species can be grown. Almost any palm will make a suitably container plant for a while but vigorous species soon outgrow their container and will need regular attention. A selection of suitable container palms is provided in the accompanying table. Virtually any of the Dwarf to Small Palms listed in the Appendix on page 257 will also make excellent container plants. Because they are grown outdoors the species must be able to tolerate the climatic regime of the area. Once a container-grown palm has become too big it can always be planted in the garden or sold.

Outdoor Conditions

Sun Container-grown palms can be used for display in sunny or shady aspects. As a general rule young palms need protection from direct, hot sun for the first two to three years of their life. Some palms such as the various species of *Phoenix* and *Sabal* will tolerate sun from a very early age while others such as *Chamaedorea elegans* and *Linospadix monostachya* need shade even when mature. The majority of plants will tolerate sun when their fronds are about 1 m high and this is an excellent size to start off a palm in a container. Tolerance to sun will also vary depending on how moist the potting mixture is kept. Palms kept well watered will tolerate much more sun than those allowed to dry out between waterings.

When a new palm is purchased from a nursery take note of how much sun it is receiving. If it has been held in a shade house or glasshouse it will need to be hardened off before being placed in full sun. Hardening consists of increasing the exposure to sun the plant receives each day while keeping it well watered. A sudden prolonged exposure, especially in summer, will lead to severe burning by the ultra violet rays of the sun.

Wind Palms generally do not like wind and those in containers should not be placed in a windy or draughty position. Cold winds may cause chilling with resultant stunted or deformed growth while hot winds cause severe dessication. Damage may also occur to the leaves and leaflets. Tall palms in tubs are also top-heavy and tend to blow over easily.

Frost Palms in containers have the advantage that they can be moved if severe environmental conditions are imminent. Frost is a major enemy of palms and only hardy species should be chosen for cold areas. A list of suitable cold-tolerant palms is included in Appendix 3.

Care of Outdoor Container Palms

Watering Watering outside containers is easier than those indoors because hoses are available and there is less need to worry about the mess. Because they are outside, however, the plants tend to be forgotten and their watering neglected. If container-grown palms are to maintain a good appearance they must be regularly watered and at no stage allowed to dry out completely. Watering will vary with the climatic conditions prevailing. In summer a daily watering may be necessary whereas in winter once or twice a week may be sufficient. Windy weather dries plants out and extra watering may be needed. Heavy rain will water the plants but do not fall into the trap of thinking that light rain will do the same. Rain needs to be fairly heavy and persistent to penetrate the potting mix and many a plant has died because the owner thought that rain had watered the plant sufficiently.

In addition to normal waterings it is a good policy to thoroughly soak the plants every two weeks. This prevents dry spots developing in the potting mixture and also leaches out excess fertiliser salts. Hosing down the foliage is also useful because it reduces the build-up of dust and discourages pests.

Potting Mixes A suitable potting mix is of tremendous importance to the successful growth of a container palm whether it be held indoors or outside. A potting mix must supply anchorage for the roots and encourage their growth by ensuring adequate aeration, moisture and nutrient supply. Two suitable potting mixes are:

Mix 1	Mix 2
5 shovels coarse sand	5 shovels coarse sand
4 shovels milled pine bark or peat moss	3 shovels peat moss
3 shovels friable loam	10 shovels milled pine bark
45 g Osmocote ® (3-4 months formulation)	70 g Osmocote ® (3-4 months formulation)
130 g Osmocote ® (8-9 months formulation)	240 g Osmocote ® (8-9 months formulation)
40 g Dolomite	60 g Dolomite
3 g Iron sulphate	5 g Magnesium sulphate
	45 g Iron sulphate
	40 g Trace element mix

Note that palms like well-rotted animal manures and these can be added to either mix.

Fertilisers Some of the fertilisers incorporated in the potting mixtures are slow release and will maintain growth for up to nine months. After this time the palm can be repotted if necessary or else treated with slow-release or liquid fertilisers as outlined on page 90.

Repotting Repotting of container-grown plants is necessary to maintain their appearance and growth. The containers eventually become filled with roots and the potting mix exhausted. Such plants are referred to as being potbound and watering them can be difficult.

Repotting will be necessary every one to two years. The plants can be put into a bigger container or if it is felt that the present container is suitable the plant can be put back into it after removal of the old potting mixture and some of the root system. Repotting is best carried out in the spring or early summer. The plants should be thoroughly watered immediately after repotting.

Pests Pests and diseases are dealt with in detail on page 64.

General Hints Certain palms such as species of *Livistona* make excellent container plants but are very prickly and are best avoided if the containers are to be placed near thoroughfares.

The containers should not be placed directly on the ground but on concrete or bricks or supported above the soil surface. This is to prevent diseases and pests (grubs, worms) from gaining entry via the drainage holes and damaging the palm's root system. It also prevents the palm roots from growing through the drainage holes and becoming entrenched in the soil.

Some palms have a prodigious root system that quickly fills a container. If these palms are not repotted regularly their roots are quite capable of bursting the container. This is particularly a problem with plastic containers but may also apply to terra cotta ones or even the large concrete containers used in shopping centres.

TABLE 8
Palms Suitable for Outside Containers

Species	Position	Climatic Conditions*	Notes
Aiphanes caryotifolia	sun or shade	Tr-STr	Prickly
Archontophoenix alexandrae	sun or shade	Tr-STr	Strong grower
Archontophoenix cunninghamiana	sun or shade	Tr-STr-Te	Strong grower
Arecastrum romanzoffianum	sun	Tr-STr-Te	Large container
Arenga engleri	sun	STr-Te	Cluster
Brahea armata	sun	STr-Te	Bluish leaves
Butia capitata	sun	STr-Te	Excellent
Caryota mitis	sun	Tr-STr	Nice foliage
Caryota urens	sun	Tr-STr	Nice foliage
Chamaedorea costaricana	shade	Tr-STr-Te	Small cluster palm
Chamaedorea elegans	shade	Tr-STr-Te	Small palm
Chamaedorea geonomiformis	shade	Tr-STr	Small palm
Chamaedorea seifrizii	shade	Tr-STr	Small palm, fast growing
Chamaerops humilis	sun	STr-Te	Very hardy, prickly
Chrysalidocarpus lutescens	sun	Tr-STr-Te	Excellent
Cyrtostachys renda	sun	Tr	Colourful
Dictyosperma album	sun	Tr-STr	Nice foliage
Hedyscepe canterburyana	shade	STr-Te	Slow growing
Howea belmoreana	sun or shade	STr-Te	Excellent
Howea forsteriana	sun or shade	STr-Te	Excellent
Laccospadix australasica	shade – some sun	Tr-STr	Excellent
Licuala grandis	sun	Tr	Spectacular
Licuala ramsayi	sun	Tr-STr	Excellent
Linospadix minor	shade	Tr-STr	Small palm

Palms Suitable for Outside Containers

Species	Position	Climatic Conditions*	Notes
Linospadix monostachya	shade	STr-Te	Small palm
Livistona chinensis	sun	Tr-STr-Te	Spreading, prickly
Microcoelum weddellianum	shade	Tr-STr	Excellent small palm
Normanbya normanbyi	sun or shade	Tr-STr	Attractive foliage
Phoenix pusilla	sun	Tr-STr-Te	Attractive foliage
Phoenix roebelenii	sun	Tr-STr-Te	Excellent
Phoenix rupicola	sun	Tr-STr-Te	Attractive
Ptychosperma macarthuri	sun	Tr-STr	Excellent
Reinhardtia gracilis	shade	Tr-STr	Excellent small palm
Rhapis spp	sun or shade	STr-Te	Excellent
Roystonea regia	sun	Tr-STr	Large container
Sabal minor	sun	Tr-STr-Te	Very hardy
Thrinax radiata	sun	Tr-STr	Long lived
Trachycarpus fortunei	sun	STr-Te	Very hardy

*Tr = tropical; STr = subtropical; Te = temperate.

CHAPTER 7
Australian and New Zealand Native Palms

THE Australian flora contains about fifty-seven species of palms in twenty-two genera. The exact number is somewhat uncertain because complex genera such as *Livistona* and *Linospadix* are still under study. For example, about twenty species of *Livistona* are known from Australia of which eight are undescribed as is also one species of *Linospadix*. New Zealand has two species of palm, both endemic.

Fifty-seven species of palm is a meagre representation of such a large, diverse group of plants especially when one considers the huge size of the Australian continent. This paucity not only illustrates the unsuitable climate but indicates that either very few species had reached Australia before the separation of the continents comprising Gondwanaland or they became extinct in a subsequent hostile climate. Expansion within Australia since its isolation by sea has been limited by the arid zones. Within the fifty-seven species there is a high degree of endemism (80 per cent of Australian palms are endemic), indicating adaptation to local topography and climatic regimes. (See Tables 9 and 10.) Australian palms are principally found on the coastal fringes of the continent with the notable exceptions being several hardy species of the genus *Livistona* which are found along inland rivers and gorges. The southernmost Australian palm is *Livistona australis* which extends into eastern Victoria. The main proliferation occurs within the tropics with most species being found in the rainforests of Queensland and a reduced westerly extension into the top end of the Northern Territory (twelve species) and the Kimberley region of Western Australia (five species).

Those palms occurring in north-eastern Queensland (thirty-four species) have strong links with nearby Pacific Islands and South-east Asia. These links are mainly at the generic level as the majority of species found here are endemic. Some species such as *Gulubia costata* and *Ptychosperma macarthurii* are common to both areas. There are no links to New Zealand which has only two species which are closely related to the only palm found on Norfolk Island. Lord Howe Island is an intriguing little refuge with four species, all endemic to the island. Two of these species, both Howeas, form a dominant component of the island's lowland vegetation.

Palms in Australia are rarely a dominant feature of the vegetation although they may be a prominent component. In north-eastern Queensland colonies of the Fan Palm *(Licuala ramsayi)* are spectacular. In breaks in the rainforest and along the margins thick stands of prickly climbing species of *Calamus* are not uncommon. Sporadic large stands of Bangalow Palm *(Archontophoenix cunninghamiana)* are scattered down the east coast while patches of *Livistona* species are localised in lowland swampy areas. Occasional hillsides in highland rainforest areas of north-eastern Queensland bear a profusion of *Laccospadix australasica*. On the whole however, Australian palms, interesting though they may be, are a very minor part of the flora.

In the following pages the Australian and New Zealand palms are presented in some detail and with a standardised layout to aid in comparison and location of specific details. The names following each genus and species are abbreviations of the people responsible for describing them.

TABLE 9
Endemism in Australian Palm Genera

Genus	Endemic	Not Endemic	Genus	Endemic	Not Endemic
Archontophoenix	X		*Laccospadix*	X	
Arenga		X	*Lepidorrhachis*	X	
Calamus		X	*Licuala*		X
Carpentaria	X		*Linospadix*		X
Caryota		X	*Livistona*		X
Cocos		X	*Normanbya*	X	
Corypha		X	*Nypa*		X
Gronophyllum		X	*Orania*		X
Gulubia		X	*Ptychosperma*		X
Hedyscepe	X		*Wodyetia*	X	
Howea	X		Total	8	14
Hydriastele		X		36%	64%

TABLE 10
Endemism in Australian Palm Species

Species	Distribution	Endemic	Not Endemic
Archontophoenix alexandrae	Qld	X	
Archontophoenix cunninghamiana	Qld, NSW	X	
Arenga australasica	Qld, NT	X	
Calamus aruensis	Qld		X
Calamus australis	Qld	X	
Calamus caryotoides	Qld	X	
Calamus hollrungii	Qld		X
Calamus moti	Qld	X	
Calamus muelleri	Qld, NSW	X	
Calamus radicalis	Qld	X	
Calamus warburgii	Qld		X
Carpentaria acuminata	NT	X	
Caryota rumphiana	Qld		X

Species	Distribution	Endemic	Not Endemic
Cocos nucifera	Qld		X
Corypha elata	Qld, NT		X
Gronophyllum ramsayi	NT	X	
Gulubia costata	Qld		X
Hedyscepe canterburyana	Lord Howe Island	X	
Howea belmoreana	Lord Howe Island	X	
Howea forsteriana	Lord Howe Island	X	
Hydriastele wendlandiana	Qld, NT	X	
Laccospadix australasica	Qld	X	
Lepidorrhachis moorei	Lord Howe Island	X	
Licuala ramsayi	Qld	X	
Linospadix aequisegmentosa	Qld	X	
Linospadix microcarya	Qld	X	
Linospadix minor	Qld		X
Linospadix monostachya	Qld, NSW	X	
Linospadix palmeriana	Qld	X	
Linospadix sp. (Mt Lewis)	Qld	X	
Livistona alfredii	WA	X	
Livistona australis	Qld, NSW, Vic	X	
Livistona benthamii	Qld, NT		X
Livistona decipiens	Qld	X	
Livistona drudei	Qld	X	
Livistona eastonii	WA	X	
Livistona humilis	NT		X
Livistona inermis	NT	X	
Livistona loriphylla	WA	X	
Livistona mariae	NT	X	
Livistona muelleri	Qld	X	
Livistona rigida	Qld, NT	X	
Livistona sp. 'Blackdown'	Qld	X	
Livistona sp. 'Cape River'	Qld	X	

TABLE 10 continued

Species	Distribution	Endemic	Not Endemic
Livistona sp. 'Carnarvon'	Qld	X	
Livistona sp. 'Cooktown'	Qld	X	
Livistona sp. 'Eungella'	Qld	X	
Livistona sp. 'Kimberlies'	WA	X	
Livistona sp. 'Paluma Range'	Qld	X	
Livistona sp. 'Victoria River'	WA, NT	X	
Normanbya normanbyi	Qld	X	
Nypa fruticans	Qld, NT		X
Orania appendiculata	Qld	X	
Ptychosperma bleeseri	NT	X	
Ptychosperma elegans	Qld, NT	X	
Ptychosperma macarthurii	Qld		X
Wodyetia bifurcata	Qld	X	
Total		45	12
Percentage		79%	21%

TABLE 11

Classification of Australian and New Zealand Palm Genera (according to Moore 1973)

Group	Genus	Number of Australasian Species	Group	Genus	Number of Australasian Species
Coryphoid Palms	*Livistona*	20	Arecoid Palms (cont'd)	*Linospadix*	6
	Licuala	1		*Laccospadix*	1
	Corypha	1		*Howea*	2
Lepidocaryoid Palms	*Calamus*	8		*Carpentaria*	1
				Normanbya	1
				Ptychosperma	3
Nypoid Palms	*Nypa*	1		*Gronophyllum*	1
				Hydriastele	1
Caryotoid Palms	*Arenga*	1		*Gulubia*	1
	Caryota	1		*Lepidorrhachis*	1
Arecoid Palms	*Orania*	1		*Wodyetia*	1
	Archontophoenix	2		*Rhopalostylis*	3
	Hedyscepe	1	Cocosoid Palms	*Cocos*	1

Archontophoenix alexandrae in fruit.

Archontophoenix alexandrae, young plant in flower.

ARCHONTOPHOENIX
H. H. Wendl. & Drude

Both the described species of this genus are endemic in eastern Australia where they are usually locally abundant in colonies. They are to be found in rainforest and moist situations in open forest. One species, *A. alexandrae*, is extremely variable and the different forms are under study to see if they warrant specific or infraspecific separation.

Archontophoenix alexandrae
H. H. Wendl. & Drude *(after Princess Alexandra)*
Alexandra Palm

Description: Solitary, feather-leaved palm; trunk 15-20 m tall, enlarged at base, then slender (15-25 cm thick) grey, often with steps at the base; crownshaft about 0.6-1 m long, light green and prominent; leaves 1-2.5 m long, arching in a crown; pinnae 30-45 cm x 2-4 cm, numerous, acuminate, entire, dark green above white or glaucous beneath; spathes 30-45 cm long, pink-ish-white; panicle 30-40 cm long, semi-pendulous, much branched; flowers about 0.8 cm across, white or cream; male flowers with 9-16 stamens; female flowers with broad segments; fruit 1-1.5 cm long, ovoid, waxy, red, mature late Jan-Dec.

Notes: A common palm within its range, usually found growing in colonies. It occurs naturally along stream banks and moist to swampy areas in rainforest, and in areas of very heavy rainfall it may also grow in drier soils. In dense colonies there may be very little undergrowth and the ground is covered with stunted seedlings. Alexandra palms form a very dense root system and are important agents in preventing erosion along stream banks. The cabbage of Alexandra palms is edible and quite tasty and was apparently collected and eaten by the Aborigines. This palm was known to the Aborigines around Cairns as 'Borum-bru' and by the Tully River tribes as 'Ko-paranga'. The expanded leaf base was closed off at one end and used as a scoop-like carrier by the Aborigines.

Alexandra palms are quite variable and there

are a number of different forms that are known (and sold in nurseries) by their area of origin (eg Kuranda, Iron Range). The best known of these is probably the Mount Lewis form which is dealt with separately. The form known as 'Beatriceae' was once described as a separate species. It was originally collected at Mount Elliott just south of Townsville and has a conspicuous swollen base of the trunk with prominent steps formed by the scars of the fallen leaf bases. It is no longer regarded as being botanically distinct but is still commonly propagated and sold in the nursery trade.

Distribution: Coastal and near-coastal areas of north-eastern Qld from Bamaga on northern Cape York Peninsula to Oyster Creek, south of Miriam Vale in central Qld, from sea level to over 1200 m altitude and often locally common.

Distinguishing Features: A tall, slender, feather-leaved palm with a prominent crownshaft; leaflet tips entire, ashy white to glaucous beneath; flowers cream to white.

Confusing Species: *A. cunninghamiana*, *A.* sp 'Mount Lewis', *Ptychosperma elegans*

Archontophoenix cunninghamiana in flower.

Cultivation: Alexandra palms are very popular subjects for cultivation, particularly in tropical and subtropical regions. They are generally rather frost sensitive and can only be grown with difficulty in temperate regions south of Sydney. They are excellent garden palms but need protection from direct sunlight for the first two years. They can be very fast growing in a good situation and respond strongly to applications of fertiliser and watering during dry periods. Well-grown plants are very handsome and look especially decorative when in fruit.

Alexandra palms are readily available from nurseries and are frequently sold for indoor decoration. They are generally unsuitable for this purpose, having high light requirements and disliking the often-dry atmosphere inside offices and dwellings. They do make a very attractive tub plant and are suitable for verandahs or patios.

Propagation: Very readily propagated from seed which is produced in large quantities. Seed usually takes one to three months to germinate. Seedlings transplant readily.

Archontophoenix cunninghamiana
(Wendl.) Wendl. & Drude *(after Alan Cunningham, prominent early Australian botanist)*
Bangalow Palm or Piccabeen Palm

Description: Solitary, feather-leaved palm; trunk 20-25 m tall, slightly enlarged at base, slender throughout (15-20 cm thick), grey; crownshaft about 0.6-1 m long, bright green to purplish-brown and prominent; leaves 2-3 m long, arching in a crown; pinnae 30-50 cm x 2-4 cm, numerous, linear, with long, thread-like points, green on both surfaces; spathes 30-40 cm long; panicle 30-40 cm long, semi-pendulous, much-branched; flowers about 1 cm across, pink to lilac; male flowers with about 9-16 stamens; fruit 1-1.5 cm long, ovoid, waxy, bright red, mature Dec-March.

Notes: A common and familiar palm usually found growing in colonies which may sometimes be extensive and dense almost to the exclusion of other plants. It grows naturally on stream banks and gullies in rainforest and also favours swampy areas in much more open situations. In dense colonies there may be little undergrowth and the ground is carpeted with stunted seedlings. The plants form a mass of cord-like roots and are

Archontophoenix cunninghamiana in fruit.

important in reducing erosion on stream banks. Bangalows are renowned for their ability to withstand strong winds and cyclones by bending and giving with the gusts, and they are often one of the few plants to survive a severe blow. Their cabbage is very tasty and was widely collected by the Aborigines and early settlers. They were known by various tribal names and the name of 'Pikki' was used by the Aborigines of Moreton Bay. This ostensibly referred to the expanded leaf base which was used as a water carrier. The name was later extended to 'Piccabeen'. The early settlers apparently regarded these palms rather fondly for they were often left during clearing operations and today it is not an uncommon sight to see a forlorn group in the middle of cleared paddocks. They were also frequently planted around early homesteads and these were probably the survivors from bush transplants. Bangalow palms are not variable despite their wide distribution.

Distribution: Endemic in coastal and near-coastal areas from north-eastern Qld (Eungella Range, Mackay) to south-eastern NSW near

Batemans Bay and in some cases extending a fair distance inland. It is generally common throughout its range.

Distinguishing Features: A tall, slender, feather-leaved palm with a prominent crownshaft; leaflets with long, thread-like tips, green beneath; flowers lilac.

Confusing Species: *A. alexandrae, Carpentaria acuminata, Ptychosperma elegans*

Cultivation: Bangalow palms are extensively grown in warmer areas such as the subtropics and to a lesser extent the tropics. They are also not infrequent in temperate regions, surviving happily as far south as Melbourne and even exhibit some hardiness in inland towns. They are commonly grown in parks, streets and private gardens and are now also frequently planted in reclamation projects in wasteland along streams, etc. They will tolerate full exposure to sun but need some protection when small. They can be fast growing in a suitable situation and respond to fertilisers and watering during dry periods. They are excellent for planting in groups and a well-grown grove is an attractive sight especially when in fruit. Occasional specimens with variegated leaves have been reported.

Bangalows are readily available from nurseries although they are not grown as frequently now as they were a few years ago. They are frequently sold for indoor decoration but are often disappointing when used this way since they have high light requirements and dislike the often-dry atmospheres found inside offices and dwellings. They do make an attractive tub plant for verandahs or patios. In nature their leaves may sometimes be disfigured by a leaf blight known as *Gleosporium palmarum*.

Propagation: Readily propagated by seed which is produced in large quantities and usually takes one to three months to germinate. Seedlings resent disturbance and are generally difficult, especially if root damage occurs.

Archontophoenix sp. Mount Lewis

Description: Solitary, feather-leaved palm; trunk 15-20 m tall, slightly enlarged at base, slender, grey to whitish; crownshaft about 0.6-1 m long, reddish to purple; young leaves bronze-coloured; leaves 2-3 m long, arching in a crown, pinnae 30-40 cm x 2-4 cm, numerous, acuminate, dark green above white or glaucous beneath; spathes 30-60 cm long, reddish; panicle 40-50 cm long, much branched; fruit 2-3 cm long, ovoid.

Notes: This palm, which may be but a form of *A. alexandrae*, grows naturally in scattered colonies in high altitude rainforests.

Distribution: Endemic on Mt Lewis in north-eastern Queensland, above about 800 m altitude.

Distinguishing Features: A tall, slender, feather-leaved palm with a crown of dark green fronds which are reddish when young; ovoid fruit 2-3 cm long.

Confusing Species: *A. alexandrae.*

Cultivation: An excellent palm for cultivation being slender, sturdy and handsome. When well grown the new fronds may be quite colourful. Plants are more cold tolerant than Alexandra Palm and succeed better in temperate districts. They need protection from direct sun while small and respond to watering and mulching.

Propagation: Fresh seed germinates readily two to six months after sowing.

ARECA ALICEAE F. Muell.

This palm was described in 1879 from a plant growing in the Brisbane Botanical Gardens. The plant was believed to have been collected in rainforest 16 km north of Trinity Bay. Researchers can find no material to back these claims and it would seem to be a case of mistaken identity.

ARENGA Labill.

Of the seventeen species of palms in this genus a solitary species is to be found in the coastal districts and adjacent islands of north-eastern Qld where it is endemic. (For exotic species of *Arenga* see page 160.)

Arenga australasica (H. H. Wendl. & Drude) *S. T. Blake (Australian)*

Description: Clumping, feather-leaved palm; trunks 15-20 m tall, moderately slender (25-

Arenga australasica.

30 cm thick), grey, usually 1-3 stems dominant, with a fringe of immature suckers; leaves 2.5-3.5 m long, dark green, widely spaced up the stem; leaf sheaths with black, fibrous margins; pinnae 20-45 cm long, pleated, with marginal notches, dark green, arranged radially around the rhachis; inflorescence 1-2 m long, interfoliar, flowering down the stem which dies when the lowermost node has produced ripe fruit; flowers about 1 cm across, arranged in threes with one female between two males; fruit about 2 cm across, globose.

Notes: A relatively uncommon palm on the mainland, always found in near-coastal and littoral rainforest usually in partially shady situations although large specimens will survive in the open. It is very common on some offshore islands. There is some possibility that *Arenga microcarpa* also occurs on northern Cape York Peninsula but the differences between the two species are at this stage poorly understood.

Distribution: Confined to north-eastern Qld between Bamaga on northern Cape York Peninsula and just south of Innisfail alway close to the coast in rainforest. Also common on many adjacent islands. A single specimen of an *Arenga* has also been found on Elcho Island in the NT (Dunlop *et al* 1975). The author has examined this specimen (which is sterile) and it is a good match for *A. australasica*.

Distinguishing Features: A tall, clumping palm with feather leaves and monocarpic stems; pinnae radiating, with notched margins.

Confusing Species: None.

Cultivation: This palm is poorly known in cultivation and is grown mainly by enthusiasts although there are some nice specimens in Brisbane parks. Plants will grow in the tropics, subtropics and even warm temperate areas but are sensitive to poor drainage. They are slow growing even in the tropics and are very tolerant of exposure to sun even when small and prefer to be grown in an open position. They respond to water during dry periods and mulches when small.

Propagation: By seed which germinates slowly and erratically from six months to two years. The flesh of the fruit contains a caustic material and the fruit should be handled with great care. Bottom heat may improve germination. This palm may also be propagated from suckers.

BACULARIA F. Muell.

This is an old name for the genus *Linospadix*. The latter name has priority and is accepted under the rules of nomenclature.

Borassus flabellifer L.
Palmyra Palm

The natural existence of this palm in Australia is very doubtful. It was originally reported in 1902 to be growing on Cape York Peninsula but this stand has never been rediscovered nor have there been any reports of other populations since then. A plant was reported to have been transplanted from the stand to Somerset, the home of Frank Jardine, near the tip of Cake York Peninsula. That a Borassus Palm was growing in this garden is not in doubt but its origin remains uncertain. This palm is still growing near Jardine's now-abandoned house.

CALAMUS L.

Of the very large number of species in this genus (375), eight are to be found in Australia. All occur in Qld with a solitary species extending to NSW. Six are endemic. They are climbing palms which form thickets along rainforest margins, tracks, roads and in breaks in the rainforest canopy. They are most noticeable because of their spiny stems and leaves and hook-bearing, entangling appendages. The fruit of some species have a thin layer of edible flesh and are eagerly sought by large fruit-eating birds. In Australia *Calamus* stems are harvested on a limited scale for furniture and basket making. Recent forestry figures indicate that 20-30 tonnes of cane are still harvested annually, but this is a very small fraction of what was cut thirty years ago. (For the exotic species of *Calamus* see page 169.)

Calamus aruensis Becc.
(from the Aru Islands near New Guinea)

Description: Vigorous climbing palm; stems few per clump, very slender, the old stems yellowish-green; fronds about 3 m long, spreading, scattered on the upper third of the stems; petiole short, unarmed, the sheathing base smooth; rhachis with a few hooks; pinnae 15-20 cm x 2-5 cm, elliptical, 30-40 per leaf, scattered and sparse, dark green, the rhachis ending in a long cirrus which is armed with recurved hooks; panicle 2-3 m long, pendulous, sparsely branched; flowers about 0.3-0.4 cm across, greenish; fruit 0.8-1.2 cm across, globular, cream.

Notes: This climbing palm forms tall, fairly slender clumps in and around the margins of monsoonal rainforest and along stream banks. The fruit are an important article of diet of the fruit-eating pigeons and have a thin layer of edible flesh around the seed.

Distribution: In Australia confined to the northern part of Cape York Peninsula extending south to the Jardine River, also New Guinea, and Aru Island.

Distinguishing Features: A climbing palm bearing cirri; leaves with 30-40 scattered, dark-green leaflets, the sheathing base smooth and unarmed.

Confusing Species: *C. hollrungii.*

Cultivation: This palm is virtually unknown in cultivation and little is known of its requirements. Seedlings make attractive pot plants with handsome, dark-green leaves and could be useful for indoor decoration. They have proved to be very sensitive to periods of cold and will not withstand even the lightest frost. They must also be kept out of direct sun. Young plants require a well-drained potting mix rich in organic matter.

Propagation: By seed which must be sown fresh soon after collection. Germination occurs within three to four months of sowing. Suckers are difficult to separate and seedlings have proved to be tricky to transplant.

Calamus australis C. Martius.
(southern)
Hairy Mary, Lawyer Cane or Wait-a-while

Description: Vigorous climbing palm; stems many per clump, slender, the old stems yellow; fronds 1-2.5 m long, fairly closely spaced over the upper half of the stems; petiole short, prickly, the

Calamus caryotoides in fruit.

sheathing base armed with numerous spines up to 8 cm long; rhachis with a few hooks; pinnae 10-30 cm x 2-3 cm, lanceolate, 25-56 per leaf, scattered and not crowded, pale to dark green, a few inconspicuous spines on the margins and along the veins; flagella 2-3 m long, bearing numerous recurved hooks; panicle 2-3 m long, pendulous, sparsely branched, the main stem and rhachillae armed with hooks; flowers about 0.3-0.4 cm across, greenish; fruit 0.8-1 cm across, globular with a small nipple, cream to white.

Notes: A common climbing palm that forms tangled thickets along rainforest margins and in gaps within the rainforest itself. The fruit have a thin layer of edible flesh and are eagerly sought after by fruit-eating pigeons. It was known as 'Jamboolum' by the Aborigines of the Barron River and was probably used by them and other tribes in various ways.

Distribution: Apparently endemic in Australia where it is common in lowland and highland rainforest in north-eastern Qld extending to altitudes of above 1000 m on the Atherton Tableland.

Distinguishing Features: A robust climbing palm bearing flagella; leaves with 30-40 scattered leaflets, the sheaths bearing numerous spines.

Calamus australis in fruit.

Confusing Species: *C. radicalis.*

Cultivation: Although prickly, this climbing palm is grown to a limited extent by enthusiasts and in collections such as are maintained by Botanic Gardens. It likes a cool, shady situation. Soils must have free drainage and mulching seems essential for its success. Once established plants are fairly tolerant of dryness but for best results should be watered at regular intervals. The species is hardy at least as far south as Sydney. Seedlings make interesting pot plants and could be suitable for indoor decoration.

Propagation: By seed which germinates readily within three to four months of sowing. Seed loses its viability quickly and should be sown soon after collection. Seedlings are difficult to transplant.

Calamus caryotoides C. Martius.
(resembling the genus Caryota)
Fish-tail Lawyer Cane

Description: Slender climbing palm; stems few per clump, very slender and wiry, the old stems greenish brown; fronds 0.5-0.7 m long, spreading, fairly widely spaced on the upper half of the stems; petiole short, prickly, the sheathing base armed with scattered spines 1-2 cm long; rhachis with a few scattered hooks; pinnae 10-20 cm x 4-6 cm, tapered, 6-12 per leaf, sparse, pale green, the apices jagged and praemorse, a few spines along the veins, the terminal ones united and fish-tail like; flagella 1-2.5 m long, very thin and whip-like, bearing recurved hooks; panicle 1-2.5 m long, pendulous, bearing a few short branches; flowers 0.3-0.4 cm across, greenish; fruit 0.8-1.3 cm across, globular, cream to yellowish.

Notes: This is the most slender of the Australian species of *Calamus* and very distinctive with its fish-tail leaflets. It grows in open areas in drier rainforests and along forest margins and stream banks. It is less offensive than other members of this genus but is the easiest to be caught by, and thickets are still best avoided as the thin, whip-like flagella grip tenaciously. The fruit have a thin layer of edible flesh and are eaten by fruit-eating birds.

Distribution: Endemic in Australia where it is found in lowland and highland rainforests of north-eastern Qld.

Distinguishing Features: A slender climbing palm bearing flagella; leaves with 6-12 fish-tail like leaflets, the sheathing base bearing scattered spines.

Confusing Species: None.

Cultivation: This is the most desirable of the Australian species of *Calamus* for cultivation but it is still only to be found in enthusiasts collections. It is an unusual, slender plant to grow under established trees. It likes shady conditions and plenty of water especially during dry periods. Plants are slow growing in their early years of establishment but then may increase in height quite rapidly. Some have a single stem for many years while others produce suckers quite early in life. It is quite cold tolerant and plants can be grown as far south as Melbourne. Seedlings make an interesting pot plant and have proved to be suitable for indoor decoration although they may become tall and in need of staking.

Propagation: By seed which germinates readily within three to four months of sowing. Seedlings and suckers are difficult to transplant. Seed loses its viability fairly quickly and should be sown soon after collection.

Calamus hollrungii Becc.
(after Udo Max Hollrung, a nineteenth-century German collector in New Guinea)

Description: Vigorous climbing palm; stems one per clump, thickish, the old stems greenish yellow usually with roots from the lower nodes; fronds 2-3 m long, fairly widely spaced over the upper part of the stems; petiole short or absent, the sheathing base armed with numerous spines up to 4 cm long; rhachis smooth with a few scattered hooks; pinnae 15-20 cm x 2-4 cm, elliptical, 20-40 per leaf, widely spaced in pairs and sparse, dark green and shiny, a few small spines present on the veins; the rhachis ending in a long cirrus which is armed with recurved hooks; panicle 3-4 m long, pendulous, much-branched; flowers small, cream-green; fruit 0.8-1.2 cm across, globular, cream to white.

Notes: A tall, sparse climbing palm which does not form thickets like many of the other *Calamus* species but straggles up through the trees. It grows in monsoonal rainforest and along stream banks. The fruit are avidly eaten by fruit-eating pigeons such as the Torres Strait Pigeon. They have a thin layer of edible flesh which surrounds the seed.

Distribution: In Australia distributed from the Iron Range on Cape York Peninsula to Mission Beach south of Innisfail and also known from Dunk Island, and New Guinea.

Distinguishing Features: A sparse, climbing palm bearing cirri; leaves with 20-40 widely spaced dark green paired leaflets, the sheathing base armed with numerous spines.

Confusing Species: *C. aruensis.*

Cultivation: This palm is little-grown except by enthusiasts. Seedlings are very handsome and look nice in a large pot or tub and could have some potential for use indoors or glasshouses in temperate regions. In the garden they need a shady situation in well-drained, organically rich soil. They respond to plenty of water during dry periods and mulching to keep the soil surface moist. They have proved to be very sensitive to frost and are best suited to tropical regions.

Propagation: By seed which germinates easily within three to four months after sowing. Seed loses its viability soon after collection.

Calamus moti showing strong growth habit.

Calamus moti Bailey
(an Aboriginal Name)
Yellow Lawyer Cane or Wait-a-while

Description: Large, vigorous climbing palm; stems many per clump, thickish, the old stems yellow; fronds 2-3 m long, often partially twisted, crowded in the upper sections of the stems; petiole short or absent, the sheathing base armed with rows of yellow, bayonet-like thorns about 2 cm long; rhachis with a few recurved hooks; pinnae 30-50 cm x 2-3 cm, linear-lanceolate, stiff, 80-100 per leaf, crowded, usually pale yellowish green, spines along the margins and veins; flagella 3-4 m long, pendulous, much branched; flowers 0.3-0.5 cm across, cream to green; fruit 0.8-1.3 cm across, globular, cream.

Notes: The yellow bayonet-like thorns of this climbing palm are not easily forgotten, especially if experienced at close range. They are quite sharp and have a nasty habit of leaving the brittle point beneath the skin to fester. The long flagella are also well armed and tenacious, so much so that the Aborigines used them as an effective fishing device. This common palm forms tangled thickets in lowland and highland rainforests, usually along the margins or where there is any break in the canopy. The canes frequently wander and loop in a haphazard fashion and to become entangled in a colony is not an enjoyable experience.

The pliant stems of this palm were used by the Aborigines for various purposes particularly related to hunting. One such use was for nooses to capture crocodiles. The fruit have a thin layer of edible flesh which is agreeable and the swollen bases of the young shoots were consumed after being skinned and pounded following roasting. The epithet 'Moti' is the name used for this palm by the Aborigines of the Barron River. Those from the Tully River referred to it as 'Bai-Kal' and in the Atherton area it was known as 'Mollu-kan'. Fruit-eating pigeons feed avidly on the ripe fruit.

Juvenile or non-climbing dormant clumps of this palm often form a prominent part of the understory of undisturbed rainforests and are quick to take advantage of any break that occurs in the canopy.

Distribution: Endemic in Australia where it forms a prominent feature of lowland and highland rainforest of north-eastern Qld extending to above 1000 m altitude on the Atherton Tableland.

Distinguishing Features: A robust climbing palm bearing flagella; leaves with 80-100, crowded, yellowish-green leaflets, the sheaths bearing long bayonet-like yellow thorns.

Confusing Species: *C. radicalis* (at a distance).

Cultivation: Although rarely seen in cultivation because of its unfriendly nature this palm nevertheless has quite a few attractive features provided that it is viewed from a distance. It likes cool, shady conditions with plenty of moisture throughout the year. It responds to fertilisers and mulches are a decided benefit. It is fairly cold tolerant and can be grown as far south as Sydney. Seedlings are very handsome, although thorny, subjects and could make an interesting conversation piece inside.

Propagation: By seed which germinates readily within three to four months of sowing. Seed loses its viability quickly and should be sown soon after collection. Seedlings are difficult to transplant.

Calamus moti showing thorns on underside of leaf rhachis.

Calamus muelleri H. H. Wendl. & Drude
(after Baron Ferdinand von Mueller, first Victorian Government botanist)
Southern Lawyer Cane or Wait-a-while

Description: Slender climbing palm; stems few per clump, slender, the old stems brownish; fronds 0.3-1 m long, scattered over the upper half of the stems; petiole short, prickly, the sheathing base armed with numerous spines; rhachis with numerous hooks; pinnae 10-20 cm x 1.5-2 cm, lanceolate to elliptical, 15-20 per leaf, sparse, dark green, spines along the margins and veins; flagella 1-2 m long, bearing recurved hooks; panicle 0.3-1 m long, pendulous, sparsely branched; flowers about 0.3-0.4 cm across, greenish; fruit about 0.9 cm across, globular, cream.

Notes: This is a widely distributed *Calamus* which grows in rainforests and moist scrubs and often forms untidy, prickly thickets. The stems are usually slender and the plants grow in shady situations although their tops may be in the canopy of the forest. The fruits are very hard and have little if any flesh. In the early days of the settlement, one chain (20 metre) lengths of stems of this palm were frequently used by surveyors for land measurement. The Aborigines used the supple stems of this palm for weaving and tying and other purposes associated with hunting. The tribes of the Brisbane river referred to it as 'Taigam'.

Distribution: Endemic to Australia where distributed between Kenilworth in Qld and Bellinger in NSW.

Distinguishing Features: A slender, climbing palm bearing flagella; leaves with 15-20 sparse, dark-green leaflets, the sheathing base armed with spines.

Confusing Species: None.

Cultivation: This is one of the more familiar species of *Calamus* being distributed in well-frequented areas and still being common close to large centres of population. It is still rarely grown and outside of Botanic Gardens is mainly to be found in the collections of enthusiasts. Garden-grown plants tend to scramble round seeking a support to climb on and they are quite prickly, especially the hooked flagella. Plants like a shady situation in deep, well-drained soil and respond to mulching and water during dry periods. Frost may damage them while young but they are sufficiently hardy to survive in a protected position as far south as Melbourne.

Seedlings make handsome pot plants and have been used successfully for indoor decoration. They will tolerate fairly dark conditions and some neglect but are best if spelled at short intervals. A potting mix rich in organic matter is most suitable. Plants are self supporting until about 80 cm tall and may then need some staking. If flagella threaten to be a nuisance they can be removed.

Propagation: By seed which germinates readily in three to four months. Suckers are difficult to remove with success. Seedlings do not transplant readily.

Calamus radicalis H. H. Wendl. & Drude
(arising from the root)
Vicious Hairy Mary

Description: Vigorous climbing palm; stems many per clump, thickish, the old stems yellow; fronds 2-3 m long, crowded in the upper half of the stems; petiole short or absent, the sheathing base armed with numerous brown spines up to 5 cm long; rhachis covered with similar spines; pinnae 30-50 cm x 2-3 cm, linear-lanceolate, 80-120 per leaf, crowded, bright shiny green, conspicuous spines on the margins and veins; flagella 2-3.5 m long, bearing recurved hooks; panicle 3-4 m long, pendulous, much branched bearing numerous spines; flowers 0.3-0.4 cm across, cream-green; fruit about 0.8 cm across, globular.

Notes: An extremely prickly climbing palm that grows in quite extensive untidy thickets. With its impressive armament of sharp, brittle spines on almost every part, supplemented with long tenacious flagella, it is little wonder that these thickets are nearly impenetrable and best avoided. They are to be found where breaks occur in the rainforest canopy or along its margins.

Distribution: Apparently endemic to Australia where found in lowland and highland rainforests of north-eastern Qld extending to about 1000 m altitude on the Atherton Tableland.

Calamus radicalis in flower (above) and (right) showing masses of brown spines on the stems.

Distinguishing Features: A robust climbing palm bearing flagella; leaves with 80-120 crowded, shiny leaflets, all parts bearing numerous long brown spines.

Confusing Species: *C. australis, C. moti* and *C. warburgii.*

Cultivation: Of all the native palms this is probably the least likely to be cultivated. It is certainly handsome but because of its formidable nature is best viewed from a distance, preferably a track in the rainforest. Seedlings make a very unusual conversation piece but are rather difficult to repot. They are sensitive to frosts but can be grown in a protected situation to temperate zones.

Propagation: By seed which germinates easily three to four months after sowing. Seedlings are difficult to transplant.

Calamus warburgii in fruit.

Calamus warburgii Schumann.
(after Otto Warburg, a nineteenth-century German collector in New Guinea)

Description: Vigorous climbing palm; stems many per clump, thickish, the old stems yellow; fronds 1-2 m long, crowded in the upper half of the stems; petiole short, the sheathing base densely armed with spines about 5 cm long; rhachis bearing scattered spines; pinnae 20-40 cm x 1.5-2 cm, linear-lanceolate, 80-100 per leaf, crowded, bright shiny green, a few spines present on the veins, the rhachis ending in a long cirrus which is armed with recurved hooks; panicle 2-3 m long, pendulous, sparsely branched, bearing some hooks and spines; flowers 0.3-0.4 cm across, greenish; fruit 0.8-1.2 cm across, globular, cream to white.

Notes: This climbing palm grows in tangled thickets in and around the margins of monsoonal rainforest. The fruit have a thin layer of edible flesh around the seed.

Distribution: In Australia found in the Iron Range on Cape York Peninsula, also New Guinea.

Distinguishing Features: A climbing palm bearing cirri; leaves with 80-100 crowded, light green leaflets, the sheathing base densely armed with spines.

Confusing Species: *C. radicalis.*

Cultivation: Seedlings of this palm have proved to be very cold sensitive and would appear to be suitable for tropical regions only. It is a rather vicious species and although plants are attractive there is little interest in its cultivation except perhaps by enthusiasts. Seedlings make attractive container plants with their spines and numerous shiny leaflets and could be an interesting addition to the indoor decor. They also make a useful glasshouse plant for temperate regions. They require a well-drained potting mix rich in organic matter. Seedlings are very sensitive to sun damage and should be kept out of direct sun for their first three to four years.

Propagation: By seed which germinates readily within three to four months. Seed lose their viability quickly and should be sown soon after collection. Suckers have proved to be difficult to transplant as also are seedlings.

CARPENTARIA Becc.

A monotypic genus of palms endemic to the Northern Territory. The species is a solitary, feather-leaved palm and is becoming widely grown in areas of tropical Australia.

Carpentaria acuminata, a graceful tropical palm.

Carpentaria acuminata in fruit.

Carpentaria acuminata Becc.
(tapering to a long point, in reference to the small, very pointed bracts at the base of each lateral branch of the inflorescence)
Carpentaria Palm

Description: Solitary feather-leaved palm; trunk 15-20 m tall, slightly enlarged at the base then tapered throughout, slender (10-15 cm thick), grey, with well-spaced rings; crownshaft 0.7-1 m long, greyish white, broader at the base; leaves 1-2 m long, curved, arching in a graceful crown, dark green; petiole about 30 cm long; pinnae 30-40 cm x 2-4 cm, linear to lanceolate, closely spaced, green on both surfaces, obliquely erect, the apices bifid or 4-lobed; inflorescence about 1 m long, infrafoliar, pendulous, much branched; spathes 60-80 cm long, broad and scoop-shaped; petiole 10-20 cm long; flower about 1 cm across, white; fruit about 1 cm long, ovoid, bright scarlet with yellow cupules, mature Nov-Jan.

Notes: An uncommon palm that grows in moist, shady jungle or heavy rainforest generally not far from streams. It grows as individuals or in scattered colonies and in nature is a very tall palm with the crown either just within the tree canopy or emergent from it. It is fairly widespread in well-watered areas and may be sometimes locally common. The Aborigines collected and ate the cabbage and the species was variously known as 'Thora' and 'Yirrgi Yirrgi'

Distribution: An edemic palm scattered over northern parts of the Top End of the Northern Territory and extending into Arnhem Land.

Distinguishing Features: A tall, slender, feather-leaved palm with a prominent crownshaft; leaves recurved; pinnae dark green, the apices deeply divided 2-4 times.

Confusing Species: *Archontophoenix cunninghamiana, Gronophyllum ramsayi.*

Cultivation: This palm is becoming widely grown in tropical towns such as Darwin and Cairns. In such places it has proved to be fast growing, hardy and highly ornamental. In Darwin it is commonly planted not only in private gardens but also in streets and landscape projects and grows well quite close to the sea. It likes well-drained soil and an abundance of water during dry periods, especially when small. Plants will tolerate considerable exposure to sun or will grow in the shade of trees. Young specimens need protection for at least the first two to three years after planting out. Cultivated specimens do not appear as if they will grow as tall as palms in the wild. Seedlings are very decorative having dark-green leaves often with reddish tinges in the veins and petiole.

Carpentaria palms are essentially for the tropics and although they can be grown in warm situations in the subtropics most specimens planted there struggle. They are especially sensitive to frost and in cold spells the leaves have dead patches of tissue. A well-grown palm is a very handsome specimen and when bearing clusters of fruit they are striking. While this palm can be grown as a specimen it is also well suited to planting in groups. Young plants are useful for indoor decoration but require a high light intensity and do not like cold.

Propagation: Easily propagated from seed which takes three to four months to germinate. Seedlings resent disturbance and may be difficult to transplant if root damage occurs.

CARYOTA L.

Of the twelve species of palms in this genus a single widespread species extends to Australia where it is found in the rainforests of Cape York Peninsula. It is a solitary-stemmed, monocarpic palm. (For exotic *Caryota* species see page 172.)

Caryota rumphiana C. Martius
(after G. E. Rumph)
Native Fishtail Palm

Description: Solitary bipinnate-leaved palm; trunk 8-20 m tall, slender, greyish, tapered from the base; leaves 3-5 m long and 2-3 m broad, scattered on the upper part of trunk, arching; petiole about 1 m long; pinnules 10-20 cm long, half-fan shaped, oblique, pleated, bright green, leathery, scattered, the margins very ragged, often produced into slender, blunt points; inflorescence 1-2 m long, consisting of a stout peduncle about 60 cm long and many pendulous spikes about 1 m long; flowers over 1 cm across, mauve in bud, flowers cream, in groups of two male and one

female; fruit 2.5-3 cm across, globular, purplish black, hard.

Notes: A relatively little-known palm that grows beside watercourses in monsoonal rainforest. The plants are monocarpic. At maturity they flower down the trunk from each successive node and when the lower-most inflorescence has matured fruit the plant dies. The fruit are avidly eaten by cassowaries even though the flesh contains oxalate raphides which produce an intense burning sensation if handled. The plants occur in scattered, loose colonies, with the individuals at various stages of maturity.

This palm is distributed throughout eastern Indonesia and New Guinea and it was originally believed that the plants found in Australia differed by having much longer inflorescence branches and hence were distinguished as var. *albertii* F. Muell. There are no clear distinctions between the palms found in Australia and those found overseas and hence the varietal name is relegated to synonymy. Some overseas varieties are distinct.

Distribution: In Australia confined to lowland monsoonal rainforests of Cape York Peninsula north of the McIlwraith Range; also New Guinea, Indonesia, the Philippines and Malaysia.

Distinguishing Features: A tall, slender, bipinnate-leaved palm with the leaflets of a fan or fishtail shape.

Confusing Species: None.

Cultivation: Although relatively unknown in cultivation this species is worthy of wider planting. It succeeds very well in tropical and warm subtropical areas but has also proved to be adaptable since it can be grown in coastal temperate regions such as the Sydney Botanic Gardens. It is similar to other Fish-tail palms grown. However seedlings demand a situation protected from direct sun for the first three to five years. It likes well-drained, organically rich soil and an abundance of water during dry periods. Best growth is probably achieved where its roots can tap ground water. Mulches are beneficial and the plants respond to side dressings of fertiliser during the growing season. Young plants have proved to be surprisingly tolerant of cold although during long cold spells dark patches may appear on the leaves. Dryness is an enemy of this palm and it is not uncommon for potted plants of this species to die completely after drying out. Specialist nurseries occasionally have plants of this species for sale. The palm is generally unsuitable for indoor decoration.

Propagation: From seed which germinates sparingly over several years. Bottom heat promotes germination as do pre-sowing treatments such as cracking the seed coat or soaking in warm water. Seedlings are difficult to transplant.

COCOS L.

A monotypic genus the species of which is naturalised on tropical parts of the east coast of Australia (*see also* page 186).

Cocos nucifera L.
Coconut

This palm is almost cosmopolitan in tropical areas and has been widely spread by man because of its usefulness. It was probably intro-duced into Australia early last century and is now widely planted and naturalised in coastal areas of tropical Qld and adjacent islands as well as those of the Torres Strait.

CORYPHA L.

A small genus of eight species of palms principally developed in the Indo-Malaysian region with a single, widespread species extending through the islands to Indonesia and northern Australia. They are solitary, monocarpic palms with large costapalmate leaves and towering terminal inflorescences.

Corypha elata Roxb. *(tall, lofty, stately)*

Description: Solitary, tall, fan-leaved palm; trunk 20-25 m tall, 35-100 cm thick, in tall specimens a substantial part covered with persistent leaf bases, the remainder grey with a spiral pattern left by the leafbases; leaves 5-7 m long, grey green to bluish, stiff, in a large, majestic crown; petiole 3-4 m long, about 4 cm across and 8 cm

Corypha elata.

Corypha elata, in fruit.

thick, channelled, the margins black and bearing stout prickles 1-2 cm long; lamina 2-3 m across, round to orbicular, grey green, thick textured, stiff, sometimes partly folded, divided half way into segments, costapalmate with a rib 1.2-1.6 m long; panicle 6-8 m long, terminal, erect pyramidal; flowers about 0.3 cm across, cream, with a strong smell, numerous; fruit 2-3 cm across, olive-green, globular.

Notes: In Australia this very distinctive palm grows in large colonies along the margins of watercourses subject to flooding. It is very common along some of the rivers flowing west from the high country of Cape York Peninsula into the Gulf of Carpentaria and in some situations forms quite extensive thickets. On a windy day a colony is quite noisy with the large leaves creaking and scraping with each movement. The colonies consist of plants in all stages of growth from seedlings to flowering and fruiting specimens and even those in the advanced stages of collapse and decay. The trees fruit once in their lifetime, expending all of their accumulated energy in one spectacular flowering from which a prodigious quantity of fruit is ripened before the tree dies. The Aborigines who lived in the area where these palms grow must have used them for various purposes but this information is difficult to obtain.

Distribution: In Australia distributed sporadically across the top end of the Northern Territory and Cape York Peninsula in northern Qld; also widely distributed throughout the Pacific and west to India.

Distinguishing Features: A large, monocarpic palm with huge fan leaves that are costapalmate; inflorescence terminal.

Confusing Species: None.

Cultivation: Easily grown in tropical areas and also useful for inland regions with a warm climate. Grows best with access to ground water, otherwise needs regular watering. Seedlings are very slow growing, staying in the rosette stage for some fourteen to twenty years. They will take exposure to direct sun while still very small. Plants are not suitable for home gardens because of their size and prickly petioles, but with their large spectacular crown are an ideal subject for parks.

Propagation: Readily propagated from seed which germinates sporadically fifteen to twenty months after sowing. Seed retains its viability for many months. Seedlings are difficult to transplant.

GRONOPHYLLUM Scheffer

One of the fourteen species of palms in this genus is endemic to the Northern Territory. (For exotic species of this genus see page 195.)

Gronophyllum ramsayi (Becc.) Moore
(after P. Ramsay)
Northern Kentia Palm

Description: Solitary, feather-leaved palm; trunk 25-35 m tall, moderately slender (10-25 cm thick), dark grey with prominent dark rings; crownshaft 0.8-1 m long, pale yellow, covered with whitish powdery bloom; leaves 1.5-2.5 m long, strongly recurved, greyish green, arching in a crown; petiole about 0.8 m long, scurfy; pinnae 30-70 cm x 3-5 cm, linear, evenly spaced along the rhachis, the lower ones held at a sharp angle, the tips acuminate; inflorescences 30-40 cm long, sparsely branched, slightly arching, borne at the base of the crownshaft; flowers about 0.6 cm across, white, male and female separate; fruit 1.2-1.5 cm long, ovoid, bright waxy red, mature Nov-Jan.

Notes: A relatively little-known palm that grows on sandstone cliffs and in flat, semi-moist areas of sandy soil in open forest. It usually grows in colonies and some of these may be quite extensive consisting of several hundred individuals. It is known from a few colonies on the mainland of the Northern Territory and a couple of islands off the coast (Croker and Melville). Most of the colonies occur on Aboriginal reserves and for this reason are rarely seen by white men.

These palms appear to be slow growing but the colonies are viable as evidenced by the numerous seedlings present. These seedlings have very broad fronds with few segments and are noticeably glaucous. As well the texture of their fronds is firm and stiff. In one colony there are a number of branched specimens which have been tagged for research. The branching varies from a simple,

Gronophyllum ramsayi, a handsome palm from the Northern Territory.

An unusually branched specimen of *Gronophyllum ramsayi.*

paired bifurcation to up to five stems arising from the one point.

Aboriginals find these palms very useful and they were probably of local significance to the tribes that lived and hunted in their habitat. The apical bud is highly esteemed for its flavour and baskets are made from the sheathing base and rhachis. The fronds were probably used for shelters but this is uncertain. It was called 'Thora' by one local tribe.

Distribution: An endemic palm scattered in colonies on Arnhem Land and adjacent areas of the Top End, Northern Territory, together with some offshore islands.

Distinguishing Features: A tall, slender, feather-leaved palm with a prominent crownshaft; leaves greyish, strongly recurved.

Confusing Species: *Carpentaria acuminata.*

Cultivation: Although relatively unknown in cultivation this species is being promoted by enthusiasts for tropical areas. It is being grown in parks and gardens of Darwin and has proved to be quite hardy and adaptable. It likes well-drained soil and an abundance of water during dry periods. Best growth is probably achieved where its roots can tap ground water. Plants will tolerate considerable amounts of sun even when quite small. They are however very sensitive to cold and it would seem that this palm is essentially one for the tropics. Young plants have proved to be useful for indoor decoration but prefer conditions of fairly high light intensity. They make excellent tub plants for verandahs or patios. The Northern Kentia is a very graceful palm and it is hoped that it will become a familiar sight in city streets and gardens of the tropics.

Propagation: By seed which usually takes six to twelve months to germinate and then comes up very sporadically. Bottom heat beds may make germination faster and more uniform. Seedlings transplant easily but should be potted before their roots become too long as they are brittle and readily damaged.

GULUBIA Becc.

A small genus of nine species of palms restricted to Indonesia, Solomon Islands, New Hebrides, Fiji and New Guinea with a widespread species extending to north-eastern Qld. They are solitary palms with tall, slender trunks and a rounded crown of finely pinnate leaves with drooping pinnae. They mostly grow as emergents in rainforest and are often in colonies. In cultivation they are best suited to tropical areas and require an abundance of water.

Gulubia costata Becc.
(ribbed – in reference to the fruit)

Description: Solitary, very tall, slender, feather-leaved palm; trunk 20-35 m tall, very slender, usually curved (15-40 cm thick), grey with white patches, conspicuously ringed; crownshaft about 1 m long, pale green; leaves 3-4 m long, spreading in a crown, the lower ones tending to droop; petiole 30-60 cm long, covered with a dense, close wool; pinnae 0.6-1 m x 2-5 cm, up to sixty pairs per leaf, the longest in the centre of the frond,

Gulubia costata in silhouette.

acuminate, very lax and drooping, green on both surfaces, those near the end of the leaf widely spaced and very narrow; inflorescence 40-60 cm long, pendulous, much branched; spathes short; peduncle 3-4 cm long; flowers about 1 cm across, cream; fruit about 1 cm x 0.5 cm, ovoid, deep maroon, in large clusters.

Notes: This palm grows in monsoonal rainforests always in quite dense colonies although these may be small and isolated. Being very tall the tops of the palms are visible above the forest conopies and this enables colonies to be located easily. Often there is little or no growth on the ground under the colonies; even very few palm seedlings. The best colonies are usually in swampy areas beside small permanent streams.

Distribution: In Australia confined to lowland forests on the north-eastern part of Cape York Peninsula; also New Guinea.

Distinguishing Features: A very tall, slender, feather-leaved palm; leaves spreading, the lower ones deflexed; leaflets drooping.

Confusing Species: None.

Cultivation: *Gulubia costata* is very sensitive to cold and will only succeed in warm, tropical regions. It is quite fast growing and needs rich soil and plenty of water especially while small (plants will grow in wet situations). Young plants are best planted in a shady position although they will take full sun when they get over 1 m tall.

Propagation: From seed which germinates readily in three to five months. Seedlings transplant readily but are best handled while small as they resent root damage.

HEDYSCEPE H. H. Wendl. & Drude

A monotypic genus of palms endemic to Lord Howe Island. The species is solitary, feather-leaved palm with stiffly arched fronds.

Hedyscepe canterburyana
(C. Moore & F. Muell) H. H. Wendl. & Drude.
Umbrella Palm, Big Mountain Palm

Description: Solitary, slender, feather-leaved palm; trunk 4-10 m tall, slender (12-18 cm thick),

Hedyscepe canterburyana is native to the mountains of Lord Howe Island.

Hedyscepe canterburyana in immature fruit.

grey, prominently ringed; crownshaft 0.8-1 m long, widest near the base, shiny bluish to silvery green; leaves 2-3 m long, stiffly arching, slightly twisted, forming a dark green, dense crown; petiole very short; rhachis curved; pinnae 20-30 cm x 2-4 cm, lanceolate, dark green, pointed, spreading or obliquely erect; inflorescence 20-30 cm long, subfoliar; panicle much branched, the branches spreading stiffly; flowers over 1 cm across, greenish white; fruit 2-3 cm long, elliptical, brownish when ripe.

Notes: This relatively unknown but very handsome and sturdy palm grows in forests on the mountains of Lord Howe Island between 400 and 800 m altitude. Plants at lower elevations tend to be taller and are usually found in the forest while those higher up are shorter and dumpier and often grow above the stunted forest. The area in which these grow is subject to almost continual winds and these are frequently strong and buffeting. Clouds also frequently cover the mountains where they grow.

Distribution: Endemic to Lord Howe Island.

Distinguishing Features: A slender, feather-leaved palm with a dense crown of dark-green stiffly arching leaves and a prominent silvery crownshaft; the stiffly branched inflorescence; the large fruit.

Confusing Species: *Howea belmoreana, Lepidorrhachis mooreana.*

Cultivation: A very slow growing palm that is mainly grown by enthusiasts. It is best suited to temperate and cool subtropical regions and will not thrive where it does not receive cool nights. It can be grown as far south as Melbourne and needs a protected situation in well-drained, organically rich soil. Plants must be shaded from hot summer sun for at least their first five years. Light frosts are tolerated.

Propagation: From seed which germinates erratically over twelve months. Seed takes about four years to mature and is difficult to tell when ripe.

HOWEA Becc.

A small genus of two species of palms both endemic to Lord Howe Island where they grow in extensive colonies. They are solitary palms with a slender trunk and attractive pinnate fronds. Both species are cultivated with *H. forsteriana* being one of the most sought after horticultural palms in the world. A significant seedling export industry has been developed on Lord Howe Island.

Howea belmoreana (C. Moore & F. Muell.) Becc. *(after M. DeBelmore, former Governor of NSW)*
Curly Palm, Sentry Palm or Kentia Palm

Description: Solitary, slender, feather-leaved palm; trunk 5-12 m tall, very slender (10-15 cm thick), expanded at the base, greyish, prominently ringed; leaves 3-5 m long, strongly arching in an erect crown; petiole 20-40 cm long, fairly slender, strongly arched, some grey fibre at the base; rhachis also arching; pinnae 30-60 cm x 2-3 cm, held erect, crowded, bright green on both surfaces; inflorescence a simple, pendulous, curved spike 0.6-1.6 m long, arising from among the lower leaves; fruit 2.5-3 cm long, ovoid, with a conspicuous beak at the apex, brownish red when ripe, hard.

Notes: This palm grows in colonies on the intermediate levels of Lord Howe Island often in association with *H. forsteriana*. Curly palm is the dominant species on volcanic soils of the mountain slopes of the island between 100 m and 300 m altitude, although in some places it also extends to the sandy flats of the lowlands. It grows very tall and slender, no doubt as the result of competition with its neighbours. Sporadic hybrids between the two species of *Howea* are known to occur on the island. An industry is established on the island selling germinated seeds of this palm and the following species.

Distribution: Endemic to Lord Howe Island.

Distinguishing Features: A tall, slender, feather-leaved palm with strongly arching leaves and erect pinnae; the absence of a crownshaft; the simple, unbranched inflorescence.

Confusing Species: *H. forsteriana, Hedyscepe canterburyana.*

Cultivation: Curly palm is a popular subject for cultivation both in Australia and overseas although it is not as common as *H. forsteriana*. It makes an excellent garden plant and is one of the best palms for indoor decoration tolerating quite dark conditions and considerable neglect. In the garden it can be grown successfully as far south as Melbourne and north into subtropical regions. The plants do very well in coastal districts withstanding considerable buffeting by salt-laden winds. There are some fine old specimens in Sydney's inner suburbs.

Curly palms appreciate some protection when young and do not like to dry out. A well-drained soil, plenty of mulch and regular watering during dry periods are the keys to success with this

Howea belmoreana is endemic to Lord Howe Island where it grows in large colonies.

Howea belmoreana in immature fruit.

species. Regular side dressings with nitrogenous fertilisers also produce a good response. This palm will tolerate considerable cold but severe frosts may kill it.

Curly palms are commonly sold in the nursery trade but are usually mixed with *H. forsteriana*. They are very slow growing especially when young and established specimens may be quite expensive. In cultivation they rarely reach more than 5 m tall except where they are crowded and have to compete with other plants. They make an excellent tub plant and can be grown as such for many years.

Propagation: From seed which germinates sporadically over one to three years. Bottom heat and fungicide treatment greatly improves germination. Seeds take three or four years to mature and are rather difficult to tell when they are ripe. Seedlings transplant easily.

Howea forsteriana (C. Moore & F. Muell.) Becc. *(after William Forster, NSW Senator)*
Kentia Palm or Thatch Palm

Description: Solitary, slender, feather-leaved palm; trunk 5-15 m tall, very slender (8-15 cm thick), greyish, prominently ringed, not enlarged at the base; leaves 3-5 m long, spreading in a very graceful crown; petiole 1-1.6 m long, slender, straight or slightly curved, the bases covered with grey fibre; rhachis slightly curved with weight; pinnae 30-60 cm x 2-4 cm, drooping, dark green on both surfaces, somewhat scaly beneath, the main veins yellowish; inflorescence about 1 m long, pendulous , consisting of a cluster of simple spikes arising from among the lower leaves; fruit 3-5 cm long, narrowly ovoid, hard, brownish red to bright red when ripe.

Notes: This palm grows in colonies on the lower parts of Lord Howe Island often in pure stands but also mixed with *H. belmoreana*. In some places it grows in dense colonies close the sea. It is mainly found on the sandy flats but also extends onto the volcanic soils up to about 300 m altitude on the northern slopes of Mount Lidgbird. Individuals in the colonies may be 1-3 m apart and the plants grow very tall and slender under these conditions. Sporadic hybrids between the two species of *Howea* are known to occur on the island. A local industry is established on the island for

Howea forsteriana grows down to the shore line on parts of Lord Howe Island.

Howea forsteriana in flower.

the collection of seeds of *Howea* palms which are then planted and sold when germinated.

Distribution: Endemic to Lord Howe Island.

Distinguishing Features: A tall, slender, feather-leaved palm with spreading leaves and drooping pinnae; the absence of a crownshaft; a clustered inflorescence of simple spikes.

Confusing Species: *H. belmoreana.*

Collecting *Howea* seed is a commercial industry on Lord Howe Island.

small palms. Their slender trunk and graceful crown of dark-green, drooping fronds make them a favourite. They do very well in coastal districts withstanding considerable exposure to buffeting, salt-laden winds.

Kentias will tolerate direct sun when 4-5 years old but they need protection while small. They like a well-drained, organically rich soil, plenty of mulch, side dressings with fertiliser and regular watering during dry periods. Mild frosts are tolerated without setback.

Kentias are commonly sold in the nursery trade and in fact young plants are exported from Australia to Europe. They are very slow growing and established specimens are very expensive. When grown in open positions they rarely reach more than 4 m tall and are the ideal palm for the small garden. Attacks by grasshoppers may be severe in subtropical regions.

Propagation: From seed which germinates sporadically over one to three years. Bottom heat and fungicide treatment greatly improves germination. Commercial growers commonly sow large beds of seed from which they remove sprouted seeds at regular intervals. Seeds take three or four years to mature and it is very difficult to tell when they are ripe as they colour slowly. Seedlings transplant easily.

Cultivation: *H. forsteriana* is probably one of the most familiar and widely grown palms in the world. It is highly favoured as an indoor plant in the United Kingdom, Europe, America and to a lesser extent Australia. In Europe the palm has been grown since the 1850s and once its qualities were realised it was much in demand by the aristocracy for beautifying their hallways, ballrooms, etc. It will grow happily, albeit slowly, in a tub for many years and can even be repotted back into the same container providing that some of the old soil mixture is replaced with fresh material. It will withstand quite dark and dry positions indoors and is tolerant of neglect. The secret for success indoors is to rest the palms at regular intervals by moving them outside into a shady, moist situation such as a bush house. Such a rest washes the dirt from the leaves, refreshes the plant and allows new growth to take place.

As a garden plant these palms can be grown outside at least as far south as Melbourne and north into coastal districts of the subtropics. They are often planted singly but they lend themselves best to group planting or mixing with other

---

HYDRIASTELE H. H. Wendl. & Drude

Of the eight species of slender clumping palms found in this genus one species is endemic in northern Australia. (For notes on exotic species of *Hydriastele* see page 196.)

Hydriastele wendlandiana (F. Muell.)
H. H. Wendl. & Drude *(after Hermann Wendland, twentieth-century palm botanist)*

Description: Clumping, feather-leaved palm; trunk 7-25 m or more tall, very slender (6-10 cm thick) grey, one usually dominant plus 2-3 others intermediate, and basal suckers; crownshaft slender, white to whitish; leaves 1.5-2 m long, dark green, in a sparse crown; petiole 20-25 cm long, with brown, scurfy hairs; pinnae 20-45 cm x 3-5 cm long, irregularly spaced, unequal, the terminal ones confluent and fish-tail like, solitary or

119

Hydriastele wendlandiana.

Hydriastele wendlandiana, ripe fruit.

in clusters of 2-3, dark green, the apices usually jagged and sometimes with protruding threads; inflorescence about 30 cm long, subfoliar, a densely branched panicle; peduncle about 3 cm long; flowers about 0.8 cm across; fruit about 0.8 cm long, ovoid, ribbed or striate, bright red.

Notes: A widely distributed and sometimes locally common palm that grows in soaks and

swamps in coastal and near-coastal districts. It is extremely slender and some very tall specimens are known with one being measured at over 26 m. Young plants are usually shaded by trees but mature plants have their crown exposed to full sun.

Distribution: Endemic to coastal and near-coastal areas of the top end of the Northern Territory and north-eastern Qld from Cape York Peninsula to just south of Tully.

Distinguishing Features: A tall, very slender, feather-leaved palm; leaflets irregularly spaced; the tips jagged, the terminal ones united and fishtail like.

Confusing Species: *Ptychosperma macarthurii.*

Cultivation: This palm is essentially tropical in its requirements. It is not commonly encountered in cultivation and is primarily a collectors palm. Young plants need protection from direct sun but will tolerate exposure once they become well established. They like plenty of water and are very sensitive to cold being quickly killed by frosts or severe cold snaps. The plants are generally slow growing while small but speed up as they mature. They are quite a decorative palm, especially when in fruit and are best planted in groups. Wet situations are quite suitable but the palm can also be established in well-drained soils providing the plants are watered during dry periods. Mulches are especially beneficial.

Small plants of this palm are quite tolerant of dark positions and survive quite well indoors. They also make an excellent glasshouse plant and will grow in a tub for many years.

Propagation: Readily propagated from seed which takes three to six months to germinate. Germination is improved by the use of bottom heat. Seedlings transplant readily. This palm can also be propagated from suckers which split off readily.

LACCOSPADIX H. H. Wendl. & Drude

A monotypic genus endemic in the rainforests of north-eastern Qld. The species is a solitary or clumping, feather-leaved palm that is highly ornamental and becoming a popular subject for cultivation.

Laccospadix australasica H.H. Wendl. & Drude
(Australian)
Atherton Palm

Description: Solitary or clumping, feather-leaved palm; trunk(s) 2-8 m tall, slender throughout (5-10 cm thick) dark green or yellowish, prominently ringed; leaves 2-2.5 m long, 6-8 scattered at the top of the trunk, arching; petiole 30-100 cm long; rhachis slightly scurfy; pinnae 30-40 cm x 2-4 cm, linear lanceolate, the tip acuminate or sometimes notched, dark, glossy-green above, paler beneath, 20-24 pairs per leaf; spathe 60-70 cm long, slender, papery; spikes 0.5-1.5 m long, slender, simple, arching, the peduncle 34-38 cm, somewhat flattened; flowers about 0.5 cm across, yellowish, successive small groups of male and female down the spike; fruit about 1 cm long, ovoid, bright red, mature Dec – Jan.

Notes: A distinctive palm that grows in shaded rainforest usually in loose scattered to dense colonies. It is commonly believed that this species is always a suckering or clumping palm however a very high percentage of the plants produce solitary trunks. These solitary plants may be scattered throughout suckering plants or there may be whole colonies which are solitary or produce very few suckers. There is a tendency for the clumping types to be found at higher elevations and as this palm grows on scattered, isolated mountain tops the clumping growth habit may represent an example of adaptation. It has been reported in the literature that the stems of this palm are relatively short-lived and are replaced by younger ones in the clump. This is entirely erroneous as the mature stems are very long lived. The new leaves are an attractive reddish colour.

Distribution: Endemic to the ranges and table-lands of north-eastern Qld above 800 m altitude and extending up to 1600 m altitude. It is usually locally common.

Distinguishing Features: A medium-sized, slender, feather-leaved palm with single or multiple trunks; inflorescence an undivided spike.

Confusing Species: None.

Laccospadix australasica.

Laccospadix australasica in fruit.

Cultivation: An easy and reward ng palm for garden culture in subtropical and warm temperate regions. It is a very ornamental palm with a pleasant appearance and because of its relatively small size is becoming more popular in cultivation. It requires shady conditions and prefers a rich, loamy soil rich in organic matter. Plants can be grown in warm situations as far south as Melbourne and will tolerate light to medium frosts. This palm appreciates mulches on the soil surface and watering during dry periods. It is an excellent palm for planting amongst ferns.

Laccospadix is not yet readily available from nurseries although it is being grown and promoted more each year. It makes an excellent plant for indoor decoration tolerating some neglect and low light intensities. It also makes an attractive tub plant for outdoor decoration but must not be exposed to too much sun.

Propagation: Readily propagated from seed which germinates easily, usually taking three to five months. Seedlings transplant very easily. This palm can also be propagated from suckers which split off fairly readily.

LEPIDORRHACHIS (H. H. Wendl. & Drude) Cook

A monotypic genus of palm endemic on Lord Howe Island where it is restricted to the mountain peaks. The species is a dumpy, solitary, feather-leaved palm.

Lepidorrhachis mooreana (F. Muell.) Cook
(after Charles Moore, first Superintendent of Sydney Botanic Gardens)
Little Mountain Palm

Description: Solitary, stout, dwarf, feather-leaved palm; trunk rarely more than 1.5 m tall, 15-20 cm thick, sturdy, prominently scarred with closely spaced rings; crownshaft not distinct but the leaf bases greatly enlarged and swollen; leaves 1-1.3 m long, in a loose crown, arching or sometimes twisted; petiole about 30 cm long, very stout; rhachis straight or curved; pinnae 25-40 cm x 2-4 cm, lanceolate, acuminate, dark green, spreading or obliquely erect; inflorescence 30-50 cm long, much branched, arising in the

Lepidorrhachis moorei (above) is confined to the mountain tops of Lord Howe Island. Right, *Lepidorrhachis moorei* in flower and immature fruit.

lower leaf axil and by flowering time this leaf has fallen; panicle branches stiffly spreading; flowers about 0.8 cm across; fruit about 1 cm across, globular, red.

Notes: This remarkable palm is restricted to the upper slopes and summits on Mounts Gower and Lidgbird on Lord Howe Island at about 750 m altitude. Here it grows in stunted moss forest in scattered colonies and is locally common. All the surrounding vegetation is reduced in stature by the bleak, windswept conditions and the infertile soil and this palm is no exception. Most plants grow in the shade but in some places are exposed to the wind and sun. Clouds frequently cover the mountain tops where this palm grows.

Distribution: Endemic to Lord Howe Island.

Distinguishing Features: A short, stout, feather-leaved palm with prominently swollen leaf bases forming a loose crownshaft; the small fruit.

Confusing Species: *Hedyscepe canterburyana.*

Cultivation: This palm is rarely encountered in cultivation and has proved to be extremely slow growing and tricky to maintain. It needs cool, moist conditions in well-drained soil and resents a dry atmosphere.

Propagation: By seed which takes six to twelve months to germinate. Germination is improved by the use of bottom heat but seedlings rot readily.

LICUALA Wurmb.

Of the 108 species of palms in this genus a single species is found in the rainforests of north-eastern Qld where it is endemic. (For notes on exotic species of *Licuala* see page 203.)

Licuala ramsayi (F. Muell.) Domin
(after P. Ramsay, original collector)
Fan Palm

Description: Solitary, slender, fan-leaved palm; trunk 6-18 m tall, slender (10-20 cm thick), dark grey, with numerous annular rings; leaves 2-4 m long, in a spectacular crown; petiole 1.5-2 m long, arching, slender (3-4 cm across), spiny at the base, the rest smooth and hard; leaf blade 1.2-

Licuala ramsayi is a magnificent Australian palm.

Licuala ramsayi leaves in silhouette.

2 m across, appearing circular, but in fact consisting of many, closely spaced groups of wedge-shaped segments forming a stiff, bright-green disc with the petiole appearing falsely peltate; each group of segments is tapered, 5-8 cm across at the end, pleated, the apex bluntly and irregularly toothed and separate from adjacent groups but with the individual segments of a group united throughout; inflorescence an interfoliar panicle 1.5-2 m long, pendulous, slender; fruit about 1 cm across, oval, brilliant orange-red.

Notes: This spectacular palm is a familiar sight in lowland coastal districts of north-eastern Qld where it grows along stream banks subject to inundation and in swampy areas. In some swamps of a particular soil type the palms form extensive pure colonies and the dark conditions created by their leaves reduce the undergrowth to a minimum. Their large fronds move and creak in the slightest breeze and to sleep under a canopy of these palms is quite an experience.

The fronds of young palms have widely spaced segments and this imparts a very different appearance to the almost circular leaves of mature specimens. Being such a spectacular component of vegetation the palms were well-known to local Aboriginal tribes who collected and ate the cabbage and more than likely made use of the leaves for thatching and weaving. This palm was known by such names as 'Moor-goo-doo' around Cairns, 'Chakoro' by the Tully River Aborigines and 'Moi-yur' by those from around the Bloomfield area. The outer part of the trunk of this palm is hard and attractively marked with dark lines.

Distribution: Endemic to lowland coastal areas of north-eastern Qld from Cape York Peninsula to near Tully, often locally common.

Distinguishing Features: A medium-sized slender, fan-leaved palm with almost circular leaves.

Confusing Species: None.

Cultivation: Despite their spectacular appearance fan palms are not widely encountered in cultivation. This may be because they are very slow growing and fairly strict in their requirements of a warm, shady situation with plenty of moisture. They resent wind and direct sun even when quite large and must be kept well sheltered at all times. They will grow in a range of soils but need mulches and plenty of water during dry periods. Although they succeed best in the tropics they have proved to be remarkably adaptable and will succeed at least as far south as Sydney. They respond in a limited way to fertilisers.

Young plants make attractive pot or tub specimens and can be used successfully for indoor decoration. Plants are usually available from specialist nurseries.

Propagation: Propagated by seed which may germinate erratically over six to twelve months. Seedlings transplant fairly readily.

LINOSPADIX H. H. Wendl.

A small genus of eleven species of palms restricted to Australia and New Guinea. They are mostly small, slender palms with entire or pinnate leaves and may be solitary or clumping. The inflorescence is a simple, pendulous spike that arises in the axils of the lower leaves. Six species are found in Australia with at least one species undescribed. All species are to be found in Queensland with a concentration in the northeast and a solitary species extending into NSW. They grow in shady situations and are excellent palms for garden or pot culture. Some species were previously included in the genus *Bacularia*.

Linospadix aequisegmentosa (Domin) Burrett
(divided into equal segments, a reference to the pinnate leaves)

Description: Small, clumping, pinnate-leaved palm; trunks 1-1.5 m tall, very slender (0.5-1 cm thick), prominently ringed, 2-4 dominant, the rest basal suckers; leaves 35-50 cm long, spreading in a dense crown; petiole 8-16 cm long; pinnae 12-13 cm x 0.5-1 cm, about 18 per leaf, dense, linear-lanceolate, falcate, the apices acuminate, dark green and somewhat shiny; inflorescence 30-40 cm long, a simple, pendulous spike arising in the lower leaf axils; flowers about 0.4 cm across; fruit 1-1.5 cm x 0.5-0.8 cm, ovoid-ellipsoid, yellow-orange or red.

Notes: A little-known, small, clumping palm that occurs as scattered individuals in intermediate to highland rainforests. Studies by A. K. Irvine indicate that this species is a form of *L. palmeriana*.

Distribution: Endemic in the mountains of north-eastern Qld.

Distinguishing Features: A small, clumping palm with slender trunks and a dense crown of fronds, each with about nine pairs of narrow pinnae.

Confusing Species: *L. microcarya, L. minor.*

Cultivation: Easily grown in a pot or the garden but requires, cool, shady, moist conditions. Best suited to cool tropical and subtropical regions. Mulches and plenty of water are necessary for good growth. Plants and seed of this species are rarely available.

Propagation: From seed which germinates readily. Seed loses its viability soon after harvest. Plants can also be propagated from suckers.

Linospadix microcarya (Domin) Burret
(with small nuts – in reference to the fruit)

Description: Small, clumping, pinnate-leaved palm; trunks 1-2 m tall, very slender (0.5-1.5 cm thick), 3-4 dominant, the rest basal suckers; leaves 40-60 cm long, spreading in a loose crown; petiole very short; pinnae 10-25 cm x 2-5 cm, about 12 per leaf, spreading, irregularly shaped, slender to broad, thin and papery, bright green, the apices obliquely rounded and toothed, the terminal leaflets confluent; inflorescence 30-40 cm long, a simple arching spike arising in the lower leaf axils; flowers about 0.4 cm across; fruit 0.7-0.8 cm x 0.5-0.8 cm, globose yellow-orange and pink to red when ripe.

Notes: A little-known, small, clumping palm that occurs as scattered individuals in lowland to intermediate rainforests of near-coastal districts, up to 1100 m altitude.

Distribution: Endemic to north-eastern Qld.

Distinguishing Features: A small, clumping palm with slender trunks and a sparse crown of fronds each with about six pairs of variable pinnae per leaf, and small fruit.

Confusing Species: *L. aequisegmentosa, L. minor, L.* sp 'Mt Lewis'.

Cultivation: Suitable for a protected, shady position in tropical and subtropical gardens. Plants and seed of this species are rarely available.

Propagation: From seed which germinates in four to six months after sowing or by removal of suckers.

Linospadix minor (F. Muell.) Burret
(smaller, lesser)

Description: Small, clumping, pinnate-leaved palm; trunks 0.8-1.6 m tall, several together but usually only 2-3 dominant, very slender (about 0.6-2 cm thick); leaves 0.6-1 m long, spreading in a loose crown; petiole 10-20 cm long; pinnae 15-25 cm long, 12-14 per leaf, irregularly shaped, broad, the ends irregularly toothed, the terminal leaflets confluent and fish-tail like; inflorescence 20-40 cm long, a simple pendulous spike arising in the leaf axils; flowers about 0.4 cm across, greenish, male and female separate; fruit 1.2-1.8 cm long, elliptical, yellow or coral pink to red when ripe, crowded.

Notes: This small clumping palm is common in rainforest and usually occurs as scattered individuals. One or two stems of the clump become dominant while the others remain as basal suckers. These elongate only when one of the main stems dies. The strings fruit are a highly ornmental feature and have a thin layer of edible flesh. The Aborigines around Cairns called it 'Jak-ar-ungle'.

Linospadix minor in fruit.

Distribution: Widespread in north-eastern Qld and perhaps extending to the Fly River area of New Guinea.

Distinguishing Features: A small, clumping, pinnate-leaved palm with slender trunks and 6-7 pairs of pinnae per leaf.

Confusing Species: *L. aequisegmentosa*, *L. microcarya*, *L. palmeriana* and *L. monostachya*.

Cultivation: Easily grown in a shady, protected situation. Likes plenty of water and a deep, well-drained, organically rich soil. Mulches are very beneficial. It is suited to tropical and subtropical areas and will also grow in a protected situation as far south as Sydney.

This species is occasionally available from specialist nurseries. Well-developed plants look really good in a large pot or tub and will tolerate some exposure to indoor conditions, especially if placed in a well lit position and sprayed when the atmosphere is dry.

Propagation: From seed which germinates readily in four to six months. Bottom heat promotes germination. Seed loses its viability soon after harvest. Seedlings transplant easily.

Linospadix monostachya in fruit.

Linospadix monostachya (C. Martius) H. H. Wendl. *(in a single spike, referring to the inflorescence)*
Walking Stick Palm or Midgin-bil

Description: Solitary, very slender, feather-leaved palm; trunk 1-4 m tall, thin (2-3 cm thick), woody, green, with numerous rings; leaves 30-120 cm long, spreading in a loose crown; petiole 20-30 cm long, the base produced into two sheathing, stipule-like lobes; pinnae irregular in shape and distribution, 10-30 cm long, tapered, the apices irregular, the terminal pair united and fish-tail like; inflorescence a simple pendulous spike 1-1.5 m long, arising from the lower leaf axils; flowers about 0.8 cm across, greenish, male and female separate; fruit about 1.2-1.5 cm long, ovoid to elliptical, waxy red or yellow-orange.

Notes: This small, slender palm is found in rainforest often along stream banks. It is usually found in quite shady positions and on suitable sites may grow in scattered colonies. It is common throughout its range.

The common name of this palm is apt because its stems make excellent walking sticks. At the base of the trunk just below the soil surface there is a knob of varying size depending on the age of the palm. This can be carved to provide an excellent hand grip. During the first World War thousands of these palms were harvested and converted into walking sticks for returning wounded soldiers. The people who did the collecting referred to them as 'Midgin-bils' or 'Midgin-balls'. The cabbage of this small palm is quite edible as are also the red fruit which have a thin, somewhat acid layer of flesh around the seed.

Distribution: An endemic palm distributed from about Gympie in southern Qld to Bulahdelah in central northern NSW, in the northern end of its range mainly found in highland regions.

Distinguishing Features: A pinnate-leaved palm with a very slender, solitary trunk.

Confusing Species: *L. minor*.

Cultivation: Walking Stick Palms are easily

grown in the garden and because of their slender habit are ideal subjects for cultivation. Their strings of red or yellow-orange fruit are a particularly decorative feature. For successful culture they need complete shade, an organically rich, well-drained soil and plenty of mulch on the soil surface. As well they appreciate watering during dry periods and light applications of fertilisers during the warm months. They will happily withstand cold climates and will grow south at least as far as Melbourne. In the tropics they are more difficult and need a cool, very shady position.

Walking Stick Palms are available from specialist nurseries. However they are very slow growing and specimens with a trunk may be quite expensive. They have limited application as an indoor plant, tolerating fairly dark conditions but they need to be rested at frequent intervals as their leaves lose lustre in dry atmospheres and may suffer from attacks by two-spotted mite. Occasional plants have been recorded with variegated foliage – these would be a collectors item indeed.

Propagation: From seed which germinates easily in four to six months after sowing. Seed loses viability within ten to fourteen days. Seedlings transplant readily.

Linospadix palmeriana (Bailey) Burret
(after Edward Palmer)

Description: Small, clumping, pinnate-leaved palm; trunks 1-1.6 m tall, very slender (0.5-1.5 cm thick), 2-3 dominant the rest reduced to basal suckers; leaves 25-45 cm long, spreading in a loose crown; petiole 15-30 cm long, erect and spreading, the sheathing bases prominently ribbed; pinnae 15-25 cm long, 2-4 per leaf, almost triangular, tapered, their bases broadly adnate to the rhachis, the apex acute, toothed, the terminal ones fish-tail like; inflorescence 15-25 cm long, a simple, pendulous spike arising in the lower leaf axils; flowers about 0.4 cm across; fruit 0.8-1 cm long, elliptical, red or yellow-orange when ripe.

Notes: A little-known species apparently confined to highland rainforests in sheltered shady situations. Studies by A. K. Irvine indicate that *L. aequisegmentosa* may only be a form of this species.

Distribution: Apparently confined to peaks of the Bellenden Ker Range in north-eastern Qld, above 800 m altitude.

Distinguishing Features: A small, clumping, pinnate-leaved palm with slender trunks and one or two pairs of pinnae per leaf.

Confusing Species: *L. minor.*

Cultivation: Easily grown in a pot or the garden but requires cool, shady, moist conditions. Best suited to temperate and cool subtropical regions. Mulches are very beneficial.

Propagation: From seed which germinates readily. Seed loses its viability soon after harvest.

Linospadix sp. 'Mt Lewis'

Description: Small, clumping palm with simple-lobed or irregularly pinnate leaves; stems 0.8-3 m tall, several together but usually 2-3 dominant, very slender (0.8-2 cm diameter);

An undescribed species of *Linospadix* which is common on Mt Lewis in north-eastern Qld.

127

leaves 30-80 cm x 12-25 cm, spreading in a loose crown, sessile; adult leaves simple and bilobed to irregularly pinnate, with 2-8 pinnae, sometimes simple on one side of the midrib, pinnate on the other; lower juvenile leaves 0.3-1 m long, simple and deeply bilobed at the apex; inflorescence 40-60 cm long, a simple pendulous spike arising in the lower leaf axils; flowers about 0.3 cm across, greenish cream to cream, male and female separate; fruit 1-1.5 cm x 0.5-0.8 cm, ovoid to cylindrical, red or orange-red when ripe.

Notes: This small, clumping palm is common in rainforest above 900 m on Mt Lewis and Mt Spurgeon where it usually occurs in large colonies in heavily shaded conditions. Plants consist of several basal suckers and 1-5 tall dominant stems which are replaced as they die or are damaged.

Distribution: Endemic to the Mt Lewis and Mt Spurgeon area of north-eastern Qld.

Distinguishing Features: The large, simple, sessile, bilobed juvenile leaves.

Confusing Species: Some forms of *Linospadix microcarya.*

Cultivation: Easily grown in a shady, protected situation but requires constant high humidity. Likes plenty of water and a deep, well-drained, organically rich soil. This species grows well in a large pot or tub and makes a striking indoor decoration where it will tolerate low light intensities but deteriorates if the atmosphere is too dry.

Propagation: From seed which germinates readily in four to six months. Bottom heat promotes germination. Seed looses viability rather quickly. Seedlings transplant readily but are slow growing.

LIVISTONA R. Br.

Of the twenty-eight species of palms in this genus about twenty are to be found in Australia and this includes about eight undescribed species. Some grow in rainforest but the majority are hardy palms growing in inland gorges or open forest in tropical regions often in extensive colonies. They are frequently to be found in wet situations or low-lying areas subject to periodic inundation but a couple of species are normal components of the forest flora. Although they are most common in the tropics, one species extends down the east coast to Victoria and is Australia's most southerly palm. Because of their abundance and habit of growing in colonies they were used by the Aborigines to construct shelters and harvested for their edible cabbage. Some records remain of this useage but for some species this is unrecorded as is also the extent to which they were used.(For exotic species of *Livistona* see page 206.)

Livistona alfredii F. Muell. *(after Alfred, Duke of Edinburgh in the late nineteenth century)*
Millstream Palm

Description: Solitary, medium-sized, fan-leaved palm; trunk 5-12 m tall, 30-40 cm thick, naked, dark grey to brownish, with prominent annular rings; leaves 2-3 m long, stiff, dull blue-green, in a large spreading crown; petiole 1.5-2 m long, erect or decurved, 6-8 cm across at the base

Livistonia alfredii is commonly known as the Millstream Palm.

tapering to 2.5 cm at the top, pale green to yellowish, white near the base, the margins armed with numerous prickles; lamina 0.8-1.2 m long, orbicular, often partially folded, dull green to slightly glaucous, stiff, divided more than half way into numerous segments; segments narrow, acuminate, stiff, the upper part not drooping; panicle 60-80 cm long, much-branched, with stiff upward-pointing branches; flowers about 0.6 cm across, yellowish; fruit 2.5-3 cm across, ovoid to globular, hard, dark chestnut brown.

Notes: This fan palm is commonly seen in the area of the Fortescue River around Millstream Station. Here it is a tropical relic that grows amongst luxuriant vegetation created by the outflow of a very large, permanent spring. The water from this spring is warm and enters the Fortescue River bed about 6.5 km above the Station thus ensuring good water levels all year round and creating a tropical oasis. The Station is a well-frequented stopping place for tourists and the palms are promoted as a significant tourist feature.

Distribution: Endemic in areas of the Pilbara region around the Fortescue and Ashburton Rivers of north-western Western Australia.

Distinguishing Features: A medium-sized, fan-leaved palm with a fairly stout trunk and a large crown of stiff, dull blue-green leaves.

Confusing Species: *L. eastonii, L.* sp. 'Victoria River'.

Cultivation: This palm is rarely encountered in cultivation except in enthusiasts' collections. Seed is occasionally available for sale from commercial seed distributors. It is a handsome palm, well suited to cultivation in inland regions but would probably require an abundance of water. Seedlings are very slow growing but will tolerate direct sun from a very early age.

Propagation: Freshly collected ripe seed germinates readily within three to six months. Seed sold commercially often will not germinate either because of incorrect storage or collection of immature fruit.

Livistona australis is widespread in eastern Australia.

Livistona australis C. Martius *(southern – the most southerly of all Australian palms)*
Cabbage Palm or Fan Palm

Description: Solitary, tall, fan-leaved palm; trunk 20-30 m or more tall, 25-35 cm thick, naked, grey with longitudinal fissures and annular ridges; leaves 3-4.5 m long, fairly stiff, with drooping tips, bright shiny green, in a large crown; petiole 2.5-3 m long, erect or decurved, 5-6 cm across at the base tapering to 2 cm at the top, the margins with numerous curved prickles; lamina 1-1.6 m across, orbicular, bright shiny green, fairly thin-textured, divided more than half way into numerous segments which form a complete circle; segments narrow, acuminate, entire or forked, the upper part drooping, part of the margin armed with teeth; panicles about 1 m long, much branched; spathes 15-25 cm long, blunt; flowers 0.25-0.5 cm across, cream to white; fruit 1-1.5 cm across, globular, black, hard.

Notes: This is the most widely distributed of all the *Livistona* species found in eastern Australia and is also the most familiar since it occurs near

129

major centres of population. It is commonly found in rainforest but also ventures into more open situations along stream banks and in swampy areas where it may form large colonies. It extends further south than any other palm in Australia. In the early days of settlement the leaves were commonly stripped, shredded, plaited and sewn into cabbage tree hats which were widely worn as protection from the sun. The leaves were also made into baskets. The early settlers collected and ate the cabbage and split lengths of the trunk for slab huts or hollowed them to provide useful feed troughs for animals such as pigs. The outer, woody part of the trunk is dark coloured and attractively marked and suitable for walking sticks and inlays. Cabbage palms were extremely useful to the Aborigines who referred to them as 'Konda' around Rockhampton and 'Binkar' around Brisbane. As well as eating the cabbage and young leaves which were just pulled out and chewed, they used the hard, outer wood for spear heads and the mature leaves for making fishing lines and nets as well as baskets and various containers for carrying. The leaves were also occasionally used to roof their dwellings.

Distribution: Endemic to Australia where distributed in a narrow coastal strip from Fraser Island, Qld south through eastern NSW with three isolated occurrences in eastern Victoria. There is some disagreement about the status of the population of the fan palm in the Eungella Range and it is included here as a distinct species.

Distinguishing Features: A tall, fan-leaved palms with a fairly stout, bulky trunk, shiny green leaves with drooping tips and cream flowers.

Confusing Species: *Livistona* sp. Carnarvon, *L. drudei*, *L. decipiens*, *L.* sp. 'Eungella', *L.* sp. 'Paluma'.

Cultivation: Very popular in cultivation, this species is widely grown in temperate and subtropical parts of Australia and in many countries overseas. It grows readily and will adapt to a variety of soils and conditions although it grows best in a well-drained, organically rich soil and takes on a lustrous, dark green appearance when grown in a semi-shaded position. It will tolerate quite wet soils although only where the water is

moving and not stagnant. In dry situations plants should be given plenty of water to ensure a good appearance. Young plants will tolerate direct sun when two or three years old but are best protected until at least 2 m tall. They are quite fast growing, especially in favourable conditions. Frosts may cause some browning on young leaves but are generally tolerated with only minor setback.

This palm is very suitable for home gardens and mixes very well with ferns. It can also be used in parks, either in group plantings or singly and as an avenue bordering roads and driveways. Young plants can be quite suitable for indoor decoration but the prickly petioles are a slight drawback. They prefer a well-lit position and are best if spelled at regular intervals. They are usually readily available from nurseries.

Propagation: From seed which germinates rapidly within one to three months. Seedlings transplant easily.

Livistona benthamii Bailey *(after George Bentham)* Fan Palm

Description: Solitary, tall, fan-leaved palm; trunk 10-16 m tall, 30-40 cm thick, covered with leaf bases which are eventually shed, grey; leaves 2-3 m long, fairly stiff, numerous in a long, extended crown, bright shiny green; petiole 1-1.4 m long, 3-4 cm wide at the base tapering to 1.5 cm at the top, dark green, bearing white scales, the lower margins with many short, straight or curved prickles; lamina 1-1.6 m long, longer than wide, bright shiny green, thin-textured, divided about one third into numerous segments, prominently folded; segments narrow, acuminate, forked and divided into slender, bristle-like points, the tips drooping; panicles 1.5-2 m or more long, spathes about 30 cm long, blunt; flowers 0.1-0.25 cm across, cream to pale yellow; fruit about 1 cm across, globose to pyriform bluish-black with a powdery bloom.

Notes: This tall, striking palm grows in colonies along streams subject to flooding and around the margins of swamps often in association with large paperbarks. It also frequently occurs in colonies along rainforest margins and in rainforest along stream banks. It is most frequent in near-coastal areas and may even grow around streams where

Livistona benthamii.

Livistona decipiens.

the water is brackish and around the margins of offshore islands. It retains its older leaves for much longer than in other species, giving the plants a large, extended head of foliage. This palm was very useful to the Aborigines who collected and ate the cabbage and used the leaves to roof their shelters. It was called 'Dre-amberi' by the Aborigines of the Wenlock River.

Distribution: Coastal districts of the top end of the Northern Territory, adjacent islands and Cape York Peninsula, Qld, extending as far south as the Massey River; also New Guinea.

Distinguishing Features: A tall, fan-leaved palm with an extended crown of bright shiny green, prominently folded, deeply divided, thin-textured leaves.

Confusing Species: *L.* sp. 'Cooktown'.

Cultivation: This handsome palm deserves to be more widely grown. It is best suited to tropical regions but can also be grown in warm areas of the subtropics. It prefers protection from direct sun for the first four or five years and appre-

ciates an abundance of water during dry periods. Mulches are beneficial and there is some response to fertiliser application. When small they make an excellent tub plant for verandahs or patios.

Propagation: From seed which usually germinates within three to four months of sowing. Seedlings are difficult to transplant.

Livistona decipiens Becc.
(deceptive, misleading)
Weeping Cabbage Palm or Ribbon Fan Palm

Description: Solitary, tall, fan-leaved palm; trunk 10-15 m tall, 20-25 cm thick, naked, grey; leaves 3-4 m long, stiff, with prominent, drooping tips, yellowish green, in a large, heavy crown; petiole 2.5-3 m long, 5-6 cm across at the base tapering to 2 cm at the top, green at the base, the margins with numerous curved prickles; lamina 1-1.5 m across, orbicular, pale yellowish green, thin-textured, divided for most of the way into numerous segments; segments narrow, very long and pointed, with long, drooping tips; panicles about 1 m long, much branched; flowers 0.1-0.25 cm across, yellow; fruit 1.2-1.8 cm across, globular, black, shiny.

Notes: This attractive palm with prominent, weeping fronds grows along stream banks in small, scattered colonies. It occurs in open areas in eucalypt forest and also along rainforest margins. It usually grows where ground water is accessible and often in sandy soils. It extends from coastal districts into the foothills of nearby ranges.

Distribution: Endemic to Qld where widely distributed between Miriam Vale just south of Gladstone to Cape Cleveland just south of Townsville and Magnetic Island.

Distinguishing Features: A tall solitary fan palm with finely divided fronds and long drooping segments.

Confusing Species: *L. australis, L. drudei, L.* sp. 'Carnarvon'.

Cultivation: This is one of the most attractive of our native palms and while it is becoming more widely grown it still has a long way to go to reach the popularity it deserves. Its attractive features are the large crown of strongly weeping fronds on a slender trunk and an attractive display of flowers during spring. It can be grown in warm-temperate, subtropical and tropical regions and is very suitable for home gardens. Well-drained but moist soils are essential together with plenty of water during dry periods. Young plants respond to application of fertilisers.

Propagation: From seed which germinates easily within three to four months of sowing.

Livistona drudei F. Muell. *(after Dr Oscar Drude, German botanist specialising in Palms)*

Description: Solitary, tall, fan-leaved palm; trunk 15-20 m tall, 20-25 cm thick, naked smooth, pale grey to whitish; leaves 3-4 m long, stiff, finely divided, bright green, in a large crown; petiole 2.5-3 m long, 5-6 m across at the base, tapering to 2 cm at the top, purplish-black at the base, the margins with curved prickles; lamina about 1 m across, orbicular, very finely divided, bright shiny green, thin-textured, divided more than half way into numerous segments; segments narrow, forked, the tips frayed, the upper part drooping; panicles about 1 m long, much branched; flowers 0.1-0.2 cm across, cream; fruit 0.8-1 cm across; globular, shiny black, hard.

Notes: A little-known palm which is becoming uncommon due to clearing of its habitat for sugar production. It grows in small colonies along stream banks and around the margins of paperbark swamps.

Distribution: Endemic to Queensland where restricted to the narrow coastal area from Paluma north of Townsville to Kurramine Beach, also Hinchinbrook Island.

Distinguishing Features: A tall, slender, fan-leaved palm with a smooth, pale trunk, finely divided, shiny leaves with black petiole bases, cream flowers and small black fruit.

Confusing Species: *L. australis, L. decipiens, L.* sp. 'Carnarvon'.

Livistona drudei.

Cultivation: This is a poorly known species which is rarely encountered in cultivation although plants have been sold in Brisbane nurseries over recent years. It grows readily and appreciates well-drained, organically rich soil and plenty of water during dry spells. The plants respond to mulches and regular applications of fertilisers and manures. They can be quite fast growing. Seedling appreciate shelter from direct sun for the first few years.

L. drudei is a very attractive palm worthy of wider cultivation. It makes a useful potplant for indoor decoration but should be spelled at regular intervals.

Propagation: From seed which germinates readily within two to three months of sowing.

The crown of *Livistona eastonii.*

Livistona eastonii C. Gardner *(after W. R. Easton, contract surveyor in Western Australia)*

Description: Solitary, slender, fan-leaved palm; trunk 5-8 m tall, 8-12 cm thick, slender, patterned with persistent leaf-bases, usually darkened from fires, swollen at the base; leaves 2.5-3 m long, in a slender, spreading crown, pale yellowish-green; petiole 1.5-2.2 m long, about 4 cm wide at the base, tapering to 2 cm at the top, hard, the margins bearing scattered thorns; lamina 0.6-0.8 m long, conspicuously folded, glaucous when young, shiny green to yellowish-

Livistona eastonii forms large colonies in the Kimberley region of north-western WA.

green when mature, divided about halfway into segments; segments stiff, not drooping, the tips forked; panicles 0.5-1 m long, stiff, much-branched; flowers about 0.4 cm across, cream; fruit about 1.5 cm across, globular, black.

Notes: A slender palm which grows in large colonies in open forest country. The trunks are very distinctive being patterned by a neat spiral of persistent leaf bases and are usually blackened by the regular grass fires that occur throughout the area.

Distribution: Endemic to the Kimberley region of Western Australia.

Distinguishing Features: A slender, fan-leaved palm with persistent leaf bases and a crown of light-green, folded leaves.

Confusing Species: *L. alfredii*, L. sp. 'Kimberlies'.

Cultivation: An attractive palm deserving of wider cultivation but little-known at this stage. Seed is occasionally available for sale from commercial seed distributors. Well suited to drier tropical areas.

Propagation: Freshly collected ripe seed germination readily within three to six months. Seed sold commercially usually performs poorly.

Livistona humilis R. Br. *(of low growth)*
Sand Palm

Description: Solitary, dwarf, fan-leaved palm; trunk 1-3 m tall 8-12 cm thick, adorned with petiole bases or bearing a skirt of dead fronds, dark brown to blackish; leaves 1-1.3 m long, bright green, spreading in a small, sparse crown; petiole 60-90 cm long, about 3 cm across at the base, tapering to 1.5 cm at the top, dark green, with numerous prickles along the margins; lamina 30-50 cm long, bright shiny green on both sides, somewhat folded, divided for more than half way into numerous segments, segments narrow, acuminate, the apex narrowly forked and thread-like, scaly beneath; panicles on female plants 1-3 m long, arching, slender, with few branches, those on male plants with prominent branches; flowers 0.2-0.4 cm across, pale yellow; fruit 1-1.5 cm long, oval, black.

Livistona humilis in flower.

Notes: This species is very common in open forest frequently growing in scattered colonies and sometimes in pure stands. It is usually but not always found in sandy soil and often where ground water is accessible. The Aborigines collected and ate the cabbage principally during the wet season. Grass fires are very common throughout the area where this palm grows.

Distribution: Widespread in the wetter parts of the top end of the Northern Territory, also adjacent offshore islands.

Distinguishing Features: A small-growing fan palm with a slender trunk and small, stiff, dark-green leaves and small, ovoid, black fruit.

Confusing Species: None.

Cultivation: This species is grown around Darwin but is rarely encountered in cultivation elsewhere. Seedlings are very slow growing and large plants are impossible to transplant. In a garden or park the species likes well-drained soil, plenty of water in dry periods and a sunny position. Seedlings will withstand direct sun even

Livistona humilis dominates some forests of the Northern Territory.

when quite small. Away from tropical areas this species has proved to be very slow growing and tricky to establish.

Propagation: By seed which takes up to six months or longer to germinate. Bottom heat speeds up the process. Seedlings are very difficult to transplant.

Livistona inermis R. Br.
(unarmed in reference to the smooth petiole)

Description: Solitary, very slender, fan-leaved palm; trunk 3-8 m tall, 8-12 cm thick, grey, with prominent annular rings, sometimes partly adorned with short, persistent sheathing bases giving a blotched appearance; leaves 1.8-2 m long, of very slender appearance, willowy, in a small, sparse crown, a skirt of dead fronds immediately below the crown; petiole 1-1.2 m long, very slender, about 2 cm across at the base tapering to 1 cm at the top, the margin smooth or with a few small prickles; lamina 60-80 cm long, pale greyish green and wispy, deeply divided almost to the base into numerous segments; segments strap-shaped, acuminate, widely divergent, the tips not drooping; panicles 20-40 cm long, sparsely branched (one major branch) drooping; flowers about 0.2 cm across, yellow; fruit 1-1.5 cm long, oval, black.

Notes: This palm is mainly found on sandstone outcrops and escarpments although occasional plants occur on the sandy soils of the coastal plain. The palm is remarkably slender and the wispy leaves make the observer wonder if the plant is in a healthy state or otherwise. Grass fires occur sporadically in the area where it grows. The correct placement of the names *L. inermis* and *L. loriphylla* has been subject to much confusion.

Distribution: Endemic in the Northern Territory where it mainly grows on sandstone escarpments, not extending east of Katherine, also the Sir Edward Pellew group of islands in the Gulf of Carpentaria.

Distinguishing Features: A very slender, fan-leaved palm with a sparse crown of grey-green wispy fronds the segments of which do not droop.

Confusing Species: *L. loriphylla.*

Cultivation: This palm is very slow growing and in fact seems a bit tricky to grow. At this stage it has mainly been tried by enthusiasts around Darwin and does not seem to flourish. It demands soils of very free drainage in a sunny situation.

Propagation: From seed which is slow and sporadic to germinate, taking from four to nine months.

Livistona loriphylla Becc.
(with ribbon-shaped leaves, in reference to the very slender leaf segments)

Description: Solitary, very slender, fan-leaved palm; trunk 3-8 m tall, 8-12 cm thick, dark grey-brown, without adherent leaf-bases; leaves 1.8-2 m long, in a slender, sparse crown, a few dead fronds hanging; petiole 1-1.2 m long, slender, about 3 cm across at the base, tapering to 2 cm at the top, the margin bearing small prickles; lamina 60-80 cm long, costapalmate, bright shiny green on both sides, deeply divided; seg-

ments slender, widely spaced at the base, the tips drooping; panicles 20-45 cm long, relatively sparsely branched, (3-4 major branches); flowers about 0.2 cm across, cream; fruit about 1.2 cm long, obovoid, dull black.

Notes: A little-known palm that grows in small colonies in open forest country. Grass fires are common in the area where it grows. The correct placement of the names *L. loriphylla* and *L. inermis* has been subject to much confusion.

Distribution: Endemic to the Kimberley region of Western Australia.

Distinguishing Features: A slender, fan-leaved palm with a sparse crown of bright shiny green, deeply divided fronds the tips of the segments of which droop.

Confusing Species: *L. inermis*, L. sp. 'Kimberlies'.

Cultivation: This palm is relatively untried in cultivation although seed is sometimes offered for sale. It appears to be slow growing and difficult to establish and is probably best suited to the tropics.

Propagation: From seed which is slow and sporadic to germinate, taking four to nine months.

Livistona mariae F. Muell.
(after Maria, Duchess of Edinburgh)
Central Australian Cabbage Palm

Description: Solitary, tall, fan-leaved palm; trunk 15-20 m tall, 30-40 cm thick, dark grey, tapering, naked; leaves 3-4.5 m long, very stiff, in a compact, dense crown, shiny green above, glaucous beneath; petiole 1-1.5 m long, about 5 cm wide at the base tapering to 2 cm at the top, hard, the margins bearing scattered thorns; lamina 2-3 m long, as wide as long, folded, bright shiny green above, glaucous and waxy beneath, reddish when young, divided about half way into numerous segments; segments linear, acuminate, entire or frayed, the tips drooping, the margins with numerous prickles; panicles 0.6-1.3 m long, drooping, much branched (9-14 branches), stout; spathes 15-30 cm long, blunt; flowers about 0.5 cm across, greenish yellow; fruit 1.5-2 cm across, globular, black.

Livistona inermis is a thin, wispy species.

Livistona loriphylla is a fan palm endemic to the Kimberley region of north-western WA.

Livistona mariae in the gorges of Palm Valley, Central Australia.

Notes: This intriguing palm is found in Central Australia and is separated from any other species of palm by more than 1000 km. It is a relic species surviving from a prior, much moister climate. Today the population consists of about 3000 plants and these are restricted to gorges where springs and seepage keep up the constant supply of moisture it needs for survival. The plants grow in small colonies around permanent water and are restricted to the Finke River and its tributaries. The Aborigines apparently ate the cabbage of this species and the very young leaves are edible.

Distribution: Northern Territory where endemic to the MacDonnell Ranges in the south.

Distinguishing Features: A solitary, tall, fan-leaved palm with a compact crown of shiny leaves which are reddish when young and the segments with numerous prickles on the margins.

Confusing Species: *L. rigida, L.* sp. 'Cape River'.

Cultivation: Despite its isolation (or perhaps because of it) this palm has aroused considerable interest and is widely grown in such diverse localities as Melbourne and Darwin and in some countries overseas. Although quite adaptable it is best suited to subtropical and tropical regions or inland areas with a drier, warm climate. Plants like a well-drained situation and plenty of water during dry periods. They will withstand full sun when quite small and generally take on a very attractive, reddish appearance. Seedlings tend to be slow growing although in Darwin they are regarded as being fairly fast. This palm looks very attractive when planted with the powder blue seedlings of *L.* sp. 'Victoria River'.

Propagation: By seed which germinates somewhat erratically over four to six months.

Livistona muelleri Bailey
(after Baron Sir Ferdinand von Mueller,
first Government Botanist, Victoria)
Dwarf Fan Palm

Description: Solitary, fan-leaved palm; trunk 2-12 m tall, 30-50 cm thick, clothed with the brown, fibrous bases of old leaf sheaths (although these may be burnt in fires); leaves about 2 m

Livistona muelleri in flower.

long, stiff, in a small, dense crown; petiole about 1 m long 5-6 cm wide at the base tapering to 2 cm at the top, dark green, hard, the basal margins bearing curved thorns; lamina 0.6-0.8 m long, dark green above, pale green or grey-green beneath, divided about half way into numerous segments; segments narrow, stiff, acuminate, the apex narrowly forked, sometimes toothed near the base; panicles 1-1.2 m long, spathes 20-30 cm long, striate, acuminate; flowers 0.1-0.25 cm across, yellow; fruit about 0.6 cm across, globular, blue-black, glaucous.

Notes: This small-growing species is found in scattered stands in open forest. It appears to be a very hardy plant and is frequent in savannah grassland that is burnt annually. The cabbage is edible, and the plant was called 'Bel-em-buna' by the Aborigines around Cairns.

Distribution: In northern Qld from just south of Innisfail to the tip of Cape York and on the western side of the Cape; also New Guinea (?).

Distinguishing Features: A fairly small growing, fan-leaved palm with a small, compact

Livistona rigida, Gregory River, northern Qld.

when young, in a large spreading crown; petiole 1.5-2 m long, erect or decurved about 8 cm across at the base, tapering to 3 cm at the top, pale green to yellowish, the margins armed with stout prickles; lamina about 1.5 m across, dull green to blue-green, stiff, divided for about one third to one half into numerous segments; segments stiff, up to 3 cm wide at the base, spreading, divided again into tips about 70 cm long; panicle about 1 m long, stout, much branched (15-17 branches), divided into short, rigid branches; flowers 0.1-0.25 cm across, sessile, in groups of 3-5, thick textured; fruit 1.5-2 cm across, globular, black, hard.

Notes: This palm is common on some inland northerly flowing rivers where it is found in large, quite dense colonies. Seedlings have dull reddish leaves. The species is similar in many respects to *L. mariae*.

Distribution: Queensland (on the Gregory River and its tributaries), also the Northern Territory at Mataranka where it grows on limestone.

Distinguishing Features: A medium to large fan palm with a large crown of stiff, spreading, dull grey to glaucous leaves.

Confusing Species: *L. mariae*, *L.* sp. 'Cape River'.

Cultivation: Uncommonly found in cultivation although it is grown by enthusiasts around Darwin. It is a very hardy and handsome palm, well-suited to cultivation in inland regions. It can also be grown in coastal tropical districts. Young plants are particularly attractive with reddish fronds sometimes with yellowish petioles. Plants can be grown in heavy clay soils but need watering during long dry periods. Seedlings are slow in their early stages but will tolerate direct sun from a very early age.

Propagation: Freshly collected ripe seed germinates within one to three months of sowing.

crown; leaf bases persistent on the trunk; fronds pale green to grey-green beneath, the fruit blue-black.

Confusing Species: None.

Cultivation: This is a very slow growing palm that seems to be rarely encountered in cultivation. It is best suited to tropical and warm subtropical regions and requires an open position in well-drained soil. Although hardy, the plants respond to water during dry periods. Seedlings are very slow to reach any size.

Propagation: By seed which takes four to eight months to germinate. Germination may be sporadic.

Livistona rigida Becc.
(stiff, rigid – in reference to the leaves)

Description: Solitary, stout, fan-leaved palm; trunk 7-20 m tall, 30-40 cm thick, dark grey to brownish; leaves 3-4 m long, stiff, dull blue-green, often with yellowish or reddish tinges

---

Livistona sp. 'Blackdown'

Description: Solitary, medium-sized, fan-leaved palm; trunk 8-12 m tall, 25-30 cm thick, naked, dark grey; leaves 3-4 m long, very stiff and flat, grey-green, dull, in a large crown; petiole 2-

3 m long, 5-6 cm across at the base tapering to 2 cm at the top, the margins with stout, curved prickles; lamina 1-1.5 m across, circular, dull grey-green, hairy beneath, thick-textured and stiff, the new leaves rusty golden-brown on the underside, divided for less than a quarter of their length; segments narrow, acuminate, forked, stiff, not drooping at the tips; panicles about 1 m long, much branched; flowers 0.3-0.4 cm across, yellow; fruit 1.2-1.5 cm across, globular, black, hard, with a glaucous bloom.

Notes: An undescribed species which grows in small, scattered colonies in rocky situations. The new leaves have an attractive, rusty appearance.

Distribution: Endemic to central Qld where confined to the Blackdown Tableland.

Distinguishing Features: A fan-leaved palm with broad, flat, stiff, dull-green leaves that are hardly divided.

Confusing Species: None.

Cultivation: Uncommon in cultivation and mainly grown by enthusiasts. A handsome palm suited to cultivation in tropical and subtropical regions and probably also temperate areas. Requires a sunny position in well-drained soil and responds to watering during dry spells.

Propagation: By seed which germinates easily within three to four months of sowing.

Livistona sp. 'Cape River'
Waxy Cabbage Palm

Description: Solitary, tall, fan-leaved palm; trunk 10-20 m tall, 25-30 cm thick, naked, dark grey; leaves 3-4.5 m long, costapalmate, very large, stiff, flat, silvery or glaucous on both surfaces, in a large, spreading crown; petiole 1.5-2.5 m long, 6-8 cm across at the base tapering to 3 cm at the top, the margins with stout, curved prickles; lamina 1.5-2.5 m across, circular, stiff and thick-textured, silvery from a thick coating of wax on both surfaces, deeply divided, with a long, pointed hastula; segments narrow, acuminate, stiff, drooping at the tips; panicles about 1 m long, much branched (21-27 branches); inflorescence bracts clothed densely with woolly hairs; flowers 0.25-0.3 cm across, cream; fruit

The very distinctive undescribed *Livistona* from the Blackdown Tableland.

2.5-3.5 cm across, globular, blackish, with small white flecks.

Notes: An undescribed species which grows in colonies along stream banks well inland from the coast. It is a very distinctive species with thick, silvery leaves that are thickly coated with wax on both surfaces. A. K. Irvine believes that the population at Ravenswood may have resulted from the planting of two palms around the old Glenroy Station.

Distribution: Endemic to Qld on the Burdekin-Ravenswood-Cape River area inland from Ayr (so far found on the tributaries of the Burdekin River but not on the Burdekin itself).

Distinguishing Features: A fan palm with large, stiff, silvery leaves thickly coated with wax on both surfaces.

Confusing Species: *L. mariae*, *L. rigida*, *L.* sp. Kimberlies.

Cultivation: At present only grown by enthusiasts but has potential for wider cultiva-

A clump of the undescribed *Livistona* from Cape River, Qld.

The undescribed *Livistona* from Carnarvon Gorge in flower.

tion. A rather distinctive palm for tropical and subtropical regions. Seedlings will tolerate direct sun when quite small. Needs well-drained soil and plenty of water during dry spells. Seedlings are fairly slow growing.

Propagation: From seed which germinates easily two to three months after sowing.

Livistona sp. 'Carnarvon'

Description: Solitary, tall, fan-leaved palm; trunk 20-35 m tall, 20-25 cm thick, naked, grey, with longitudinal fissures and annular ridges; leaves 3-4.5 m long, fairly stiff, with drooping tips, bright shiny green, in a large, heavy crown; petiole 2.5-3 m long, 5-6 cm across at the base tapering to 2 cm at the top, the margins with curved prickles; lamina 1-1.5 m across, bright shiny green, stiff, thin-textured, divided more than half way into numerous segments; segments up to 3 cm wide at the base, acuminate, forked, the upper part drooping; panicles about 1 m long, stout, much branched, divided into short,

rigid branches; spathes with woolly tomentum; flowers 0.3-0.5 cm across, bright yellow, solitary or in pairs; fruit 1.5-2 cm across, globular, black, hard, glossy.

Notes: This palm, although undescribed, is familiar to many people as it is common in the Carnarvon Gorge National Park and adjacent areas. It grows in large colonies along stream banks and flood terraces, also extending to the rocky gorges. It is very similar in appearance to *L. australis* and easily confused with it.

Distribution: Endemic in central-western Queensland on the Dawson River and its tributaries around Theodore and Taroom (Carnarvon and Isla Gorges).

Distinguishing Features: A tall, fan-leaved palm with a slender trunk, shiny green leaves with drooping tips and bright yellow flowers.

Confusing Species: *L. australis, L. decipiens, L. drudei.*

Cultivation: Easily grown requiring similar

141

conditions to *L. australis.* Not common in cultivation although many plants have been introduced into Brisbane by enthusiasts. Seedlings are fairly slow growing but will tolerate full sun when quite small.

Propagation: Easily grown from seed which takes two to four months to germinate.

Livistona sp. 'Cooktown'
Cooktown Fan Palm

Description: Solitary, tall, fan-leaved palm; trunk 20-30 m tall, 25-35 cm thick; petioles persistent on young palms up to 5 m tall, rapidly shed on older plants; leaves 2.5-3 m long, light green, in a large crown; petioles 1.2-2 m long, 2.2-2.6 cm wide in the mid area, 5-6 cm across near the base, the basal margins with blackish spines 0.3-0.5 cm long, the distal part smooth; lamina 1.5-1.8 m across, with a broad central area of fused segments, light green on both surfaces; segments 70-78 per leaf, the tips awn-shaped, prominently drooping at the ends; inflorescence 1.6-

The undescribed *Livistona* from Cooktown.

1.9 m long, much branched, the rhachis bracts glabrous; flowers about 0.16 cm across, cream; fruit 1-1.1 cm x 1-1.1 cm, globose, occasionally ovoid (when 1.3-1.4 cm long) black, shiny, mature Oct – Nov.

Notes: In the past this species has been confused with *L. benthamii* but collections by A. K. Irvine in November 1981 have shown that it is quite distinct from that species. It occurs along stream banks in open forest and rainforest in near-coastal areas often close to mangroves.

Distribution: Endemic on Cape York Peninsula in the vicinity of Cooktown (Flinders Islands near Bathurst Bay, Kennedy River near Lakefield, tributaries of the Endeavour River and south towards Gap Creek near the Bloomfield River).

Distinguishing Features: The leaves of similar light green colouration on both surfaces, the broad central area of fused segments in the lamina.

Confusing Species: *L. benthamii, L. drudei.*

Cultivation: This species is little known in cultivation except in some parts of Cooktown. It can be grown in open or shady situations but is likely to be frost tender and suitable only for tropical and coastal subtropical regions.

Propagation: From seed which takes three to six months to germinate. Seedlings transplant readily but are sensitive to significant root damage.

Livistona sp 'Eungella Range'
Eungella Fan Palm

Description: Solitary, tall, dioecious, fan-leaved palm; trunk 15-30 m tall, up to 50 cm thick, mostly 25-35 cm; male and female plants markedly dimorphic, the males having a shorter, narrower petiole, with a wider lamina; petiole 1.5-1.8 m long, 1.7-3 cm wide in the mid part, 6-9 cm across at the base, the basal margins with stout blackish spines 0.3-0.5 cm long, smooth in the upper part; lamina 0.4-1 m across, a broad central area of fused segments, dark green above, paler beneath; segments 76-80 per leaf, the tips of female plants erect, those of the males lax and drooping, the segments nearest the petiole compound; inflorescence 1.2-1.6 m long, the main rhachis bracts with whitish scaly hairs; flowers 0.3-0.4 cm across, cream; fruit 1.2-1.9 cm x 1.2-1.8 cm, globose, black, on stalks 0.1-0.3 cm long.

Notes: This species has been referred to by some authorities as *L. australis* but A. K. Irvine believes it is distinct. It grows in rainforest and wet sclerophyll forest and in some areas forms extensive, dense stands.

Distribution: Endemic to the Eungella Range near Mackay, above 500 m altitude.

Distinguishing Features: The leaf blade has a circular profile with the segments nearest the petiole compound; male and female plants have dimorphic leaves.

Confusing Species: *Livistona australis, L.* sp. 'Paluma Range'

Cultivation: A hardy palm, easily grown in open and shady situations. Frost hardy and suitable for warm temperate, subtropical and tropical climates. Attractive as an indoor plant.

Propagation: From seed which germinates in three to five months, with sporadic germination for up to twelve months. Seedlings transplant readily but are sensitive to significant root damage.

Livistona sp. 'Kimberlies'

Description: Solitary, medium-sized, fan-leaved palm; trunk 5-8 m tall, 15-20 cm thick, naked, grey; leaves 2.5-3.5 m long, dull green, with partly drooping segments; petiole 1.5-2 m long, slightly hairy, 5-6 cm across at the base, tapering to 2.5 cm at the top, the margins armed with prickles; lamina about 1 m long, dull green, deeply divided into segments; segments more than 2.5 cm wide, the upper half drooping; panicle about 0.5 m long, much branched; fruit about 1.5 cm across, pyriform, black.

Notes: An apparently undescribed palm that grows in sparse colonies or small groups in open forest country where grass fires are frequent.

Distribution: Endemic to the central Kimberley region of Western Australia.

Distinguishing Features: A solitary, fan-

leaved palm with a moderately stout trunk and a crown of deeply divided, dull-green leaves with drooping tips.

Confusing Species: *L. eastonii, L. loriphylla, L.* sp. 'Cape River'.

Cultivation: This species is virtually unknown in cultivation but its requirements are probably similar to those of *L. eastonii*.

Propagation: From seed.

Livistona sp 'Paluma Range'.
Paluma Fan Palm

Description: Solitary, tall, fan-leaved palm; trunk 15-30 m tall, 25-45 cm thick, stout near the base; leaves 3.1-3.5 m long, dark green, in a dense crown; petiole 2-2.7 m long, 2.9-3.3 cm wide in the mid area, 9 cm across near the base, the basal margins with bronze-green to blackish spines 0.6-0.9 cm long, the distal part smooth except for a few small spines near the lamina; lamina 0.9-1.5 m across, a broad central area of fused segments, dark shiny green above, slightly paler beneath; segments 73-81 per leaf, the tips awn shaped, erect on palms to 14 m tall, tending to hang on taller palms, the lowest segments compound; inflorescence 2-2.7 m long, the main rhachis bracts bearing whitish, scaly hairs; flowers about 0.3 cm across, cream; fruit black, globose.

Notes: This species has been referred to by some authorities as *L. australis* but studies by A. K. Irvine show that it is quite distinct. It grows in wet sclerophyll forest and rainforest.

Distribution: Endemic near Townsville on Mt Elliot and the southern end of the Paluma Range, above 500 m altitude.

Distinguishing Features: The leaf has a circular profile with a distinct sector at the base of the circle lacking segments; the lowest segments near the petiole are compound; the flowers are distinct with blunt petals which are held flat.

Confusing Species: *Livistona australis, L.* sp. 'Eungella Range'.

Cultivation: A hardy palm easily grown in both open and shady conditions. Faster growing than

L. australis in the tropics. Very frost tolerant and suitable to warm temperate, subtropical and tropical climates. Attractive indoors.

Propagation: From seed but information on germination lacking. Seedling transplant readily but are sensitive to significant root damage.

Livistona sp. 'Victoria River'

Description: Solitary, slender fan-leaved palm; trunk 5-8 m tall, 15-20 cm thick, naked, grey-black, swollen at the base; leaves 2-3 m long, in a stiff spreading crown, dull green to blue-green; petiole 1.5-2 m long, about 5 cm wide at the base, tapering to 3 cm wide at the top, hard, the margins bearing numerous dark thorns; lamina about 1 m long, costapalmate, dull green to blue green on both surfaces, divided about halfway into segments; segments stiff; panicles about 0.5 m long, branched; fruit about 1.5 cm across, black.

Notes: An apparently undescribed species that grows in scattered colonies in open forest country. In some areas it is abundant, growing in ranges and gorges. Seedlings and young plants have striking, stiff, brilliant blue-green leaves. Grass fires are frequent in the area where it grows. It is allied closely to *L. alfredii*.

Distribution: Endemic in the region of Victoria River and adjacent areas on both sides of the Northern Territory-Western Australian border.

Distinguishing Features: A medium-sized, fan-leaved palm with a slender trunk and a crown of stiff, dull, blue-green leaves.

Confusing Species: *L. alfredii.*

Cultivation: Although little-known in cultivation this palm has tremendous potential for drier tropical regions. It is grown in Darwin and the young plants have stiff, upright leaves which are a striking powdery blue colour. They grow well in a sunny aspect in well-drained soil.

Propagation: From seed which germinates in six to eight months.

A young plant of the very handsome undescribed *Livistona* from the Victoria River.

NORMANBYA F. Muell

A monotypic genus of palms endemic to the rainforests of north-eastern Qld. The species is a solitary, feather-leaved palm with the leaflets in a radiating arrangement.

Normanbya normanbyi (W. Hill.) L. H. Bailey
(after the Marquis of Normanby)
Black Palm

Description: Solitary, feather-leaved palm; trunk 15-20 m tall, enlarged at the base, slender throughout, light grey, the wood very hard, black flecked with red markings; crownshaft 0.5-1 m long, mealy white, somewhat inflated near the base; leaves 2-2.5 m long, arching in a crown, the petiole very short; rhachis stout, covered with white, mealy hairs; pinnae 30-45 cm x 2-3 cm, arranged in groups to give a whorled or feathery appearance, dark green above with prominent veins, white beneath, the apices jagged; spathes 15-30 cm long; panicle 15-35 cm long, the rhachillae flattened; flowers about 1.5 cm across, white to pinkish, with pink anthers; fruit 3-3.5 cm

Normanbya normanbyi is a beautiful Australian palm.

Normanbya normanbyi showing the silver underside of the fronds.

long, ovoid to pyriform, deep pink to scarlet, mature Dec-Feb.

Notes: A very distinctive palm, easily recognised by the light grey trunk and crown of feathery fronds. It grows in coastal rainforests often near swampy areas and usually in scattered colonies. The outer wood of the trunk is very hard and dark, almost black with cream streaks. It is attractively marked with red and polishes beautifully, being used for walking sticks and fancy inlays. The Aborigines used the wood for making spear shafts since it is long-grained and very hard. The cabbage is also quite tasty and the expanded leaf base was used for carrying items. The palm was known as 'Dowar' by Aborigines of the Cape Bedford area.

Distribution: Endemic to coastal areas of north-eastern Qld.

Distinguishing Features: A tall, slender, feather-leaved palm with the leaflets radiating in all directions; leaflets dark green above, whitish beneath, the tips jagged.

Confusing Species: *Wodyetia bifurcata.*

Cultivation: Black palms, despite their attractive appearance, are not widely grown and seem to be mainly planted by enthusiasts. The species grows well in tropical and subtropical regions but can only be grown outside in warm coastal districts further south. Plants succeed quite well in the Sydney Botanic Gardens. The plants are sensitive to frost and in long cold periods get black patches on the leaflets. They are very sensitive to sunburn when small and need a shady, protected position for the first three to five years. They are rather slow growing in the subtropics but faster in tropics, and like a rich, loamy soil. They are a very handsome palm and deserving of much wider cultivation.

Black palms are not commonly available from nurseries although they may often be sold by specialist native plant nurseries. They can make a successful indoor palm tolerating fairly dim conditions but resent a dry atmosphere.

Propagation: Propagated from seed but germination is sporadic and this species is difficult to raise in large quantities. Seed usually takes two to three months to germinate with stragglers appearing for up to twelve months. Seedlings transplant readily.

NYPA Steck

A monotypic genus of palm widely distributed around tropical coastlines between Malaysia and northern Australia. The species is a feather-leaved palm with a forking, subterranean trunk. It grows in brackish water and has an unusual inflorescence and compound fruiting head.

Nypa fruticans Wurmb.
(shrubby or bush-like)
Mangrove Palm

Description: Clumping, maritime, feather-leaved palm; trunk prostrate, much branched, 5-30 cm thick, usually below water, rooting from the lower surface; fronds 4-9 m long, in an erect crown; petiole 1-1.4 m long, stout, powdery; pinnae 0.6-1.3 m x 5-8 cm, 100-120 per leaf, rigid, shiny, dark green above, powdery white beneath; inflorescence 1-2 m long, arising direct from the rhizome; peduncle bearing many small, papery spathes and one larger and strap-like; male flowers bright yellow borne on catkins on the lateral part of the inflorescence; female flowers borne on a spherical head 20-25 cm across; individual fruit 10-15 cm x 5-8 cm, angular, fibrous, chestnut brown, packed in a globular head, 30-45 cm across.

Notes: An unsual palm which grows as a mangrove in inundated mud around the margins of sheltered bays, coves and along the estuaries of large coastal rivers. It is an important component of coastal stabilisation and ecology. The zone where Mangrove Palm seems to succeed best in Australia is on the smaller estuarine tributaries where the water is brackish and can sometimes be fresh.

In some overseas countries such as the Philippines it inhabits large, marshy areas and the plant has many important economic products such as sugar, vinegar and alcohol from the sap of the fruit stalk, petioles and leaves for building and thatching. The seed is also edible when

The Mangrove Palm, *Nypa fruticans* in north-eastern Qld.

young and soft. The outcrops of Mangrove Palm in Australia are fairly small and scattered and there is little indication that the Aborigines made use of them. It is recorded that the tribes of the Herbert River collected and ate the unripe seeds. The palm was known to the tribes around Cardwell as 'Ki-bano' and further north on the Pascoe River as 'Tacannapoon'. The fruits float on sea water and are distributed by ocean currents. The bases of *Nypa* leaves contain air spaces to aid in bouyancy.

This palm is widely distributed and when it was discovered in Australia in 1880 it was described as a separate variety (var. *neameana* F. M. Bail. after its discover, Arthur Neame). There are however no distinctions between the palms found in Australia and those found overseas and hence the varietal name was relegated to synonymy.

Distribution: In Australia sporadically distributed on coastal mudflats of north-eastern Qld and the NT and adjacent islands, localised in colonies; also widely distributed throughout the Pacific Islands and South-east Asia.

Distinguishing Features: A clumping, maritime, feather-leaved palm; the large, spherical female head.

Confusing Species: None.

Cultivation: Mangrove Palm grows best in a salt marsh or tidal mudflat habitat and it has been successfully introduced into such areas. In the tropics it can also be grown around freshwater swamps. One such colony has thrived in Bogor for at least 100 years, flowering and fruiting. Plants are also growing in a tropical glasshouse at Kew Gardens, England, in the waterlily pool. Generally plants are very cold sensitive and slow growing.

Propagation: By seed which germinates best in the presence of brackish water. Divisions may be established in suitable areas.

ORANIA Zipp.

Of the sixteen species of palms in this genus only one species is native to Australia and is found in the rainforests of north-eastern Qld. (For exotic species of *Orania* see page 214.)

Orania appendiculata Domin
(with an appendage, in this case on the petals)

Description: Solitary, feather-leaved palm; trunk 5-12 m tall, moderately slender to quite stout (20-40 cm thick), grey to greenish, prominently ringed; leaves 2-4 m long, spreading in a graceful crown; pinnae 50-75 cm x 3-4 cm, 140-160 on each leaf, linear to lanceolate, dark green above, white, grey or golden-brown beneath, with two green lines near the midrib, the midrib forming a ridge; inflorescence interfoliar; spathes 3-4, yellowish, the largest 40-60 cm x 15-20 cm; panicle 50-75 cm long, much branched, the ends drooping; flowers about 0.8 cm across, white, the petals with a prominent, triangular appendage; fruit 3-3.5 cm across, globular, bright yellow.

Notes: This palm grows in dense rainforests in creek beds or on slopes above the streams. It is commonest at high elevations and here the trunks are often short and stout and the plants with massive greyish crowns. It also extends to fairly low elevations in near-coastal districts but here it is relatively uncommon. It always grows

Orania appendiculata is endemic to the rainforests of north-eastern Qld.

where it is protected by the canopies of rainforest trees. In general appearance this palm resembles a dwarf or stout coconut. Many exotic species of *Orania* have very poisonous fruits but the toxicity of the Australian species appears to be unknown.

Distribution: Confined to north-eastern Qld between the Big Tableland near Helenvale and the south-east of Innisfail, and extending from about 100 m altitude to over 1200 m altitude.

Distinguishing Features: A stout, feather-leaved palm with a conspicuous large crown of spreading fronds which are silvery or golden-brown beneath; terminal leaflets united at the base and fan-like.

Confusing Species: *Cocos nucifera.*

Cultivation: A fairly difficult palm to grow very successfully. It appreciates cool, moist conditions in deep organically rich soil and does not like to dry out. It must be protected from direct sunlight at all times and seems to grow best in hilly to mountain districts where these conditions exist. It has proved to be quite cold tolerant and grows steadily, but slowly, in a protected position in temperate regions. Plants are generally quite slow growing especially in their very young stages. This palm is not commonly encountered in cultivation and is mainly a collectors item.

Propagation: From seed which germinates sparingly over several years. Bottom heat does not promote germination but pre-treatments such as cracking the shell or heating in warm water may enhance it. Seedlings may be tricky to transplant.

PTYCHOSPERMA Labill.

Of the twenty-eight species of palm in this genus three are found in northern Australia, two of which are endemic. (For notes on exotic species of *Ptychosperma* see page 231.)

Ptychosperma bleeseri Burret
(after Florenz A. K. Bleeser, 19th & 20th Century botanical collector in the Darwin area)

Description: Slender clumping, feather-leaved palm; trunks 5-8 m tall, very slender (3-5 cm

thick) green with prominent leaf scars, procumbent or supported by the surrounding vegetation; crown of a mature stem of 3-4 leaves only; leaves 1.3-1.5 m long; petiole 20-30 cm long; pinnae 20-30 cm x 2-3 cm, 30-40 per leaf, lanceolate, dull pale green above, slightly shiny below, tapered to the base, the distal pinnae attached by a broad base, the lower ones opposite to subopposite, the upper ones alternate, the apex irregularly truncate; inflorescence 20-30 cm long, subfoliar, yellowish, sparsely branched; fruit 1.2-1.5 cm x 0.8-1 cm, ovoid, bright red, with a short apical point.

Notes: This palm was described in 1928 from near Darwin and has been virtually lost to science since the original collection. The type was apparently destroyed during the Second World War. Recent botanists have wrongly equated *P. bleeseri* with *Carpentaria acuminata.* The species has recently been rediscovered, however, in wet rainforest near Darwin growing with *Carpentaria acuminata* and *Livistona benthamii.* It is a very distinct and unique palm. The mature stems are too weak to support themselves and rely on the surrounding vegetation to remain erect. Those that do not manage to obtain support become quite prostrate or lie at an acute angle to the forest floor. Another distinct feature is the very small crown consisting of only three or four fronds.

Distribution: Endemic to a small area of rainforest near Darwin where localised and rare.

Distinguishing Features: A clumping palm with very slender, weak stems and a small crown of three or four fronds.

Confusing Species: None.

Cultivation: Cultural requirements are unknown but the habitat suggests a shady situation in the tropics and the plants should be kept well watered.

Ptychosperma elegans (R. Br.) Blume
(elegant, graceful)
Solitaire Palm

Description: Solitary, feather-leaved palm; trunk 5-10 m tall, slender and tapered throughout (7-12 cm thick), grey, with conspicuous rings; crownshaft 30-40 cm long, whitish green, enlarged at the base; leaves 1-2.5 m long, arching

Ptychosperma elegans, the Solitaire Palm.

in a crown; pinnae 50-60 cm x 3-8 cm, 40-60 on each leaf broadest near the middle, the apex oblique and erose, green on both surfaces, paler beneath, usually held stiffly erect, the terminal leaflets united and fish-tail like; inflorescence infrafoliar; spathes two, 30-35 cm long, greenish; panicle 30-50 cm long, semi-pendulous, much branched, the rhachillae flattened; flowers about 0.8 cm across, white, fragrant; fruit 1.5-2 cm long, globular to oblong, bright red.

Notes: Restricted to eastern Qld, this species is sometimes locally common in the lowland tropics near the coast. It may grow in moist, sheltered gullies in scattered colonies and is also found on ridges in high rainfall areas. It is usually shaded by the canopies of the rainforest trees. In some areas it extends right down to the sea and may grow in decomposing coral.

Distribution: Endemic to coastal and near-coastal areas of eastern Qld from Cape York Peninsula to Sandy Cape, Fraser Island.

Distinguishing Features: A tall, slender, feather-leaved palm with a short crownshaft;

leaflet tips obliquely erose, pale green beneath.

Confusing Species: *Archontophoenix alexandrae, A. cunninghamiana, Hydriastele wendlandiana, Ptychosperma macarthurii.*

Cultivation: Solitaire palms are popular subjects for cultivation in tropical areas of Australia and overseas. Although they can be grown in the warmer parts of the subtropics and even as far south as Sydney they often do not thrive and resent cold spells (they are somewhat sensitive to frost). They are excellent palms for parks or gardens but need protection from direct sunlight for the first two to four years. They can be very fast growing and like a rich, loamy soil for their growth. Well grown plants are very handsome with their crown of stiff, spreading, dark-green fronds and look especially decorative with their large clusters of bright red fruit.

Solitaire palms are commonly available from nurseries and are frequently sold for indoor decoration. In this they are only suitable if given high light intensities and warm, humid conditions. Thus they can be successful in the tropics but are difficult elsewhere. They can be grown in tubs for outside decoration. Frequently nursery-grown plants of this palm suffer a blight on their leaves which causes dead, brown blotches. These may be unsightly but have a minor effect on the plant's growth. This fungus is often worse in subtropical regions.

Propagation: Readily propagated from seed which is produced in large quantities. Seed usually takes five to six months to germinate but may be speeded up by bottom heat. Seedlings transplant readily.

Ptychosperma macarthurii (H. H. Wendl. ex Veitch) H. H. Wendl. ex Hook. f. *(after Sir W. MacArthur of New South Wales)*
MacArthur Palm

Description: Solitary or clumping, feather-leaved palm; trunks 3-8 m tall, slender (3-10 cm thick), tapered from the base, greenish-grey to whitish, with prominent, annular rings; crownshaft 50-70 cm long, slender, bright green; leaves 1-2 m long, arching in a loose crown; petiole 30-50 cm long; pinnae 15-35 cm x 3-5 cm, 30-50 per leaf, lanceolate, bright green above,

Ptychosperma macarthurii is a popular, neat, clumping palm for the tropics.

Distinguishing Features: A clumping, slender feather-leaved palm; leaflet tips truncate, as if bitten off, the terminal ones very narrow and separated.

Confusing Species: *Hydriastele wendlandiana, Ptychosperma elegans.*

Cultivation: MacArthur palm is a very popular subject for cultivation, especially in tropical regions. The plants will tolerate full sun even while quite small and when grown make a neat, compact clump with a pleasant appearance. They require a free-draining soil and plenty of water during dry periods and respond to regular dressings of nitrogenous fertilisers. Although somewhat cold sensitive they can be grown in subtropical districts and even as far south as Sydney but they are very slow growing in these areas and suffer during cold spells.

Young plants make a decorative tub specimen for a patio or verandah and can also be used indoors for limited periods. Grasshopper attacks may be severe on this species.

Propagation: From seed which germinates readily within two or three months of sowing. Suckers can also be removed and successfully established as separate plants.

paler beneath, the apex irregularly truncate; inflorescence 20-35 cm long, subfoliar, yellowish; spathe 15-20 cm long, cream to yellowish; panicle sparsely branched; flowers about 0.8 cm across, greenish-yellow; fruit 1-2 cm long, elongated, pointed at one end, bright waxy red.

Notes: MacArthur palm is uncommon in Australia although it may grow in localised colonies. It is found along overflow channels and areas subject to periodic inundation in near coastal districts. The plants are usually protected by the canopies of large trees such as Melaleucas or other palms such as *Livistona benthamii* or grow in the rainforest itself. In the wild the plants appear quite different to cultivated specimens, the most notable feature being the much narrower leaflets. Most cultivated plants are probably grown from seed originating in overseas gardens where hybridisation has probably occurred.

Distribution: In Australia confined to the central and northern parts of Cape York Peninsula and the top end of the Northern Territory; also New Guinea.

Ptychosperma sanderianum Ridley

Although reported as being native to Australia in some publications, a recent review has established that the species is of New Guinean origin. (For description see page 233.)

RHOPALOSTYLIS H. H. Wendl. & Drude

A small genus of three species of palm with two endemic to New Zealand (one in the Kermadec group of islands). They are solitary, feather-leaved palms with a distinctive silhouette. (See also *R. baueri* page 239.)

Rhopalostylis cheesemanii Becc. *(after T. F. Cheeseman, prominent New Zealand botanist)*
Kermadec Nikau Palm

Description: As for *R. sapida* but the inflorescence larger, being about 40 cm long and more branched, bearing longer branches and the fruit larger (1.5 cm or more long) and globose.

Notes: This species is basically similar to *R. sapida* and could perhaps be regarded as an insular development of it although it is often regarded as being closer to *R. baueri* from Norfolk Island and is sometimes included as a variety of that species *(R. baueri* var. *cheesemanii)*.

Distribution: Endemic to Raoul Island of the Kermadec Group, off the coast of New Zealand.

Distinguishing Features: A slender, feather-leaved palm with a bulging crownshaft and a crown of obliquely erect fronds, fruit globose, about 1.5 cm long.

Confusing Species: *R. sapida, R. baueri.*

Cultivation: Rare in cultivation and its requirements are largely unknown. Mainly of interest to enthusiasts. Would probably grow well in temperate and subtropical regions requiring similar conditions to *R. sapida*.

Propagation: As for *R. sapida*.

Rhopalostylis sapida H. H. Wendl. & Drude
(pleasant to taste, a reference to the edible inflorescence)
Nikau Palm

Description: Solitary, medium-sized, feather-leaved palm; trunk 6-10 m tall, 20-25 cm thick, naked, smooth, with prominent, closely spaced rings, green when young; crownshaft 40-60 cm long, bright green and glossy, prominently bulging at the base; leaves 2-3 m long, stiffly erect in a crowded crown, dark green; petiole very short; pinnae 0.8-1 m x 1-1.5 cm, linear to lanceolate, erect and stiffly ascending, dark green on both surfaces; inflorescence about 30 cm long, bearing numerous stiff branches, arising at the base of the crownshaft; spathes 20-30 cm x 10-15 cm boat-shaped, pink-yellow; flowers lilac to cream; fruit about 1 cm long, elliptical, deep red.

Notes: A very distinctive palm widely distributed in lowland forests and often growing in dense, dark situations. It is the southernmost naturally occurring palm in the world. In parts, particularly on the west coast of the South Island,

The distinctive 'feather-duster' silhouette of the Nikau Palm *(Rhopalostylis sapida)* native to New Zealand.

it grows on forested slopes facing the Tasman sea. The plants grow as individuals or as scattered colonies and are very distinctive with their 'feather-duster' silhouettes. It appears that they were often retained during land clearing for they are not an uncommon sight in open paddocks. The Maoris made considerable use of the Nikau palms, eating the young inflorescence and the heart, and plaiting the leaflets into baskets and other utilities. The leaves were used to thatch huts known as whares and when properly constructed these were waterproof. The fruit are extremely hard and it is recorded that they were used as bullets when shot was scarce.

Distribution: Endemic in New Zealand where it is widely distributed over the lowland parts of the North Island and in the South Island extending south to Bank's Peninsula and Greymouth.

Distinguishing Features: A slender, feather-leaved palm with a bulging crownshaft and crown of obliquely erect fronds; fruit ovoid, about 1 cm long.

151

Confusing Species: *R. baueri, R. cheesemanii.*

Cultivation: A very cold-hardy palm ideally suited to temperate regions but can also be successfully grown in cooler parts of the subtropics. It is generally slow growing and plants do not form a trunk before they are 15 years old nor flower until about 30 years of age. Young plants need shady, moist conditions and protection from direct sun for the first five or six years. Even mature plants look best in a sheltered position as the fronds are easily damaged by wind. They need well-drained soil and plenty of organic mulches. Fruiting inflorescences provide a brilliant patch of colour. Solitary specimens are capable of setting fruit.

Propagation: Easily propagated from seed which takes three to four months to germinate. Seedlings are very slow growing.

WODYETIA A. K. Irvine

A monotypic genus restricted to the Melville Range in north-eastern Qld. The single species is a solitary palm with pinnate leaves in which the central primary pinnae each divide into many linear secondary pinnae, which are ribbed on both margins. The inflorescence arises at the base of the crownshaft. The genus has been very recently described and is named after Wodyeti, the last male Aboriginal with traditional knowledge of the Bathurst Bay-Melville Range area, who died in 1978 at about seventy-eight years of age.

Wodyetia bifurcata A. K. Irvine
(in reference to the secondary forking of the pinnae and the forking of the outer endocarp fibres of the fruit)

Description: Solitary, feather-leaved palm; trunk 6-15 m tall, 20-25 cm thick, slightly bottle-shaped, prominently ringed; crownshaft 80-120 cm long, light green, with grey-white bloom; leaves 2.6-3.2 m long, 6-10 in the crown; petiole 29-42 cm long, about 5 cm thick; pinnae mostly divided into secondary linear pinnae, the central primary pinnae each divided into 11-17 secondary pinnae; primary pinnae 90-107 per leaf, regularly arranged; secondary pinnae 765-950, the margins ribbed, 45-70 cm x 2-4.8 cm, glossy light

The recently described *Wodyetia bifurcata* from Cape York, north-eastern Qld.

green above, dull green beneath with a faint whitish sheen, the apex lacerate or obliquely praemorse; inflorescence 75-112 cm long, arising at the base of the crownshaft; flowers in threes, the female in the centre; male flowers about 1.5 cm across; female flowers 0.8-1 cm across; fruit 6-6.5 cm x 2.7-3.7 cm, ovoid to globose, orange-red.

Notes: This species forms prolific stands in loose granitic sandy soils, among huge granite boulders. It grows in open woodland communities, containing rainforest elements, with the main canopy being the palms themselves. It extends a short distance along open forest creeks at the foot of the granitic hills at altitudes of 60-400 m above sea level. The climate has a prolonged dry season.

Distribution: Endemic to the Melville Range, near Bathurst Bay on Cape York Peninsula, north-eastern Qld.

Distinguishing Features: A solitary, feather-leaved palm with a slightly bottle-shaped stem;

Wodyetia bifurcata fruit.

primary pinnae regularly arranged and the middle ones divided into 11-17 secondary pinnae which are ribbed on the margins; outer endocarp of fruit with conspicuous strongly forked black fibres.

Confusing Species: *Normanbya normanbyi.*

Cultivation: Experience in cultivation is limited to seedlings about two years old. Seedlings initially concentrate their energy into developing a deep root system, an adaptation needed to survive in their seasonally dry habitat. The first leaf remains as a spear for some three to six months before opening into a V shape. The palm is very likely to be frost sensitive, but would probably be suitable for planting in open conditions in dry tropical towns, both coastal and inland, where frosts are not severe. In its natural habitat between the granite boulders, seedlings experience intense heat when the sun is overhead. Deep pots would be best for seedlings.

Propagation: From seed which germinates in two to three months from sowing, with odd batches still appearing after seven to twelve months. Seedlings can be transplanted successfully but deep digging is necessary to avoid extensive damage to the root system.

CHAPTER 8

Alphabetical Arrangement of Exotic Palms for Australian and New Zealand Gardens

THIS chapter contains details of all palms commonly grown in Australia and New Zealand and many collectors items which are mainly grown by enthusiasts. It also includes some species with obvious appeal that have not yet been introduced but which are likely to be. Because of the tremendous enthusiasm shown by palm collectors the species in this chapter can in no way be considered as being exhaustive of the palms grown in Australia and New Zealand.

Acoelorrhaphe

A monotypic genus distributed from Florida to Central America. Its species is a clumping, fan palm uncommon in cultivation.

Acoelorrhaphe wrightii
Silver Saw Palmetto

This tough, fan palm which extends from Florida to Central America and the West Indies usually grows in damp, sandy soil where it can tap ground water reserves. It is a clumping species, the most distinctive features of which are its prominent, silvery fan leaves and an intricate fibrous sheath around the trunk. A few trunks may dominate the clump and are surrounded by a dense growth of suckers. The plants are tropical or subtropical in their requirements and will tolerate full sun when quite small. Coastal conditions suit them admirably. They need plenty of water and are best grown where their roots can reach ground water. Once established, plants are quite hardy. Seeds are fairly small and germinate erratically sometimes taking over twelve months from sowing. The species was previously known as *Paurotis wrightii*.

Acrocomia

A genus of twenty-six species of palms distributed in South America and various islands of the Caribbean. They are solitary palms with a crown of arching, pinnate leaves, the leaflets of which have a plumose arrangement. The trunks are usually spiny. Each inflorescence is subtended by a large, woody spathe. Plants are uncommon and rarely grown in Australia but

Acoelorrhaphe wrightii.

have excellent features and should be more widely planted.

Acrocomia aculeata
Macaw Palm

Although best suited to the tropics this species could possibly be also grown successfully in a

154

warm position in subtropical zones. It is a tall, solitary palm growing to 12 m, with a stout grey trunk covered with numerous spines which are especially obvious on young specimens. Plants have a handsome, dense crown of dark green fronds which are slightly paler beneath due to a covering of white hairs. Single plants can produce fertile seed. Native to the Caribbean islands of Dominica and Martinique,. plants of this species require a sunny aspect and for good growth must be planted in well-drained soils and supplied with plenty of water. This palm has a stately appearance and lends itself well to landscaping, being suitable for such uses as lawn specimens and for avenue planting. Seeds may be difficult to germinate and respond to cracking of the seedcoat and soaking in warm water.

Acrocomia media

Native to Puerto Rico this stately palm has much to offer for landscaping in tropical regions. The trunk is erect, fairly stout (a drawback is the numerous long, black spines on its surface) and supports a graceful crown of fronds which are each about 3 m long. These fronds are finely divided with the pinnae having a plumose arrangement. Each segment is slender, shiny green above and silvery grey beneath. The whole appearance of a mature plant is graceful and the species should be excellent for parks and private gardens. The species could also make a useful avenue palm. It would be a wise policy to remove spines from the trunk for a height of about 2 m. Seeds may be difficult to germinate.

Actinokentia

A monotypic genus of palms endemic in New Caledonia. The single species is a slender, solitary, feather-leaved palm and is rare in cultivation.

Actinokentia divaricata

A choice, slender palm from the lowland rainforests of New Caledonia which is unfortunately at this stage a rare collectors item in Australia. Its very slender trunk to about 4 m tall is crowned by only four or five spreading, pinnate leaves, each of which has curiously arched leaflets. The new leaves are bright red and the mature ones a dark, glossy green. In cultivation the species likes a shady aspect and deep, well-drained soil. This palm would probably make a very attractive container specimen.

Actinorhytis

A small genus of two species of palm one found in Malaysia and the other in New Guinea and the Solomons. They are solitary, feather-leaved palms with a crownshaft.

Actinorhytis calapparia

A widespread New Guinea palm which is an inhabitant of dense rainforest. The plants grow tall (12 m or more) with a slender, grey-brown trunk topped with a bright green crownshaft and a spreading crown of finely divided fronds. The pinnae are glossy green and arch out from the rhachis in an attractive manner. The ovoid fruit, which are about 8 cm long, are reddish when ripe and are carried on a large, complex infructescence. Although this species is hardly known in Australia its ornamental features give it great potential for the tropics.

Aiphanes

A relatively large genus of thirty-eight species of palms found in the West Indies, Central and South America. They are solitary, pinnate palms which have long, dark spines on the slender trunks and other parts including the pinnae of some species. The leaves are coarsely divided into broad leaflets and produce a distinctive silhouette. Despite their spiny nature these palms have tremendous horticultural appeal and are popular with enthusiasts. Most species are tropical in their requirements. Many species were previously well known under the genus *Martinezia*.

Aiphanes acanthophylla

This Puerto Rican palm is a slender species with a graceful crown of pinnate leaves that have fairly crowded segments. Each segment is irregular at the end and a much darker green above than below and with black spines on both surfaces. Its trunk is adorned with rings of long, black spines and these are the only drawback to the cultivation of an otherwise very decorative palm. It succeeds best in tropical and to a lesser degree subtropical regions and needs protection from direct sun when small. Plants thrive in organically rich soils and need plenty of water during dry periods. Seeds germinate easily but early growth is slow.

Aiphanes caryotifolia
Coyure Palm

Although formidably armed with long, black,

brittle spines on the trunk, petioles and leaflets this palm has been a firm favourite in cultivation for well over 100 years. It was a popular glasshouse palm in England during the nineteenth century. In the garden it can be grown outside in subtropical and tropical regions. Although small plants need protection from direct sun larger specimens will happily tolerate partial shade to full sun. Its solitary trunk is ringed with black spines which are quite sharp and should be removed from ground to eye level. The crown consists of many graceful pinnate leaves the leaflets of which are broad and jagged similar to those of the genus *Caryota,* but with irregularly spaced leaflets, each of which has spines on the lower surface. Coyure palm likes a rich, damp, well-drained soil and plenty of water during dry periods. It is native to Columbia, Venezuala and Ecuador and grows naturally in rainforests. Propagation is from seed which germinates readily within two months of sowing although seedlings are slow growing in their early years. Clusters of orange-red to scarlet fruit on the tree are quite decorative and are reportedly edible.

Aiphanes erosa

The long, narrow, triangular leaf segments with their irregularly lacerated margin and the long brown spines on the petioles and veins give immediate clues to the identity of this palm which hails from the island of Barbados in the West Indies. It is a slender species with a crown of bright green pinnate leaves of delightful symmetry. As well as being spiny, the leaf petioles are covered with a white, mealy powder. Inflorescences are crowded with cream, fragrant flowers and are followed by red fruit. The species is not common in cultivation and is mainly to be found in enthusiasts' collections. It is strictly tropical in its requirements, being very cold sensitive. Propagation is from seed which germinates readily but early growth is slow.

Allagoptera

A genus of five species of palms restricted to South America. They are cluster palms with subterranean trunks and pinnate leaves. Plants are rarely grown in Australia.

Allagoptera arenaria

This palm, which is little-known in Australia, is tolerant of extreme coastal exposure and should

Aiphanes caryotifolia, young plant.

prove to be a very useful species for coastal tropical and subtropical planting. In nature it grows on the sand just above the high tide mark of Brazilian beaches. Plants in cultivation overseas have performed very well but require exposure to sun. The plants form a clump of erect pinnate fronds to about 2 m tall and have a branching, subterranean trunk. The pinnae are dark green above and silvery beneath and are in an attractive whorled arrangement. The small, greenish-yellow fruits are edible.

Areca

A relatively large genus of about forty-eight species of palms widely distributed from India through Malaysia to the Solomon Islands and New Guinea. They are solitary or clumping palms with pinnate leaves and are excellent horticultural plants for the tropics. In the early days the genus *Areca* was the dumping ground for many palms which are now in other genera. Some of these errors are maintained by horticulturists such as the use of *Areca lutescens* for *Crysalidocarpus lutescens.* For a note on *Areca alicae* see page 102.

Areca catechu.

Areca catechu
Betel Nut Palm

A tropical palm the seeds of which form the basis of a huge industry (see Edible Seeds page 47). As a consequence this palm, which probably originated in either Malaysia or the Philippines, is a familiar sight in tropical regions around the world. It is characteristically a very tall, slender palm with a crownshaft and a small, crowded crown of semi-erect, silverly, pinnate fronds. The fruit, if they are allowed to ripen, are quite large and colourful, varying from orange to scarlet. The species is reputedly cold sensitive and will only thrive in the warm tropics although healthy plants are known from as far south as Brisbane. It likes deep, well-drained soils and plenty of water during dry spells. Young plants will tolerate considerable exposure to sunshine and will also grow in the shade. Although very wind resistant the crown becomes very tattered following strong blows. Seed germinates readily within two to three months and seedlings grow rapidly in good conditions. Betel Nut Palms are somewhat variable and many different varieties and forms are known.

Areca concinna

This species is very rare in cultivation and most plants sold as it are in fact *A. triandra*. The true *A. concinna* is restricted to lowland rainforests of Ceylon whereas *A. triandra* is much more widespread. *A. concinna* succeeds best in a shady situation in the tropics and likes an abundance of moisture. The fruit are borne in clusters and are scarlet when ripe. In Ceylon they are used as a Betel Nut substitute. It is a very attractive palm well worth growing if true seed of the species can be obtained.

Areca guppyana

An attractive, small, slender palm from New Guinea and the Solomon Islands which grows in rainforests. Its thin, solitary trunk may grow to about 3 m tall and is supported at the base by stilt roots and terminated by a light crown of short fronds each of which has about five pairs of widely spaced, broad pinnae. The palm also has a slender, smooth crownshaft and bears bright red fruits which may be used by the natives as a substitute for Betel Nut. A highly ornamental species this palm is rarely grown if at all. In the Solomon Islands it is regarded as a sacred plant and may be grown on graves.

Areca hutchinsoniana

An attractive palm from the Philippines which is useful because of its short, compact growth habit. The slender trunk grows no more than 4 m tall and about 15 cm thick and has prominent, pale, annular rings. The crownshaft bulges somewhat and the fronds are dark green and spread in a graceful crown. The fruits are about 3 cm long, elliptical and an attractive yellow when ripe. Responses in cultivation indicate that this palm grows best in the tropics and the plants are quite cold sensitive. Small plants should be protected from direct, hot sun.

Areca ipot

In some respects this palm resembles a reduced version of the Betel Nut Palm *(A. catechu)*. It is a solitary species which does not grow to more than 4 m tall and with a trunk 8-12 cm in diameter. This trunk is ringed and topped by a short, but somewhat inflated crownshaft. The infructescence is densely crowded with large, ovoid fruit which measure about 5 x 3 cm and are red when ripe. Highly ornamental in all respects this palm

Areca triandra.

is becoming much sought after by enthusiasts. Native to the Philippines it succeeds best in a shady situation in tropical gardens.

Areca macrocalyx
Highland Betel Nut Palm
As the common name suggests this palm is cultivated around villages in the highlands of New Guinea and is used as a Betel Nut substitute. It is a solitary, fairly tall palm with a thick, dark-green crown and bears dense, club-like clusters of fruit. Although it is not known to be grown in Australia it appears to be an attractive palm worthy of trial in tropical and subtropical areas.

Areca macrocarpa
A cluster palm from the Philippines which forms clumps of slender, elegant stems and overlapping crowns of dark green leaves. The large, elongated fruit (up to 7 x 3.5 cm) are sometimes used as Betel Nut substitute in the area where it grows. Although it is highly ornamental this palm is mainly to be found in the collections of enthusiasts. It needs hot, humid conditions in deep, organically rich soil and plenty of water for good appearance.

Areca ridleyana
A dwarf, highly ornamental palm that is native to Malaysia where it grows as an understory plant on hillsides in rainforest. Each palm has a solitary, slender trunk that grows no more than 1 m tall and has a crown of dark-green leaves about 30 cm long. These are deeply notched at the tip and may be entire or divided into one or two broad leaflets. Brilliant-red, elliptical fruit about 0.5 cm long are carried on a short, sparsely branched inflorescence. This is a very ornamental little palm that makes a delightful addition to any tropical garden requiring a sheltered, shady position.

Areca triandra
A delightful palm that forms a dense clump of slender, pale-green stems and deep-green pinnate fronds. It is very tropical in its appearance and is the perfect neat, cluster palm for the home garden growing well in the tropics and subtropics. Clusters of fruit are an additional decorative feature being bright orange-red when ripe and they follow pale-coloured flowers which have a strong lemon perfume. Native to India and Malaysia the species likes a situation sheltered from wind and direct sun when small. Deep, rich, organic soils and plenty of water ensure fast growth and an attractive appearance. Propagation is by seed which takes six to ten months to germinate or by removal of basal suckers.

Areca vestiaria
The most attractive feature of this slender palm is its crownshaft which is invariably of a brilliant orange colouration. Native to the Celebes and Moluccas, it is a clumping palm with prominent stilt roots. Plants are becoming widely distributed and well known in cultivation. Although succeeding best in the tropics, plants have also been grown as far south as Brisbane suburbs. They require a shady position and like an organically rich soil. In a good position they can be quite fast growing. Trunks may be 10-12 cm thick and the leaves have very broad, dark-green leaflets. Fresh seed germinates quite rapidly. Fruit are deep orange, about 2 cm long and carried in tightly packed bunches. The species was previously known as *A. langloisiana*.

Areca whitfordii
A Philippine species which grows in semi-

Areca vestiaria showing orange leaf bases.

Areca vestiaria showing stilt roots.

swampy areas of the lowlands. It develops trunks to 20 cm thick and more than 5 m tall and these may be conspicuously ringed. The crownshaft is prominent, somewhat swollen and the fronds arch upwards and out in the crown. Fruit are 4-5 cm long and up to 2 cm thick, elliptical in shape and brownish when ripe. This species is mainly to be found in collections in the tropics.

Arecastrum

A monotypic genus endemic to Brazil. The species is commonly grown in tropical and subtropical areas around the world and is a familiar horticultural subject. It is a solitary, pinnate palm which has radiating leaflets which impart a plumose appearance to the leaves. Plants of this species are naturalised in parts of Qld. *Arecastrum* may hybridise with species of *Butia*.

Arecastrum romanzoffianum
Queen Palm

A familiar sight in tropical and subtropical parts of Australia where it is planted by the thousands, this palm has proved to be surprisingly adaptable as mature specimens are known from as far south

Arecastrum romanzoffianum, the very popular Queen Palm.

as Melbourne. In the tropics it will grow in inland areas and also thrives on the coast, withstanding quite a deal of salt-laden wind. It is planted in parks and in streets as well as home gardens for its decorative value. This palm is fast-growing and is especially responsive to nitrogenous fertilisers. The grey trunk is fairly slender and grows up to 15 m tall and is crowned by spreading, feathery-looking fronds. The species originates in Brazil where it is usually found in coastal districts. Plants are monoecious and fruit can be produced on solitary trees. It is often sold in the nursery trade as *Cocos plumosus*. This palm has a couple of drawbacks, notably the retention of untidy dead fronds and the large mass of fruits which when ripe attract bats and cockroaches. Large plants can be shifted readily, often with little setback. The species is somewhat variable, the typical form having fat fruit 2-2.5 cm long while in the var. *australe* they are quite slender and up to 3 cm long.

Arenga

A genus of seventeen species of palm mainly found in the Indo-Malaysian region with a few extending to New Guinea and one in north-western Australia. They are solitary or clumping, feather-leaved palms with the solitary species being monocarpic and the clumping ones hapaxanthic. Some species are of local commercial significance for the production of starch, sugar and fibre. Many species, especially some of the clumping palms, have tremendous horticultural appeal and have proved to be quite hardy in warmer-temperate regions. Others are tropical in their requirements. *Arenga* fruit contain caustic calcium oxalate crystals and should be handled with care. For notes on the native species of *Arenga* see page 102.

Arenga ambong

Native to the Philippines this palm has a very short, branching trunk which is largely subterranean and it thus forms spreading clumps. These may reach 5-6 m tall and spread for considerable distances. The fronds are erect with very broad leaflets which are prominently lobed along the margin. These leaflets, which may reach 70 cm long, are dark green above and silvery white beneath. This is a very beautiful palm and deserves to be more widely promoted. It will succeed in subtropical and tropical zones in sunny or

partially shaded positions. Seed may be slow and difficult to germinate.

Arenga caudata

A delightful, clumping *Arenga* from Thailand which has distinctive wedge-shaped leaflets with variously lobed and lacerated margins and a long, drawn-out tail at the apex. The leaflets are glossy green above and silvery white beneath and provide a pleasant contrast when stirred by the wind. The palm itself forms dense, bushy clumps to about 2 m tall with slender trunks, and is a decided acquisition to any garden. It will succeed in tropical and subtropical areas in a semi-protected position where it will receive some sun. A dwarf-growing, compact form is sometimes available and is sold as 'Nana Compacta'. The palm was previously known as *Didymosperma caudata*.

Arenga engleri

This palm has proved to be exceedingly adaptable in cultivation growing well in both tropical and temperate regions. It originates in Taiwan and the Ryukyu Islands to the north, and will withstand exposure to light frosts. It is an attractive, clumping palm that rarely grows more than 3 m tall but may spread as much as 5 m. It has long, graceful, pinnate leaves which are frequently partially twisted. These have numerous, crowded leaflets which are dark green on top and silvery beneath. It is an excellent palm for a large garden providing that it has room to spread. It is sufficiently tough to be grown under established trees and will tolerate a semi-shady or sunny position. Good drainage is necessary and the plants respond to fertiliser applications. Propagation is from seed or by division which can be difficult. Seeds germinate slowly and erratically, taking up to two years to appear. Presoaking for three to five days promotes more rapid germination. Ripe fruit should be handled carefully as the pulp contains caustic chemicals.

Arenga listeri

An interesting palm that is endemic to Christmas Island where it grows in sheltered situations in rainforests. Although still reasonably prevalent on the island, its future is considered vulnerable because of phosphate mining, and the activities of seed eating crabs. The palm is a solitary slender species of a medium size and should be ideal for garden cultivation. Plants have terminal inflorescence and die after flowering. Seeds of the species have been collected and germinated in north-eastern Queensland. The palm is probably tropical in its requirements of warmth, moisture and a shady position.

Arenga microcarpa

A rather coarse, clumping palm which deserves to be more widely grown, although its trunks may reach more than 7 m tall. They are prominently ringed, dark green and bear a crown of spreading leaves which are dark glossy green above and silvery white beneath. The clumps are usually quite dense with a few stems dominating and other stages present down to new suckers on the periphery. Interestingly, the flowers are dark purple. The species is native to New Guinea and succeeds best in tropical regions.

Arenga pinnata
Sugar Palm or Gomuti Palm

The origin of this palm is somewhat uncertain as it is now widely cultivated throughout tropical Asia for its saleable products. It probably came

Arenga pinnata in flower.

from either Indonesia or Malaysia. It is a very distinctive monocarpic palm with a thick, black, fibrous trunk, long spines on the leaf bases and a dense crown of finely pinnate leaves with drooping, dark-green leaflets which are satiny white beneath. The flowers and fruit are carried in large, drooping panicles and the purple flowers have an unpleasant odour. The palm succeeds best in the tropics where it can be quite fast growing, reaching maturity within ten years. It can also be induced to grow in cooler areas of the subtropics and warm temperate regions but is much slower. It needs rich, well-drained soil and plenty of water throughout the year. Plants will tolerate direct sun when quite small. Seed germinates readily, usually within two months of sowing and seedling growth is rapid. Ripe fruit should be handled very carefully as the pulp contains caustic chemicals. The species was previously known as *A. saccharifera*.

Arenga tremula

A handsome cluster palm which may form clumps 3-4 m tall. It has proved to be quite adaptable, surviving well as far south as Sydney and also succeeding in tropical areas. The trunks are slender and green with prominent pale rings. Each supports a handsome spreading crown of fairly broad fronds which are dark green above and dull, glaucous green beneath. The leaflets are quite narrow, of nearly uniform width throughout and with a few small teeth along the margin. The inflorescences are quite large and held well above the foliage. *A. tremula* is native to the Philippines and is an excellent garden palm. It succeeds in partially protected situations where it receive some sun during the day.

Arenga undulatifolia

One of the most ornamental of all palms this species, which originates in Borneo, forms a neat, dense clump of fronds which are a lustrous, blue-green colour. These arch out from a short, stocky trunk or cluster of trunks and may reach more than 2 m tall. The leaflets are fairly long and crowded on the fronds and have toothed, characteristically wavy margins which give rise to the appropriate specific epithet. Large plants are very decorative indeed. For cultivation, a tropical climate is probably most suitable although plants would be well worth trying further south in the subtropics. It makes a handsome lawn

Arenga undulatifolia, a magnificent palm for the tropics.

specimen and can also be mixed with other palms in a collection. Seed germination may be erratic.

Arenga westerhoutii

This palm forms open clumps consisting of about four stems each with a massive crown. The stems are covered with black fibres which arise on the leaf sheaths and the individual fronds may be nearly 8 m long. These are flat, with stiff, oblong leaflets and are green above and greyish-white beneath. Fruit are oblong, 5-7 cm across and blackish when ripe. Like most *Arenga* species this is a handsome palm well worthy of cultivation. It is native to Malaysia where it is a common palm in rainforests. Plants thrive in warm, tropical conditions and are sensitive to cold.

Arenga wightii

An Indian palm which forms small clumps consisting of a few crowded, black, fibrous trunks each with a crown of arching leaves 2-3 m long. The leaves have long, narrow, linear leaflets which have small teeth and lobes along the margins. These leaflets are up to 30 cm long, are sil-

very beneath and spread in almost a flat plane on either side of the rhachis. This species is a collectors palm which will grow in a sheltered position in the tropics.

Arikuryroba

A monotypic genus of palm endemic in Brazil. The species is a solitary, pinnate palm which is uncommon in cultivation.

Arikuryroba schizophylla

Although mainly a collectors palm this species has proved to be fairly adaptable and more cold tolerant than its Brazilian habitat would suggest. It is a solitary, pinnate palm the most conspicuous feature of which is the long, black leaf bases which cover the trunk. These are very spiny near the base. Its crown consists of numerous, dark-green, pinnate leaves which have very slender petioles and arch pleasantly, sometimes with a slight twist. The species can be grown in tropical and subtropical regions and needs protection from direct sun at least when small. Young plants make attractive tub specimens. Seed germinates readily within two months of sowing.

Arikuryroba schizophylla

The spiny inflorescence and frond bases of *Astrocaryum mexicanum*.

Astrocaryum

A genus of forty-seven species of palm restricted to the West Indies, Central and South America. They are solitary or clumping palms with simple or pinnate leaves. A few species are very prickly. The fruit of some species such as *A. standleyanum*, have unusual, star-like markings on the endocarp. Only one species seems to be grown in Australia.

Astrocaryum aculeatum

A graceful palm from South America which has a slender grey trunk copiously armed with black spines and an almost round crown of bright green leaves. These are quite long (about 5 m) and are finely divided into numerous leaflets which are plumose and arranged in groups. The leaf stalks, rhachises and midribs of the leaflets are all armed with sharp black spines. Clusters of large, orange fruit are a decorative feature and as a bonus are edible. This species is best suited to the tropics in large gardens or parks. Seed may be difficult and sporadic to germinate and may respond to cracking or soaking in warm water prior to sowing.

Astrocaryum mexicanum

This tough-looking palm is formidably armed with prickles and yet has an interesting appearance. Young plants in particular are quite appealing with their large, simple or sparingly divided leaves and spiny petioles and rhachises. In older plants the fronds are distinctly pinnate with a marked variation in the size of the leaflets. The terminal pair tend to be united and fish-tail like. All leaflets are dark green above and silvery beneath. The spathe subtending the inflorescence is interesting, being deeply cup-shaped and densely spiny. The fruit are also spiny, about 3 cm across and the seeds have an edible kernel. Native to Mexico and adjacent Central American countries this palm is mainly grown in botanical collections. Plants are of a very manageable size, rarely exceeding 2.5 m in height. They grow very well in subtropical regions.

Bactris

A large genus of 239 species of pinnate-leaved palms widely distributed in South America and the West Indies. They commonly grow in rainforest and may have solitary or multiple trunks. Some species have edible fruits and are of local significance. They are rarely encountered in cultivation, probably because they are liberally coated with ferocious spines. As a group they prefer tropical conditions.

Bactris gasipaes
Peach Palm or Pejibaye

This palm is widely grown in some tropical countries for its fruit which are eaten after cooking and also for its edible cabbage. The fruit are yellow with an attractive appearance like a peach and hang in pendulous clusters. Two crops are produced each year and seedless forms are known. The palm is clumping with slender prominently ringed spiny trunks and a crown of deep green, pinnate fronds which are also liberally covered with spines. It is best suited to hot, humid tropical regions although plants have been grown as far south as Brisbane. In the tropics plants can be very fast growing and are appreciative of regular watering and feeding. Young plants need protection from direct sun. Seeds germinate readily within two months but should be sown very soon after collection as they rapidly lose their viability. The species was previously known as *Guilielma gasipaes*.

Bactris jamaiciensis

Palms of this genus are mainly collectors items because of both their rarity in cultivation and the rather unfriendly nature of their slender trunks and leafbases which are very spiny. They are clumping palms with pinnate leaves and are quite attractive when well grown. This palm, as the name suggests, comes from Jamaica where it may grow in thickets. It is very tropical in its requirements and succeeds best in a partially protected position. Seeds germinate readily within two months of sowing.

Bactris major

The clustered trunks of this palm may grow to 8 m tall and are no more than 5 cm thick. They are spiny when young but the spines are shed with age and the older trunks are smooth with prominent white rings. Each trunk is crowned

Balaka seemannii.

with a cluster of dull green, pinnate fronds. Clusters of purple fruit are quite showy and have a juicy flesh which is edible or can be made into wine. The species is only to be found in botanical collections and succeeds best in the tropics. Once established, plants will tolerate full sun, but need protection while small. Seed germinates readily and should be sown soon after collection. In nature this palm grows on the margins of estuaries at the extreme of tidal influence.

Balaka

A genus of nineteen species of solitary, pinnate-leaved palms restricted to the islands of Fiji and Samoa. All are very handsome palms but are rarely encountered in cultivation in Australia.

Balaka seemannii
Spear Palm

The slender, hard, straight trunks of this palm were prized as spear shafts by the Fijians and were later harvested by Europeans and made into walking sticks. The palm is very common in some dense forests of Fiji and is widely planted there and in many countries overseas for its ornamental qualities. Its trunk, which may grow to 4 m tall, is usually less than 2 cm thick and is prominently ringed. At its apex it has a sparse crown of a few pinnate leaves which have very few triangular leaflets. This palm succeeds best in the tropics and requires well-drained soil in a shady to semi-shady position. Once established growth can be fast, especially if the plants are supplied with plenty of water. Propagate from seed.

Basselinia

A small genus of nine species of palms all endemic to New Caledonia. They are feather-leaved palms and may be solitary or clumping. Most species have very slender stems and are small growing while a couple of species are quite robust. All species would appear to have tremendous horticultural potential but they are virtually unknown in cultivation in Australia due to lack of seed. There are some reports indicating that they may be difficult to grow in cultivation.

Basselinia eriostachys

A choice collectors palm from New Caledonia where it grows in dense rainforest. It is exceptionally colourful, rivalling even the brilliant Sealing

Wax Palms for gaudiness. The leaves are dark green and glossy, the sheaths and crownshaft are dark red with blue tinges, the petioles purplish and the rhachis yellowish-green. The species is a clumping palm with several slender stems arising in close proximity. It is extremely rare in cultivation in Australia and reports indicate that it is not easily grown. A couple of specimens have been planted in Royal Botanic Gardens, Sydney. It appears to require cool, shaded, moist conditions in well-drained soil. Seed germinates easily within two to three months of sowing.

Bentinckia

A small genus of two species of solitary, feather-leaved palms found in India and the adjacent Nicobar Islands. One species is fairly commonly grown in tropical regions.

Bentinckia nicobarica

Superficially this palm closely resembles the widely cultivated Bangalow Palm but can be immediately distinguished by the longer crownshaft and the leathery leaflets which are lobed at the tip. It is a very tall, slender species reaching upwards of 15 m and has a graceful crown of dark-green, pinnate fronds. It is endemic to the Nicobar Islands in the Indian Ocean and is fairly widely grown in tropical countries. Being very cold sensitive it is best suited to the hot, humid lowlands and once established is quite a fast-growing species. Seed germinates readily within two months of sowing.

Bismarckia

A monotypic genus endemic to Madagascar. The species is a large, very handsome fan palm with a solitary trunk and costapalmate leaves. At this stage it is rarely grown in Australia.

Bismarckia nobilis

A magnificent fan palm from Madagascar with a large, heavy crown of leaves. The lamina may be in excess of 3 m across and is strongly costa-palmate with rigid, blue-green segments. It is supported by a very thick petiole which is covered with a waxy, woolly material. The petiole splits at the base where it is attached to the trunk. The trunk itself is stout, clear of petiole bases and may reach 60 m tall in nature. Separate male and female trees are necessary to produce fruit which is about 3 cm across and brown when ripe. In cultivation the palm is reputed to be fast growing. It requires a sunny aspect in well-drained soil and grows best in the tropics.

Borassus

A small genus of seven species of very distinctive, solitary palms all of which have broad crowns of large costapalmate leaves. They are found in drier tropical regions and for a small genus are very widespread around the world in such places as Africa, Madagascar, India, Indonesia and New Guinea. At least one species, *B. flabellifer*, is of considerable economic importance and others are of local significance. *Borassus* species prefer drier tropical conditions and are well suited to large parks or gardens. Because they germinate with a long sinker they are best sown into a large container or in situ. For notes on the possible occurrence of *Borassus* in Australia see page 103.

Borassus flabellifer
Palmyra Palm

This tall palm is frequently noticeable in drier tropical regions where it grows to perfection. It is native to India and Malaysia and is widespread

Borassus flabellifer prefers drier tropical regions.

and common in open situations frequently in dry, sandy soils near the coast. The hard, black trunks are often curved and bear a dead skirt beneath the crown of large, rigid, blue-green, fan-shaped leaves. In its native state the very old plants are cut for their hard, black timber and also the sap is tapped to yield palm sugar. When fresh the large, black seeds (almost as large as coconuts) are surrounded by a layer of orange, fibrous flesh which is sweet and juicy. Palmyra palms greatly resent disturbance and the seeds are best sown in their permanent position in the ground. They like a sunny aspect in well-drained soil and are very sensitive to cold. Seed takes two to six months to germinate.

Brahea

A small genus of twelve species of hardy palms found in the southern states of the USA and Mexico. They are solitary, fan-leaved palms that grow in colonies in open, often rocky situations. In cultivation they have proved to be very adaptable and will succeed from tropical to temperate areas. All species of the genus *Erythea* are now included in *Brahea*.

Brahea aculeata

The large, green, fan leaves of this palm (the fans are up to a metre across) are supported by a slender petiole which looks too thin to carry the weight. The petioles are toothed along their margins which is unusual for this genus of palms. This species is a robust, squat-growing palm to about 10 m tall. It bears masses of small, brown to black fruit in heavy, hanging clusters. The plants will grow in temperate, subtropical and tropical regions and need an open, sunny position in well-drained soil. Seed germinates readily within three to four months of sowing.

Brahea armata
Blue Hesper Palm

The most distinctive feature of this palm is its stiff, blue-green, fan-shaped leaves which radiate in a crown from the apex of the trunk. These leaves persist after death as a brown skirt. The relatively slender trunk grows up to 12 m tall and the species produces arching inflorescence 4-6 m long. This palm is very decorative with its bluish leaves but is uncommonly grown in Australia. It is very hardy and is best suited to temperate or subtropical regions. It withstands severe frosts without damage and is hardy as far south as Melbourne. For best leaf colour the plants should be grown in a sunny situation. It will grow in poor soils but will not tolerate bad drainage. The plants are relatively slow growing but may flower while quite small. The species is native to California, USA. Seed usually takes three to four months to germinate.

Brahea brandegeei
San José Hesper Palm

The tallest of the Hesper Palms, this species can reach more than 25 m in height. As the common name indicates it is native to the San José area of Mexico but is now fairly widely grown although it is still uncommon in Australia. The crown is quite large and dense and the leaves are green above and white beneath. Frequently a petticoat of dead leaves persists below the crown. This palm is well suited to temperate and subtropical regions. It needs well-drained soil and plants will tolerate direct sun from an early age. The cabbage is edible and was collected by the local people in its native area. Seed may take twelve months or more to germinate.

Brahea dulcis
Rock Palm

The small, yellow fruits of this palm hang in large clusters up to 2 m long. They have a layer of succulent flesh which is quite sweet and tasty and were eaten by the Indians of Mexico where the palm is native. As its common name suggests, the species grows in poor, skeletal soils in rocky areas. It is quite a stout palm with a large crown of deeply divided, stiff, fan-shaped leaves which are covered with a mealy white powder at least while young. Although relatively slow growing the species is adaptable, succeeding in temperate and tropical regions. It needs well-drained soil and once established is quite hardy. Seeds take from three to six months to germinate and seedlings appear sporadically.

Brahea edulis
Guadalupe Palm

When in fruit this palm bears prodigious quantities of small, round, black fruit which have a fleshy, sweet pulp around the seed. This pulp is edible and in some palms is very acceptable and tasty. Native to Guadalupe Island off the coast of

Brahea armata is prized for its bluish leaves and long arching flower spikes.

Brahea edulis, the Guadalupe Palm, is noted for its large impressive fan leaves.

Mexico the palm is now promoted for its large, handsome, fan leaves, its hardiness and its tasty fruit. Mature specimens are very ornamental with the large crown of fronds and as well as have proved to be very adaptable in cultivation, succeeding from subtropical to temperate areas and even withstanding frosts. Young plants tolerate exposure to full sun but well-drained soils are essential for success. Plants are generally slow growing. Seed germinates readily within four to six months of sowing.

Brassiophoenix

A genus of two species of palms endemic to the rainforests of New Guinea. They are slender, solitary, feather-leaved palms which can be readily recognised by the unusual wedge-shaped leaflets which have three prominent points at the apex. Unfortunately they are rarely seen in cultivation.

Brassiophoenix drymophloeiodes

Rainforests of eastern New Guinea are the home of this very attractive, slender palm which may grow as much as 10 m tall. It bears a neat crown of fronds (which have unusually shaped leaflets) above a prominent crownshaft. The inflorescen e is densely covered with white, woolly tomentum and this feature together with the dark red fruit serves to distinguish this species from the following. A number of attractive features make this palm a very desirable subject for cultivation and it must surely become more widely grown in the future. Partial shade in a well-watered, tropical garden are its requirements.

Brassiophoenix schumannii

This New Guinea palm occurs in north-eastern and eastern New Guinea where it grows in rainforest. Like the previous species it is a slender palm with excellent ornamental prospects but unfortunately is virtually unknown in Australia. From the climate where it grows and reports about its performance in America it would appear to like a partially shaded position in the tropics. It can be distinguished from the previous species by its pale, yellow-orange fruit and dark, scaly hairs on the inflorescence.

Butia

A small genus of five species of South American palms which have solitary trunks and pinnate

Butia capitata is a hardy palm which will grow in a wide range of climates.

fronds. One highly ornamental species is commonly grown in Australia and is a familiar sight in tropical as well as temperate regions. In general they are hardy, sun-loving palms with high horticultural appeal. *Butia* species may hybridise sporadically with species of *Arecastrum* and *Syagrus*.

Butia capitata
Wine Palm or Jelly Palm

An eye-catching and distinctive palm readily recognised by its stout, woody trunk to 5 m tall and graceful crown of arching, bluish-green, pinnate fronds. It is native to South America where it is widespread in the drier regions and is sometimes locally common. Plants are monoecious and a single specimen is capable of producing fruit. The fruits are very decorative, being 2-3 cm across, somewhat flattened and yellow or reddish when ripe. They are edible with a fruity flavour but rather fibrous consistency. This palm is very hardy and will thrive in temperate and subtropical regions as well as inland districts. It requires a sunny position in well-drained soils, and will tolerate well-structured clay or limey soils.

Young plants make a very decorative and hardy tub specimen. The species can be distinguished from its close relatives by the glaucous, glabrous spathes of the inflorescence, the long spines on the petioles (8-11 cm long) and the small flowers (3-8 mm long) and the fruit (1.5-2.5 cm long). Seed of this palm is often difficult to germinate as it has a very hard, woody coat. Cracking the seed coat and soaking in warm water are useful techniques to hasten germination.

Butia eriospatha

Although basically similar to *B. capitata* this species can be distinguished by the spathes which are densely covered with brown wool. The plants are also more slender with a trunk about 50 cm across and the fronds are greener than in *B. capitata*. The fronds have a stout, spiny petiole which may reach 1 m long while the rhachis can be 2-2.5 m long. Fruit are globular, about 2 cm across and yellow when ripe. The plants grow up to 6 m tall and are very hardy in cultivation, requiring a sunny aspect in well-drained soil. The species is native to Brazil and is uncommon to rare in cultivation in Australia.

Butia eriospatha.

Butia yatay
Yatay Palm

This handsome palm from Argentina is little-known in cultivation, being mainly grown by enthusiasts. It will grow in tropical and sub-tropical regions and also seems to be hardy enough for inland districts. Its trunk tends to be taller (to 12 m) and more prominent than in most Butias and is adorned with dark, persistent leaf bases. Its bluish fronds are in an attractive crown and the large, yellowish fruit (3-4 cm long) are reportedly edible. Well-drained soils in a sunny position are essential for success. Plants are generally slow growing and seed is slow and erratic to germinate, taking from six months to two years. Cracking the hard outer shell may speed up germination. The species can be distinguished from its close relatives by the glaucous, hairy spathes of the inflorescence, the short spines on the petioles (about 3 cm long) and the larger flowers (10-16 mm long) and fruit (3-4 cm long).

X Butiarecastrum

A hybrid genus of palm originating from crosses between the genera *Arecastrum* and *Butia*. Sporadic plants occur in batches of seed obtained where the parent genra grow in proximity to each other.

X Butiarecastrum nabonnandii

This palm is an intergeneric hybrid between *Butia capitata* and *Arecastrum romanzoffianum*. It was apparently produced orginally as a deliberate cross by a French horticulturist using the *Arecastrum* as the pollen donor. Crosses also occur where mature plants of the parents grow in close proximity and show up in batches of seed raised from these plants. Seedlings and larger plants of the cross have characters intermediate between the parents. A couple of large plants are known in Brisbane's municipal gardens and are also in the collection of enthusiasts. They are quite adaptable to cultivation but are sterile.

Calamus

A large genus of about 375 species of palms widely distributed in tropical regions of the world but particularly well developed in South-east Asia. Many species are climbing palms with thin, tough stems and spreading pinnate leaves but a number are shrubby and some even stemless. *C. arborescens* from Burma forms erect, unsupported

X *Butiarecastrum nabonnandii* is a sporadic hybrid between *Butia capitata* and *Arecastrum romanzoffianum*.

clumps with stems to more than 7 m tall. Climbing in other species is aided by thorns on the rhachises and petioles and spines on the young stems. Plants also produce specialised, hook-bearing extensions of the rhachis (cirri) or flagella which are modified inflorescences and arise in the leaf axils.

As a group these palms are known as rattans because the slender, pliable stems are harvested for furniture construction. Some species have very thin, whippy stems while others are quite stout. They mainly climb in breaks in the forest canopy and are common along roads, trails, and so on. Many species have fruit with a thin layer of edible or thirst-quenching flesh surrounding the seed. Drinking water can be collected from the cut stems of some species and young suckers and their starchy base can be eaten after cooking.

Because of their prickly nature very few species are grown and they are mainly to be found in botanical collections and those of enthusiasts. Some species make striking pot plants and are suitable for indoor decoration. Young plants of many species are very sensitive to sun damage

and may be readily killed by over exposure. As a group they are best grown in semi-shady conditions and appreciate organic mulches and litter. Seed seems to germinate readily provided that it is fresh. Seed of some species may lose its viability quite rapidly. For notes on the Australian species of *Calamus* see page 103.

Calamus ciliaris

A slender climbing palm native to Java and Sumatra where it climbs by hooked extensions to the leaves. Although the species lacks garden appeal the young plants are graceful and make an interesting pot plant. The species has been cultivated for display in English glasshouses for many decades. In this species the pinnate leaves are verdant green and the narrow segments are quite hairy. In pots it likes a well-drained mixture rich in organic matter and as it is rather sensitive to cold may need to be kept in a glasshouse. The plants must not be allowed to dry out as they may easily die. Seed germinates within two to four months of sowing.

Calamus discolor

This is a rather attractive climbing palm as the pinnate leaves are green above and silvery white beneath. It is not as vigorous as many climbing species and plants can be held in a pot for considerable periods. The slender stems are spiny and the thorny extensions can be removed if a nuisance. Native to the Philippines it is best suited to tropical and perhaps subtropical regions.

Calamus maximus
Rattan Palm

A vigorous climbing palm with slender, sinuous stems which in nature may exceed 60 m in length. Its pinnate fronds bear many hooks which aid in climbing and the young stems are clothed with spines. The white fruit are about 1 cm across, scaly and with a thin layer of edible flesh. This is a fast-growing palm native to the Philippines and its stems are harvested for rattan cane. It is hardly suitable for garden culture nevertheless its seeds are frequently offered for sale. It succeeds best in tropical conditions.

Calamus ornatus
Limuran

This climbing palm from the Philippines and South-east Asia bears clusters of red, scaly fruit each up to 3.5 cm across. These have edible flesh and are sometimes sold in the local markets. The palm itself has large, dark-green, pinnate leaves and spiny stems. It is quite an attractive species but prickly. It probably fruits best in tropical areas and should be planted in a shady position in well-drained soil.

Calamus reyesianus
Apas Palm

A vigorous climbing palm from the Philippines, this species suckers freely and forms spreading clumps. Its long, pinnate leaves are bright green and finely divided and bear a long, prickly cirrus at each tip. When young the leaves are bright pink and are most decorative. Large white fruit up to 2 cm across are borne in long, hanging clusters. Although vigorous this palm makes an attractive pot subject as it suckers early in its development. Prickly extensions can be removed if a nuisance. It should be planted in a shady situation where it can climb and is probably best grown in tropical regions.

Calamus viminalis

A vigorous climbing palm from India and Malaysia which has succeeded very well in the Royal Botanic Gardens, Sydney. It has fairly stout, prickly stems with woolly white leaf sheaths and spreading, pale-green leaves about 1 m long which are divided into numerous narrow leaflets. These leaflets are not spread evenly but rather are grouped in small clusters along the rhachis. The stems climb with the aid of flagella. Its fruit are about 1 cm across, yellow when ripe and are globular with a prominent beak.

Calyptrocalyx

A genus of about forty species of small to medium sized palms restricted to Melanesia, with the principal development in New Guinea. They may be solitary or clumping and are mostly found in rainforest. All have tremendous horticultural potential but are rarely encountered in cultivation. The above estimation of members in the genus includes the New Guinea species of *Linospadix* and *Paralinospadix*. These await further study and not all combinations have been made, hence in this publication three species are included under the genus *Paralinospadix*.

Calyptrocalyx lauterbachianus

A New Guinea gem which rarely grows to 3 m tall

and which is found in shaded rainforest at moderate altitude. The plants may have solitary or multiple stems and have erect, dark-green leaves, the pinnae of which radiate in many directions to give a plumose appearance. Newly emerging leaves are reported to be reddish. The inflorescences are long, unbranched, pendulous spikes carried in small groups and after flowering bear fairly large, bright-crimson fruit. All in all this is a very decorative palm which would make an ideal subject for a shady nook in a tropical garden.

Calyptrocalyx spicatus

A rarely grown, collectors palm from the island of Amboina in the Moluccas. It has a handsome crown of drooping, green, pinnate fronds reminiscent of the Kentia palm *(Howea forsteriana)* and a long, pendulous, simple spike as its inflorescence. The trunk, which may grow to more than 12 m tall, is prominently ringed. This species is essentially a palm for the tropics and needs shade for best appearance. It deserves to be far more widely grown than it is at present and should be tested for its suitability as an indoor plant. Seed germination fairly readily within one to two months of sowing.

Calyptronoma

A small genus of three species restricted to the West Indies and adjacent areas. They are solitary, feather-leaved palms that lack a crownshaft. Species are rarely seen in cultivation and are mainly collectors items.

Calyptronoma dulcis

A Cuban palm with a solitary trunk and large, spreading crown of dark green fronds. In general appearance plants resemble those of the coconut but with stiffer leaflets. The leaflets droop towards the margins and have a prominent midrib. Fruit are about 2.5 cm long. The species grows well in wet situations and is most suitable for the tropics.

Calyptronoma rivalis

This Puerto Rican palm is considered to be endangered in its natural state as it is known only from about three localities on the island. Fortunately seed was distributed to palm enthusiasts some years ago and these have generally germinated and the plants grown very well in cultiva-

Calyptronoma rivalis, a young plant.

tion. They require a shady aspect with plenty of water and succeed in tropical and subtropical regions. The palm is attractive with finely pinnate leaves and is quite fast growing.

Caryota
Fishtail Palms

A small genus of twelve species of very distinctive palms with a peak development in Indo-Malaysia and a solitary species extending to north-eastern Australia. Their most distinctive feature is the bipinnate fronds with unusual-shaped leaflets. All species have monocarpic stems which may be solitary or clumping. Some are of local importance for products such as sago, sugar and fibre. All species have tremendous horticultural appeal and a few have become commonly grown. The fruit contain caustic crystals of calcium oxalate and should be handled with care and on no account eaten. For notes on the Australian species of *Caryota* see page 111.

Caryota cumingii
Fishtail Palm

In general appearance this palm resembles a very vigorous form of *C. urens*, having a thicker but deeply ringed trunk, larger leaves and huge inflorescences with very large and prominent spathes. It is native to the Philippines and is not commonly encountered in cultivation. It is very tropical in its requirements and succeeds best in the hot, humid lowlands. Cultural requirements are as for *C. urens*. Mature plants have been recorded at about 12 m tall. Germination of this species is very haphazard with some seedlings taking ten to twelve months to appear.

Caryota maxima

This giant palm from the mountains of Java, Sumatra and Malaysia is truly an imposing palm. Plants may grow to more than 30 m tall, with a solitary trunk and a huge, elongated crown of fronds. Individual fronds may be up to 3 m long and 2 m wide and are dull green with prominently drooping pinnae and pendulous leaflets. The fruit are bright pinky red and most contain only one seed. These are carried on a massive infructescence which may be more than 2 m long and is composed of numerous pendulous spikes. Unfortunately this majestic palm appears to be unknown in cultivation in Australia but it would make an impressive addition to a park or large garden. Taxonomically this species has had a very confused history and has been known under the names *C. aequatorialis*, *C. obtusa* var. *aequatorialis* and *C. rumphiana* var. *javanica*.

Caryota mitis
Clustered Fishtail Palm

A very widespread palm which extends from India to the Philippines and the island of Java in Indonesia. As well it is widely cultivated in many tropical and subtropical regions of the world and is a familiar garden palm. It forms a characteristic cluster of closely placed stems and the crowns together produce a crowded mass of the attractive, bipinnate leaves with their unusual fish-tail leaflets. It is an excellent garden palm and while plants in the tropics may reach more than 5 m tall those in cooler districts rarely achieve these proportions. It is sufficiently hardy to be grown in a warm position in temperate regions. It is quite a long-lived palm and although each stem is monocarpic and dies when the fruit matures on the lowermost inflorescence each is replaced by new basal suckers. Requirements are well-drained, rich soil and plenty of water. The plants are especially responsive to applications of

A suckering clump of *Caryota mitis*.

An inflorescence of *Caryota mitis*.

nitrogenous fertilisers. They will tolerate full sun when quite small and are fast growing. Young specimens make excellent indoor plants but disliked dry, dusty atmosphere. They can be propagated by division of the suckers or from seed which usually takes four to six months to germinate. The fruit should be handled with care as they contain stinging crystals.

Caryota no
Giant Fishtail Palm

This is the biggest of all the fishtail palms and is a true majestic giant in all respects. Plants may grow to more than 25 m tall and have a crown of obliquely arching to horizontal fronds which have stiff pinnae and pendulous leaflets. Individual fronds may grow to 4 m long and be nearly 3 m wide. The grey trunk is stout and bulging in a manner reminiscent of *Roystonea regia*. Inflorescences which may measure over 2.5 m long carry cream flowers or large black fruit each of which contains two seeds. The species is native to lowland areas of Borneo. This species appears to be unknown in Australia but would be an excellent palm for the tropical lowlands. It has also been known as *Caryota rumphiana* var. *borneensis*.

Caryota obtusa
Fishtail Palm

This palm from mountainous regions of northern India is a solitary species similar in many respects to *C. urens*, but its leaflets are blunt and rounded at the tips. It is not commonly encountered in cultivation and if anything is more cold tolerant than most of the other species in this genus with the possible exception of *C. ochlandra*. It is monocarpic and requires similar cultural conditions to *C. urens*. Propagation is from seed which may germinate erratically. This palm has also been known as *C. rumphiana* var *indica*.

Caryota ochlandra
Chinese Fishtail Palm

This is probably the most cold tolerant of all the species of *Caryota*. It is a solitary palm with a large crown of bluish green, bipinnate leaves and may grow to about 8 m tall. The leaflets tends to be narrower and blunter than in most other species and with jagged margins. They are densely clustered at the base of each frond. Like other solitary *Caryota* species it is monocarpic, usually beginning to flower after ten to fifteen years. As the

173

common name suggests it is native to China, being found in the region of Canton. Young plants appreciate protection from direct sun but once established will tolerate considerable exposure. Light to medium frosts cause little obvious damage. Propagate from seed which may germinate sporadically over six to eight months. Fruit contain stinging crystals and should be handled with care.

Caryota rumphiana
Fishtail Palm

This is a variable palm which extends from the Moluccas through New Guinea to Australia. The typical form is from the Moluccas and is a large, solitary fishtail palm with stiffly spreading fronds and round fruit each containing a solitary seed. In New Guinea the species is represented as the var. *papuana* which is basically similar to the form found in Australia (var. *australiensis* see page 111). Forms of *C. rumphiana* from countries west of the Moluccas are referable to other species (see *C. maxima* and *C. no*).

Caryota urens
Solitary Fishtail Palm

Although native to the tropics (India, Burma and Sri Lanka) and widely grown there, this large, impressive palm has proved to be sufficiently adaptable to survive in warm, temperate regions. It is a solitary species with a large, thick, ringed grey trunk and a head of arching, bipinnate fronds. Unfortunately these majestic palms are monocarpic and die once the fruit on the lowermast inflorescence matures. They are however an excellent and impressive garden plant and add that tropical flavour. They will tolerate sun when quite small and like a deep, rich soil with plenty of water. They are also very responsive to applications of nitrogenous fertilisers. Once established in good conditions they can be quite fast growing and can easily reach 20 m tall. Young plants make very useful tub specimens for indoor and foyer decoration. In their native countries of India and Malaysia the sap is tapped via the inflorescence and used to make alcoholic drinks or palm sugar. The trunk also contains an edible sago. Propagation is from seed which germinates in two to four months. The fruit contain stinging crystals and should be handled with care and on no account eaten.

Caryota urens.

Chamaedorea

A large genus of 133 species of palms restricted to Mexico, the West Indies and South America. They are small to tall, slender palms, with leaves that may be entire or pinnate with few to many pinnae. Their stems may be solitary or clustered and are cane or bamboo-like. The plants are dioecious with the inflorescence of the male plants being a spike and those of the female a panicle. In some of the solitary species the male and female plants have a slightly different morphology. They mainly grow in shady conditions such as in rainforests. As a group they have tremendous horticultural appeal and because of their size make excellent garden plants. A few are grown in Australia but there is plenty of scope for the introduction of more species. There is considerable confusion amongst horticulturists as to the correct names of some of the species that are grown and hybridism is common, adding to the difficulty. The genera *Collinia*, *Eleutheropetalum* and *Neanthe* are now included with *Chamaedorea*.

Chamaedorea ahrenbergiana

Widespread from Guatemala to Panama, this

elegant *Chamaedora* may grow in excess of 2.5 m tall. It is a solitary species with a slender, prominently stepped trunk about 2.5 cm thick, ending in a sparse crown of about six leaves which may be nearly 2 m long. Each leaf has up to fifteen pairs of widely scattered, broad leaflets which can grow to 30 cm long and over 15 cm wide. These are a dull, deep-green colour. Flower spikes are orange and the ovoid fruit, about 0.8 cm long are black when ripe. A shady situation in the tropics or subtropics is most suitable for this species.

Chamaedorea brachypoda

A slender, clumping palm from Guatemala which at least in the tropics grows in fairly rapidly spreading clumps (it is slow elsewhere). It likes a shady, moist position in organically rich soil and grows to about 2 m tall. Spread is by underground shoots which emerge at intervals from the parent plant. The trunks are very slender (about 1 cm thick) and bear entire, satiny, glaucous, green leaves which are deeply notched at the apex. This is a lovely garden palm that at present is mainly to be found in the collections of

enthusiasts. It deserves to become widely grown but will probably be restricted by lack of propagating material at least until a reliable seed source can be obtained. Plants of this species are sometimes incorrectly sold as *C. stolonifera*, a distinct species from Mexico.

Chamaedorea cataractarum

A trunkless Mexican palm each growth of which splits and separates to form two growths and eventually develops into sparse, slowly spreading clumps. Each crown bears two to six upright to arching, dark-green, pinnate leaves, the terminal leaflets of which are undifferentiated from the rest. The flowerstalk, which grows to about 50 cm tall, arises from the basal axils and bears yellowish flowers. The reddish fruit are about 0.4 cm across. At present this interesting palm is essentially a collectors item but a well-grown plant resembles a clump of small Kentia palms and looks most attractive in a large pot. As the species grows well inside houses it should become a very popular palm for home and office decoration in the future. Outside it needs shady, moist conditions in well-drained, organically rich soil and is

The clumping palm, *Chamaedorea brachypoda*.

The inflorescence of *Chamaedorea cataractarum*.

an ideal garden palm. There seems to be confusion between this species and *C. atrovirens* also from Mexico.

Chamaedorea concolor

A small, solitary palm from Mexico which develops a slender stem (2 cm thick) which is ridged at each node and bears a few aerial roots. It grows 1-2 m tall and bears shiny, bright-green, pinnate leaves scattered near the top. These have broad leaflets with drawn-out, slender tips. Its flowers are bright orange and are followed by red fruit about 0.5 cm long. The species is best suited to tropical and subtropical regions and has proved to be rather sensitive to cold. It requires shady, moist conditions for best growth and appearance.

Chamaedorea costaricana

In general appearance this clumping palm from Costa Rica closely resembles both *C. microspadix* and *C. erumpens*. The former species has bright orange fruit while those of the others are black. *C. costaricana* has longer, more closely spaced leaves

that are dull rather than shiny dark green. Plants of *C. costaricana* tend to be more cold tolerant and survive quite happily in a protected situation in temperate regions. They will grow in full shade (in fact young plants demand this protection) but once established will withstand considerable exposure to sun, especially if kept well watered and mulched. It can be propagated readily by seed or division of the clumps. One interesting characteristic of this species is the formation of suckers or lateral growths above ground level. As a tub plant it is quite handsome and is very useful for indoor decoration.

Chamaedorea elatior
Climbing Chamaedorea

Unusual for this genus, this palm is a climber with its slender, solitary trunk threading its way through surrounding vegetation and being supported by spreading, somewhat-recurved, dark-green, pinnate leaves. It is rarely encountered except in botanical collections and seems best suited to a shady position in tropical and subtropical regions. As its stem needs support it is

Chamaedorea costaricana is a strong-growing, clumping palm.

Chamaedorea elegans, the very popular indoor Parlour Palm.

best grown among shrubbery or over a suitable frame or tree. Plants can be quite fast growing and for seed production should be planted in clumps. The round fruit are black when ripe and about 0.7 cm across. It is native to Mexico and Guatemala.

Chamaedorea elegans
Parlour Palm

This slender, dwarf palm is very popular for indoor decoration and is propagated by the thousands each year in the nursery trade. It is native to Mexico and Guatemala and the solitary trunk which may grow to 3 m tall is very slender and woody with numerous closely spaced growth rings. The pinnate leaves are dark green and ascend in an upright crown. The leaf sheaths frequently have a prominent, white margin. The fruit are about 0.5 cm long and black when ripe. Plants are diocious and a single specimen is incapable of producing fruit. As well as being ideal for indoor decoration the plants can also be grown outdoors in a cool, moist position protected from hot sun and drying winds. It can be grown from temperate to tropical regions although severe frosts may damage the leaves. A fine-leaf form with narrow pinnae is much in demand. *C. elegans* is frequently sold in the nursery trade as *Neanthe bella* and is sometimes also placed in the genus *Collinia*.

Chamaedorea ernesti-augusti

Distributed from Mexico to Honduras, this small palm grows as an understory plant in shady rainforest. The slender, solitary trunk grows to about 1 m tall and has numerous, prominent, pale, annular rings. Its leaves are simple and like those of *C. geonomiformis* are deeply notched like a fishes tail. When in flower it is quite spectacular with panicles of bright-scarlet flowers. This little slow-growing palm is rare in cultivation and is a collectors gem. It can be grown in warm-temperate and subtropical regions and likes a shady, moist situation. It can be propagated from seed which may take three to four months to germinate. There seems to be considerable confusion in Australia between the identity of this species and *C. geonomiformis* which is very rare in cultivation.

Chamaedorea erumpens

Palms sold in Australian nurseries as this species are usually *C. microspadix*, a similar but quite dis-

Chamaedorea ernesti-augusti, a male plant in flower.

Chamaedorea ernesti-augusti, a female plant in flower.

tinct species. The true *C. erumpens* seems to be rarely grown and can be distinguished by its shorter, glossy leaves (45-50 cm long) and its black fruit about 0.6 cm across. Like *C. microspadix* it is a clumping palm with fairly broad, somewhat falcate leaflets that are glossy green on both surfaces. The stems grow to about 4 m tall and the plants form an attractive clump for the garden. Native to Guatemala and British Honduras the species appears best suited to tropical and subtropical conditions.

Chamaedorea geonomiformis

This delightful, small palm consists of a single, slender trunk that may grow to 1.5 cm tall and a crown of dark-green, simple leaves each of which resembles a large fishes tail. The leaves are shiny, thin-textured and have prominent veins. Small branching racemes or spikes are borne at regular intervals from the lower leaves and carry cream flowers followed by reddish fruit. This palm makes an attractive pot plant and also looks good planted in a shady pot, especially among ferns. Once established the plants are quite hardy. Although originating in Honduras the species has proved to be adaptable, growing in warm-temperate regions as well as the tropics. Seed germinates easily but early plant growth is very slow. There seems to be considerable confusion in Australia between the identity of this species and *C. ernesti-augusti* and most plants are of the latter.

Chamaedorea glaucifolia

This slender, single-trunked, Mexican palm may get quite tall, reaching to over 6 m in height (and less than 2.5 cm thick) although plants in cultivation are usually much less. Its most conspicuous feature is the nearly 2 m long pinnate leaves which have numerous narrow leaflets that are covered by a powdery bloom on both surfaces. These leaflets are spaced unequally and are borne in several ranks. The fronds spread in a loose crown from the top of the slender trunk which is ridged at each node. Fruit are relatively small (0.6 cm long) and green when ripe. The species is best suited to tropical and subtropical regions and requires shady conditions.

Chamaedorea karwinskyana

A collectors palm that originates in the shady forests of Mexico. It is a slender, clumping species with bamboo-like stems which grow 2-3 m tall and bear pinnate leaves scattered along their length. These are 40-60 cm long and have 12-16 pairs of leaflets the terminal ones of which are hardly differentiated from the others. These leaflets are bright, shiny green on both surfaces, lanceolate in outline and come off the rhachis at an oblique angle. In general appearance this species is similar to many of the other clumping Chamaedoreas. Like them it prefers shady, moist conditions in the tropics or subtropics.

Chamaedorea klotzschiana

Essentially a collectors items in Australia and New Zealand this small palm grows readily in shady positions. It is native to Mexico and will grow as far south as Sydney. It has a slender, solitary trunk enlarged at the nodes and a small crown of leaves which have broad, dark-green leaflets arranged in sporadic groups along the rhachis. Palms of this species also make attractive pot plants.

Chamaedorea metallica is an extremely decorative small palm.

The leaves of *Chamaedorea metallica* have a metallic sheen.

Chamaedorea microspadix is the very commonly grown Bamboo Palm.

The colourful fruit of *Chamaedorea microspadix*.

Chamaedorea metallica

The dark blue-green leaves of this small palm have an interesting metallic sheen that particularly shows to advantage when wet. They are simple and roughly heart-shaped with a deeply notched apex and are mottled and barred with dark green markings. The slender, solitary trunk grows to about 1 m tall and bears aerial roots at intervals along its length. The flowers are generally inconspicuous and the black fruit are about

0.5 cm long. It likes a cool, shady situation with plenty of water and is best suited to tropical and subtropical regions. Young plants of this palm are highly ornamental and look most attractive if closely planted in groups or in pots. Male and female plants have a slightly different and distinctive appearance. This species has been confused with *C. tenella*.

Chamaedorea microspadix
Bamboo Palm

A wonderful, clumping palm that makes an admirable plant for either indoor decoration or for a shady spot in the garden. Under good conditions it is quite a fast grower and forms a dense clump spreading by suckers. The stems which are bamboo-like and grow to about 3 m tall have pinnate, dull-green leaves scattered along their length. The terminal pair of pinnae are united and fishtail-like. The stems bear clusters of bright orange-red fruit at intervals through the warmer months of the year. This palm is quite hardy once established but for best appearance needs plenty of water during dry periods. It is equally at home in a shady situation in the tropics or in a protected position in temperate regions. Large clumps transplant easily and can also be divided into new plants. The seeds germinate readily within two to three months of sowing. It is native to Mexico. Plants of this species are readily available in Australia but are often mistakingly sold as *C. erumpens* (this species has glossy leaflets and black fruit).

Chamaedorea oblongata

A slender, solitary palm that is widespread from Mexico to Nicaragua, growing in shady forests. The trunk, which may grow to 3 m tall, is about 2 cm thick and prominently ridged at each node. The pinnate leaves with rather broad, bright, shiny-green, somewhat-twisted or contorted leaflets are borne in a small, sparse crown. Flowers are bright orange and are followed by fruit which are about 0.6 cm long and dark green when ripe. This is an attractive small palm suitable for mingling in a shaded shrubbery or the like. It will succeed in warm-temperate, subtropical and tropical regions.

Chamaedorea pinnatifrons

Shady forests of Venezuela are the natural habitat of this slender, solitary palm which may

The shiny leaves of *Chamaedorea oblongata*.

grow to 3.5 m tall. Young plants are fast growing and often flower within two years of germination. They have a pale-green trunk 4-5 cm thick and in the young stages this may have attractive cream to white tonings. Pinnate leaves may reach 50 cm long and have numerous thin-textured, pale-green, lanceolate leaflets. Inflorescences are ivory white and later as they mature become pinkish and bear small, ovoid, reddish-black fruit. A very easy and rewarding palm to grow, this species favours moist, shady conditions. It is best suited to group planting. Many plants, believed to be this species, have been sold in Queensland nurseries in recent years.

Chamaedorea radicalis

An unusual habit of this small palm is that the inflorescences arise from below or just near ground level and are erect with bright yellow to orange flowers. Native to Mexico, this palm grows in cool, shady rainforests where it forms a sparse clump with the trunks usually remaining short or being absent. The pinnate leaves are dark green and are usually held fairly stiffly erect. The terminal leaflets are enlarged and fishtail-like. Fruit are about 0.6 cm across and orange. The species is easily grown in a shady, moist position and will succeed in temperate and subtropical regions. It can be propagated by seed which may take three to four months to germinate or by division of the clumps. Plants can flower when very young.

Chamaedorea seifrizii

This elegant Mexican palm has been something of a collectors item but in recent years has become more common. In Australia many wrongly labelled plants are passed as it. The species can be readily recognised by its stiff, erect, clumping habit and the dark-green, finely pinnate leaves scattered up the stems (leaflets less than 2 cm wide). The clumps are generally narrow and the stems are a pale bluish green which provides a pleasant contrast to the dark leaves. Bright-orange flowers are followed by greenish-black fruit about 0.4 cm long. It is indeed an attractive palm and one well worthy of garden culture or as an indoor plant. Clumps will grow to 3 m tall and prefer shady conditions with plenty of water during dry periods. Propagation is from seed which germinates readily or by division of the clumps. This species hybridizes freely with other members of the genus.

Chamaedorea sp
Elfin Palm

An undescribed palm from Costa Rica which is truly a collectors delight. It is dwarf in every respect, being trunkless and having a crown of fronds which are no more than 30 cm long. These arch from the ground in a rosette and impart a strong, fern-like appearance to the plant. They are symmetrically pinnate, a bright, glossy green and have an attractive wing along the rhachis. Any doubt about the plant being a palm is dispelled upon the appearance of the inflorescences which are a simple, fleshy spike. At fruiting these are brilliant orange and carry shiny black, rounded fruit that are quite large for the size of the plant. In nature this species inhabits shady forest floors. It grows easily in cultivation and deserves to become widely grown; at this stage its spread is limited by lack of propagating material.

Chamaedorea tenella

A small, slow-growing palm from Mexico which rarely reaches more than 80 cm tall. It has a slen-

Chamaedorea radicalis is a small trunkless palm.

Chamaedorea seifrizii is colourful in fruit.

der trunk and a crown of broad, pinnate leaves which are shiny and fairly thick textured. The leaflets have sparse teeth along the margins. In cultivation it requires shady, moist conditions and is best suited to tropical and subtropical regions. This species has been confused with *C. metallica*.

Chamaedorea tepejilote

A very slender palm from Mexico with an interesting trunk which has swollen nodes and closely resembles bamboo. The trunks are solitary with numerous annular rings and produce conspicuous aerial roots from the lower nodes. In very humid situations these roots eventually contact the soil and grow normally. The trunks can grow to 3-7 m tall and at the apex have a loose crown of dark green pinnate fronds which may be nearly 1 m broad. Flowers are orange and the fruit (about 1.5 cm long) are black when ripe. A shady position is essential and the species can be quite fast growing. Tropical and subtropical regions are most suitable.

Chamaerops

A monotypic genus of palm found in southern Europe and northern Africa. The species is a tough, fan palm which may have solitary or multiple trunks. It is very decorative as well as hardy and is a familiar sight in municipal gardens of temperate Australia.

Chamaerops humilis
European Fan Palm

This handsome palm is widespread around the Mediterranean coast of southern Europe and northern Africa. It is the most widespread palm native to Europe and is a widely cultivated and very hardy species. It is extremely variable in growth habit and plants may have one to many trunks, be dwarf or tall and with green or glaucous leaves. The form most commonly met with in Australia forms a low, bushy clump with several trunks and glaucous green leaves. The petioles are strongly spined and rather unfriendly. This palm is very hardy and best suited to temperate regions, being slow and somewhat difficult in the tropics. It is cold tolerant and remains unaffected by heavy frosts. The palms prefer a sunny position and are adaptable to a variety of soils but will not tolerate poor drainage. The species is dioe-

A typical clump of *Chamaerops humilis* (above) and (below) *Chamaerops humilis* in fruit.

cious and male and female plants are necessary to produce seed. Plants of the variety *elatior* have solitary, tall trunks.

Chambeyronia

A small genus of two species of palms restricted to New Caledonia where they grow in rainforests. They are solitary, very attractive, feather-leaved palms and are deserving of much wider cultivation. They are closely related to Kentia palms and part of a fairly confused group.

Chambeyronia macrocarpa

This handsome New Caledonian palm is rarely grown in Australia, probably because of lack of propagating material. It is a striking species with a slender trunk and a crown of dark-green, curved, pinnate fronds. These are a brilliant reddish-orange when young and are quite spectacular. Plants are very slow growing and each new frond may take up to five months to expand. Plants take many years to mature and produce fruit which are crimson when ripe. Its neat habit makes it a very desirable garden subject. The plants like well-drained, organically rich soil and need a shady position at least for the first few years. Although fairly tropical in its requirements plants are known to succeed as far south as Sydney.

Chrysalidocarpus

A genus of twenty species of palms restricted to Madagascar and nearby islands. They are solitary or clumping, feather-leaves palms with many attractive features. Only a couple of species are commonly grown but these have proved to be excellent horticultural subjects and more should be tried. The commonest species grown, *C. lutescens*, is often sold in nurseries as *Areca lutescens*.

Chrysalidocarpus cabadae
Cabada Palm

A suckering palm which forms large, spreading clumps to more than 7 m tall and 5 m across. It is reputedly a fast-growing species and could be an ideal palm for parks. At this stage it is mainly to be found in botanical collections. The crown on each trunk is quite long and drawn out by comparison with *C. lutescens* and the leaves and leaf-bases are dark green. The trunks are also green, much thicker and prominently swollen at the base. Native to Madagascar the species seems most suitable for tropical regions.

Chrysalidocarpus lucubensis

In nature this palm is restricted to the island of Nossi Be which is off the coast of Madagascar. The species is in fact closely related to *C. madagascariensis* and is included as a variety of it by some authors. Despite its fairly remote natural occurrence the species was introduced into cultivation many years ago and is now widely grown and

esteemed as a horticultural subject. It thrives best in the tropics but can also be successful in the subtropics, although plants may suffer cold damage in their early years. In the tropics it is a very fast growing palm and appreciates deep, rich soils and plenty of moisture. Most plants have a solitary trunk but occasional specimens branch to form a pair. Mature plants have a stately, graceful appearance and the palm is ideal for home gardens as well as for parks and avenues. They are also very useful in coastal districts tolerating a fair degree of exposure to salt-laden winds. Seed germinates readily.

Chrysalidocarpus lutescens
Golden Cane Palm or Butterfly Palm

The common name of this palm arises from the clumps of slender, golden stems and leaf stalks that each plant produces. These grow up to 10 m tall and each is topped with a crown of twisted, yellowish green, pinnate fronds. New canes are produced from the base of the clump as the older canes mature. This spineless and very decorative palm is native to Madagascar where it grows in thickets. The golden colouration is especially pronounced in starved specimens or those grown

Chambeyronia macrocarpa.

Chrysalidocarpus lucubensis.

Chrysalidocarpus lutescens is a large clumping palm adaptable to a wide range of climates.

in a very hot, sunny position. The plants are dioecious and male and female are necessary for seed production. Golden Cane palm is very popular in the tropics but can even be grown in temperate regions as there are some large clumps in old Melbourne gardens. It is, however, rather cold sensitive when young. It prefers a sunny position in rich, well-drained soils. It is often sold in the nursery trade as *Areca lutescens*. Seed germinates easily but may take four to five months.

Chrysalidocarpus madagascariensis

As the specific name indicates this species is native to the island of Madagascar where it is widespread and locally common. It is a clumping palm with fairly thick, prominently ringed grey stems which may grow to 8 m or more tall. Each stem has a fairly sparse crown of plumose fronds. Although this species and the previous one are both clumping palms the habit of each is very different. *C. lutescens* forms a dense crowded clump while those of *C. madagascariensis* are open and sparse by comparison. The latter species is uncommonly grown in Australia but will succeed

in tropical, subtropical and perhaps warm-temperate regions. *C. lucubensis* bears many similarities to this species and is sometimes regarded as being a single-trunked variety of it.

Clinostigma

A genus of thirteen species of palm distributed through various Pacific islands. They are solitary palms with finely divided, pinnate leaves and a conspicuous crownshaft. A few species, previously placed in the genus *Exorrhiza*, have prominent stilt roots at the base of the trunk. As a genus they are handsome palms but are rarely grown.

Clinostigma samoense

An incredibly beautiful palm from Samoa where it grows in protected situations in high rainfall forests. The most notable feature of the species is its crown of very finely divided fronds. These spread gracefully and have strongly drooping, long-pointed leaflets. This graceful crown tops a prominent, pale-green crownshaft and a slender, prominently ringed grey trunk which grows to about 12 m tall. Inflorescences are intricately and finely branched and the fruit are small and unusually humped. The performance of this lovely palm in cultivation is largely unknown. A few plants are in the collections of enthusiasts and it is to be hoped that they succeed with its culture. In nature it grows in well-drained soils in an area with an extremely high and evenly spread annual rainfall.

Coccothrinax

An interesting genus of twenty species of solitary, fan palms which are predominately developed in the West Indies and have a couple of species found in adjacent areas. Although they are uncommonly grown in Australia some species are extremely attractive and deserve to be more widely known. Most species are ideally suited to garden culture, having a slender trunk and being of only moderate size. Species are often confused with those of the genus *Thrinax* but can be readily distinguished by the solid, non-splitting leaf bases and the fleshy, purple-black fruit.

Coccothrinax alta

A slender palm from Puerto Rico which grows to approximately 8 m tall. It has a naked trunk which is 10-15 cm thick and a graceful crown of broad leaves which have prominent, drooping segments. These are dark green above and silvery beneath. Like most species of *Coccothrinax* this palm has small, blackish fruit. Plants are very slow growing and take many years to make a trunk. They like an open, sunny situation and can be grown in subtropical and tropical zones.

Coccothrinax argentata
Silver Palm

Although mainly grown in enthusiasts collections this fan palm is deserving of much wider cultivation. It has many interesting features including a trunk covered with woven fibres, and deeply divided leaves which have drooping leaflets which are dark green and glossy above and silvery white beneath. These contrast attractively when the leaves move in the wind. Silver Palms are fairly slow growing and this is their main drawback although they may flower when quite small. They will tolerate sun when quite small and need an open, sunny position in very well-drained soil. Plants will withstand almost as much coastal exposure as the coconut. Once established the plants are quite hardy but for best appearance should be watered during dry periods. Seeds germinate within two to three months of sowing but seedling growth is slow. This palm is native to Florida and the Bahamas and succeeds best in tropical conditions.

Coccothrinax argentea

Although similar in name and general appearance to *C. argentata* this species is quite distinct. It is endemic to the West Indian island of Hispaniola where it grows in colonies in open situations. Its fan leaves are deeply divided into segments which are dull green above and silvery beneath. In old specimens the trunks may reach 10 m tall but plants in cultivation are always much less than this. This palm has proved to be quite adaptable and will grow in temperate as well as tropical regions. It needs well-drained soil in a sunny position. Seed germinates two to four months after sowing and seedling growth is slow.

Coccothrinax crinita

The trunk of this palm is truly remarkable, being completely covered with a thick layer of brown, woolly hair and what is more, this hair is quite conspicuous when the plants are only 10 cm tall. The palm's crown is rather nondescript by comparison to the hairy trunk, consisting of drooping, fan-shaped leaves which are greyish beneath and shiny green above. This palm is a collectors dream and is uncommon to rare in cultivation. It seems to succeed best in tropical regions but may adapt to the subtropics. Young plants are quite tolerant of sunshine and need well-drained soil. Seed germinates fairly readily within two to four months of sowing.

The silvery leaves of *Coccothrinax argentea*.

Coccothrinax dussiana

A graceful fan palm from Guadeloupe which has a slender trunk to 10 m or more tall and a crown of large, fan-shaped leaves which are a shiny, silvery white beneath. Most of the trunk is naked but thick fibre adheres to the upper part just below the leaves. The leaves are not deeply divided into segments and are most attractive as their surfaces alternate in windy weather. This palm succeeds best in tropical regions and needs a sunny position in well-drained soil. Seed germinates two to four months after sowing and grows slowly.

Coccothrinax miraguama

Cuba is the home of this elegant palm, the leaves

Coccothrinax dussiana.

of which make a graceful silhouette against the sky. These leaves are relatively small but very rigid and with the segments widely spaced allow plenty of light to pass through giving the characteristic appearance. They are a shiny, dark-green above and greyish hairy beneath. The majority of the trunk is covered with a closely woven, woollen fibre which adds greatly to the palm's decorative appeal. Although slow growing the species is easy to grow and is suited to tropical and subtropical regions. It is primarily a collectors palm but deserves to be more widely grown. Seeds may take four to six months to germinate.

Coccothrinax readii

Described as recently as 1980, this species hails from the Yucatan Peninsula of Mexico where it is common in near-coastal rainforests and also extends to exposed situations on sand dunes. It is a typical *Coccothrinax* with a slender trunk and a sparse crown of deeply segmented fan leaves carried on very slender, arching petioles. A ready means of identification is that the narrow, triangular hastula is frequently notched at the apex. Although rare in cultivation in Australia seeds of

this species have been distributed to enthusiasts. It would probably require similar cultural conditions to *C. dussiana*.

Cocos

A monotypic genus of palms the solitary species of which (the Coconut) is widespread throughout the tropics. Other palms have previously been included in the genus *Cocos* but have now been transferred to other genera (for example, *Acrocomia, Arecastrum, Butia* and *Microcoelum*). Many nurserymen still sell plants of *Arecastrum* and *Microcoelum* under the incorrect name of *Cocos*, probably because it is shorter and easier to spell. For the occurrence of the Coconut in Australia see page 112.

Cocos nucifera
Coconut

The coconut is of tremendous significance to man not only because of its large, edible nuts but also because of the other numerous uses to which its parts can be put (see page 38). Although most familiar in its natural habitat lining tropical sandy beaches, the Coconut will also grow in warm inland areas and on near-coastal tablelands (eg Atherton Tableland). The secret for its success seems to be a warm climate and access to underground water. Coconuts are widely planted in coastal districts as far south as Sydney but they rarely fruit in the subtropics or further south. There are numerous varieties of Coconuts suited to different climatic regions, bearing nuts of different sizes and tall or dwarf growing. They make an excellent street tree (although the plants tend to lean) and are widely planted in gardens of the tropics. Their ability to withstand severe coastal conditions is unparalleled in palms. Coconuts germinate readily in warm temperatures after five to six months and their subsequent growth is quite fast.

Copernicia

A genus of twenty-five species of palms distributed in Cuba, Central and South America. They are solitary or clumping with stiff, deeply divided, fan-shaped leaves. Most species are impressive or indeed spectacular palms but are rarely grown in Australia or New Zealand and seem to be restricted to botanical collections or those of enthusiasts. One species is of commercial significance in the production of wax.

The Coconut *(Cocos nucifera)* is commonly naturalised on the beaches of northern Qld.

The colourful fruit of the Coconut cultivar Malay Dwarf.

Copernicia baileyana

The most spectacular feature of this palm is its huge, deeply segmented, bright-green fan leaves which are at first stiffly erect then as they age are held at greater angles, the tips of the segments eventually becoming lax and drooping. The crown of the palm is large and crowded with the leaves almost overlapping. Plants about ten years old look most impressive then as they begin to develop a trunk they take on a different appearance. Native to Cuba the plants prefer a sunny position in tropical or subtropical regions although they will grow in partial shade. Well-drained soil is essential for success. Seeds germinate in about three to four months and seedlings grow slowly.

Copernicia macroglossa
Cuban Petticoat Palm

This must be one of the most spectacular of all palms and its a pity that it is only a collectors item in Australia and New Zealand. The plants bear a spiral crown of closely packed, almost stalkless, glossy-green leaves but the most remarkable feature is the dense brown petticoat formed by the

187

dead leaves. This petticoat is a solid mass of closely packed, dead leaves and in plants up to about twenty-five years old extends right to the ground. Individual leaves are about 2 m across and are deeply divided into stiff, pointed segments. The Cuban Petticoat Palm likes a sunny aspect in well-drained soil. It should be grown in subtropical and tropical regions. Seeds are reported to germinate readily but plants are very slow growing. This species was previously known as *C. torreana*.

Copernicia prunifera
Carnauba Wax Palm

In Brazil where this palm is native, it is widely grown in commercial plantations for the production of carnauba wax. This wax is harvested from the leaves and used for a wide variety of purposes. The export is worth millions of dollars to Brazil and research programmes are underway to produce high-yielding cultivars. The palms grow to about 10 m tall and have a large, rounded crown of deeply divided, fan-shaped leaves held on long petioles. The trunk is very hard and patterned with the bases of fallen leaves. Although quite ornamental this palm seems to be rarely grown

Corypha umbraculifera, a young plant.

outside its natural habitat and has only recently been introduced into Australia. It is probably well suited to subtropical conditions. Seed takes eight to ten months to germinate. This species was previously known as *C. cerifera*.

Corypha

A genus of eight species of palms distributed from India to the Philippines with a single widespread species extending to northern Australia. They are solitary palms with large costapalmate leaves. All species are monocarpic, producing a terminal panicle containing numerous, small, bisexual flowers. Plants of this genus are rarely grown in Australia. For notes on the species of *Corypha* in Australia see page 112.

Corypha umbraculifera
Talipot Palm

This giant palm is suitable only for very large gardens, parks and acreage planting since it develops into an immense plant before eventually flowering, fruiting and dying. Individual leaves may be more than 5 m across (the broadest of all palms) and hence one can imagine the space occupied by a single plant. The large, leathery, bright-green, costapalmate leaves are carried on a stout petiole about 4 m long. This petiole has numerous small teeth along the margin. Younger parts of the trunk are covered with persistent leaf bases. Plants grow for thirty to eighty years, achieving heights of 12 to 25 m before flowering. Flowering plants are an impressive sight indeed with a terminal panicle more than 6 m high and bearing millions of tiny, cream flowers. These are followed by dull-green, rounded fruit which mature about twelve months after flowering (after which the palm dies). Talipot palms are quite hardy in cultivation but have limited appeal because of their awesome size. They are also very slow growing. Once established, plants are very hardy to dryness and other adverse conditions. The species is native to India and Ceylon and grows best in tropical zones.

Cryosophila

A small genus of eight species of palms native to Mexico and Central America. They are solitary, fan-leaved palms and one species is well known because of root spines on its trunk. They are primarily of interest to collectors and are rarely encountered in Australia.

Cryosophila warscewiczii
Rootspine Palm

The trunk of this palm is its most distinctive feature being covered with short spines which are in fact aerial roots. These are called rootspines and are frequently branched. If in contact with the soil the lowest ones may take root. The palm is native to Panama and is a tall, slender species with a crown of large, fan-shaped leaves. These may be 2 m across and are dark green above and greyish beneath. Plants are rather cold sensitive and are best suited to the tropics but will also succeed in a warm position in subtropical regions.

Cyphophoenix

A monotypic genus endemic to New Caledonia and similar in appearance to *Howea*. The species is a handsome, solitary, feather-leaved palm that is rarely grown.

Cyphophoenix elegans

A rather tough-looking but elegant palm which grows on windswept ridges of New Caledonia, sometimes extending to more than 1200 m altitude. It is rarely grown in Australia probably because of lack of propagating material but is deserving of much wider recognition. Its slender trunk is topped by a relatively small, neat crown of greyish green, spreading fronds each of which has a recurved tip. These fronds are relatively stiff and tough, apparently withstanding wind quite well. The plants appreciate a well-drained, organically rich soil and need a shady position at least for the first few years. They are apparently fairly adaptable to different climates and will grow as far south as Sydney.

Cyphosperma

A monotypic genus of feather-leaved palm restricted to New Caledonia.

Cyphosperma balansae

This is a very rare and little-known collectors palm from New Caledonia where it grows in dense rainforest. It is a handsome, feather-leaved palm with a solitary trunk and a crown of dark-green fronds which have long, pointed pinnae. Its inflorescences are widely spreading and much-branched and are carried at the base of the crownshaft. Little is known about the cultural requirements of this palm as there are no mature plants in Australia. It probably requires shade, certainly when young, and a well-drained, organic soil with water during dry periods.

Cyrtostachys

A small genus of eight species of palm mainly developed in New Guinea and the Solomon Islands. They are clumping, feather-leaved palms and a couple of species are renowned for their colourful crownshafts. Most species are ornamental but are very sensitive to cold and therefore strictly tropical.

Cyrtostachys glauca

A clumping palm from the rainforests of New Guinea which should be an attractive acquisition to tropical gardens. Like some other species in this genus it has a prominent crownshaft but in this case it is markedly glaucous rather than brightly coloured. The leaves have spreading or drooping, bright-green pinnae and the small, dull-brown fruit are borne in clusters below the crownshaft. The species probably requires similar cultural conditions to others in the genus.

Cyrtostachys peekeliana

Although this species does not appear to be grown in Australia it should be for it has excellent prospects in tropical areas. Native to the island of New Britain in New Guinea it is a solitary palm with a slender, prominently ringed trunk and a conspicuous crownshaft below an upright crown of dark green fronds. This combination gives the species a very elegant and tropical appearance. The palms bear a massive, intricately branched inflorescence which at fruiting time carries masses of small, slender black fruit.

Cyrtostachys renda
Sealing Wax Palm or Maharajah Palm

The brilliant, glossy, scarlet leaf bases and petioles which characterise this tropical species make it one of the most colourful and ornamental of all palms. With this colour contrasting with its dark green leaflets and added to the neat, clumping habit it is perhaps surprising that it is not more widely grown than it is at present. There is some suggestion that it is not an easy plant to establish and it is certainly tropical in its requirements. It will grow in shade or full sun and requires plenty of water at all times. The clumps grow to about 4 m tall. The palm is native to Malaysia and grows in near-coastal swamps.

A clump of the beautiful Sealing Wax Palm, *Cyrtostachys renda*.

The brilliant crownshafts of *Cyrtostachys renda*.

Seed should be sown soon after collection as it loses its viability rapidly. Germination usually takes place within two months of sowing. The species was previously very well known as *C. lakka*.

Daemonorops

A large genus of 115 species of palms widely distributed in the Indo-Malaysian regions. They are mostly climbing palms with long, slender, spiny stems and spreading pinnate leaves each with a thorn-bearing cirrus at the tip. A few are dwarf, clumping palms. The fruit are scaly and in some species have a thin layer of edible flesh around the seed. In some countries their slender, flexible stems are harvested for rattan cane, used in furniture manufacture. Very few species of *Daemonorops* are grown in Australia or New Zealand.

Daemonorops angustifolia

A vicious climbing palm from Malaysia where it is common on stream banks frequently forming tangled thickets. Its slender climbing stems are prickly and the spreading, bright-green leaves are divided into numerous, narrow, crowded segments. Each leaf ends in a slender cirrus which is effective at entangling in surrounding vegetation. When damaged the stems of this species bleed white sap. Because of its decidedly unfriendly nature this palm has little to offer for cultivation. Enthusiasts may find some attraction in the graceful fronds. The species succeeds best in tropical regions.

Daemonorops calicarpa

A dwarf clumping palm from Malaysia and Sumatra where it is very common in hilly country and frequently forms colonies in rainforest. The plants are actually trunkless with the stems branching beneath the soil, each bearing a rosette of erect, prickly leaves to 5 m long. The inflorescences are unusual and each terminates an axis which dies after fruit has ripened, and is replaced by new suckers. The flowering axis is a compact, crowded structure borne among the leaf bases and contains reduced leaves, the axils of which bear the dumpy inflorescence. Plants may be male or female. Although unknown in cultivation in Australia this species would be a very interesting palm for a shady position in the tropics.

Deckenia

A monotypic genus of palm endemic to the Seychelles. The single species is a tall, solitary, pinnate-leaved palm with spiny petioles, leaf sheaths and inflorescence spathes.

Deckenia nobilis

A tall palm from the Seychelles which has a slender trunk which may reach more than 35 m in height. This is topped with a graceful crown of dark-green, pinnate leaves. Individual leaflets are slender with a long, pointed tip and are hairy beneath. Sheathing bases and petioles are prickly but this is only obvious on young plants. Ovoid fruit are dark purple when ripe. In its native country of the Seychelles this species is becoming rare, partly through cleaning of its habitat and also because its edible cabbage is collected. In cultivation the palm only grows well in tropical regions and is very sensitive to cold. Many plants grown and sold as this species in Australia are in fact wrongly identified.

Dictyosperma

A monotypic genus of palms from Mauritius and the Seychelles. It is a tall, slender, solitary palm with a crown of pinnate leaves and is fairly commonly grown in Australia in tropical and subtropical regions.

Dictyosperma album
Princess Palm or Hurricane Palm

A rather cold-sensitive palm which is well suited to tropical conditions but will also succeed in subtropical and warm-temperate areas especially in near-coastal districts. It is an excellent palm for the coast, tolerating salt-laden winds quite happily without the burning usually suffered by palms in such areas. In fact, it is frequently called hurricane palm because of its ability to survive such winds. It is a solitary palm with dark-grey, ringed trunk which grows to more than 10 m tall and has a prominent, bright-green, white or reddish crownshaft. The pinnate fronds spread in a graceful crown and when young are frequently reddish. This trait is usually obvious on young plants. The flowers of this palm are large, fragrant and quite showy, being reddish, and are followed by purplish-black fruits in large clusters. One characteristic feature which often serves to identify this species is the habit of the youngest developing frond to stand erect like

Dictyosperma album is an excellent palm for coastal districts in the tropics.

a sentinel. Princess palm originates in Mauritius and the other Mascarene Islands, and is somewhat variable, some having bright-green leaflets with white veins and a whitish crownshaft while others are darker with reddish veins and a coloured crownshaft. These forms have been named as botanical varieties but are really just colour variations of no botanical standing. In cultivation this species needs well-drained, rich soil and a warm, sunny position. Plants respond to nitrogenous fertilisers and water during dry periods. When young they make excellent specimens for indoor decoration. Seed germinates readily within two to three months of sowing. *D. aureum* is also included as a form of this species.

Drymophloeus

A genus of about fifteen species of palms from Indonesia, Samoa and New Guinea. They are solitary, rather slender palms with a crownshaft and broad leaflets which are irregularly cut and notched on the apex. Some species have excellent prospects for cultivation in the tropics, requiring shade and lashings of water. The genus includes those species previously placed in *Coleospadix*.

Drymophloeus beguini

A slender, Indonesian palm which is rarely grown in Australian collections. The plants may grow to about 5 m tall and bear a small but elegant crown of fronds. These have widely spaced, broad segments the apices of which appear as if they have been roughly trimmed. In cultivation the plants need a shady position and liberal applications of mulch and water. They are reported to be cold sensitive and therefore should be grown in the tropics. The juice from the fruit is reported to be irritant.

Drymophloeus oliviformis

As with the previous species, this neat, small, elegant palm is unfortunately little known in Australian collections. It is sincerely hoped that this will be changed soon for the plant has all the hallmarks of a decorative pot or garden subject. It is smaller and more slender than the previous species and the leaflets impart a ruffled appearance to the fronds. It is very sensitive to sunburn and requires a shady, moist position in tropical regions.

Dypsis pinnatifrons is a delightful small palm for the tropics.

Drymophloeus pachychladus

This is a tall, slender palm native to the Solomon Islands. In the rainforest, where they grow naturally, plants may reach 12 m tall and have an elegant, if somewhat untidy, crown of arching or even twisted fronds which have distinctively broad segments. These are shiny green above and dull grey beneath. The crownshaft is prominent and bright green. Mature fruit, about 2 cm long, are elliptical in shape and red when ripe. A few plants are in the collections of enthusiasts in Australia but at this stage the cultural requirements of the species are hardly known. It would probably grow best in the warm, moist, tropical lowlands.

Dypsis

A genus of twenty-one species of palms restricted to the islands of Madagascar where they grow on shady forest floors. They are small, solitary or clumping palms, with entire or pinnate leaves and slender, cane-like stems. As a group they have much to offer horticulture but unfortunately they are rarely seen probably because of the lack of propagating material.

Dypsis pinnatifrons

A delightful Madagascan palm with a sturdy, erect, yet very slender trunk (about 1.5 cm thick) which may exceed 5 m in height. It has pinnate fronds with broad, attractively clustered or whorled leaflets which are dark, shiny, lustrous green. The fronds are scattered up the stem and may sometimes be produced at irregular intervals. The youngest frond is usually pointed and erect, forming the perfect tip to the spear-like stem. Young plants of *D. pinnatifrons* make very attractive pot plants and are also excellent for garden culture in the tropics. Being very sensitive to sun damage they should be grown in a shady, protected position and provided with plenty of moisture. The species was previously known as *D. gracilis*.

Elaeis
Oil Palms

A small genus of two species of palms from Africa and South America. They are solitary, feather-leaved palms with an unusual, large, fruiting body. The seeds and pulp of the fruit are rich in oil and one species is widely grown in plantations in the tropics for this product. The genus *Corozo* from South America is included under *Elaeis*.

Elaeis guineensis is planted commercially for oil production and is also very ornamental.

The fruiting heads of *Elaeis guineensis*.

Elaeis guineensis
African Oil Palm

This palm is extremely important to the economies of countries such as Nigeria because high quality oils are extracted from both the fruit pulp and the kernel of the seed. These oils are exported to industrialised countries where they are used in manufacture and as a lubricant. Oil palm plantations were established in north-eastern Qld before the second world War but did not persist because of the slow growth of the plants. Oil palms are a tough, distinctive plant and a large, healthy specimen is quite ornamental. The large, solid trunk is very rough and bears a crown of spreading, graceful, shiny, green, pinnate fronds. Male and female flowers are borne on separate inflorescences on the same tree and each type is very distinctive. The male inflorescence is a cluster of furry, simple spikes which resembles a hand while the female inflorescence is a dense, compound head. Oil palms thrive best in the tropics but are sufficiently hardy to grow in cool, subtropical areas where their rate of growth is, however, much slower. Once established they are a hardy palm but for best appearance should be watered during dry spells. Epiphytes such as ferns and orchids can be successfully grown on the rough trunks. They do very well in coastal districts and will withstand some salt spray. Well-drained soil is essential and the palms grow well where their roots can tap ground water. The large seeds have a thick shell which may need cracking before satisfactory germination can be achieved. Pre-soaking in hot water and bottom heating of sowing medium are beneficial.

Elaeis oleifera
American Oil Palm

Whereas the trunk of the African Oil Palm is erect, that of its American relative creeps across the ground for many metres before turning upright and growing vertically. Even so, an erect trunk rarely achieves more than 2 m in height. The trunk is covered with the remains of leaf bases and spiny petioles. Leaves grow to about 4 m long and are very wide with the leaflets themselves often being more than 1 m long. The dark-orange fruit are carried in congested heads. They have an oily flesh from which an oil can be expressed and although it is generally inferior to that obtained from the African species. *E. oleifera* originates in Central and South America and grows best in tropical zones. It was previously known as *Corozo oleifera*.

Eleiodoxa

A monotypic genus of Malaysian palms closely related to *Salacca* but with massive terminal inflorescences. The species is a trunkless, clump-forming palm with erect, prickly feather leaves.

Eleiodoxa conferta

E. conferta is a prickly palm from Malaysia where it forms thickets in swampy lowland areas, usually in or near rainforest. The trunks are subterranean and branch freely to form spreading clumps. Each trunk, at its apex, bears a tuft of tall, erect, willowy fronds which have coarse, broad leaflets which are silvery beneath. The petioles, rhachises, and even the midribs of the leaflets are liberally coated with long, sharp, black spines imparting a very formidable appearance. The fruit are about 3 cm long, somewhat pear shaped and covered with overlapping scales which, when ripe, are dull yellow. In cultivation this species likes a hot tropical climate and must be provided with plenty of water. The species was previously called *Salacca conferta*.

Eugeissona

A small genus of about seven species of palms found in Borneo and Malaysia. They are clumping, feather-leaved palms and each steam bears a terminal inflorescence. Plants are interesting but are rarely encountered in cultivation in Australia.

Eugeissona tristis

A rather untidy palm from Malaysia where it is widespread from the lowlands to about 800 m altitude. It usually grows in timbered areas and in favourable sites may dominate the vegetation. Each clump is large and dense and usually contains numerous dead leaves giving an untidy appearance. Individual leaves are held stiffly erect, are crowded, and may grow to 8 m tall. The leaf stalks are spiny. Inflorescences may rise to 3 m tall and carry brownish flowers (with purple pollen) and large fruits (to 10 cm x 5 cm). Immature fruits are edible and the leaves are prized locally for thatching huts. *E. tristis* is a very hardy and interesting palm which will grow in a sunny or shady position in tropical regions.

Euterpe

A genus of eighteen species of palms all found in tropical America. They are solitary, feather-leaved palms with a prominent crownshaft and some species bear a marked, superficial resemblance to species of *Roystonea*. They mainly grow in rainforest and some species have been exploited heavily for their edible cabbage. One species is commonly grown in Australia.

Euterpe edulis
Jucara Palm

Native to Brazil where it is locally common, this palm is widely grown around the world and is a very useful species for indoor decoration, tolerating dark conditions and neglect. It develops a slender, tall trunk that is topped by a prominent crownshaft and graceful, dark-green pinnate fronds which have crowded, drooping leaflets. It bears masses of small, round, brown to black fruit on drooping clusters. The plants are easy to grow and seem best suited to subtropical and temperate regions. They like rich, well-drained soil and young plants need protection from direct sun for the first few years. Seed germination can be markedly improved by leaching in water held at 30°C for seventy-two hours (eighty per cent germination compared with thirty per cent germination untreated after twenty-four days).

Euterpe oleracea
Assai Palm or Acai Palm

The common name of this palm is derived from a thick, refreshing drink which is concocted from the ripe fruit in its native country of Brazil. This

Eugeissonia tristis is a common Malaysian palm.

material can also be used to flavour ice cream and is a very popular product. As well the cabbage is highly regarded so this palm is a very useful member of the community. It is a solitary species with a tall, slender trunk and a graceful crown of finely cut, drooping leaves. Plants can be quite fast growing and revel in deep, rich soils and will also tolerate poor drainage. They will grow very successfully in subtropical and tropical regions and look most attractive when planted in groups.

Gastrococos

A monotypic genus of palm confined to Cuba. The single species is a solitary, feather-leaved palm with a remarkable bulging, spiny trunk. It is rarely grown in Australia.

Gastrococos crispa
Corojo Palm or Cuban Belly Palm

A distinctive palm with a trunk which is supported on a slender base. The trunk itself is very woody and armed with rows of flat spines, a row on each annular ring. The crown of arching fronds is quite dense towards the centre. Individual fronds have numerous leaflets which are

Gaussia attenuata.

dark, glossy green above and prominently glaucous beneath. Each inflorescence is subtended by a large, persistent woody spathe which is covered with brownish fur and spines. The flowers are bright yellow and showy. Solitary plants are capable of setting fruit. *G. crispa* grows well in tropical and subtropical regions. Plants are generally slow but may grow in spurts. They like well-drained soil and plenty of water during the warm months of the year. Native to Cuba, this species was previously known as *Acrocomia armentalis* and *A. crispa*.

Gaussia

A small genus of two species of palm native to Cuba and Puerto Rico. They are solitary, feather-leaved palms which lack a crownshaft. They have an unusual trunk that is swollen near the base and then tapers throughout. They also have a relatively small crown compared to their height and the leaflets are crowded. In nature both species grow in very harsh conditions in skeletal, limestone soils on cliffs and steep slopes. They are rarely to be seen in cultivation in Australia.

Gaussia attenuata

The trunk of this palm is widest at the base (sometimes bulging prominently) and then tapers throughout until it is quite slender just below the crown. It is also unusual because its roots wander prominently across the surface of the soil. Native to Puerto Rico it may reach 30 m tall in nature. Its crown is usually rather depauperate and disappointing as if the plant could do with a good dose of fertiliser. The fruit are round, orange, about 1 cm across and carried in large clusters. In cultivation this palm has proved to be very hardy, succeeding in tropical, subtropical and perhaps even warm-temperate areas (plants are known from Cairns, Brisbane and Sydney). Young plants will tolerate exposure to full sun. An annual dose of lime may be beneficial since in nature this species is restricted to limestone soils. Seeds germinate readily six to eight weeks after sowing.

Gronophyllum

A genus of fourteen species of palms mostly found in New Guinea, Indonesia and the adjacent islands with one in northern Australia and four also being found in the Philippines. They are solitary, generally tall, pinnate-leaved palms with a long crownshaft. Few species are known in cultivation. For notes on the Australian species see page 113.

Gronophyllum chaunostachys

This tall, elegant palm is to be found in the highlands of New Guinea where it juts above the forest canopy. It is a very prominent, stately palm with a crown of attractively arching fronds which have erect and spreading slender leaflets. The trunk is slender, ringed and grey and the crownshaft covered with woolly brown hairs. Bright red, smallish fruit are carried in dense clusters. This palm has many features to offer the enthusiast and should be tried in tropical and subtropical regions.

Heterospathe

A genus of about thirty-two species of palms widespread among the Pacific Islands (New Guinea, Solomons, Philippines, Mariana Islands, etc) and extending to India. They are solitary, feather-leaved palms lacking a crownshaft. As a group they are generally cold sensitive and will succeed only in tropical climates.

Heterospathe elata
Sagisi Palm

This tall, slender palm from the Philippines and adjacent islands is rather cold sensitive and succeeds best in lowland tropical regions although plants are known from the subtropics. It has a large crown of gracefully curving, dark green fronds, and long, tapering leaflets. The young fronds are an unusual pale pink or brownish colour. Small white fruits are borne in dense, hanging clusters among the leaves. In good conditions this palm can be fast growing and young plants may then have an extended crown of graceful fronds. It is mainly of interest for the collector living in the tropics. Seed germinates within two to three months of sowing.

Heterospathe humilis

An attractive New Guinea palm which deserves to be more widely cultivated in tropical gardens. It is a dwarf clumping palm with thin, cane-like stems and small, pinnate or simple leaves. Pinnate and simple-leaved forms may grow side by side in a population and it seems uncertain as to

whether these are juvenile and mature leaves or simply different growth forms. The species grows in shady positions in rainforest.

Heterospathe negrosensis

A slender Philippine palm which occurs naturally in shady rainforests. Its trunk can grow to 5 m tall and reach a diameter of about 5 cm. Pinnae of the leaves are 35-40 cm long and 2.5 cm broad and are generally dark green and shiny. Unlike the other species its inflorescence is sparse, usually with only two branches. An attractive palm for culture in the tropics. Seed takes one to two months to germinate.

Heterospathe philippinensis

The slender trunk of this palm is 2-3 cm thick and can reach 3 m tall. It is a graceful species with the leaves divided into numerous leaflets which are 25-30 cm long. New leaves are a pinkish-bronze colour. The fruit are ovoid and suddenly contracted at the apex into a small point. As the specific name suggests the palm is native to the Philippines where it grows in rainforest at medium altitudes. As with the others species it needs a shady position in a tropical or subtropical area.

Heterospathe sibuyanensis

This is one of the tallest of the Philippine *Heterospathe* species with the trunks growing to 10 m with a thickness of 12 cm. It is characterised by having small brown scales on the underside of the leaflets and a branched inflorescence bearing pointed, conical fruit. It requires a shady aspect in moist soil and is best suited to the tropics.

Heterospathe woodfordiana

New leaves of this slender palm are deep red and colourful, much as those of the delightful *Chambeyronia macrocarpa*. As each matures it becomes deep green and a new frond provides a colourful contrast. The palm has a slender brown trunk which grows about 4 m tall and the leaf sheaths have distinct dark blotches. Pinkish flowers are followed by brilliant red fruit each about 1 cm long. Native to the Solomon Islands the species is only suitable for the tropics.

Hydriastele

A small genus of eight species of palm restricted to New Guinea and northern Australia. They are solitary or clumping feather-leaved palms usually found in swampy situations. Their leaves have a disjunct arrangement of broad pinnae and this imparts a distinctive appearance to the crown. The stems, although slender, may grow very tall. Most species are basically similar in appearance and there is confusion as to their correct names, especially some of those in cultivation. All species are very tropical in their requirements. For notes on the Australian species see page 119.

Hydriastele beccariana

A tall slender palm found in hot steamy lowland jungles of New Guinea. The stems are about 8 cm thick and are topped with a small but dense crown of six to eight fronds. These fronds are dark green, a little over a metre long and more than 65 cm wide. The end pinnae are conjoined and fish-tail like. The trunk also has quite a long, greyish crownshaft and dense, drooping inflorescences arise at its base. This is a solitary palm and is not commonly seen in cultivation. It deserves to be more widely grown and is best suited to lowland tropical regions.

A young Bottle Palm, *Hyophorbe lagenicaulis*.

Hydriastele microspadix

A New Guinea palm which is widespread and common in moist to wet forested areas. It grows in clumps of tall, slender stems and the short leaves have oddly clustered, sharply truncate pinnae. White flowers are produced in mass from short, branched inflorescences and are followed by round, bright-red fruit. The species deserves to be widely grown but unfortunately it is hardly known. It would be best suited to tropical districts.

Hydriastele rostrata

A clumping palm from New Guinea where it grows in lowland swamps in hot, humid conditions. Its slender trunks may grow to more than 10 m tall and have a dull green crownshaft which has a roughened texture and a small crown of few fronds. The fronds may be 2 m long and have well-scattered, irregularly placed leaflets which are dull green and have irregularly cut tips. This is a rather tall but impressive palm that should be more frequently grown. It would appear to be rather cold sensitive and suitable only for tropical regions. The plants like wet conditions.

Hyophorbe

A small genus of five species of palms which are endemic to Madagascar and Mauritius. All are interesting species with a solitary trunk (which may be grotesquely swollen) a prominent crownshaft and a fairly small crown of pinnate leaves. A couple of species are popular subjects for cultivation which is fortunate because all species must be considered to be endangered in their native state. (*H. amaricaulis* is today known only from a solitary plant.) The genus was previously known as *Mascarena*.

Hyophorbe lagenicaulis
Bottle Palm

An intriguing palm from the Mascarene Islands which gets its common name from the unusual bloated trunk which in some specimens resembles a bottle. As well as the distinctive trunk the dark green pinnate fronds have a prominent twist which is characteristic, and the crown consists of a small number of expanded fronds (usually four to six) at any one time. Bottle palms are rather cold sensitive and are best suited to tropical conditions. They grow very well in coastal districts and will tolerate considerable exposure to salt-

Hyophorbe lagenicaulis in fruit.

laden winds. They like a sunny aspect and are very slow growing. Mature or even large specimens are extremely rare in Australia. Plants are readily propagated from seeds which usually germinate within six to eight months of sowing.

Hyophorbe verschaffeltii
Spindle Palm

As the common name suggests the trunk of this palm is fusiform or spindle-shaped, being narrow at either end and with a prominent bulge in the middle. The trunk is usually grey and topped with a bright green crownshaft which may be expanded at the base. The crown consists of six to ten arching, feathery, dark-green fronds which are most attractive. The inflorescences when young are carried in unusual, erect, curved, horn-like spathes and usually several at a time appear near the base of the crownshaft. This palm is rather popular in cultivation, especially in tropical areas. It will withstand some cold and also coastal exposure. A sunny position is essential for success. Young plants make excellent tub specimens and they can be held in the same container for many years. Plants are generally slow growing and although hardy they are best

watered during dry periods. Seeds germinate readily within six months of sowing.

Hyphaene

A genus of forty-one species of palm widely distributed in Africa with one species found in each of Madagascar and India. They are solitary, fan palms and are unique because their trunks have the ability to branch by forking but the degree of branching varies with the species. The fruit are generally quite large, of unusual shape and are borne in large clusters. Species of *Hyphaene* are interesting palms but are rarely seen in cultivation in Australia.

Hyphaene petersiana
Elala Palm

This species grows along stream banks of southern Africa and unlike the Doum Palm branches sparsely if at all. The surface of the trunk is rough and covered with old leaf bases and the crown is fairly small and compound of bright-green, deeply divided, fan-shaped leaves. The pear-shaped fruit are yellowish when ripe and about 5 cm long. This palm should be well suited to cultivation in temperate regions and it is known that it also grows in the tropics. The plants require a well-drained soil in a sunny position. This species has been known as *H. ventricosa*.

Hyphaene thebaica
Doum Palm or Gingerbread Palm

Native to northern and eastern Africa this palm is famed for its regularly forking trunk so that an old plant consists of many branches each ending in a small crown of leaves. The leaves are stiffly fan-shaped, grey-green to glaucous and strongly costapalmate. They are borne on strong petioles which have thick, black teeth along the margins. The pear-shaped fruit are bright orange when ripe (about 8 cm long) and have a mealy flesh which is edible and reported to taste like gingerbread. Doum Palms may reach 15 m tall and may be nearly as far across. They are a botanical curiousity because of their branching and are rarely seen in cultivation in Australia. They will grow in warm-temperate, subtropical and tropical regions and need an open, sunny position. Germination is erratic and may take eight to ten months to occur. The seeds should be sown in a deep container as a long shoot develops before the leaves emerge. This shoot is edible and rich in starch.

Hyphaene petersiana in flower.

The Spindle Palm, *Hyophorbe verschaffeltii*.

Hyphaene thebaica showing branching habit.

Johannesteijsmannia altifrons in its natural state, Malaysia.

Iguanura

A small genus of twenty-one species of palm native to Malaysia, the Philippines and Indonesia. They are mostly small-growing palms with a solitary or clumping habit and pinnate fronds. Few species are grown in Australia.

Iguanura geonomiformis

A common, small, Malaysian palm which forms congested clumps up to 3 m tall (occasional plants have solitary stems). The stems are very slender and sometimes have clusters of stilt roots at the base. The leaves, which are about 1 m long, arise at a steep angle to the stem and are divided into irregular-shaped, folded leaflets which are green above and grey beneath. The inflorescence is a simple, pendulous spike which, after flowering, carries small red fruit. The fronds trap litter, which builds up around the crown. This is a delightful, small palm suitable for tropical gardens where it needs a sheltered, shady position. It should also make an attractive pot plant.

Iguanura wallichiana

This palm is similar in many respects to *I. genomiformis* but can be distinguished by the inflorescence which has up to ten branches. It also is a small, suckering palm native to the Malaysian rainforests and has excellent potential as a garden plant for the tropics. Its leaves are variable, usually being divided but with coarse or fine leaflets. Occasionally however, they are entire.

Johannesteijsmannia

A genus of four species of palms endemic to Malaysia and Sumatra. The species have an underground or shortly emergent trunk and huge, simple leaves. They are litter-collecting palms found in shady rainforests. The genus was previously known as *Teysmannia*.

Johannesteijsmannia altifrons
Litter Collecting Palm

This relatively small palm with the big name grows on the floor of rainforest and jungles of Malaysia and Sumatra. It is a litter-collecting plant with the large, simple leaves directing falling litter to form piles in the centre of the plant. This litter covers the underground stem and developing crown of the palm and the palms roots grow into the litter as it decays. The palm is well known in the area where it grows because the large fronds (to 4 m or more tall) provide an

Fronds of *Johannesteijsmannia altifrons* used for thatching in Malaysia.

Jubaea chilensis is a stout palm which grows well in temperate regions.

excellent shelter for a sudden downpour. They are also ideal for thatching huts. This palm is most decorative and unusual with its large, simple, paddle-shaped fronds. It is a rarity in Australia because of the lack of propagating material. Plants are best suited to the tropics or warm subtropics and apparently grow quite readily in well-shaded, moist sitations. They would make a very interesting tub specimen.

Jubaea

A monotypic genus of palm endemic to Chile. The species is a solitary palm with a crown of pinnate leaves and a massive, woody trunk. Once common, this palm is now considered to be endangered because of over exploitation for wine and a local delicacy known as palm honey.

Jubaea chilensis
Chilean Wine Palm or Coquito Palm

This distinctive palm is readily recognised by its stout, grey trunk crowned with feathery, spreading fronds. It is native to Chile where it is apparently becoming uncommon because mature plants are cut down for their sugary sap which is distilled to make the delicacy known as palm honey. Palms are now protected in their native state. Jubaea palms are monoecious and solitary specimens are capable of setting fruit. This palm grows well in temperate climates but is more difficult in the tropics. It is very tolerant of cold and can withstand severe frosts even while small. Plants are slow growing when young but accelerate after a trunk is produced. They required a sunny position in well-drained soil and respond to nitrogen-rich fertilisers. Mature plants grow up to 25 m tall. Seeds take six to fifteen months to germinate. The species was previously known as *J. spectabilis*.

Jubaeopsis

A monotypic genus endemic to South Africa. The single species is a solitary, feather-leaved palm very rarely encountered in cultivation.

Jubaeopsis caffra

An African palm that bears a strong, superficial resemblance to *Jubaea chilensis*, hence the similarity of the generic name. The stiff, dark-green leaves have a slight twist in the rhachis imparting an attractive appearance to the crown. The trunk is short and woody, usually not growing to more than 6 m tall. Individual leaflets are stiff, very slender and are unequally emarginate at the apex. The fruit, which are about 3 cm long, are globose and resemble a miniature coconut. In nature this palm is restricted to South Africa where it grows on rocky cliffs near rivers and in alluvial flood plains. It is hardly known in cultivation in Australia but is deserving of introduction. Some reports indicate that plants are very slow growing and seed germination may be difficult. They can be grown in warm temperatures and subtropical regions and particularly favour sandy soils where ground water is available.

Kentiopsis

A monotypic genus of palm endemic to New Caledonia. The species is a solitary, feather-leaved palm rarely encountered in cultivation.

Kentiopsis oliviformis

At first glance this palm could easily be mistaken for *Howea forsteriana* but a mature specimen can be distinguished readily by the vastly different inflorescence which resembles a straw boom. Native to New Caledonia this palm could one day become very popular in cultivation but at present is mainly a collectors item because of lack of seed. It is endemic to New Caledonia where it is apparently rare and grows along stream banks in heavily leached soils. It is not as easy as *Kentia* to grow and requires moist, shady conditions. There are several plants growing in the Royal Botanic Gardens, Sydney.

Latania

A genus of three species of solitary, fan palms which are confined to the Mascarene Islands. They are handsome palms with large, striking leaves. They have proved to be very hardy, although slow growing, and are deserving of much wider cultivation. All species commonly grown in Australia are basically similar in

The crown of *Latania loddigesii* showing split petiole bases.

Latania lontaroides, the Red Latan Palm, is a striking palm for the tropics.

appearance and can usually be distinguished on colouration in the leaves and petioles and the size and shape of the hastula. Hybridisation is frequent in cultivated plants of this genus.

Latania loddigesii
Blue Latan Palm

The large, very glaucous, fan leaves of this palm spread stiffly from the crown and in mature plants the petioles and basal parts of the leaves are covered with a thick white wool which adheres strongly. The plants develop a slender trunk to more than 8 m tall and this is topped by a rounded, dense crown of the fronds each of which may be over 4 m long. Large, shiny-brown, plum-like fruit are carried on inflorescences nearly 2 m long and ripen slowly. This very attractive palm, which is native to the Mascarene Islands, is deserving of much wider cultivation since it has proved to be adaptable to a range of climates. It also grows well in warm-temperate areas as well as the tropics. Plants will tolerate sun from a very early age and need freely draining soil. Seeds germinate readily within two to four months of sowing and the seedlings are surprisingly fast growing.

Latania lontaroides
Red Latan Palm

Young plants of this palm have a striking red colouration in the leaves and often also have bright red petioles. Older plants have greyish-green leaves with streaks of red (actually red veins) in the leaves and along the petioles. The leaves also have a prominently pointed hastula which is raised above the leaf surface. In mature plants the trunk is grey and naked throughout. This is a hardy palm which needs a sunny position in well-drained soils. Plants will succeed as far south as Sydney and can also be grown in the tropics. This species has also been known as *L. borbonica* and *L. commersonii*.

Latania verschaffeltii
Yellow Latan Palm

A robust fan-palm native to the Mascarene Islands and similar in many respects to *L. loddigesii*. Its petioles and leaf bases are also covered with a dense, white wool at least on mature trees but the leaves are green rather than glaucous. In young plants the leaf veins and petioles are an attractive bright orange colour with this coloura-

A young plant of the Golden Latan Palm, *Latania verschaffeltii*.

tion even extending to the leaf lamina of some plants. The leaves also have a short, blunt hastula which is quite different to the other species. Cultivation and propagation details are as described for *L. loddigesii*.

Licuala

A large genus of ornate palms consisting of 108 species. They are distributed from India to New Guinea with a solitary species in north-eastern Australia. All are typically shade-loving palms, found around the margins of swamps and in rainforest sometimes in colonies. The trunks may be solitary or multiple and the fan-leaves may be deeply divided or entire. Although a few species are fairly commonly grown, there is a large range with tremendous horticultural potential that awaits introduction to cultivation. New Guinea alone has thirty-six species, some of them small-growing palms. As a group Licualas are generally tropical in their requirements. For notes on the Australian species of *Licuala* see page 123.

Licuala glabra

This fan palm may be stemless or with a stout trunk that can reach 2 m tall. It has a crown of spreading leaves that have slender petioles up to 3 m long, each topped with a dark-green, orbicular blade which may be 60 cm across. The blades are divided into twelve narrowly triangular, overlapping segments with the central part split to the base. Long, slender inflorescences (sometimes reaching more than 3 m) arch above the foliage and carry small, dull-orange fruit. This palm is very decorative and is common in the lowland forests of Malaysia. In cultivation it needs a shady position in the tropics.

Licuala grandis
Fan Palm

Some palms are prized horticultural subjects and this species is one of the most sought after. It originates in the New Hebrides and grows in lowland tropical jungles. It has become popular because of its wonderfully symmetrical, glossy dark green leaves and neat habit of growth. The circular, pleated leaves are up to 1 m across and have notched margins. The species is essentially tropical in its requirements and is rather sensitive to cold although it can be grown in a warm, protected position in the subtropics. The plants are generally slow growing and make excellent subjects for tub culture. They require shaded conditions and protection from strong winds. Propagation is from seed which may take three to five months to germinate. Bottom heat is beneficial.

Licuala lauterbachii

A small to medium sized, fan palm from New Guinea which carries its leaves on very slender petioles nearly 2 m long. The leaves themselves are about 1 m across, circular, bright green and are divided to the base into thirty to thirty-five narrowly triangular segments which have pointed tips. Bright red fruit 2-3 cm long are carried on long, arching peduncles. This attractive fan palm is widespread throughout New Guinea growing in shady forests. A distinct variety (var *bougainvillensis*) occurs in the Solomons. Tropical conditions are needed for the culture of both.

Licuala longipes

Because this palm is often trunkless its long

Licuala grandis, is a prized garden palm.

Licuala grandis in fruit.

leaves seem to erupt from the ground in a very spectacular fashion. The slender petioles may be more than 3.5 m long and are topped with a circular blade which may be nearly 2 m across. This is dark green and divided into diverging wedge-shaped segments the basal ones of which are narrow and well separated. A much-branched inflorescence to more than 1 m tall is carried among the leaf bases. This startling palm is native to India and Malaysia, growing in shady places on the rainforest floor. It is very tropical in its requirements.

Licuala orbicularis

This fan palm from Borneo rivals *L. grandis* in its beauty but unfortunately it does not yet appear to have been introduced to cultivation. Like *L. grandis* its orbicular leaves are undivided but they are held stiffly and flat. It is a small, trunkless palm which grows in rainforest and its horticultural potential is tremendous. In its native country its leaves are cut and used as rain shelters.

Licuala paludosa

A Malaysian palm which grows in wet, sandy soils close to the coast often in colonies. The plants develop a trunk to about 3 m tall and have an open crown of dark green, orbicular leaves which may be close to a metre across. These are carried on slender petioles about 60 cm long with the margins armed with numerous, small, black thorns. The leaves are divided into six to nine pleated segments which are toothed on the ends. The fruit are small, round and dull coloured.

Licuala rumphii.

Little is known about this palm's cultural requirements but it seems to be suited to the tropics.

Licuala peltata

This very tropical palm forms impressive clumps up to 5 m tall and spreading a similar width. Its leaves are orbicular, nearly 1.5 m across and are divided into numerous, narrow, dark-green, widely spaced segments. These are cut squarely across at the ends and are toothed, the whole arrangement imparting a splendid symmetrical impression. The blade is carried on the end of a petiole over 2 m long, which is triangular with very sharp marginal spines. The inflorescences arch well above the leaves and carry bunches of orange, elliptical fruit each about 1 cm long. In their native countries of Burma and India the leaves are made into hats.

Licuala rumphii

A little-known species from the islands of the Celebes and the Moluccas to the east of New Guinea. Plants have radiating leaflets similar to *L. spinosa* and thorny petioles. In cultivation they have proved to be very slow growing and would probably be best suited to the tropics although they will withstand conditions as far south as Brisbane.

Licuala spinosa

The slender trunks of this clumping palm may grow to more than 4 m tall and yet are usually less than 10 cm thick. Superficially they resemble a *Rhapis* species but can be quickly distinguished by the spines on the petiole and the shiny, square-ended leaf segments. The palm is native to Malaysia, India and neighbouring countries, and grows in rainforest often close to the sea. Well-grown clumps are very attractive and are a frequent sight in tropical countries. In cultivation it likes warm, moist conditions but will withstand some cold periods and can be grown in subtropical regions. It prefers a shady or partially protected position and if grown in full sun without adequate water the leaves may bleach or burn. Plants take considerable coastal exposure without obvious detriment. When in fruit clumps are quite spectacular with long, arching inflorescences carrying clusters of brilliant scarlet fruit. This palm is excellent not only for home gardens but also for parks. Seed is slow to germinate, taking six to eight months for seedlings to appear.

Licuala spinosa.

Livistona

A familiar genus of palms comprising twenty-eight species that are found in various countries from India to Australia. They are solitary, fan-leaved palms with stout thorns on their petioles. One species or another will grow in regions from the tropics to the temperate zones and they are a familiar sight in municipal gardens in many parts of Australia. Most species are hardy, sun-loving palms that grow easily and are tolerant of neglect. For notes on the Australian species of *Livistona* see page 128.

Livistona chinensis
Chinese Fan Palm

This fan palm has prominently drooping tips which adorn the broad, glossy or yellowish leaves of all but very young plants. The leaves often have a fresh green lustre and this together with the weeping segment tips provides a decorative combination. As the common name suggests the species is native to China. It is monoecious and a single plant is capable of producing fruit. Chinese Fan Palm is hardy and is a popular subject for cultivation in tropical and temperate regions. It

makes an excellent tub plant and when young is very useful indoors, even tolerating dark positions. It tends to be slow growing in temperate Australia and rarely reaches 4 m tall. The plants are tolerant of poor soil but respond to applications of fertiliser. They will grow in full sun or semi-shade and may flower while quite small. Seed germinates readily within one or two months of sowing.

Livistona jenkinsiana

A popular pot and glasshouse palm in Europe where it has been grown for a long period, this palm is virtually unknown in Australia and New Zealand. It is native to northern India and has achieved some prominence through the unusual jhapee hats which are made from its leaves and worn by the Assamese people. It is a typical *Livistona* with a thick, rounded crown atop a fairly slender trunk which may reach 10 m tall. Its large, fan-shaped leaves have numerous bilobed segments which are bluish green on the underside. Fruit are carried in dense, hanging clusters and when ripe are about 2.5 cm across and of a leaden blue colouration. In cultivation this palm should succeed in temperate and subtropical localities requiring soils and cultural conditions similar to other Livistonas.

Livistona robinsoniana

This collectors palm has a slender, green trunk which has contrasting broad, pale annular rings at regular intervals along its length. The fan-shaped leaves are quite large and bright green with drooping tips and at least when young have a twist in the lamina. Unlike most *Livistona* species the petioles of this species are smooth and unarmed. Native to the Philippines it will grow in tropical and subtropical regions even tolerating some cold. For best appearance it needs a shady position or at least protection from direct sun for part of the day. Mature fruit are yellowish orange. Seeds germinate readily within two to four months of sowing.

Livistona rotundifolia
Footstool Palm

The distinctive, round, glossy leaves of young plants earn this species its popular name. These leaves when young are only shallowly divided with softly drooping tips. As a tub plant at this stage of growth the plants are excellent and can be successfully employed for indoor decoration. Leaves on mature plants, however, lose much of their appeal especially when they have been tattered by the wind. Those plants grown in a deeply shady situation will retain the juvenile leaves much longer than plants grown in the open. Footstool Palm is native to Malaysia and may grow to about 10 m tall. In its native state the cabbage is collected and eaten and the dark-violet fruit is eaten by children. It is ideal for tropical climates and needs protection from direct sun when small. Rich soils promote strong, vigorous growth. In districts with a cold winter the plants struggle and are very slow growing.

A very striking variety is native to the Philippine island of Luzon. This is known as var. *luzonensis* and has a slender trunk with prominent white rings. If anything this palm is more tropical in its requirements and tends to be slower growing than the typical variety. Fruiting plants are very decorative, bearing masses of brick-red

Livistona chinensis is commonly grown in various parts of Australia.

Livistona robinsoniana, native to the Philippines, is a handsome palm for the tropics.

207

fruit. Both forms can be propagated from seed which germinates within two months but seedling growth is very slow.

Livistona saribus
Taraw Palm

A widely spread South-east Asian palm which grows as an emergent plant in dense tropical jungle, its trunks reaching to more than 25 m tall. It is a typical fan palm with deeply segmented green leaves and reddish to orange petioles which have large, very prominent thorns along the margins. Its most distinctive and striking ornamental feature is the large clusters of brilliant blue fruit which follow the flowers. Individually these are not much more than 1 cm long but in mass are very colourful. The palm is rather tropical in its requirements but will succeed in the subtropics and tolerate some cold in the winter. Young plants need protection from hot sun and are generally strong growers. Seeds germinate readily within two to four months of sowing.

Livistona speciosa

A palm of the mountains of India, Burma and Malaysia usually growing above 600 m altitude. It has a slender, rough trunk to 18 m tall and a large, dense crown of leaves. These leaves are not flat but rather are irregularly folded with stiff, spreading segments and are bright green above and bluish green beneath. The inflorescence may be nearly 3 m long and is subtended by chocolate brown spathes. The fruit, which are fairly narrow grow to about 2.5 cm long and are jade green at maturity, ageing to black. Like other *Livistona* this species should prove to be reliable and hardy in cultivation.

Lodoicea

A monotypic genus of palms endemic to the Seychelles Islands. The species is a solitary palm with large, fan-shaped leaves and bears huge fruit.

Lodoicea maldivica
Coco-de-Mer or Double Coconut

Famed for its huge fruit which contains the largest seed produced by any plant in the world, this palm is endemic to two islands of the Seychelles (Praslin and Curieuse) where it grows in extensive colonies. It is a fan-palm with huge, strongly costapalmate leaves which are dark green and glossy above and with stiffly spreading segments. The trunk is slender (about 25 cm thick) and in nature may reach in excess of 25 m tall. Plants in cultivation however have proved to be exceedingly slow growing and a specimen of this height must be of great age indeed. The base of the trunk fits into a round, wooden bowl and the roots grow through holes in this bowl into the surrounding soil. This bowl is extremely resistant to rotting and persists in the soil long after the plants have disappeared. Its purpose is unclear but since the base of the trunk moves relative to it, it may ensure stability and cushion the effects of severe winds. The fruit are truly enormous and may weigh in excess of 20 kg. They are entirely taken up by the seed which, when sliced crossways, resembles two coconuts joined in the middle, hence the common name Double Coconut. Infertile and dead fruit float while viable ones sink and hence this palm is not distributed by the oceans currents as is the Coconut. In early times the fruit were regarded as a mystical object and fetched considerable sums of money. The seed was regarded as being a highly potent aphrodisiac and may be still held in that light today.

A clump of the Sago Palm, *Metroxylon sagu*.

Double Coconuts are rare in cultivation and many of those planted do not survive. Some areas, such as the Peradeniya Gardens in Sri Lanka, achieve considerable success while others report difficulties. A tropical climate is essential as is a deep soil since the palm sends out a long radicle when germinating. Germination may take from six to eighteen months and the plants from thirty to sixty years before they flower. Male and female plants are necessary to produce fruit and the fruit takes five to seven years to mature on the plant. A few Double Coconut seeds have recently been introduced into Australia and it is hoped that they become successfully established. Seeds of *Lodoicea* must be sown in their permanent position since they produce a sinker over 4 m long.

Metroxylon

A small genus of eight species of palm mainly found from New Guinea to Malaysia. They are solitary, feather-leaved palms which are monocarpic and produce a terminal inflorescence. In nature they form colonies, usually in marshy ground. Some species are commonly grown for sago which forms an important part of the diet of the local people. They are generally tropical in their requirements and have limited horticultural appeal.

Metroxylon sagu
Sago Palm

High-quality sago is obtained from the trunk of this monocarpic palm which is felled just as the tree is about to flower. This sago is a staple part of the diet of millions of people in Asia and as well generates revenue via its sale to Europe and other countries. Sago palms are widely cultivated in various tropical countries of the world and are a large impressive palm. The thick trunk, which may grow to 8 m tall, bears an impressive crown of spreading, dark-green, pinnate fronds at its apex. At maturity a large, terminal, spiny panicle is thrust above the leaves and the flowers are followed by attractively patterned, round fruits which may be up to 5 cm across. Once these fruit mature, the plant dies. Sago palms are very cold sensitive and like the hot, humid conditions of the tropical lowlands. They are quite fast growing and like a sunny situation with plenty of water. Seeds germinate very slowly and sporadically, taking six to twelve months. Bottom heat speeds up the process and it is also reported that pre-soaking in warm water may be beneficial. Spiny and spineless forms of the Sago Palm are known.

Metroxylon salomonense

This sago palm is native to the Solomon Islands where it is widespread, forming clumps in swampy ground. Young plants are very handsome with a graceful, arching crown of dark-green, pinnate leaves. On older plants the armament becomes more obvious with clusters of yellowish spines on the trunk which may be nearly 40 cm long. The terminal inflorescence bears many flat, spreading or drooping branches and creamy flowers. These are followed by large, brownish green, scaly fruit which are nearly round and about 8 cm across. This palm is very tropical in its requirements and will only succeed in areas with a climate similar to Cairns.

Metroxylon warburgii

Flowering plants of this sago palm are striking as the huge, stiff terminal inflorescence carries thousands of bright yellow flowers which makes the plants stand out, even from a distance. The flowers are followed by pear-shaped, brown fruit about 8 cm long, each of which is covered by an intricate pattern of scales. Native to the Solomon Islands where the trunks are harvested for sago and the leaves used for thatch, this palm is rarely cultivated. Like the other species of this genus it thrives only in tropical conditions.

Microcoelum

A small genus of two species of palm endemic to Brazil where they grow in shady rainforests. They are solitary, pinnate palms with a slender trunk. Both are excellent garden plants and one species is also frequently used for indoor decoration. At various times they have been included in the genera *Cocos* and *Syagrus* and even today it is not uncommon to see them advertised under the former name.

Microcoelum insigne

A small, neat-growing palm from Brazil that is adaptable in cultivation, growing from the warm tropical regions to protected positions in the subtropics or as a pot plant in a heated glasshouse. The plants grow to about 2 m tall and have a rough trunk only 4.5 cm thick. The crown is composed of small, neat fronds that are silvery

Microcoelum insigne is a decorative small palm.

advanced specimens are usually expensive. The species is native to Brazil. Seed germinates readily within two to four months of sowing. There is some confusion about the correct name of this palm with some authorities claiming it should be *Microcoelum martianum*. It has also been included in the genera *Cocos* and *Syagrus*.

Nannorrhops

A monotypic genus of palms native to northern India and Afghanistan. They are tough, fan-leaved palms with branching trunks which may be subterranean or emergent. Like species of *Corypha*, to which they are related, the branches bear a terminal inflorescence.

Nannorrhops ritchiana
Mazari Palm

Mostly the trunk of this palm is subterranean and branches freely so that the plants form dense clumps. Occasionally however the trunk is erect, and while it still branches it may exceed 5 m tall. Native to northern India and Afghanistan this very hardy palm is abundant in scattered colonies in infertile, stony soils often on treeless plains. It is of considerable importance to the

beneath. Once established, plants will tolerate considerable sun but while young they need protection. Potted specimens are useful for indoor decoration. This palm is usually seen only in the collections of enthusiasts but will probably become more widely grown. Seeds take six to eight months to germinate and benefit from the use of bottom heat. Seedlings of this species often appear in batches of seed of *M. weddellianum* and can be readily distinguished by their broad, undivided seedling leaves.

Microcoelum weddellianum

A small, graceful palm that is one of the best for indoor decoration. It will tolerate quite dark conditions and its slender, graceful, dark-green, shiny leaves make it a very attractive addition to the decor. Plants can be grown in a large tub and appreciate a well-drained mix rich in organic matter. In the garden the species demands a semi-shady to shady position in a frost-free area. Plants are rarely seen over 2 m tall and the very slender trunk may be no more than 4 cm thick. It has the disadvantage of being extremely slow growing, especially in the first few years and

Microcoelum weddellianum, a popular small palm.

Young plant of *Microcoelum weddellianum* showing beautiful, shiny fronds.

local inhabitants who eat the very young leaves as a vegetable, the flesh of the fruit and use other parts for building, thatching, weaving and as fuel for fires. Mazari Palm extends into the mountains of Afghanistan and plants may be covered with snow for long periods during the winter. An interesting feature of its growth is that each crown is monocarpic, producing a single terminal inflorescence. As this matures fruit it dies back down the trunk to the next branch, which replaces it. Each trunk is thick and densely covered with old leaf bases which carry orange wool. The leaves are fan shaped, stiff to rigid and an attractive grey-green colouration. The terminal inflorescence may be 2 m tall and single plants are capable of producing fruit. In cultivation this species has proved to be very slow growing but hardy and extremely cold tolerant. It will grow in a sunny position in temperate and subtropical regions.

Nenga

A small genus of five species of palms from Indochina, Malaysia, Indonesia and Thailand. They are clumping palms with pinnate leaves and a prominent crownshaft. Because of their manageable size they are ideal for garden culture but are rather tropical in their requirements. The genus is closely related to *Pinanga*.

Nenga pumila

A specimen of this palm resembles a cluster of dwarfed bangalows crowded together. A graceful, arching crown of dark green pinnate leaves (1-1.5 m long) tops a prominent, bright purplegreen crownshaft on each stem. Clusters of oval

fruit about 2.5 cm long are bright orange when ripe and a very decorative feature. This is a graceful and highly ornamental palm that because of its manageable size is ideally suited to garden cultivation. Plants have proved to be rather cold sensitive and succeed best in the tropics. Young plants require protection from direct, hot sun.

Nengella

A genus of about nineteen species all restricted to New Guinea where they grow in rainforests. They are solitary or clumping, pinnate palms with slender stems. They have tremendous horticultural potential but are virtually unknown in Australia. Their requirements are probably tropical. Plants are extremely variable in their characteristics and a botanical investigation would reduce the number of species, possibly by a large number.

Nengella flabellata

This prized collectors palm from New Guinea grows in shady, moist situations under dense rainforest. It is a very slender, clumping palm reminiscent of both *Linospadix* and *Chamaedorea* and the bamboo-like stems may reach more than 5 m tall. The leaves are scattered up the stem and are divided into a few leaflets which are usually irregularly cut and toothed on the ends. The end pair are usually united and fishtail-like. Flowers and fruit are carried on simple, unbranched spikes and may be quite colourful. This delicate, highly ornamental palm likes deep shade, plenty of moisture and tropical or subtropical conditions. Seeds take four to five months to germinate and seedlings are very slow growing.

Neodypsis

An interesting genus of palms comprising fourteen species endemic to Madagascar. They are solitary palms with pinnate leaves. One remarkable species is occasionally found in cultivation.

Neodypsis decaryi

A spectacular and distinctive palm from Madagascar which can be readily recognised by the prominent three-sided trunk caused by the arrangement of the leaf bases in three rows. As well, the pinnate fronds are held stiffly erect, drooping only at the tips and the lowermost leaflets are developed into filamentous extensions

Neodypsis decaryi, an attractive palm which succeeds well in tropical and subtropical regions.

The trunk of *Neodypsis decaryi.*

which hang to the ground. The chalky white bloom on the trunk and grey leaflets add to the character of this most unusual palm. It is essentially a collectors item and in fact is quite rare in cultivation. It succeeds best in tropical and subtropical regions and requires a sunny position. Garden-grown plants have proved to be adaptable and quite fast growing. Seed germinates rapidly, usually within a month of sowing.

Neoveitchia

A monotypic genus endemic to Fiji. The species is an attractive, solitary palm with pinnate leaves. It is mainly to be found in botanic gardens and in the collections of enthusiasts.

Neoveitchia storckii

This palm was of local economic significance to the island of Viti Levu where it grew in large stands on riverine plains. The immature fruits of this tall, elegant Fijian palm may have been collected and eaten by the locals, and the trunks were certainly cut to form the supporting poles of the dwellings so characteristic of the area. Today it is a very rare species. It is a handsome palm very reminiscent of many species of *Veitchia* but with a heavy crown of twisted, pinnate fronds the leaflets of which are very pointed, and with a loose, open crownshaft. It is essentially a palm for the collector and being very cold sensitive requires tropical conditions. In nature the plants grow to more than 20 m tall. Propagation is from seed which may take six months to germinate.

Nephrosperma

A monotypic genus of palms endemic to the Seychelles. The species is a solitary, feather-leaved palm and is rare in cultivation.

Nephrosperma vanhoutteanum

Another of the remarkable palms native to the Seychelles Islands. This species develops a slender trunk with a prominent, bright-green crownshaft and a graceful crown of arching or drooping, dark-green fronds. Young plants have prominently spiny petioles but these are much less obvious on larger plants. The small, round fruit are red when ripe. Solitary plants are capable of setting fruit. Essentially a collectors palm in Australia this species requires shady conditions in the tropics or perhaps a warm, sheltered aspect in a subtropical garden.

Oenocarpus

A genus of sixteen species of palm restricted to Central and South America with one species extending to the West Indies. They are solitary or clumping, feather-leaved palms with slender stems.

Oenocarpus distichus

A little-known palm from the Amazon region of Brazil. Seeds have been distributed to palm enthusiasts but not much is known about its biology or cultural requirements. It is a solitary species with a fairly slender trunk and is unusual because its leaves are arranged in a single plane, imparting a distinctive flat appearance. It is probably best grown in tropical zones.

Oenocarpus panamanus

As the specific name suggests, this palm originates in Panama where it grows in dry rainforests. It is a clumping species with slender stems which may grow to nearly 18 m tall. These are smooth and unarmed and superficially resemble bamboo. Leaves are about 2 m long with widely spaced, slender leaflets which are split at the apex. Round black fruit are borne in heavy clusters. This palm will possibly one day be widely planted for its attractive appearance, but at present is limited to botanical collections.

Oncosperma

A small genus of five species of palms from Southeast Asia. They grow in large, dense clumps and most organs are armed with long, black, brittle spines. They form impressive clumps but are uncommon to rare in cultivation. Most species seem to be very tropical in their requirements.

Oncosperma fasciculatum

Endemic to Ceylon, this palm is basically similar to the more widely cultivated *O. tigillarium* but grows in narrower clumps with less stems and rarely reaches more than 15 m tall. Each stem grows to about 15 cm thick and is liberally armed with long, black, brittle spines. The leaves, which are about 2.3 m long, have spiny petioles and fairly broad leaflets (5 cm) which droop at the tips. Inflorescences are not spiny. Large clusters of black fruit, which are only about 0.5 cm across, are a feature of this palm. Like the other species in this genus it is essentially for parks and large gardens in the tropics.

A large clump of *Oncosperma fasciculatum*.

Oncosperma horridum

Like the other species in the genus, this palm forms impressive, but very prickly, clumps. Native to Malaysia and Sumatra it occurs naturally in swampy conditions. A clump consists of thirty to forty slender stems which may reach 5 m tall. Each stem is liberally armed with black spines and bears a relatively sparse crown of leathery fronds. The fruit, which are 2-2.5 cm across, are spherical and purple-black when ripe. Outdoor cultivation of this palm is restricted to the tropics, as it is very sensitive to cold and likes warm, humid conditions.

Oncosperma tigillarium
Nibung Palm

An eye-catching palm which grows in tall, slender, very dense clumps which may reach more than 25 m high. Each trunk is only 10-15 cm across (and covered with black spines) but up to fifty may be together in a clump and are so crowded that they almost touch at the base. The upper part of the clump is a mass of the dark-green, pinnate fronds which crown each trunk. These have characteristic, leathery, drooping

Oncosperma tigillarium is a large clumping palm suitable for the tropics.

leaflets and the petioles (and inflorescence) are covered with long black spines. The palm is very widespread in South-east Asia and grows in coastal swamps. It is a handsome species but because of its size and rather formidable nature is suitable only for large municipal parks and gardens. It thrives in the hot, humid conditions of the tropical lowlands. Seeds lose their viability quickly after collection. When sown fresh they take two to three months to germinate. The species was previously known as *O. filamentosum.*

Opsiandra

A small genus of two species of palms restricted to Central America. They are solitary, pinnate-leaved palms one of which is occasionally grown. The flesh of the fruit contains caustic raphides of Calcium oxalate and should be handled with care.

Opsiandra maya

This palm grows in the rainforests of Mexico, Guatemala and British Honduras. It is a pinnate-leaved species with a tall, slender trunk and

the unusual flowering characteristic of delayed development (that is, the inflorescences grow to a certain stage but develop no further until several others form above them). After some triggering mechanism flowering begins in order of maturity and a plant may have fifteen or more inflorescences present at the one time, all in different stages of development. This odd characteristic is further complicated by the persistence of viable male flowers for long periods on the inflorescence and also the ability of sections of the inflorescence to flower much later than others and produce succeeding crops of fruit. This flowering habit adds to the species ornamental appeal although it is mainly a palm for the collector. It will grow in tropical and subtropical zones and there are also instances of it succeeding in warm-temperate areas (for example, the Royal Botanic Gardens, Sydney). It likes shade, and plenty of water and mulch. Seeds germinate within four months of sowing. Fruit should be handled carefully as the flesh contains needle-like, stinging crystals.

Orania

A genus of sixteen species of palms distributed between the Philippines, Indonesia and New Guinea with a single species in north-eastern Australia. They are solitary, feather-leaved palms with a fairly large crown of spreading fronds. The fruits are generally round and may have one, two or three seeds. Some species are known to be quite poisonous and the cabbage and seeds of all species should be treated with caution. The genus has been recently reviewed by Essig (1980). For notes on the species of *Orania* in Australia see page 147.

Orania disticha

Although relatively unknown in cultivation this New Guinean palm is to be found close to centres of population such as Port Moresby where it grows on forest margins, stream banks, and such. It is a tall species (to 15 m) with a moderately slender trunk (10-15 cm thick) and a large, graceful crown. The fronds, which are dark green, arch out in a pleasant fashion and have prominently drooping leaflets. The basal leaflets of each frond are the largest and overlap to give the centre of the crown a crowded appearance.

Orania glauca

A New Guinea palm which is characterised by its

Orbignya cohune native to Central America.

Orania palindan

Native to the Philippines this palm is common in forested valleys ascending from the lowlands to mountains at medium altitudes. The plants grow to about 5 m tall with a slender, prominently ringed, very hard trunk and a graceful crown of pinnate leaves, the leaflets of which are drooping and with shredded tips. The spherical fruit, 5-6 cm across, are yellowish when ripe. This is a very decorative palm suitable for tropical and warm subtropical regions. Young plants are slow growing and require protection from direct sun for the first few years. The fruits and cabbage of this species are poisonous. Seeds germinate readily within two to three months of sowing.

Orbignya

A genus of twenty-four species of palm which are found in Mexico, Central and South America. They are solitary, feather-leaved palms, few species of which are to be found in cultivation. In general their requirements are tropical.

Orbignya cohune
Cohune Palm

This massive palm is frequently included in the genus *Attalea* but is more correctly placed here. Native to the South American countries of Honduras and British Honduras, it is characterised by an enormous crown of dark-green, pinnate fronds which are held stiffly erect. These crown a trunk which may be more than 15 m tall and the result is a very impressive palm which because of its size is best suited to parks and public gardens. In some tropical countries they are also planted in rows to line streets and driveways. In young, trunkless plants the erect fronds seem to erupt out of the ground. The large, egg-shaped fruit yield cohune oil, valued for its lubricating properties. This palm is best suited to the hot, humid tropics and will withstand direct sun when quite small. Plants may be slow growing until they form a trunk. Seeds germinate readily, usually within two months of sowing.

Parajubaea

A small genus of two species of South American palms which grow in dense forest at fairly high altitudes in the Andes mountains. They are solitary, feather-leaved species and are rarely encountered in cultivation.

erect, stiff leaves which seem to thrust through the surrounding vegetation. The crown consists of relatively few leaves but each is large and quite broad with attractively drooping leaflets. The trunk is fairly stout and prominently ringed. When in flower the inflorescence is most impressive, being nearly 4 m long with the stems glaucous from a waxy covering (from which the species gets its name). *O. glauca* is native to the West Sepik district of New Guinea, growing in lowland forest. It is an impressive palm that is probably very tropical in its cultural requirements.

Orania lauterbachiana

This species and *O. macropetala*, both native to New Guinea, are very similar in general appearance but are separated on botanical features. Both are widespread throughout lowland areas growing in rainforests. They have a slender, grey trunk which may grow to 20 m tall and a large crown of obliquely erect, dark-green fronds which have prominent drooping leaflets. The round fruit are up to 6 cm across and orange when ripe. Like most palms from the lowlands they are very tropical in their cultural needs.

Parajubaea cocoides is a handsome palm which succeeds well in temperate regions.

Parajubaea cocoides

A little-known palm which will grow and fruit successfully in Sydney. It is native to Ecuador and Colombia where it is found at high altitude. It is quite an attractive species with a solitary trunk (to 8 m tall) and a graceful crown of bright-green, pinnate leaves which are silvery beneath. It requires well-drained soil and the plants will tolerate exposure to sun when quite small. Seeds are usually slow and difficult to germinate. Germination may be improved by pre-soaking in water for two days and sowing the seeds shallowly in a very open material such as sphagnum moss.

Paralinospadix

A genus of twenty-one species of elegant palms endemic in New Guinea where they grow in dense rainforest and jungles frequently along stream banks. They are solitary, feather-leaved palms and are mostly of small to medium growth. In some species the fronds are quite wide relative to their length and this feature makes them very ornamental when grown in containers. *Paralinos-*

padix species should be much more widely grown than they are but their popularity is limited by lack of propagating material. They are best suited to shady positions in tropical regions. The status of this genus is somewhat uncertain and botanists agree that it should be included in *Calyptrocalyx.*

Paralinospadix hollrungii

A slender, clumping palm found on the Huon Peninsula of New Guinea where it grows as an understory plant in rainforest. It is remarkable for the variability in its leaves with some being scarcely divided into coarse, broad segments while others are finely divided. Whatever the leaf shape, it is a highly desirable palm for a shady position in a tropical garden and would make an extremely decorative plant for a large container.

Paralinospadix micholitzii

This extremely beautiful palm which originates in the dense rainforests and jungles of New Guinea has been grown in England as a glasshouse plant for many years. The plants form a crown of arching, broad, bright-green, pinnate fronds and when well grown make a delightful tub specimen. The young leaves are deep purplish and this colour gradually fades as they expand. The plants like a rich, well-aerated, organic soil mix and should not be allowed to dry out. They can be grown outside in tropical areas but require shady, moist conditions. The species is virtually unknown in Australia but very deserving of introduction.

Paralinospadix petrickiana

An elegant New Guinean palm which was apparently described from plants growing in Kew Gardens early this century. Its pinnate leaves are deep purplish brown when young and expand to over 2.5 m long and nearly 1 m across. The plants form an erect clump of many fronds and are an eye-catching tub specimen for glasshouse decoration. In tropical regions they can be grown outside but require a very shady position and plenty of water during dry periods. They also like plenty of mulch and organic matter in the soil. Little is known about this species' germination.

Pelagodoxa

A monotypic genus of palm endemic to the Marquesas Islands. The species is a solitary palm with large, simple leaves and unusual tuberculate fruit. It is a highly prized collectors palm.

Pelagodoxa henryana

A spectacular palm restricted in its native state to the islands of the Marquesas where it is uncommon to rare. Its most handsome feature is its large, entire leaves which may be 2 m long and 1 m wide. These are bright green above and silvery beneath but unfortunately are readily shredded by the wind and only those plants in sheltered positions retain entire leaves. The trunk grows to 7 m tall and is fairly slender. The fruit are large (up to 10 cm across) and are covered with rough, tubercular projections. Solitary plants are capable of setting seed. Odd plants of this unique palm are known from many botanical collections throughout the world. Tahiti probably has the most plants in cultivation and also has an active program underway to increase numbers. The palm is very cold sensitive and the large leaves are subject to wind damage. Plants need a semi-protected position in well-drained soil. Seed is somewhat slow and erratic to germinate.

Phoenicophorium

A monotypic genus endemic to the Seychelles islands where the palm is very common. It is a distinctive, solitary species with large, entire leaves. These leaves are pinnately veined and may shred in the wind to give a false pinnate appearance. The generic name has an interesting derivation, alluding to the theft of one of these palms from Kew Gardens late last century. The genus was previously known as *Stevensonia*.

Phoenicophorium borsigianum

An interesting palm valued for its arching, simple leaves which may be more than 2 m long and nearly 1 m wide. Young plants are particularly distinctive and make excellent tub specimens. The margins of the leaves are deeply indented, giving a toothed appearance. The petioles and trunk are very spiny when young but become smooth with age. In its native forests of the Seychelles this palm may reach more than 15 m tall. In cultivation it is quite slow growing and demands warm, shady, moist conditions. It is very cold sensitive and best suited to tropical regions. In Australia it is strictly a collectors palm.

The handsome, but rare, *Pelagodoxa henryana*.

Phoenicophorium borsigianum

Phoenicophorium borsigianum showing the beautifully symmetrical leaves.

Phoenix canariensis is a very hardy palm which grows well in inland regions.

Phoenix
Date Palms

A genus of seventeen species of palms found in tropical Africa and Asia. They are solitary or clumping, feather-leaved palms and some species are widely planted and of commercial significance. A number of species are familiar park and garden plants in Australia. The fruit is a berry and the lowermost leaflets on each leaf are reduced to sharp spines. The leaves also have a terminal leaflet. In general they are hardy, sun-loving palms and adapt well to cultivation. Species hybridise freely and this should be noted when collecting seed from cultivated plants.

Phoenix acaulis

The trunk of this palm is very short, swollen (sometimes grotesquely) and densely covered with persistent petiole bases. At its apex it bears a crown of arching, pinnate fronds 1-2 m long. The leaflets, which are dark green, are 30-45 cm long and grouped in small bundles. The inflorescence (30-60 cm long) often trails over the ground and may be partially buried. After flow-ering it carries clusters of bright-red, oval fruit which have a sweet, edible flesh. The palm is widespread in parts of India and Burma, usually growing on poor, stony ground. It is attractive and very hardy and will grow well in subtropical and tropical regions.

Phoenix canariensis
Canary Island Date Palm

The Canary Islands are the home of this familiar palm which is now widely cultivated throughout the world. In Australia it is a familar sight and has proved to be especially hardy in inland districts, tolerating the heat and dry conditions without setback. It is especially adaptable since it can be grown in temperate, subtropical and tropical regions and in coastal as well as inland areas. It is very frost hardy and will thrive in quite poor soils although it does not succeed where the drainage is poor. This palm is dioecious and male and female plants are necessary to produce seed. The stout, woody trunk grows up to 20 m tall and is crowned by long, pinnate, light-green fronds which are spiny at the base. Large clusters of

seed or suckers. Suckers usually transplant readily while seeds may take four or five months to germinate. (For further details on Date Palm see page 39.)

Phoenix farinifera
Flour Palm

In nature this palm grows close to the sea and frequently forms impenetrable, spiny thickets. It is native to parts of India and the northern area of Sri Lanka. The trunk grows to about 1 m tall and has a floury pith which may be harvested and eaten after baking or other suitable preparation. The fronds are short, deep green and with the lower pinnae very sharp and spiny. The fruit, which are about 1.5 cm long, have a sweet, mealy flesh. Because of its spiny nature this palm has limited horticultural appeal, however it can be successfully grown in a sunny position in tropical or subtropical regions.

Phoenix loureirii

This species, although named in 1841, has been confused with *P. roebelenii*, especially in horticul-

golden fruits are especially colourful in inland districts. Seed germinates readily, usually one to two months after sowing.

Phoenix dactylifera
Date Palm

The Date Palm is famous for its succulent, edible fruit but in Australia these are only produced in dry inland tropical and subtropical areas. Despite this drawback the palm is widely planted throughout Australia in temperate and tropical regions and is a very hardy and quite ornamental plant. It is an excellent coastal plant, tolerating full exposure and heavy buffeting by salt-laden winds. It also succeeds very well in hot inland districts and in some parts has become naturalised. In cold-temperate regions the plants grow happily but rarely produce flowers. Date palms produce suckers both on the trunk and around the roots but in parks and gardens these suckers are rarely allowed to persist. The basal leaflets of a Date Palm leaf are very sharp and spiny. The crown is a graceful spreading one and the leaves are usually grey-green. Trees are either male or female and if fruit are required at least one of each sex is necessary. Dates can be propagated from

Phoenix dactylifera, the Date Palm, is adaptable to a range of climates and soils.

ture. They are very similar in general appearance and in many important features. Both grow in Indochina but *P. loureirii* is more widespread, extending also to India and Hong Kong. Plants of it can be distinguished from the very commonly grown *P. roebelenii* by the leaflets which are carried in several planes (those of *P. roebelinii* are flat and in one plane). In nature plants may grow to 4 m tall but this is unusual in cultivation. Fruits are oblong, about 12 mm long and dark purple when ripe. This palm has also been known as *P. humilis* and *P. hanceana*.

Phoenix paludosa
Mangrove Date Palm

As the common name suggests, this palm which is native to India, Indochina and Malaysia commonly grows in low-lying wet areas adjacent to mangrove communities and along river deltas, and so on. It also grows inland and frequently forms dense, almost impenetrable, thorny, thickets. It is a suckering species, very reminiscent of *P. reclinata*, and like that species makes a very decorative lawn specimen for areas such as parks and large gardens. The trunks often do not grow more than 2 m tall (but may sometimes double that height) and the leaves are spreading with somewhat flaccid leaflets which are green above and grey beneath. Leaf sheaths are covered with coarse fibre and the petioles have long, yellowish thorns. The fruits, which are about 1 cm long, may be orange or black when ripe. The species is best suited to tropical and subtropical areas although in southern parts it has proved to be rather cold sensitive.

Phoenix pusilla
Ceylon Date Palm

Although a native of hot, moist, lowland tropical areas, this palm has proved to be surprisingly tolerant of cold and will grow quite successfully in temperate regions. It is a fairly slender but coarse palm, the trunk of which is rough and covered with densely packed leaf bases. In cultivation plants do not grow much more than 3 m tall. The fronds are green or more commonly glaucous and spread in an arching crown. They are distinctive because the leaflets radiate in many planes. The fruit are interesting, ripening to a red or violet colour and with a sweet pulp. Two plants are necessary to produce fertile seed. This palm is very easily grown and adapts to

Phoenix pusilla.

most well-drained soils. A sunny position is essential. This species has been well known as *P. zeylanica*.

Phoenix reclinata
Senegal Date Palm

This handsome palm forms a large clump consisting of many slender trunks curving away from each other and crowned with bright-green, attractively curved, pinnate fronds. Numerous basal suckers form a green rosette around the bottom of the trunks. The palm is native to tropical Africa along the margins of streams and soaks, often close to the coast, and is a most impressive species for cultivation. It grows readily in tropical or temperate regions and seems quite tolerant of cold and frosts. Excellent for park planting, it looks particularly attractive when sited near water. Young plants respond markedly to regular watering, mulches and side dressings with fertiliser rich in nitrogen. A sunny position is most suitable. Two plants are necessary for fertile seed production. The brown fruit are edible but rather astringent. Propagation is by seed which germinates easily, or by removal of suckers.

A delightful clump of *Phoenix reclinata*.

The Dwarf Date Palm, *Phoenix roebelenii* is commonly grown in Australia.

The handsome *Phoenix rupicola*.

Phoenix sylvestris can be grown from tropical to temperate regions.

Phoenix roebelenii
Dwarf Date Palm

The origin of this palm has been uncertain for many years but has recently been established as being Laos. It has become extremely popular in cultivation and is commonly grown, particularly in coastal districts of the subtropics although it will also grow happily in temperate regions. It will grow in a sunny or shady position and is quite hardy and drought tolerant once established. When young it makes an excellent tub specimen and is also useful for indoor decoration, although its spiny leaves are somewhat of a drawback. The trunk is slender and rarely grows more than 2 m tall while the dark-green fronds are generally curved or arch gracefully. Regular watering and side dressing with nitrogenous fertilisers promotes strong, lush growth. The plants are dioecious and two are needed for seed production. Seeds germinate readily within three months of sowing. The fruit is edible but has only a thin layer of flesh.

Phoenix rupicola
Cliff Date Palm

This small to medium sized palm is native to India where it grows among rocks on cliffs and gorges. It is similar in many respects to *P. roebelinii* but is much more robust and with longer fronds which arch in a graceful crown. It also bears bright yellow fruits that are very decorative in mass. This palm is not as commonly grown as other species of *Phoenix* although occasional specimens are seen in tropical and subtropical regions. The trunk grows to 8 m tall and this combined with the neat crown makes this palm an excellent one for gardens. It will grow in a sunny or shady position and is ideal for mingling with ferns in a bush house. The plants are dioecious and two are needed to produce fruit. Seed germinates readily, taking two to three months.

Phoenix sylvestris
Silver Date Palm

A native of India where it is common in scattered stands, this palm is similar in general appearance to the Canary Island Date Palm, *P. canariensis*. It is generally much faster growing, however, and has a crown of grey-green or glaucous fronds. In its native state the flower stalks are tapped for their sap which is boiled down to make date sugar. The yellow fruit are reputedly edible but are very acid and if at all green are also astringent. This hardy palm will grow in tropical or temperate regions and in inland and coastal districts. It requires a sunny position in well-drained soil. The plants are dioecious and two are necessary for seed production. Seed germinates easily, usually within three months of sowing.

Pigafetta

A monotypic genus of palms restricted to the Celebes, Moluccas and New Guinea. The solitary species is a feather-leaved palm rather uncommon in cultivation and reputed to be extremely fast growing.

Pigafetta filaris

One of the most graceful and beautiful of all palms, this species is very fast growing and with a slender, straight trunk which is greenish with grey rings. Native to The Celebes, Moluccas and New Guinea, plants are reported to reach a towering 50 m tall. The pinnate fronds are arching and with the dark green leaflets held obliquely erect. Golden spines cover each leaf base, petiole and rhachis. The round yellowish fruit are about 1 cm across and are patterned with overlapping brown scales. Studies by John Dransfield have shown that the species is a pioneer palm colonising disturbed earth, embankments, roadsides etc, but being absent from dense forests. Seedlings in fact die if they are too shaded. *Pigafetta* seems to be rather uncommon in cultivation and is best suited to lowland tropical regions. Young plants require an open, sunny position and are very sensitive to shading. Seed loses it viability quickly. Fresh seed germinates rapidly, often within a month of sowing. The species was previously known as *P. elata*.

Pinanga

A large genus of tropical palms numbering 120 species widely distributed throughout South-east Asia and the Indo-Malaysian region. They are solitary or clumping palms with pinnate or rarely entire leaves and a crownshaft. The stems are slender and bamboo-like and are often colourful. The leaves generally have few, widely spaced leaflets and are rather variable in shape. Frequently the inflorescence and fruit are of bright, contrasting colours. Pinangas grow in jungle and rainforest and like shady positions in the tropics. In recent years they have become more popular

The highly desirable tropical palm *Pigafetta filaris* is extremely sensitive to cold.

and have much to offer gardeners in tropical regions. Pinangas are often difficult to identify with accuracy and many species in Australia are sold as *Pinanga* sp. and others are wrongly named.

Pinanga barnesii

A small, clumping palm from the Philippines with slender, greyish-green, prominently ringed stems 2-5 cm across and usually not more than 2 m tall. The leaves have ten to twenty fairly broad segments which are dark green above and ash-coloured beneath and often have some yellow marbling and purplish petioles. They are unevenly spaced and are deeply incised on the tips. Ovoid fruit 2-3.5 cm long are large for such a small palm and brilliant red when ripe. This is a much-sought-after, neat palm that is an ideal subject for tropical gardens. Plants need protection from long periods of hot sun and require plenty of water during dry spells. Seed germinates within one to two months of sowing.

Pinanga coronata

An attractive cluster palm with slender trunks

Pinanga coronata.

each of which is topped by a graceful crown of fronds. Each leaf is bright green and pinnate with fairly broad segments which have prominent ribbed veins. Clusters of fairly small fruit are red when ripe. Native to Java this palm is very tropical in its cultivation requirements. Plants grow best under the canopy of shady trees and like an abundance of water especially during dry times. They have proved to be very cold sensitive. Occasional nice plants of this palm are to be seen in gardens of north-eastern Queensland.

Pinanga dicksonii

An Indian palm which is common in cool, humid, mountainous gullies. Plants may be solitary or clumping with smooth, slender, green stems to 5 m tall and less than 5 cm thick. The pinnate leaves are about 1 m long and carry numerous, broad, sessile leaflets which may be up to 60 cm long. The fruit are about 2 cm long and reddish when ripe. This *Pinanga* has proved to be adaptable in cultivation and more cold tolerant than many of its relatives. As well as the tropics it will succeed in subtropical areas. A shady position seems preferable.

Pinanga disticha

Native to Malaysia, this dwarf palm is commonly encountered in dry rainforest growing in extensive, spreading patches. Its shiny brown stems are thin and sinuous and grow to about 1 m tall. Plants sucker freely and the clumps spread quickly under good conditions. The leaves are simple or divided into a few small, narrow leaflets. These are very dark green and are attractively marbled with paler blotches and spots. Small, red, elliptical fruit are carried on slender, simple spikes about 10 cm long. This little gem of a palm would appear to have tremendous potential for garden culture. It should succeed in subtropical as well as tropical areas in a shady position.

Pinanga elmeri

This species is very similar to *P. philippinensis* but can be immediately distinguished by the rusty-brown scales on the leaf sheaths. It also is a small to medium sized palm with slender, ringed stems that reach 2-4 m tall and 2-5 cm thick. Its fronds have numerous, pointed, dark-green pinnae and spread in a graceful crown. Native to lowland rainforests of the Philippines it is an attractive palm for the tropics and subtropics, apparently succeeding best in a sheltered position. Seed germinates within two months of sowing.

Pinanga genonomiformis

A small palm from the Philippines which is uncommon to rare in its natural habitat but is now becoming fairly widely grown in the tropics. It forms a neat, suckering clump of thin stems to about 1.5 m tall and the small, bright-green fronds are entire or bear one or two pairs of leaflets which contrast nicely with the unusual purple, bamboo-like stems. The palm makes an excellent pot plant and in the garden likes a moist, shady position. It grows well in the tropics and can also be grown as a glasshouse plant further south. Seed germinates readily but may take up to five months to appear.

Pinanga gracilis

A graceful palm from India where in parts it is reported to be common in moist forests. It is a clumping species with stems only 2 cm thick and 3-5 m tall. The pinnate leaves are about 1 m long, dark green and with deeply cleft leaflets which are about 30 cm long. Plants in fruit are very

The attractive leaves of *Pinanga kuhlii*.

Pinanga kuhlii in fruit.

decorative, having clusters of scarlet to orange fruit each about 1 cm long. This is a slender palm with many ornamental features and thus deserving of wide cultivation in tropical and warmer subtropical regions. It needs a protected position in moist soil.

Pinanga insignis

Pinangas are mostly medium-sized, slender palms but this Philippine species is an exception, developing a large, woody trunk. Its fronds are also relatively large and have numerous, sword-shaped pinnae which are distributed evenly along the rhachis. These are stiffly spreading to almost rigid and have deeply notched, acuminate apices. The ovoid fruit are about 2.5 cm long and reddish when ripe. This species is occasionally encountered in collections and is suitable mainly for tropical regions. Seed takes three to four months to germinate.

Pinanga kuhlii
Ivory Cane Palm

A handsome cluster palm which forms a neat clump of slender, yellowish trunks to about 8 m tall. Each trunk has a short, swollen crownshaft and the leaves are scattered apart rather than in a dense crown. The pinnate leaves are just over 1 m long and bear six to eight pairs of variable-shaped, rather-broad, falcate, prominently ribbed leaflets. It is native to Indonesia and grows in shady rainforest. This is a very attractive and desirable palm. It has proved to be rather cold hardy although plants need some protection, especially when young. It grows well in the tropics and subtropics and can perhaps be induced to grow in warm, protected positions further south. Given plenty of water and fertiliser the plants can be quite fast growing. It prefers a shady position rather than full sun. Seed germinates quickly, especially if provided with bottom heat.

Pinanga limosa

The pale stems and fleshy, waxy pink or white fruits of this palm are useful diagnostic features as well as adding to its ornamental appeal. It is a solitary species with a very thin trunk which may be no more than 1 cm thick and yet which may grow to more than 4 m tall. The leaves, which are about 40 cm long, can be entire with a deeply forked tip or divided into narrow leaflets. The fruit are about 1 cm long and are carried in two opposite rows on a simple spike 10-12 cm long. This species is a common and conspicuous palm of Malaysian rainforests. It is an ornamental, small palm suited to a shady situation in the tropics.

Pinanga maculata
Tiger Palm or Tamy's Palm
The young leaves of this Philippine palm are spotted and blotched with dark green or purple markings (sometimes yellow blotches) and present an unusual and attractive appearance. It is a solitary, feather-leaved palm with a slender, smooth trunk and an attractive crown of bright green leaves which are simple or with one or two pairs of leaflets or sometimes with many leaflets. Plants prefer warm tropical conditions and need dense shade when young. For best appearance they require plenty of water during dry periods and an organically rich soil. Young plants make an attractive pot subject. When mature they bear dense clusters of quite large, bright-red fruits.

Tiger palm is becoming popular in tropical regions where it is being planted in streets, parks and home gardens. It is adaptable to cultivation and quick growing. Seed germinates quickly (one to two months) especially if provided with bottom heat. This palm has also been included in the genus *Pseudopinanga*. *Pinanga copelandii* is a synonym of this species.

Pinanga malaiana
A slender, clumping palm with ringed, bamboo-like trunks which may reach more than 5 m tall. Its crown consists of a few, short, pinnate leaves with equally spaced broad leaflets. In young plants the leaflets are distinctly notched at the apex but this feature disappears in older plants. The crownshaft is prominent, being flushed with bronze or pink tonings. The infructescence is particularly showy having pinkish-red rhachillae and purplish-red fruit set in a black calyx. This species is an excellent garden palm but is best suited to the tropics. It likes a shady or protected position and appreciates rich soil, plenty of organic mulches and water during dry periods. Seed germinates easily, usually within two

Pinanga malaiana.

Pinanga malaiana in fruit.

months of sowing. The species is native to Malaysia where it is common in lowland rainforests.

Pinanga philippinensis

The trunks of this Philippine palm do not get any more than 3 cm thick and have prominently stepped nodes. The crownshaft is very conspicuous, being pale coloured and somewhat swollen, and the short fronds are held erect in a manner reminiscent of Betel Nut Palm. The leaf sheaths are covered with a thick, grey wool and the leaves have numerous, broad, pointed, dark-green segments. Its fruit, which are about 1.5 cm long, are carried in two opposite rows on the rhachillae. This is an ornamental, small to medium sized palm suitable for tropical conditions. Seed takes three to four months to germinate.

Pinanga polymorpha

As the specific name suggests, this palm is somewhat variable and can adopt different forms. Its most variable feature is its leaves which may be divided into narrow or broad leaflets. The leaves of this species are generally short and crowded into a dense crown. They are dark green above with conspicuous, attractive, yellow mottling and are greyish green beneath. Its stems, which are generally less than 2 cm thick, grow to about 3 m tall and lean and twist through the surrounding vegetation. Conspicious aerial roots are produced at the base of each stem. This palm is native to the highlands of Malaysia and is very common, growing in extensive thickets in moist areas. Plants in fruit are very decorative as the

A clump of *Pinanga simplicifrons*.

fruit are dark bluish green. They are also edible and follow cream flowers. A useful ornamental palm, this species grows best in a protected, shady position in the tropics.

Pinanga punicea

A little-known species from eastern New Guinea where it grows in lowland rainforest. It is a single-stemmed palm, the trunks of which are fairly slender (4-8 cm thick) and may grow to 6 m tall. The crown consists of a few finely divided fronds atop a bright green crownshaft. Ripe fruit are bright red. Cultural requirements of this species are largely unknown but are probably similar to other tropical species.

Pinanga simplicifrons

As the specific name suggests, the leaves of this palm are simple and undivided (although they are occasionally pinnate). They are oblong in shape with a deeply forked apex, and are scattered along the stems. The stems are very slender and sinuous and the palm forms spreading clumps to about 1 m tall. It is native to Malaysia and Sumatra and is locally common in lowland

Pinanga polymorpha, immature fruit.

forest, frequently along the floodplains of streams where it thrives in the alluvial soils. It is an attractrive, small palm for a pot or a shady tropical garden. Small, scarlet, horn-shaped fruit are borne sporadically throughout the year. This species can be propagated from seed, suckers or by aerial layers.

Pinanga speciosa

A slender, solitary palm from the island of Mindanao in the Philippines where it grows in shady rainforests. The plants grow to about 10 m tall and have a spreading crown of dark-green leaves about 2.5 m long. Small, blackish fruit each about 0.4 cm long are carried in clusters. The species is best suited to cultivation in tropical regions where it needs a shady, moist position for best development.

Polyandrococos

A monotypic genus of palms endemic to Brazil. The species is a solitary, feather-leaved palm which in the future should become more widely grown.

Polyandrococos caudescens
Buri Palm

A Brazilian palm that deserves to be much more widely grown but at this stage is only known in botanical collections. Good features include a medium size suitable for home gardens, a large, graceful crown of dark-green, pinnate leaves which are whitish beneath, showy yellow flowers and deep orange, edible fruit. At this stage in Australia it is only grown in tropical regions but would be worthy of testing in cooler climates. Plants seem to thrive in rich, well-drained soils and will tolerate a sunny position. They are, however, adaptable as to soil type and will grow in sandy soils of coastal districts.

Pritchardia

A genus of thirty-six species of fan palms of handsome and exotic appearance. They are native to various islands of Hawaii and Fiji and usually grow in near-coastal areas. They are solitary palms renowned for their large, stiff, pleated leaves which are carried in a heavy crown. They epitomise the tropics and some species are widely planted in parks and gardens in tropical regions of the world. Only two species are familiar in Australia with many more worthy of introduction.

Pritchardia beccariana

This beautiful, very symmetrical palm is native to the island of Hawaii where it occurs in rainforest on the windward slopes up to 1200 m altitude Plants have a slender stem to 18 m tall and large, handsome leaves which are bright green but somewhat scaly on the underside. A useful diagnostic feature is the large fruit which is variable, from 2.5-5 cm long. It varies from oval to spherical in shape and is black and shiny. Plants grow well in the tropics and in warmer areas of the subtropics in a sunny position.

Pritchardia gaudichaudii

Native to the Hawaiian island of Molokai where it grows in large colonies on vertical cliffs near the sea, this palm is a very attractive subject for cultivation. The plants have large, heavily pleated fan leaves which are more than 1 m across. Young leaves and the upper part of the crown are covered with attractive, white wool and as the leaves mature the wool is shed and the leaves are bright green. This fan palm succeeds admirably in subtropical regions and there are many attrac-

The decorative and symmetrical leaves of *Pritchardia gaudichaudii*.

tive specimens around Brisbane. A sunny aspect is essential and the plants prefer soils with free drainage.

Pritchardia hillebrandii

A handsome Hawaiian palm which will withstand some coastal exposure although not severe conditions. It succeeds best in tropical districts but can also be induced to grow in warmer subtropical areas. Interestingly this species was described from material cultivated by Hawaiian islanders and to this date has not been discovered in the wild. The plants grow 5-7 m tall and their leaves have bluish-green petioles which are densely woolly beneath.

Pritchardia kaalae

Native to the island of Oahu, this fan palm grows in rocky areas. It can be distinguished by its long inflorescences (more than 2 m long) which hang well clear of the canopy, and its small, black fruit which are usually about 2.5 cm across. The plants grow to about 10 m tall and have a sturdy crown of large leaves which are deep green on

Pritchardia maideniana is a rare species unknown in the wild.

both surfaces, and with drooping segment tips. Tropical and warm subtropical climates are suitable for its cultivation. It is a slow growing species but plants are decorative from quite a young age.

Pritchardia maideniana

Only two specimens of this palm are known in the world and these are to be found in the Royal Botanic Gardens, Sydney. It is believed that the original seeds were collected somewhere in the Hawaiian Islands by J. H. Maiden but the palm has not been relocated in the wild, probably because of the destruction of its habitat. The species was described in 1913 by Beccari from the plants growing in Sydney. Of the two palms in Sydney one has fruited but this plant was subsequently damaged in a storm. The existence of this species is very tenuous indeed and it is hoped that it can be rediscovered in the wild or at the very least fertile seed produced from the Sydney plants. Despite its apparent tropical origin the plants seem well suited to the Sydney climate and soils. It is characterised by leathery, glaucous, waxy, deeply segmented leaves, short, rigid inflorescences and small globular fruits. Two fruiting plants in the Jardin Botanique gardens in Tahiti have a close affinity with this species (see Hodel, 1982).

Pritchardia martii

A dwarf fan palm which rarely grows more than 3 m tall although it has a stout trunk and fairly large, stiff, grey-green leaves which spread in a rounded crown. Native to the Hawaiian Islands it is rarely encountered in cultivation in Australia and would seem to be a palm for the collector. Subtropical and warm-temperate regions offer suitable climatic conditions for its cultivation. It is a slow-growing species and seedlings will tolerate sun from an early age. Small plants make a very decorative container specimen. Seed appears to germinate within three to four months of sowing.

Pritchardia pacifica
Fiji Fan Palm

As the common name suggest Fiji is one of the areas of origin of this handsome fan palm which is also found in a few other islands of the Pacific. It is now widely cultivated in tropical and to a much lesser extent subtropical regions and is an

Pritchardia pacifica is a beautiful palm for the tropics.

excellent palm for coastal districts. The leaves on young plants are especially impressive, being up to 1.8 m long and nearly as wide, deeply pleated and with a brown, hairy surface when young. The plants may grow to about 9 m tall but are generally rather slow growing even in the tropics. They need very well drained soil and some protection when small. In Fiji the leaves of this palm were once made into fans which were for the exclusive use of the chiefs. Propagation is from seed which germinates readily after about two to three months. Bottom heat is beneficial.

Pritchardia thurstonii

Another handsome Fijian fan palm which is reported to grow on limestone cliffs close to the sea. It can be recognised by its long inflorescences which hang well clear of the stiff, dark-green leaves. It is an excellent palm for coastal districts and although it thrives only in tropical conditions it can also be induced to grow in warm conditions further south. It is sometimes grown as a glasshouse palm and is prized for its huge, stiff, pleated leaves. The plants need well-drained soil in a sunny position. The richer the

soil the better their growth. Seed germinates within three months of sowing.

Pseudophoenix

A genus of four species of insular palms with their distribution centred on the Caribbean Island of Hispaniola. All are solitary, feather-leaved palms found on well-drained, alkaline or saline soils in areas of low and erratic rainfall. Although they are virtually unknown in Australia, when cultivated in other countries they have proved to be very hardy and adaptable as well as ornamental.

Pseudophoenix sargentii

This palm, which is virtually unknown in Australia, is tolerant of considerable coastal exposure and should prove to be an excellent species for coastal tropical and subtropical planting. It is native to coastal Mexico, the Florida Keys and various Caribbean Islands and grows on limestone or sandy soils and will tolerate not only salt-laden winds but also salt water inundation of its roots. Though hardy and able to grow in extreme conditions this palm is ornamental and a decided acquisition wherever it is planted.

Pseudophoenix vinifera
Cherry Palm

As the specific name suggests this palm has been used for wine making on the island of Hispaniola where it is native. It grows on dry limestone hills in areas where rainfall is low and erratic. It is thus a very hardy palm and as well is extremely ornamental. It has a stout, bulging trunk which abruptly narrows below the crown. The feathery leaves are dark green and arch attractively. Huge clusters of large, bright-red fruit are a most decorative feature. In cultivation this palm has proved to be very hardy and ideal for drier subtropical and tropical regions.

Ptychococcus

A small genus of seven species of palms, six endemic to New Guinea and the other found in the Solomons. They are solitary, feather-leaved palms with a crownshaft and grow in protected forests and rainforests. The various species are poorly understood botanically and little-known horticulturally although they would appear to have excellent prospects.

Ptychococcus lepidotus

A small to medium sized, solitary palm native to New Guinea where it is found in rainforest at moderate altitude. The plants grow to about 5 m tall with a slender, grey trunk and a spreading crown of dark green fronds which have blunt leaflets. The crownshaft is quite prominent and greyish from a coating of soft hairs. The fairly large fruit (3.5-5 cm long) are bright red when ripe and follow green flowers. In New Guinea the natives use the trunk for making spears, bows and tipping their arrows. Although virtually unknown in cultivation in Australia this palm has potential for planting in tropical and subtropical areas.

Ptychosperma

A genus of twenty-eight species of pinnate-leaved, solitary or cluster palms found principally in New Guinea and the surrounding islands extending as far as the Caroline Islands. Two species are found in northern Australia. All are attractive, slender palms worthy of cultivation. As a group they are tropical in their requirements and will grow in sunny or semi-shady positions. Hybrids are known in the genus and in cultivation there are some confusing forms and errone-ous names. The genus has been recently revised (Essig 1978). For notes on Australian species of *Ptychosperma* see page 148.

Ptychosperma ambiguum

Although restricted to West Irian this small cluster palm is in cultivation and hopefully will become more freely available in the future. In its native state it grows on limestone hills and is locally common. In cultivation it grows readily enough but is very tropical in its requirements. Because of its compact growth habit plants make an excellent subject for containers or tubs. The stems will eventually grow to 5 m tall but are less than 2.5 cm thick. The species can be readily recognised by its slender pinnae arranged in clusters along the rhachis. The leaves grow to about 1.3 m long. Infructescences can be very colourful with the black fruit contrasting with the bright red rhachillae and cupules.

Ptychosperma angustifolium

Although this name is widely applied to plants in cultivation the species true identity cannot be determined because of inadequate descriptions and true specimens. As such it is a confused entity with no botanical standing.

Ptychosperma caryotoides

The mountains of New Guinea are the home of this palm which may be locally common in rainforest. It is a dwarf to small-growing species with a single, slender stem and small leaves with unusual, wedge-shaped pinnae. The flowers are yellowish and are followed by brilliant-red fruit. Unfortunately the species does not appear to have been introduced into cultivation. It would prove an excellent acquisition for tropical gardens.

Ptychosperma hospitum

This palm was originally described from a plant cultivated at Bogor Botanic Gardens. It is now considered to be merely a delicate form of *P. macarthurii* with narrow leaflets and is not specifically distinct. Plants are still grown and sold under this name.

Ptychosperma lineare

Plants of this palm usually form clumps but occasionally they remain solitary and are then very slender. In nature the trunks have been recorded as being up to 15 m tall and with a diameter of

A clump of *Ptychosperma lineare*.

Ptychosperma lineare in fruit.

only 4 cm. Each trunk bears a crown of spreading fronds about 2.5 m long. These have the narrow leaflets evenly arranged throughout, with the basal ones being short and somewhat crowded. Young leaf sheaths are woolly white. Purplish-black fruit, each 1-1.5 cm long, are borne in large clusters. This palm is native to New Guinea and is basically very similar in appearance to *P. macarthurii*. It can be grown in tropical regions in similar condition to that species.

Ptychosperma microcarpum

A New Guinea cluster palm of generally similar appearance to *P. macarthuri* but readily distinguished by its strongly clustered pinnae. It is a common species of central New Guinea where it grows in swamps and lowland rainforest. It is a very ornamental palm but rather cold sensitive and best suited to the tropics. Young plants make attractive tub specimens.

Ptychosperma nicolai

Essig (1978) has concluded that this palm is of hybrid origin and was originally described from juvenile material in cultivation. As such it is a confused entity with no botanical standing. Plants are still grown and sold under this name.

Ptychosperma propinquum

This attractive clumping palm is native to the Aru Islands of Indonesia and possibly extends as far as West Irian. It is a very similar in appearance to *P. macarthurii* but the stems of the inflorescence are densely covered with dark hairs, its fruit are larger and the pinnae are irregularly clustered along the rhachis. This species demands more tropical conditions than *P. macarthurii* but otherwise its requirements are similar. Seed germinates readily within three months of sowing.

Ptychosperma salomonense

This palm, which is common in lowland and highland rainforest throughout the Solomon Islands, is very tropical in its requirements and likes climatic conditions similar to those of Cairns. It is a handsome but variable species which strongly resembles *P. elegans* but has broader, relatively shorter pinnae and arching fronds. The trunk may reach 12 m tall and 8 cm thick. Young leaf sheaths are covered with white, woolly hairs but these are quickly shed as the leaves mature. Leaves have been measured at more than 3.5 m long and are carried in a graceful crown. The basal leaflets are crowded and this gives the crown a more crowded appearance than that of *P. elegans*. When ripe the fruit are bright red and very decorative. A number of forms exist within this species, probably the best known of which is the palm cultivated as *Strongylocaryum latius*. This is a smaller growing form with spreading leaflets and dark-orange fruits on purple rhachillae. Seed germinates one to two months after sowing.

Ptychosperma sanderianum

This palm is apparently only known from cultivation and is believed to originate in the Milne Bay area of New Guinea. It is a clumping palm similar in most respects to *P. macarthurii* but with shorter leaves and much narrower leaflets. It is rare in cultivation but from observation it seems to require similar conditions to *P. macarthurii* except that it is much more sensitive to cold. The seeds are less than 1 cm long and germinate readily. Seed takes two to three months to germinate.

Ptychosperma schefferi

Many plants of this species that are in cultivation may be of hybrid origin and are not typical of wild plants which are to be found in wet areas on the north coast of New Guinea. Plants may be solitary or clumping with stems to 7 m tall and up to 6 cm across. Young leaf sheaths are covered with white hairs which impart a woolly appearance. The leaves are 1.5-1.8 m long with about twenty-five pairs of regularly arranged pinnae which are dark green. Mature fruit (1.5-1.8 cm long) are dark purple and contrast with the yellowish-orange rhachillae. In cultivation this palm has similar requirements to *P. macarthurii*.

Ptychosperma waitianum

A small, solitary palm from New Guinea which promises to become widely grown for its neat, compact habit. Large plants may grow to 5 m tall but those in cultivation are usually much less. Leaves are much less than 1 m long and spread in a graceful crown. They have bright green, broad, wedge-shaped leaflets arranged evenly along the rhachis but with those at each end clustered. The flowers are very distinctive, being deep red and densely scaly. They are followed by fleshy black fruit nearly 2 cm long. Plants like a shady position and will succeed in the tropics or subtropics.

A clump of *Ptychosperma microcarpum*.

The very slender *Ptychosperma salomonense*.

Raphia

A genus of about thirty species of palms confined to Africa and Madagascar. They are suckering palms with upright crowns of feathery leaves and form colonies in wet situations. Raffia fibre is made from the leaflets of some species. *Raphia* palms are spectacular but are rarely seen in Australia.

Raphia farinifera
Raffia Palm

A spectacular Madagascan palm which colonises wet areas and spreads by suckers. Each trunk may grow to 3 m tall and bears an impressive crown of stiffly upright, feathery fronds. These are the largest fronds produced by any palm and indeed are the largest leaf in the plant kingdom, with individuals measuring over 20 m long. Each trunk is monocarpic but the colonies spread by the continual production of new suckers. The inflorescence is unusual and is similar to that described for *R. vinifera*. The fruit are most attractive, being about 6 cm long and are covered with overlapping, shiny brown scales. Raffia fibre, which today has decreased in importance, was made from the leaf bases of this palm. Raffia palms are far from common in cultivation and because of their size are restricted to parks and large gardens. They succeed best in the tropics but have also been successfully grown as far south as Brisbane. They grow best in wet soil and must be given sufficient room to spread. The species was previously known as *Raphia ruffia*.

Raphia vinifera
African Bamboo Palm

An interesting palm readily recognised by its upright crown of tall, dark-green, feathery leaves. The trunks are usually short and stout and sucker from the base and hence the plant eventually develops into a clump. Each trunk dies after flowering. The inflorescence is a most unusual structure best described as a thick, sausage-like growth. When it emerges it is erect but later becomes pendulous and may reach more than 3 m long. In Nigeria, where this species originates, the inflorescences are cut off as they emerge and the collected juice fermented into wine. Raphia palms are far too big for the home garden and can only be grown on acreages where they can spread. They are tropical in their requirements but can be successfully grown as far

south as Brisbane. Plants need to be grown where they can receive plenty of water. Seeds are difficult to germinate and begin emerging sporadically three to six months after sowing.

Reinhardtia

A small genus of five species of palm distributed from Mexico to South America. They are dainty, clumping palms with entire or pinnate leaves which have a unique pattern of small slits or openings near the base of each pinna. In nature they grow in shady positions in rainforest. Being small palms with a fairly compact habit they are excellent subjects for gardens or pots. They will tolerate some cold and will grow successfully in subtropical areas. The genus was previously known as *Malortiea*.

Reinhardtia gracilis
Window Pane Palm

This dainty, small palm grows in dense rainforests from Mexico to central America always in protected, shady positions. The plants grow in small clumps with thin stems up to about 1.5 m tall. The small, irregularly pinnate leaves have prominent veins and small gaps or 'windows' between the main veins at the base of each leaflet. These 'windows' create interest in the species and it has become a popular small palm to be grown mainly in subtropical regions. It makes an excellent container plant or if to be grown in the ground it likes a shady, protected position in good soil. Plants are fairly slow growing and can be propagated from seed which germinates readily or by suckers. *R. gracilis* is an extremely variable species and a number of varieties have been named based on leaflet numbers and the number of stamens in the flowers (var. *tenuissima*, var. *gracilior*, var. *rostrata*).

Reinhardtia latisecta

This species is the giant form of the window-pane palm with trunks that may grow to nearly 6 m tall. These are slender (about 6 cm across) and carry the attractively drooping leaves, scattered up the stems. Each leaf may be up to 1.3 m long and is divided into broad, conspicuously pleated pinnae which have slits or openings at the base. The leaflet tips are toothed and the terminal leaflets are united with a deeply notched apex. Black, ovoid to obovoid fruit about 2 cm long contrast with the bright red rhachillae. Native to

The Window Pane Palm, *Reinhardtia gracilis*, is a popular dwarf species for pots or ferneries (var *gracilior* is illustrated).

British Honduras this attractive palm forms sparse clumps in very shady situations. In Australia it is essentially a collectors item requiring a shady position in the tropics.

Reinhardtia simplex

Widely distributed from Honduras to Panama this small palm grows in shady situations on the forest floor. The plants form a sparse cluster of slender stems to about 1 m tall and have simple, deep-green leaves which are variously lobed and with prominently toothed margins. The leaves are generally small (10-15 cm long) and held at right angles to the stems. Unlike the commonly grown species in this genus, its leaves lack the slits or windows in their fronds. Essentially a collectors palm, this species favours protected, shady positions.

Rhapidophyllum

A monotypic genus of palms found in a few states of south-eastern USA. The species is a clumping palm with fan leaves. In cultivation it has proved to be a very hardy, cold-tolerant palm although it

will also succeed in the tropics. Plants are rarely seen in Australia.

Rhapidophyllum hystrix
Needle Palm or Blue Palmetto

Unfriendly is the best term for this palm which grows in dense clumps that are impenetrable because of the long, black spines which stick out from the petiole. Despite its nature the palm is an interesting species and has proved to be adaptable, growing in such diverse climates as those of Sydney and Darwin. Its creeping trunk (sometimes erect) branches freely to form clumps and the fan-shaped fronds are deep bluish green and silvery beneath. Flowering and fruiting takes place within the clump. The palm is native to the USA in the states of South Carolina, Georgia and Florida and grows in lowland areas of peaty soil. Plants will tolerate exposure to sunshine when quite small but are sensitive to frost. Seed takes about six months to germinate.

Rhapis

A small genus of twelve species of palms distri-

buted from southern China to Indonesia. They
are generally dwarf to small, clumping palms
with fan leaves that are deeply divided into
spreading, finger-like segments. The leaves are
scattered along the very slender stems which at
least in the young parts are covered by woven
fibres arising from the leaf bases. Rhapis palms
are highly prized horticultural subjects but only
two species are commonly grown in Australia.
Seeds are rarely produced by plants in Australia
and most propagation is by division of the
clumps. The various species are dioecious, male
and female plants being necessary for seed production.

Rhapis excelsa
Lady Palm

A multi-stemmed fan palm from southern China
that forms dense clumps or thickets that are leafy
to ground level. The leaves have five to eight
widely spaced segments that are stiff and spreading or held erect and with no tendency to droop.
The leaves are light green and generally take on
a yellowish hue if the plants are starved or grown
in full sun. The stems are very slender and
covered with woven brown fibre. *R. excelsa* is one

The Lady·Palm, *Rhapis excelsa,* is one of the most
popular dwarf palms.

of the best garden palms but because of its very
slow growth plants tend to be expensive and
hence the species is not as widely planted. It is
very cold tolerant and will grow well in temperate
areas. Plants can also be induced to grow in the
tropics. It will tolerate considerable exposure to
sun, even full sun, but the leaves bleach badly
and may even burn, especially if not watered regularly. For best appearance this palm should be
grown in a semi-protected position where it only
receives partial sunlight during the day. It can be
established under large trees and will make satisfactory growth providing it is mulched and kept
moist. As a tub plant it is unsurpassed and will
remain in the same container for years without
the need for repotting. Indoors the plants are
very decorative and will last for long periods
without the need for spelling. Most propagation
is by division of the clumps. Seedling grown
plants are sometimes available and these are usually raised from imported seed. A number of cultivars with variegated leaves are known but these
are strictly a choice collectors item in Australia.
Most apparently originated in Japan and have
silvery-white bands running along the leaflets.
They must be propagated by division.

Rhapis excelsa in flower.

Rhapis humilis
Slender Lady Palm

A lovely garden palm that was very popular early
this century and was widely planted in private
gardens as well as botanic and other municipal

gardens. It is probably native to China and forms a spreading clump that may extend to more than 2 m across and 4 m high. The clumps consist of numerous, slender stems densely covered with a closely woven, brown fibre and attractive palmate leaves scattered up their length. The leaves are deeply divided into numerous, dark-green, drooping segments and impart a very ferny appearance to the palm. In contrast to the Lady Palm the clumps tend to be taller and more open at the base and the leaves much deeper green. Plants will tolerate some sun but for best appearance like a moist position in deep shade. They grow very well in temperate and subtropical regions and are an excellent palm for mingling with or providing protection to ferns. Clumps also grow very well in tubs and seem to go for years without the need for repotting. They are also excellent for indoors tolerating considerable darkness and neglect. In the garden they like a well-drained soil with plenty of organic matter and regular watering. Female plants of this species are unknown and all plants in the world have resulted from vegetative propagation by division.

Rhapis humilis is a delightful clumping palm.

The dwarf *Rhapis*, which makes an excellent container plant, is probably an undescribed species.

Rhapis sp
Dwarf Lady Palm

This palm is fairly widely cultivated in Australia and in recent years has become a common nursery plant especially in subtropical districts. It is usually sold as *R. excelsa* 'Dwarf' but appears to be quite distinct from that species. It can be distinguished by the fewer leaf segments (three to six) which are widely spaced and often elliptical in shape and the different inflorescence. Plants do not grow much more than 1 m tall and develop into handsome clumps with dark, somewhat-glossy green leaf segments. It is an excellent palm for tub culture and indoor decoration. It is believed to have originated in Japan and comes true from seed. Large quantities of seed are available from overseas merchants.

Rhopaloblaste

A small genus of seven species of palms restricted to Malaysia, the Philippines and Indonesia. They are solitary, feather-leaved palms with a crownshaft and vary from small-growing species to very tall plants. Some species were previously included in the genus *Ptychoraphis*.

Rhopaloblaste singaporensis

When dried, lacquered and polished the slender stems of this palm make handsome walking sticks. Native to Singapore and Malaysia, it is a very common species of rainforests and moist, open forests. Clumps usually consist of two or three mature stems which may reach 3 m tall. These stems are supple and whippy and usually less than 2.5 cm thick. Leaves grow to 1.6 m long and have numerous stiff, narrow leaflets which are 35-45 cm long. Fruit are very colourful being about 1.2 cm long, fleshy and brilliant orange when ripe. All in all this is a very attractive and ornamental slender palm for a shady or semi-protected position in a tropical garden. It was previously known as *Ptychoraphis singaporensis*.

Rhopalostylis

Of the three species found in this genus of palms, two are endemic to New Zealand and the other to Norfolk Island. They are solitary palms with a prominent, inflated crownshaft and obliquely erect fronds which impart a distinctive silhouette. For notes on the species in New Zealand see page 150.

The delightful, small, tropical palm *Rhopaloblaste singaporensis*.

Rhopalostylis baueri
Norfolk Palm

This 'feather duster' palm closely resembles the Nikau Palm of New Zealand but is generally thicker and more robust in all its parts and the two can be readily separated when growing side by side. In particular, the crownshaft of the Norfolk Palm is stout, bulging and very prominent and the trunk and petiole thicker. Seedlings and young plants have distinct reddish tonings in the leaves. It is native to Norfolk Island where it is still common in the remnant vegetation. In cultivation it is quite a fast growing and handsome palm but for best appearance should be protected from the wind as the fronds readily become shredded. It is most successful when grown in moist, shady conditions and is an ideal palm for mixing with ferns. It succeeds quite admirably in temperate regions and can also be grown in the subtropics but its tolerance to tropical conditions is doubtful. Seeds germinate readily within three months of sowing and seedlings grow quite fast.

Roystonea
Royal Palms

A genus of six species of palms distributed from Florida to South America. They are solitary, feather-leaved palms with a prominent crownshaft. Some species are excellent horticultural subjects and are widely planted in tropical and subtropical areas. They especially make excellent subjects for park and avenue planting. A few of the species are very similar in their main features and are easily confused. Palms of this genus are often sold under the old generic name, *Oreodoxa*.

Roystonea borinqueana
Puerto Rican Royal Palm

Native to Puerto Rico this Royal Palm is basically very similar to *R. regia* but has a trunk that is prominently bulging above the middle and pale brown rather than purple fruit. Its dark green fronds have a feathery appearance due to the arrangement of the leaflets in many ranks. It is rarely grown in Australia and seems to be quite cold sensitive and best suited to tropical conditions.

Roystonea elata
Florida Royal Palm

In its natural state this palm occurs in the low

Rhopalostylis baueri is native to Norfolk Island.

swampy ground of Florida and today is still present in the Everglades region. It is a tall palm with a slender, ash-grey trunk and a large crown of dark-green leaves above a prominent, bright-green crownshaft. Its inflorescences are much longer than wide. It is uncommonly grown in Australia except by enthusiasts. Plants will tolerate some cold but are not as hardy as *R. regia*. They can be grown in subtropical and tropical regions. Seed germinates readily within three months of sowing.

Roystonea oleracea
South American Royal Palm

This is the tallest of the Royal Palms with trunks being recorded at more than 30 m high. They are smooth, of uniform width throughout (often with a conspicuous bulge at the base) and topped by a bright, shiny green crownshaft and a large crown of dark-green, spreading fronds. The leaves appear flat from the placement of the leaflets and in this feature and the flexuose rhachillae, the species differs from other Royal Palms. It is uncertain just how widely grown this species is in Australia because of confusion with others in the

Roystonea regia makes an excellent avenue palm.

Sabal bermudana.

genus but there are some nice specimens in the Rockhampton Botanic Gardens. It can be grown in tropical regions and also in warm-temperate districts as far south as Sydney. Seed germinates readily within three months of sowing.

Roystonea regia
Cuban Royal Palm

The bulging trunks are a useful guide to the identity of this palm although this feature is not always noticeable. Superficially the plants have a strong resemblance to the Queen Palm *(Arecastrum romanzoffianum)* as both are tall and stately with similar, feathery fronds. The inflorescences and fruit of the two species are, however, quite distinct and the prominent crownshaft immediately identifies the *Roystonea*. Cuban Royal Palm is essentially a tropical species and is very commonly grown in the tropical areas of eastern Australia. It is frequently planted in rows beside driveways, roads and avenues and makes a uniform and stately palm for this purpose. Plants can be grown as far south as Sydney but are generally very slow. A sunny position in well-drained soil is essential for success although plants may

grow rapidly in wet soils where the water is not stagna. Like Queen Palm the plants respond to heavy applications of fertiliser. The species is native to Cuba. Seed takes three to five months to germinate.

Sabal
Palmetto Palms

A genus of fourteen species of solitary fan palms found in the USA, Mexico and the West Indies. All species are unarmed and growth habit varies from those with a subterranean trunk to lofty species. Sabal palms are notoriously difficult to identify, particularly those of cultivated origin. Hybridism is common and a number of characteristics used to separate species are not constant. Most species are hardy, sun-loving palms and are excellent subjects for cultivation. They lend themselves well to municipal gardens and various species will succeed from the tropics to temperate regions.

Sabal bermudana

A fan palm from Bermuda which has proved to be adaptable in cultivation with mature specimens growing in the Melbourne Botanic Gardens. It is a fairly slender palmetto (to 50 cm thick) with a grey trunk and a sparse crown of shortish, blue-green leaves. As a garden plant it is fairly nondescript. Young plants will tolerate sun from a very early age. They are generally slow growing and require soil of unimpeded drainage.

Sabal causiarum
Puerto Rican Hat Palm

The hallmarks of this species are a very stocky, grey trunk which may rise to more than 10 m tall and be more than 1 m across and a dense, heavy crown of fan leaves which always seems to be too small for the massive trunk. Although of ungainly appearance the palm is nevertheless impressive and an excellent choice to line a driveway or scatter in open parkland. Native to Puerto Rico it is now widely planted in many countries of the world. It will grow well in tropical and temperate regions and also thrives on the drier atmosphere in inland districts. Its deeply divided leaves are usually dull green but may be bluish and after flowering the long inflorescences carry masses of small, black fruits that hang well clear of the leaves. In cultivation it needs very well drained soil and responds to added fertiliser. Once established the plants are very hardy to dry conditions. Seed germinates readily within two months of sowing but the seedlings are slow growing in their first couple of years.

Sabal domingensis
Palmetto Palm

In general appearance this species resembles a drawn out version of *S. causiarum* with a more open crown. Its grey trunk, although quite stout and woody, is usually much more slender than that massive species and grows taller (to 20 m high in nature). This species also has much larger fruit and the inflorescences remain hidden within the leaves which are strongly costapalmate and divided for about half way. Native to Santo Domingo in the Dominican Republic there is much confusion about plants in cultivation labelled as either this species, *S. blackburnia* or *S. umbraculifera*. Whatever the identity the palm thrives on hot, dry climates and succeeds admirably in inland districts. It can also be grown in many other regions and climates both temperate

The sturdy *Sabal causiarum.*

Sabal domingensis, a hardy palm for inland towns.

241

The slender, graceful Savannah Palm, *Sabal mauritiiformis*.

Plants of *Sabal minor* may have an underground or shortly emergent trunk.

and tropical. Good drainage is essential. Seed germinates readily within two to four months of sowing.

Sabal etonia
Scrub Palmetto

This is one of the easier *Sabal* species to identify with certainty since it has a subterranean trunk, and strongly costapalmate, green leaves which have many threads hanging from the segments near the division. It is native to southern Florida and seems to be relatively uncommon in cultivation. It grows well in tropical areas but its adaptability to colder climates is unknown. It likes a sunny position in well-drained soil. Seeds germinate readily within two to four months of sowing but seedlings are very slow growing.

Sabal mauritiiformis

This species of *Sabal* (native to Colombia, Trinidad and British Honduras) is quite a distinctive and attractive palm. It has a slender, grey trunk (to 15 cm thick) which may grow to more than 10 m tall and has a fairly open crown

of fan-shaped leaves. These are bright green above and silvery to glaucous beneath and the open appearance of the crown is enhanced by the widely separated segments, many of which are divided to the base (the divisions are variable). The inflorescence extends beyond the leaves and is branched complexly. This palm is best suited to tropical and subtropical regions and prefers some protection when young. Seed germinates within four months of sowing and seedling growth is slow. *Sabal glaucescens* and *S. nematoclada* are synonymous with this species.

Sabal mexicana
Rio Grande Palmetto or Texas Palmetto

Extending from Guatemala to northern Mexico and southern Texas along the valley of the Rio Grande river this fan palm frequently grows in large, pure stands. It is readily confused with other *Sabal* species and seems to be distinguished by its light-green, strongly costapalmate leaves that are deeply divided, and its rounded, relatively large (1.2 cm) brown fruits. It is an extremely hardy palm, well suited to culture in

Sabal palmetto (above) is from south-eastern USA. *Sabal palmetto* in flower (below).

inland areas where its crowns provide dense shade. It also succeeds in near-coastal districts and is adaptable since it can be grown from tropical to temperate climates. Plants are generally slow in their early stages but once established grow steadily. They require a sunny position in well-drained soil. Seed germinates readily within two months of sowing. *Sabal texana* and *S. guatemalensis* are synonymous with this species.

Sabal minor
Dwarf Palmetto Palm

Trunkless palms are relatively rare in Australian gardens but the Dwarf Palmetto is fairly widely grown, at least in subtropical regions. The trunk is usually subterranean and the leaves arise in a crown at the surface although some specimens may have a trunk 1-2 m tall. The leaves are fan-shaped, fairly stiff and usually of a bluish-green colouration. Plants are generally precocious and flower while quite young. The inflorescence is relatively slender and arches out from the rosette of leaves. Small, white, fragrant flowers are followed by black, shiny fruits and a succession of inflorescences is produced during summer. The Dwarf Palmetto is native to some southern states of the USA and makes an excellent garden plant. It is hardy in subtropical and temperate regions and succeeds best in a sunny position. It can be

propagated readily from seed which germinates in six to eight months.

Sabal palmetto
Palmetto Palm

A peculiar twist in the large, palmate leaves of this palm provides a ready means for its identification. This twist is imparted by the curved extension of the petiole which extends well into the leaf lamina. The leaves are dark green often with yellowish tonings, usually hanging and the segments are split at the tips. This rather impressive palm is native to the Carolina Islands and Florida, often growing in near-coastal areas. It succeeds well in sandy soil, tolerating some coastal exposure and looks good when planted in groups. It is particularly successful in subtropical and tropical regions and may be fast growing in good conditions. The plants generally flower and fruit when they are quite young. Seed germinates readily within three to ten months of sowing. *Sabal viatoris* is a synonym of this species.

Sabal parviflora
Cuban Palmetto Palm

The stout trunks of this Cuban palm sometimes bulge grotesquely. They bear a heavy crown of stiff, almost-round leaves which are divided about one third of the way and bear numerous, hanging threads along the margins. The inflorescences are completely hidden within the crown. The species is little-known in cultivation and would appear to be best suited to tropical regions. Seed germinates quickly after sowing.

Sabal princeps

Massive is the best word to describe this palm with its large, thick trunk and crown of huge, bluish-green, fan-shaped leaves. It is easily the biggest of the palmetto palms but its origin is uncertain and its botanical history confused. It is also known as *S. beccariana* but as both species were named from cultivated plants their identity is open to question. Names aside, the palm is impressive because of its stature and huge spreading crown. It grows too large for the average home garden but is ideal for parks and large municipal gardens. It likes a sunny aspect in rich, well-drained soil. Seed germinates readily within two to four months of sowing.

Sabal uresana
Sonoran Palmetto

A Mexican palm which is essentially a collectors item in Australia. Young plants are particularly decorative forming a cluster of large, deep bluish-green, fan leaves. These are deeply divided into stiff, spreading segments which have a few long, cottony threads near the sinuses. The leaves are

Sabal princeps is a massive palm.

Sabal uresana, the leaves of a young plant.

strongly costapalmate. Older plants develop a fairly stout trunk but their leaves are not as prominently glaucous. The species is very hardy, especially when established, and can be grown in subtropical and warm-temperate regions. Well-drained soil and a sunny position are necessary for its culture.

Salacca

A group of fifteen species of unique palms restricted to Malaysia, Indonesia and the Philippines where they form colonies in swampy ground. The branching trunks are subterranean while the tall, pinnate fronds are held erect. The large fruits are covered with overlapping scales and some species have a succulent, edible flesh. Although spiny these palms are imposing and ornamental. They will not tolerate cold and succeed well only in the tropics. *S. conferta* is now placed in the genus *Eleiodoxa*.

Salacca affinis

A prickly clumping palm from Malaysia and Sumatra where it grows as scattered individuals in shady forests. Leaves grow to about 3 m long and are green on both sides. They are held erect and arise in rosettes from the short trunks. All parts are well armed with long spines. The fruit grow to about 2 cm long and are scaly with a sweet, edible pulp. Plants are best suited to a position in the tropics. They need shade and plenty of water.

Salacca wallichiana

This palm is similar in general appearance and growth habit to the preceding species but its erect fronds, 5-7.5 m long, have narrow, grouped leaflets which appear to be whorled and are green on both surfaces. It has a smaller but edible, orange-brown fruit that is usually cooked before eating. The species is quite widespread, being found naturally in Thailand, Burma and Malaysia. Like *S. zalacca* it is cultivated for its fruit and is best suited to the tropics.

Salacca zalacca

The large, pear-shaped fruit of this spiny palm have an edible layer of pale yellow, succulent flesh surrounding the seed. In parts of South-east Asia these fruit are sold in the market place and are reported to be a popular article of diet. The palm itself forms huge clumps, spreading by branching subterranean trunks. Each trunk, where it emerges, carries a crown of long, erect, pinnate fronds with broad leaflets that are white beneath. Numerous sharp spines clothe most of the above-ground parts. The palm is native to the Indonesian island of Java where it grows in thickets in wet, swampy soil. Despite its vicious spines this palm is cultivated for its interesting

Salacca affinis, a spiny clumping palm for the tropics.

Salacca zalacca is valued for its tasty, edible fruit.

habit and its edible fruit. It is very tropical in its requirements and succeeds best in lowland tropical areas. The plants like plenty of water and it has been observed that they like regular dressings of fertiliser. Plants will tolerate full sun from a very early age. Seeds are fairly large and may be slow and erratic to germinate. This palm was previously known as *S. edulis*.

Satakentia

A monotypic genus endemic to the Ryukyu Islands. The species is a solitary, feather-leaved palm well worthy of cultivation. It was previously included in the genus *Gulubia* and is also closely related to *Clinostigma*.

Satakentia liukiuensis
Satake Palm

A handsome palm with many features reminiscent of a coconut. It is becoming popular in some states of the USA but at this stage is only a collectors item in Australia. It is a clean-cut palm with a neat, ornamental appearance. Cultivated plants probably will not grow much more than 10 m tall and have a crown of deep-green, graceful fronds. Newly emerged inflorescences are a colourful pink. The palm is native to the Ryukyu Islands and should prove to be adaptable to a variety of climates.

Scheelea

A genus of forty-two species of palm mostly found in South America and with some in the West Indies. They are solitary palms with a stout trunk and a crown of erect, long, pinnate leaves. Plants of this genus are rarely grown in Australia.

Scheelea butyracea

This is one of a group of more than fifty palms in four genera that have basically similar physical characteristics. As the genera are split up on the basis of floral features the identification of palms in this group on vegetative characters is fraught with difficulty. *S. butyracea* is a handsome palm from Colombia with tall, erect, dark-green fronds. In young plants these seem to erupt in a clump from the ground. Older plants develop a fairly stout trunk. The palm grows best in the tropics and requires a partially protected position when young.

Schippia

A monotypic genus of palm endemic to British Honduras. The species is a slender, elegant, solitary fan palm that deserves to become widely grown.

Schippia concolor

This palm must surely be one of the most graceful of all the fan palms. It has a slender trunk to about 10 m tall and an open crown of delicately segmented leaves. These are carried on long, slender, smooth petioles which are divided at the base. The leaves themselves are dark, glossy green above and deeply divided into slender, arching segments. Fruit are about 2.5 cm across, rounded and white when ripe. In nature the species grows in the shaded forests of British Honduras. Cultural requirements are largely unknown but it has been reported that plants will stand exposure to sun. Tropical and subtropical regions would probably be most suitable.

Serenoa

A monotypic genus the species of which is widespread in the south-eastern USA, growing in colonies. It is a fan palm with a branching, subterranean trunk and is very attractive when well grown.

Serenoa repens
Saw Palmetto

Native to various states of the south-eastern part of the USA the Saw Palmetto grows in huge colonies and is most common on the coastal plain. It is a fan-palm with a trunk that is usually subterranean but sometimes emergent and reaching 3 m tall. The leaves are extremely variable in colour, often being green or yellowish but in some forms being a splendid silvery-white. They are held stiffly erect and form quite an impassable barrier. Saw Palmettos are an attractive palm for cultivation and do extremely well in coastal districts, tolerating considerable exposure to salt-laden winds. They are rather cold sensitive however and succeed best in tropical or warm subtropical regions. The plants need a sunny aspect and will withstand full sunshine even when quite small. Once established they are very hardy, especially if their roots can tap ground water. Seed germinates readily within three to six months of sowing.

Serenoa repens, the Saw Palmetto of south-eastern USA.

Siphokentia

A small genus of two species of palm restricted to Indonesia and nearby islands. They are solitary, feather-leaved palms with a crownshaft and are collectors items.

Siphokentia beguinii

A shade-loving palm from the Molucca group of islands. It is a slender species with a shiny-green, prominently ringed trunk about 10 cm thick and a crown of shiny-green fronds, each about 2 m long. These are divided rather irregularly into narrow and broad leaflets with the terminal part undivided and prominent. The inflorescence is erect with creamy-white flowers followed by red, cylindrical fruit about 2 cm long. An ideal garden palm with a slender, manageable habit, this species is unfortunately rarely grown. It is best suited to tropical regions.

Syagrus

A genus of thirty-four species of palms distributed through South America usually in drier regions. They are solitary, pinnate palms with an attractive appearance but are rarely encountered in cultivation in Australia. Species of the genera *Arecastrum*, *Butia* and *Microcoelum* may be included in *Syagrus* by some authors. Species of *Syagrus* occasionally hybridise with *Butia* species.

Syagrus coronata

One of the more conspicuous features of this interesting Brazilian palm is its adherant leaf bases that form a loose spiral up the trunk. It is a fairly neat-growing palm that could be expected to grow about 5 m tall in cultivation. Its pinnate leaves arch in an erect crown and have the dark-green, leathery leaflets arranged in small clusters. Tropical regions are most suitable for its culture as it is very cold sensitive. Once established, plants will tolerate full sun. Seed is slow and germinates erratically over six to eight months.

Synechanthus

A small genus of two species of palm from South America. They are slender, pinnate-leaved palms found naturally in shady forests. They are very closely related to species of *Chamaedorea* but are monoecious whereas plants of *Chamaedorea* are dioecious.

Synechanthus fibrosus

In general appearance this species could easily be mistaken for a *Chamaedorea*. *S. fibrosus* is a solitary palm with a slender, shiny-green trunk and a crown of arching, pinnate leaves. These have thin, flexible, bright-green leaflets with the terminal pair united and fish-tail like. The inflorescence is a small panicle which emerges from among the lower leaves. Fruit are about 1 cm long and orange when ripe. In cultivation this palm likes shady conditions in deep, organically rich soil. It is rather sensitive to dryness and should be liberally watered. Plants have been very successfully grown in Brisbane gardens. The species is native to Costa Rica and Guatemala.

Thrinax
Thatch Palms

A small genus of four species of palms native to the islands of the Caribbean region between Florida and the West Indies and coastal areas of the adjacent mainland. All are fan palms with a

Synechanthus fibrosus, a small palm ideal for subtropical gardens.

solitary, very-slender trunk and they are commonly known as Thatch Palms. The leaf bases are split, the petioles unarmed and the fruit are white. They grow only on alkaline soils, particularly those derived from coral, and are in near coastal conditions. There is uncertainty about the names of cultivated plants and some are probably erroneous. As a group they are attractive horticultural palms which should be more widely grown. Very few plants are to be seen in Australia. The genus has been revised fairly recently (Read 1975).

Thrinax excelsa

This slender palm is endemic to Jamaica where it grows in exposed, rocky situations, always on limestone. It can be distinguished from other species of this genus by the leaves which are silvery white beneath from a dense covering of fringed scales. The inflorescence branches and flowers are colourful, being pink to purple. The leaves are very striking, nearly circular in outline, sometimes to more than 3 m across, and with stiffly pointed segment tips. Although rarely grown this is a handsome palm and is deserving of much wider recognition. It is best suited to the tropics and requires a semi-protected position in well-drained soil.

Thrinax morrisii
Brittle Thatch Palm

Although basically similar to other *Thrinax* species, *T. morrisii* can usually be distinguished by the presence of rows of numerous, small, white dots on the underside of the leaves. There is also a tendency for the leaves to be blue-green to grey beneath. The inflorescences arch well out from the leaves and are longer than in other species. Small white fruit are borne in dense clusters and are most attractive. The plants grow well in coastal conditions and are best suited to tropical and subtropical regions. Although plants of this species are rarely seen in Australia it deserves to be more widely planted, especially in coastal districts. Seeds are small but germinate readily. The species has had a confused botanical history and has been known by a variety of names, among them *T. microcarpa*.

Thrinax parviflora
Thatch Palm

A variable palm endemic to mountainous areas

Thrinax morrisii is a very slender palm.

of Jamaica where it grows in soils derived from limestone. It has the heaviest-textured leaves of the genus and these often have a corrugated appearance. Some plants have a very sparse, open crown of small leaves (ssp. *parviflora)* while others are thick and lush. The flowers and inflorescence branches are white and are followed by clusters of small, white fruit. As the common name suggests, its leaves were used for thatching dwellings in the area where it occurs naturally. It is an elegant fan palm, useful in a variety of districts and tolerating infertile, sandy soil. It is fairly frost sensitive and best suited to warm-subtropical and tropical regions. Plants need well-drained soils and will tolerate full sun when quite small. Plants of the subspecies *puberula* have a dense crown of leaves with broad blades and a prominent hastula to 4.4 cm long.

Thrinax radiata

In nature this palm always grows within the range of salt-laden winds in near-coastal areas. It is widely distributed in the Caribbean regions and also extends to southern Florida. It is an excellent palm for cultivation in exposed coastal districts and although restricted to calcareous soils in nature, cultivated plants will succeed in a wide range of soil types. The species is best suited to subtropical and tropical regions but can be induced to grow in a warm-temperate climate. Plants are very intolerant of wet soils and will happily take exposure to full sun from a very early age. They also make a very attractive and long-lived tub plant. The species has also been known as *T. floridana* and *T. martii.*

Trachycarpus

A small genus of four species of palms restricted to the Himalayan region of eastern Asia (India, Burma, China) and extending north to Japan. Only one species is commonly grown in Australia and New Zealand and that is widespread and familiar in temperate regions. All species are fan palms and most have solitary trunks (the Chinese species *T. caespitosus* is clumping). They are generally easy and rewarding palms to grow.

Trachycarpus fortunei
Chinese Windmill Palm or Chusan Palm

This palm, familiar in temperate Australia, is readily recognised by the fan-shaped leaves and slender trunk covered with persistent, dark-

The popular Chinese Windmill Palm, *Trachycarpus fortunei,* in flower.

brown fibre. It grows up to 10 m tall and the dark-green leaves are glaucous beneath. Some older leaves often persist on the upper part of the trunk as a skirt. This palm is native to China where it grows in cold mountainous regions. The fibre can be stripped from the trunk in pads and provides a very useful lining material for hanging baskets. The plants are reputedly monoecious but solitary specimens rarely produce seeds. This hardy palm thrives in temperate regions even in southern latitudes (Tasmania and South Island of New Zealand) but is somewhat difficult in the tropics. It requires a sunny position in well-drained soil. Young plants are generally slow growing. It has also been known as *T. excelsus* and is frequently sold in nurseries as *Chamaerops excelsa*. The seeds germinate readily, usually within three months of sowing.

Trachycarpus martianus
Windmill Palm

This species is generally similar to the preceding one and the two are rather difficult to tell apart. The most obvious feature of this species is the naked trunk, caused by the fibrous leaf sheaths falling with the leaves. Because of this the trunk appears quite slender and it also tends to impart a heavier aspect to the crown. The leaves are dark green and shiny and the flowers of this species are white and not as showy as the bright yellow ones of the Chinese Windmill Palm. *T. martianus* is reputed to be the slower growing of the two, however neither are fast-growing palms. This species is best suited to subtropical and temperate regions and likes an open, sunny aspect in rich, well-drained soil. It is native to the Himalayan region of northern India and Burma. Seed germinates within three months of sowing.

Trithrinax

A small genus of about five species of solitary or clumping, fan-leaved palms restricted to South America (principally Brazil). All have stiff, spreading leaves and an intricate, fibrous and spiny surface on the trunk. Only one species is commonly grown in Australia.

Trithrinax acanthocoma
Spiny Fibre Palm

A relatively little-known palm which can be readily recognised by the intricate webbing of brown fibre which covers the trunk. This fibre is

Trithrinax acanthocoma is a hardy palm for subtropical and warm temperate regions.

attached to the leaf bases which adhere to the trunk long after the leaves fall. Unfortunately the leaf-bases also bear numerous long, slender spines and these detract somewhat from the palms popularity. The combination of fibre and spines, however, does give the species a very distinctive, if formidable appearance. The leaves are fan-shaped and grey-green above. The species is native to Brazil and will grow in tropical, subtropical and temperate regions at least as far south as Sydney. It requires well-drained soil and a sunny position. These palms often flower when quite young and single plants are capable of producing fruit. Propagation is from seed which takes about eight months to germinate.

Trithrinax campestris

A little-known Argentinian palm which forms a compact clump to about 2 m tall. It has stiff, spreading leaves that are woolly white on the upper surface and glossy green beneath. The trunks are covered with a woven webbing in which are embedded spreading spines. This species is slow growing and quite showy when in flower and fruit. It is virtually unknown in Australia and is mainly to be found in botanical and enthusiasts collections.

Veitchia

A genus of eighteen species of palms, the vast majority of which are found on the islands of the New Hebrides, Philippines and Fiji. All are solitary, pinnate-leaved palms with a clean-cut, tropical appearance. Most are slender and are ideal garden plants although somewhat cold sensitive.

Veitchia arecina

Very tropical in its cultural requirements, this New Caledonian *Veitchia* is a graceful species with a very stout and sturdy inflorescence that spreads out stiffly from the base of the crownshaft. Small, pale-coloured flowers are followed by beaked, crimson-red fruit 2.5-5 cm long. The plants grow to more than 8 m tall with leaves about 2.5 m long. These have numerous, dark-green drooping leaflets which are obliquely cut at the tips. Seeds take two to three months to germinate.

Veitchia arecina.

Veitchia joannis

An elegant palm which in nature may attain heights of more than 30 m. Its slender, grey trunk is crowned with graceful arching, dark-green fronds more than 3 m long and which have prominently drooping, square-ended leaflets. Large clusters of red fruit are borne at the base of the bright-green crownshaft and are most decorative. This palm is common throughout Fiji and is now widely grown throughout the tropics. It is quite a fast-growing palm and has proved to be relatively cold tolerant, surviving in frost-free, temperate areas. When young it prefers a semi-shaded position but mature plants thrive in full sunshine. They like an organically rich, well-drained soil and respond to side dressings of nitrogenous fertilisers. Seeds germinate readily within two to three months of sowing.

Veitchia merrillii
Manila Palm or Christmas Palm

A familiar tropical species which is native to the Philippine Islands. It is becoming widely planted, especially in tropical areas and is favoured because of its neat habit and compact crown of arched, bright-green, feathery fronds. Its ornamental appeal is enhanced by large clusters of bright, glossy-red fruit which in the USA

The colourful fruit of the Christmas Palm, *Veitchia merrillii.*

Veitchia montgomeryana.

ripen about Christmas time, hence the alternative common name. It is an ideal species to plant in the lawn of the average suburban garden. Plants will grow happily in a sunny position and can be planted out when small. They are fast growing and may flower when quite young. Although they will survive in subtropical areas they are very cold sensitive and have their best appearance in the warm tropics and are excellent for coastal districts. Potted plants are reputed to be good for indoor decoration. Seeds germinate readily, usually within one to two months of sowing.

Veitchia montgomeryana
The identity and origin of this palm is subject to much confusion and it would seem to be an imperfectly understood species. There are even doubts as to whether in fact it is distinct from *V. joannis* and all plants seem to be of cultivated origin. They are known from gardens in many countries of the world. Cultivation and propagation notes are as for *V. joannis*.

Veitchia winin
A fast-growing palm from the New Hebrides

which has a prominently ringed trunk, a glossy-green crownshaft and a crown of spreading, pinnate, dark-green fronds the leaflets of which are not as drooping as in the more common *V. joannis*. It is a handsome palm which will succeed in tropical and subtropical conditions. Young plants need protection from direct sun but seek the sun as they grow older. For best growth they need lashings of water and a deep, organically rich soil. Seeds germinate soon after sowing and the young plants establish quickly.

Verschaffeltia
A monotypic genus of palms restricted to the Seychelle Islands. The species is extremely ornamental with some interesting characteristics. It succeeds best in the tropics.

Verschaffeltia splendida
Stilt Palm
An extremely ornamental palm prized by collectors for both its beauty and its interesting growth characteristics. Its leaves are simple and undivided and in young specimens are quite majestic, being bright-green, broad and pleated with conspicuously red rhachises. Unfortunately in mature palms the entire leaves readily split and appear as if pinnate. They are still, nevertheless unusually broad and form an attractive crown. Other interesting features of this palm are the long, black spines on the trunk and the cluster of stout, aerial roots which support the base of the trunk and are visible above ground. Stilt palms are native to the Seychelles Islands and grow in colonies on rocky slopes. Young specimens are extremely decorative and make fantastic plants for indoor or glasshouse use. In the garden they need shelter at least while young, and are best protected from strong winds. Warm, humid conditions with gentle air movement seem to suit them best. Seed germinates within two to four months of sowing.

Wallichia
A small genus of six palms restricted to the Himalayan region of northern India, Bangladesh and southern China. They are solitary or clumping palms with pinnate fronds the leaflets of which are folded upwards. In the clumping species the leaflets are generally broad with ragged margins, and somewhat resemble those of *Caryota* species. Most species are tolerant of cold

The tropical palm *Verschaffeltia splendida*.

Verschaffeltia splendida showing stilt roots.

but are rarely encountered in cultivation. *W. disticha* is an intriguing species with the leaves in a vertical row down each side of the trunk.

Wallichia caryotoides

An Indian palm which forms dense clusters about 3 m tall and spreading a similar distance. The trunks are virtually subterranean and bear at their apex a cluster of erect or arching fronds which have very irregular-shaped leaflets scattered along their length. These vary from oblong to fishtail shaped and are bright green above and silvery beneath. The inflorescences are borne on slender stalks a bit shorter than the leaves and carry a dense cluster of purplish-black fruit each about 1.5 cm long. In cultivation this palm has proved to be adaptable and ornamental. It is hardy once established and is suitable for tropical and subtropical regions. A semi-shaded position is favoured with the plants receiving exposure to some sun for part of the day.

Wallichia densiflora

The most outstanding feature of this small palm is its cluster of long, arching or erect fronds with

unusual leaflets not unlike those of a Fishtail Palm but bright green above and silvery-white beneath. As these fronds wave lazily in the breeze the contrast between the upper and lower surfaces is quite apparent. Each clump consists of a few short, broad and very crowded trunks with the leaves arising from near the end. Native to the Himalayas where it grows in shady, moist gullies this palm is very cold tolerant and well suited to temperate and subtropical areas. In cultivation it likes a shady aspect in well-drained, organically rich soil. Propagation is by seed which germinates fairly erratically and slowly.

Wallichia disticha

In Latin 'distichus' means arranged in two ranks and this epithet describes to perfection the leaves of this unusual palm which are placed in two vertical rows each on opposite sides of the trunk. This combination results in a very flat profile when the plant is viewed from the side. Native to the Himalayas where it grows up to 600 m altitude, this intriguing palm is unfortunately both rare in cultivation and short-lived. In cultivation the plants may reach 7 m tall taking ten to

A clump of *Wallichia densiflora*.

fifteen years, at which stage they begin to flower and then die four or five years later when they have matured all their clusters of dull-red fruit. Despite their curtailed life the plants are well worth growing. The leaves arch stiffly from the trunk and have long leaflets which are grouped in bundles. These are dark green above and greyish beneath, with a few short lobes and teeth near the apex. The trunk is invisible, being covered with persistent leafbases and their associated layers of fibre. Plants are best suited to tropical regions although they may be induced to grow in warm situations in the subtropics. Seedlings are fairly sensitive to cold.

Washingtonia

A small genus of two species of palm native to the southern states of the USA and Mexico. They are solitary, fan-leaved palms the old leaves of which clothe the trunk with a persistent, fibrous covering. Both species grow in colonies in fairly arid areas. They are popular subjects for cultivation in Australia and are widely grown in most climates and well-drained soils. Avenues of them are a familiar sight in many inland towns. The identification of the two species is subject to confusion in Australia. *Washingtonia* are commonly sold in the nursery trade but are unsuitable for indoor use.

Washingtonia filifera
American Cotton Palm

A widely grown and familiar palm that will succeed admirably in a range of soils and climates from the tropics to southern temperate regions as well as inland and coastal districts. It is a tall, distinctive palm with a fat, grey trunk and a spreading crown of grey-green, fan-shaped leaves. The old leaves persists as a petticoat covering the trunk and this may be right to ground level. Unfortunately, few palms in Australia survive with a petticoat as this feature is generally burnt. The name cotton palm arises from the white, cottony threads found on and between the leaf segments. It originates in the USA where it forms colonies in canyons of California and Arizona, also extending to Mexico. They grow to 16 m tall and a solitary specimen is capable of fruiting.

This palm has proved to be very hardy in Australia and is a fine palm for street, avenue and parkland planting. Once established the plants are very drought resistant. They prefer a sunny position although they respond to the use of fertilisers. Plants will tolerate exposure to direct sun even when quite small. Seed germinates rapidly, usually within two months of sowing.

Washingtonia robusta
Washington Palm or Skyduster
This species is frequently confused with *W. filifera* but it grows taller and with a much thinner trunk. There is also a tendency for the leaves to be much greener and on mature palms the leaf segments lack the adornment of the cottony threads. Like the former this species is also a very hardy and adaptable palm. It grows very well in cool, temperate regions as far south as Melbourne and also in the subtropics and tropics. Overseas literature records that this species is not as cold tolerant as *W. filifera*. It makes an excellent palm for avenues, driveways and in parklands. It is native to north-western Mexico. Seed germinates readily within two months of sowing.

Wissmannia
A monotypic genus of palm restricted to tropical east Africa. The species is a tall, solitary, fan-leaved palm very reminiscent of many *Livistona* species.

Wissmannia carinensis
African palms are generally uncommon in collections in Australia. This species was introduced a few years ago and seems to be quite hardy and suited to a tropical or subtropical climate. Native to tropical east Africa it was originally collected in the Somali Republic where it grows in protected positions always near permanent water. The plants usually grow in colonies, and are a tall, slender, fan palm that may reach 20 m in height. The leaf blades are deeply cut into segments and the petioles are armed with stout thorns. The fruit are rounded and up to 5 cm across. In cultivation plants have proved to be slow growing.

Zombia
A monotypic genus endemic to the Caribbean island of Haiti. The species, which is rarely

A tall specimen of *Washingtonia filifera*.

The Washington Palm, *Washingtonia robusta*.

Wismannia carinensis, young plant.

grown in Australia, is a fan palm with multiple stems.

Zombia antillarum

The strange name matches this unusual, clustering, fan palm which is native to Haiti where it grows in open, dry areas. Its trunks bear rings of downward-pointing spines and these are enmeshed in a woven mat of fibres which completely envelopes the trunk. Its leaves, which tend to droop, are deeply cut into segments which are dull green above and silvery beneath. *Zombia* is a rare palm in cultivation and succeeds best in a sunny position in the tropics. Seed germinates within two to four months of sowing.

APPENDIX I

A selection of Dwarf to Small Palms Suitable for Australian and New Zealand Gardens

Dwarf to small palms are popular subjects for gardens and containers since they don't take up much room. As a general rule they dislike direct, hot sun and prefer shady, moist conditions. They mingle well with other plants especially ferns and for best appearance should be planted in clumps. Once established they are very hardy plants but appreciate mulching and regular watering during dry periods.

Species	Clumping	Solitary
Allagoptera arenaria	X	
Areca ridleyana		X
Arenga engleri	X	
Arenga tremula	X	
Asterogyne martiana	X	
Balaka seemannii		X
Calyptrogyne ghiesbreghtiana		X
Chamaedorea atrovirens	X	
brachypoda	X	
cataractarum	X	
concolor		X
costaricana	X	
elegans		X
ernesti-augusti		X
erumpens	X	
geonomiformis		X
glaucifolia		X
klotzschiana		X
metallica		X
microspadix	X	
oblongata		X
radicalis	X	
seifrizii	X	
tenella		X
tepejilote		X
Dasystachys deckeriana		X
Dypsis gracilis		X
hildebrandtii	X	
Geonoma decurrens		X
elegans		X
gracilis		X
interrupta		X
Hedyscepe canterburyana		X
Hyophorbe lagenicaulis		X
Iguanura geonomiformis		X
Laccospadix australasica	X	X
Lepidorrhachis mooreanum		X
Linospadix minor	X	
monostachya		X
Microcoelum insigne		X
weddellianum		X
Nannorrhops ritchiana	X	
Nengella flabellata	X	
Paralinospadix petrickiana	X	
micholitzii	X	
Pelagodoxa henryana		X

Species	Clumping	Solitary
Phoenicophorium borsigianum		X
Phoenix loureirii		X
pusilla		X
roebelenii		X
Podococcus barteri		X
Ptychosperma macarthurii	X	
propinuum	X	X
sanderianum	X	
Reinhardtia gracilis	X	
simplex	X	
Rhapis excelsa	X	
humilis	X	
Rhopaloblaste singaporensis		X
Sabal etonia		X
minor		X
Serenoa repens	X	
Siphokentia beguinii		X
Synechanthus fibrosus	X	
warscewiczianus	X	
Wallichia densiflora	X	

APPENDIX II

Palms for Coastal Districts

Although many palms don't grow well in coastal districts certain species are very successful. These are species which will withstand buffeting, salt-laden winds and do not mind growing in sandy soils. The following list is far from exhaustive but is a good guide. The very hardy species tolerant of front-line exposure are marked with an asterisk.

Species	Region
Allagoptera arenaria*	Str-Tr
Arecastrum romanzoffianum	Str-Tr
Brahea edulis	Str
Butia capitata	Te-Str
Carpentaria acuminata	Str-Tr
Chamaerops humilis*	Te-Str
Chrysalidocarpus lucubensis	Str-Tr
madagascariensis	Str-Tr
Coccothrinax argentata*	Str-Tr
Cocos nucifera*	Str-Tr
Copernicia torreyana	Str-Tr
Dictyosperma album*	Str-Tr
Elaeis guineensis	Str-Tr
Hyophorbe lagenicaulis*	Str-Tr
Hyphaene thebaica	Str-Tr
Latania loddigesii	Te-Str
Licuala paludosa	Str-Tr
spinosa	Str-Tr
Livistona chinensis	Te-Str-Tr
Phoenix canariensis	Te-Str
dactylifera	Te-Str
paludosa	Str-Tr
roebelenii	Te-Str-Tr
rupicola	Te-Str
Pritchardia pacifica	Tr
Pseudophoenix sargentii*	Tr
Rhopalostylis baueri	Te-Str
sapida	Te-Str

Roystonea elata	Str-Tr
*Sabal etonia**	Te-Str
*minor**	Te-Str
mexicana	Str-Tr
*palmetto**	Str-Tr
*Serenoa repens**	Str-Tr
Thrinax microcarpa	Tr
radiata	Str-Tr
*Trachycarpus fortunei**	Te-Str
Veitchia merrillii	Tr
Washingtonia filifera	Te-Str
robusta	Te-Str

Te = temperate; Tr = tropical and Str = subtropical.

APPENDIX III
Palms for Temperate Regions

A surprising number of species of palms can be grown in temperate regions. While large collections are generally uncommon in such areas some species are a familiar sight in parks and gardens. In the list below, the very hardy, cold-tolerant species are marked with an asterisk.

Acoelorrhaphe wrightii	*Phoenix canariensis**
*Achontophoenix cunninghamiana**	*dactylifera**
*Arecastrum romanzoffianum**	*pusilla*
Bismarckia nobilis	*reclinata**
*Brahea armata**	*roebelenii*
edulis	*rupicola*
*Butia capitata**	*sylvestris**
Calamus muelleri	*Rhapidophyllum hystrix**
Caryota ochlandra	*Rhapis excelsa**
Chamaedorea costaricana	*humilis**
elegans	*Rhopalostylis baueri*
*Chamaerops humilis**	*sapida**
*Chrysalidocarpus lutescens**	*Sabal bermudana**
Hedyscepe canterburyana	*causiarum*
Howea belmoreana	*etonia*
forsteriana	*louisiana*
*Jubaea chilensis**	*mexicana*
Laccospadix australasica	*minor**
Latania commersonii	*palmetto*
loddigesii	*Serenoa repens*
verschaffeltii	*Trachycarpus fortunei**
Linospadix monostachya	*Trithrinax acanthocoma*
*Livistona australis**	*campestris*
chinensis	*Washingtonia filifera**
*Nannorrhops ritchiana**	*robusta**

APPENDIX IV
Popular Tropical Palms

In view of the fact that the vast majority of palms are found naturally in the tropics the range of species that can be grown there is overwhelming. The following list is only intended as a guide to some of the popular species that will succeed in these regions.

Aiphanes caryotifolia	*spinosa*
Archontophoenix alexandrae	*Livistona chinensis*
Areca catechu	*decipiens*
Arecastrum romanzoffianum	*rotundifolia*
Arenga engleri	*Neodypsis decaryi*
pinnata	*Oncosperma tigillarium*
Borassus flabellifer	*Opsiandra maya*
Carpentaria acuminata	*Phoenix dactylifera*
Caryota cumingii	*roebelenii*
mitis	*sylvestris*
rumphiana	*Pinanga barnesii*
urens	*kuhlii*
Chamaedorea cataractarum	*maculata*
elegans	*Pritchardia pacifica*
erumpens	*thurstonii*
glaucifolia	*Ptychosperma elegans*
microspadix	*macarthurii*
Chrysalidocarpus lutescens	*Reinhardtia gracilis*
lucubensis	*Rhapis excelsa*
Cocos nucifera	*humilis*
Corypha elata	*Roystonea elata*
Cyrtostachys renda	*oleracea*
Dictyosperma album	*Sabal causiarum*
Elaeis guineensis	*palmetto*
Hydriastele wendlandiana	*Salacca edulis*
Hyophorbe verschaffeltii	*Serenoa repens*
Licuala grandis	*Veitchia joannis*
ramsayi	*merrillii*

APPENDIX V
Palms for Wet Soil

The following palms will grow in very wet conditions and are especially tolerant of wet soil where the water is moving and is not stagnant.

Acoelorrhaphe wrightii	*Nypa fruticans*
Archontophoenix alexandrae	*Oncosperma fasciculatum*
cunninghamiana	*horridum*
Arecastrum romanzoffianum	*tigillarium*
Cyrtostachys renda	*Opsiandra maya*
Eleiodoxa conferta	*Phoenix paludosa*
Hydriastele beccariana	*reclinata*
microspadix	*Ptychosperma elegans*
rostrata	*macarthurii*
wendlandiana	*Raphia farinifera*
Licuala paludosa	*taedigera*
ramsayi	*vinifera*
spinosa	*Rhopalostylis sapida*
Livistona australis	*Roystonea regia*
chinensis	*Salacca affinis*
decipiens	*wallichiana*
drudei	*zalacca*
Metroxylon sagu	*Serenoa repens*
salomonense	

APPENDIX VI
Palms Suitable for Avenue Planting

Some tall palms make an impressive display when planted in rows along avenues or driveways. Most palms used for this purpose are solitary, feather-leaved species but fan palms can also be used. Some tall, clumping palms can also be employed for this purpose but generally create a different effect. The palms recommended here for avenue planting can also be used as specimens for lawns, parks, and so on.

Species	Region
Archontophoenix alexandrae	Str-Tr
cunninghamiana	Te-Str
Arecastrum romanzoffianum	Te-Str-Tr
Borassus flabellifer	Tr
Chrysalidocarpus lucubensis	Str-Tr
lutescens	Te-Str-Tr
Cyrtostachys renda	Tr
Dictyoperma album	Str-Tr
Howea belmoreana	Te-Str
forsteriana	Te-Str
Livistona australis	Te-Str
benthamii	Str-Tr
chinensis	Te-Str-Tr
decipiens	Str-Tr
drudei	Str-Tr
rotundifolia	Str-Tr
Lodoicea maldivica	Tr
Normanbya normanbyi	Str-Tr
Oncosperma tigillarium	Tr
Orbignya cohune	Tr
Phoenix canariensis	Te-Str
dactylifera	Te-Str
sylvestris	Te-Str
Pigafetta filaris	Tr
Pritchardia pacifica	Tr
thurstonii	Tr
Ptychosperma elegans	Tr
Roystonea boringuena	Str-Tr
elata	Str-Tr
oleracea	Str-Tr
regia	Str-Tr
Trachycarpus fortunei	Te-Str
Veitchia joannis	Tr
Washingtonia filifera	Te-Str
robusta	Te-Str

Te = temperate; Tr = tropical and Str = subtropical.

APPENDIX VII
New Guinea Palms

Australia's closest palm-rich neighbour is without doubt New Guinea where some thirty genera and 270 species of palms are to be found. Like most of its flora, New Guinea palms are only just beginning to be explored botanically and they are even less well known horticulturally. Many New Guinea palms deserve to become more widely grown in gardens of tropical Australia or as pot plants. Some species are already

grown but these are often incorrectly named. It is hoped that the inclusion of a list of those species with apparent potential will stimulate palm enthusiasts to secure more of these gems from such a close neighbour. At present it is extremely difficult to obtain any material from West Irian so only New Guinea species are listed. A complete list of New Guinea palms has been compiled by Essig (1977).

Actinorhytis capparia   highly ornamental
Areca   eleven species, some slender and decorative
Arenga microcarpa

Brassiophoenix   two species of ornamental palms

Calyptrocalyx   seventeen species of highly ornamental palms
Cyrtostachys   eight species, some appear ornamental

Drymophloeus   four species of ornamental palms

Gronophyllum   seven species of majestic palms
Gulubia   six species

Heterospathe   sixteen species, many dwarf and attractive
Hydriastele   seven species of slender, clumping palms
Licuala   thirty-six species, many in West Irian, includes many attractive dwarf types
Linospadix   five species, slender and decorative

Nengella   nineteen species, variable but highly ornamental

Orania   eight species, some attractive

Paralinospadix   twenty-one species of highly desirable palms
Physokentia avia
Pigafetta filaris
Pinanga punicea var *papuana*
Ptychococcus   seven species; some appear decorative
Ptychosperma   twenty-three species of slender, attractive palms

Rhopaloblaste   three species

APPENDIX VIII
Palm Look-Alikes

Many plants have a similar appearance to palms and are confused with them by the gardening public. Most of these are not even closely related to palms, although that vernacular is often applied to them. The commonest of these are listed here.

Beaucarnea recurvata   Pony Tail 'Palm'

Carludovica palmata   Panama Hat 'Palm' also commonly referred to as a Cyclanth
Cordyline spp   Frequently referred to as 'Palm' Lilies
Curculigo spp   'Weevil Lilies'
Cycads   Frequently referred to as 'Fern Palms'

though in fact unrelated to either

Cycas revoluta   Sago 'Palm'

Musa spp   Sometimes referred to as Banana 'Palms'

Pandanus spp   Frequently referred to as Screw 'Palms'

Ravenalea madagascariensis   Travellers 'Palm'

APPENDIX IX
Synonym List

The following list is intended only as a guide to the more recent or important name changes affecting palms grown in Australia. Australian species are dealt with in more detail than the exotics.

Actinophloeus bleeseri Burret = *Ptychosperma bleeseri* Burret

Actinophloeus macarthurii Wendl. ex Veitch = *Ptychosperma macarthurii* (Wendl ex Veitch) Wendl. ex Hook f.

Adonidia merrillii = *Veitchia merrillii*

Archontophoenix beatriceae F. Muell. see under *A. alexandrae* Wendl. & Drude

Archontophoenix jardinei F. M. Bail = *Ptychosperma elegans* (R. Br.) Blume

Areca appendiculata F. M. Bail. = *Orania appendiculata* Domin

Areca langloisiana = *A. vestiaria*

Areca lutescens is correctly *Chrysalidorcarpus lutescens*

Areca monostachya Mart. = *Linospadix monostachya* (Mart.) Wendl.

Areca normanbyi F. Muell. = *Normanbya normanbyi* (W. Hill) L. H. Bailey

Arenga saccharifera = *A. pinnata*

Attalea cohune = *Orbignya cohune*

Bacularia minor F. Muell. = *Linospadix minor* (F. Muell.) Burret

Bacularia monostachya (Mart.) F. Muell = *Linospadix monostachya* (Mart.) Wendl.

Calamus jaboolum F. M. Bail. = *C. australis* Mart.

Calamus obstruens F. Muell. = *C. australis* Mart.

Calyptrocalyx australasicus Scheff. = *Laccospadix australasica* Wendl. & Drude

Caryota albertii F. Muell. = *C. rumphiana* Mart.

Caryota rumphiana var. *australiensis* Becc. = *C. rumphiana* Mart.

Chamaerops excelsa – plants cultivated under this name are usually *Trachycarpus fortunei*

Chrysalidocarpus madagascariensis var. *lucubensis* = *C. lucubensis*

Clinostigma mooreanum F. Muell. = *Lepidorrhachis mooreanum* (F. Muell.) O. Cook

Cocos australis – plants cultivated under this name are usually *Butia capitata*

Cocos normanbyi W. Hill = *Normanbya normanbyi* (W. Hill) L. H. Bailey

Cocos weddelliana = *Microcoelum weddellianum*

Collinia elegans = *Chamaedorea elegans*

Corozo oleifera = *Elaeis oleifera*

Corypha australis R. Br. = *Livistona australis* Mart.

Copernicia cerifera = *C. prunifera*

Copernica torreana = *C. macroglossa*

Cyrtostachys lakka = *C. renda*

Denea belmoreana (Moore & F. Muell.) O. Cook = *Howea belmoreana* (Moore & F. Muell.) Becc.

Dictyosperma aureum = *D. album*

Dictyosperma rubrum = *D. album*

Didymosperma caudata = *Arenga caudata*

Drymophloeus normanbyi Benth. & Hook. = *Normanbya normanbyi* (W. Hill) L. H. Bailey

Erythea – all species of this genus are now included under *Brahea*

Erythea armata = *Brahea armata*

Erythea brandeegei = *Brahea brandeegei*

Grisebachia belmoreana Wendl. & Drude = *Howea belmoreana* (Moore & F. Muell.) Becc.

Grisebachia forsteriana Wendl. & Drude = *Howea forsteriana* (F. Muell.) Becc.

Gulubia ramsayi Becc. = *Gronophyllum ramsayi* (Becc.) Moore

Hydriastele costata F. M. Bail. = *Gulubia costata* Becc.

Hydriastele douglasiana F. M. Bail. = *Hydriastele wendlandiana* (F. Muell.) Wendl. & Drude

Hyphaene ventricosa = *H. petersiana*

Jubaea spectabilis = *J. chilensis*

Kentia acuminata Wendl. & Drude = *Carpentaria acuminata* Becc.

Kentia belmoreana F. Muell. = *Howea belmoreana* (Moore & F. Muell.) Becc.

Kentia canterburyana F. Muell. = *Hedyscepe canterburyana* Moore & F. Muell.

Kentia forsteriana F. Muell. = *Howea foresteriana* (F. Muell.) Becc.

Kentia macarthurii Hort. = *Ptychosperma macarthurii* (Wendl. ex Veitch) Wendl. ex Hook. f.

Kentia minor F. Muell. = *Linospadix minor* (F. Muell.) Burret

Kentia monostachya (Mart.) F. Muell. = *Linospadix monostachya* (Mart.) Wendl.

Kentia mooreana F. Muell. = *Lepidorrhachis mooreanum* (F. Muell.) O. Cook

Kentia ramsayi Wendl. & Drude = *Gronophyllum ramsayi* (Becc.) Moore

Kentia wendlandiana F. Muell. = *Hydriastele wendlandiana* (F. Muell.) Wendl. & Drude

Licuala muelleri Wendl. & Drude = *L. ramsayi* (F. Muell.) Domin

Linospadix intermedia (White) Burret this species is apparently a form of *L. minor* (F. Muell.) Burret

Linospadix sessilifolia (Becc.) Burret – this species is apparently synonymous with *L. microcarya* although the description of its fruit matches *L. minor*

Livistona leichhardtii F. Muell. = *L. humilis* R. Br.

Livistona ramsayi F. Muell. = *Licuala ramsayi* (F. Muell.) Domin

Martinezia – palms in this genus are now included under *Aiphanes*

Mascarena – all species in this genus are now included under *Hyophorbe*

Mascarena lagenicaulis = *Hyophorbe lagenicaulis*

Mascarena verschaffeltii = *Hyophorbe verschaffeltii*

Metroxylon laeve = *M. sagu*

Metroxylon rumphii = *M. sagu*

Microcoelum martianum = *M. wedellianum*

Neanthe bella = *Chamaedora elegans*

Oncosperma filamentosum = *O. tigillarium*

Orania beccarii F. M. Bail. = *O. appendiculata* Domin

Oreodoxa – palms in this genus are now included under *Roystonea*

Paurotis wrightii = *Acoelorraphe wrightii*

Phoenix humilis = *P. loureirii*

Phoenix zeylanica = *P. pusilla*

Pigafetta elata = *P. filaris*

Pinanga copelandii = *P. maculata*

Ptychosperma alexandrae F. Muell. = *Archontophoenix alexandrae* Wendl. & Drude

Ptychosperma capitis – yorkii Wendl. & Drude = *Ptychosperma elegans* (R. Br.) Bl.

Ptychosperma cunninghamii Wendl. = *Archontophoenix cunninghamiana* (Wendl.) Wendl. & Drude

Ptychosperma laccospadix Benth. = *Laccospadix*

australasica Wendl. & Drude

Sabal beccariana = *S. princeps*

Sabal texana = *S. mexicana*

Sabal umbraculifera = *S. domingensis*

Saguerus australasicus Wendl. & Drude = *Arenga australasica* (Wendl. & Drude) S. T. Blake

Salacca conferta = *Eleiodoxa conferta*

Seaforthia cunninghamii – a name used by nurserymen in the early 1900's for *Archontophoenix cunninghamiana* (Wendl.) Wendl. & Drude

Seaforthia elegans – this name has caused considerable confusion amongst palm botanists and horticulturists in Australia and overseas, for it was applied to two different palms by two prominent botanists. *S. elegans* Hook. is generally regarded as being a synonym of *Archontophoenix alexandrae* Wendl. & Drude, while the more commonly used *S. elegans* R. Br. is the basionym of *Ptychosperma elegans* (R. Br.) Bl.

Stevensonia borsigniana = *Phoenicophorium borsigianum*

Syagrus weddelliana = *Microcoelum weddellianum*

Teysmannia altifrons = *Johannesteijsmannia altifrons*

Thrinax radiata this name is of cultivated origin and is impossible to assign with certainty to any species.

APPENDIX X

Lists of Palms to be found growing in Australia's major Botanic and Municipal Gardens as at 1982.

Species marked with an asterisk are grown in glasshouses. The following lists are of palms that are to be found in the major botanical and municipal gardens of Australia. They have been included to help intending palm growers and enthusiasts to locate species in an area and also to illustrate how adaptable some palms are to different climatic regions and soil types. It should be stressed that seed may not be collected from any of the various gardens without the permission of the personnel in charge. Thanks are expressed to the various directors, town clerks and superintendents for providing the information.

Adelaide Botanic Garden

Archontophoenix cunninghamiana
Arecastrum romanzoffianum
Brahea armata
Butia capitata
Chamaedorea elegans
  radicalis

Chamaerops humilis
Chrysalidocarpus lutescens
Howea forsteriana
Jubaea chilensis
Livistona australis
  chinensis

mariae
Phoenix canariensis
  reclinata
  dactylifera
  roebelenii
Rhopalostylis sapida

Rhapis excelsa
  humilis
Sabal spp.
Trachycarpus fortunei
Washingtonia filifera
  robusta

Brisbane Botanic Gardens

Acoelorraphe wrightii
Aiphanes caryotifolia
Archontophoenix alexandrae
  cunninghamiana
Arecastrum romanzoffianum
  romanzoffianum var. australe
  romanzoffianum var.
  botryophorum
Arenga australasica
  engleri
  pinnata

tremula
Astrocaryum mexicanum
Brahea armata
  brandegeei
  edulis
  elegans
Butia capitata
  capitata var. odorata
  eriospatha
Calamus muelleri
Carpentaria acuminata

Caryota mitis
  urens
Chamaedorea cataractarum
  elegans
  tenella
Chamaerops humilis
  humilis var. arborescens
Chrysalidocarpus lutescens
  lucubensis
  madagascariensis
Cocothrinax argentata

argentea
  dussiana
Cocos nucifera
Corypha umbraculifera
Croysophila nana
Dictyosperma album
Elaeis guineensis
Howea belmoreana
  forsteriana
Hyophorbe verschaffeltii
Latania loddigesii

Licuala peltata
ramsayi
spinosa
Linospadix monostachya
Livistona australis
chinensis
chinensis var. amanoii
decipiens
drudei
mariae
muelleri
rotundifolia

saribus
Metroxylon sagu
Microcoelum martianum
Normanbya normanbyi
Phoenix canariensis
dactylifera
pusilla
reclinata
roebelenii
rupicola
sylvestris
Pinanga kuhlii

Pritchardia gaudichaudii
hillebrandii
Ptychosperma macarthurii
elegans
Raphia farinifera
Rhapis excelsa
humilis
Rhopalostylis sapida
Roystonea oleracea
regia
Sabal bermudana
causiarium

mexicana
minor
palmetto
princeps
umbraculifera
uresana
Thrinax morrisii
Wallichia densiflora
Washingtonia filifera
robusta
Wissmannia carinensis

Darwin Botanic Garden

Acoelorraphe wrightii
Actinorhytis calapparia
Aiphanes caryotifolia
erosa
Archontophoenix alexandrae
cunninghamiana
Areca catechu
concinna
triandra
Arecastrum romanzoffianum
Arenga caudata
engleri
obtusifolia
tremula
Bactris major
Bentinckia nicobarica
Borassus flabellifer
Butia capitata
yatay
Carpentaria acuminata
Caryota mitis
urens
gigantea (?)
sp. (Malaysia)
Calyptrocalyx spicatus
Chamaedorea elegans
erumpens
metallica

microspadix
costaricana
Chrysalidocarpus lutescens
lucubensis
Coccothrinax crinita
Cocos nucifera
'Malay Dwarf'
'Rennell Island'
Corypha elata
Cyrtostachys renda
Dictyosperma album
Dypsis decipiens
Elaeis guineensis
Gronophyllum ramsayi
Hedyscepe canterburyana
Heterospathe elata
Hydriastele wendlandiana
beccariana
Hyophorbe lagenicaulis
verschaffeltii
Hyphaena crinita
Laccospadix australasica
Latania loddigesii
verschaffeltii
Licuala grandis
spinosa
Livistona alfredii
australis

benthamii
chinensis
decipiens
eastonii
gigantea
humilis
inermis
loriphylla
mariae
muelleri
paludosa
rotundifolia
saribus
sp. (Mataranka)
sp. (Victoria R.)
Neoveitchia storckii
Normanbya normanbyi
Oncosperma tigillarium
Orbignya cohune
Phoenix canariensis
dactylifera
humilis
reclinata
roebelenii
sylvestris
Pholidocarpus majadum
Pinanga kuhlii
Pritchardia thurstonii

Ptychosperma ambiguum
elegans
hospitium (= P. macarthurii)
macarthurii
praemorsum
propinquum
sanderianum
Rhapidophyllum hystrix
Rhapis excelsa
Roystonea oleracea
regia
Sabal deeringiana (= S. minor)
domingensis
mauritiiformis
minor
palmetto
mexicana
Salacca zalacca
Serenoa repens
Thrinax parviflora
radiata
Veitchia joannis
merrillii
Verschaffeltia splendida
Washingtonia filifera
robusta

Flecker Botanic Gardens, Cairns

Acoelorrhaphe wrightii
Aiphanes caryotifolia
erosa
Archontophoenix alexandrae
cunninghamiana
Areca alicae
catechu
concinna
vestiaria
Arecastrum romanzoffianum
romanzoffianum var. australis
Arenga australasica
caudata
engleri
microcarpa
pinnata
tremula
Arikuryroba schizophylla
Bactris jamaiciensis
Bentinckia nicobarica
Borassus flabellifer
Brahea aculeata

armata
serrulata
Butia yatay
Calamus australis
caryotoides
moti
sp.
sp.
sp.
Calyptronoma occidentalis
Carpentaria acuminata
Caryota mitis
rumphiana
rumphiana var. moluccana
no
urens
sp.
Ceratolobus glaucescens
Chamaedorea brachypoda
elegans
erumpens
glaucifolia

geonomiformis
microspadix
radicalis
seifrizii
tenella
tepejilote
sp.
Chamaerops humilis
Chrysalidocarpus cabadae
lucubensis
lutescens
Coccothrinax argentata
dussiana
miraguama
sp.
Cocos nucifera
'Malay Dwarf'
Copernicia alba
baileyana
macroglossa
prunifera
Corypha elata

Cryosophila warscewiczii
Cyrtostachys renda
Daemonorops sp.
Deckenia nobilis
Dictyospermum album
Elaeis guineensis
Gaussia attenuata
Howea belmoreana
Hydriastele aff microspadix
aff wendfordianum
wendlandianum
sp.
Hyophorbe lagenicaulis
verschaffeltii
Hyphaene schatan
ventricosa
Jessenia bataua
Laccospadix australasica
Latania loddigesii
lontaroides
Licuala grandis
lauterbachii

pumila
ramsayi
spinosa
Linospadix microcarya
  monostachya
Livistona alfredii
  australis
  benthamii
  chinensis
  decipiens
  drudei
  humilis
  mariae
  muelleri
  saribus
  sp.
Metroxylon sagu
Microcoelum insigne
  weddellianum
Neodypsis decaryi
Neoveitchia storckii
Normanbya normanbyi
Nypa fruticans
Oncosperma tigillarium

Opsiandra maya
Orania appendiculata
  sylvicola
  sp.
Orbignya cohune
Paralinospadix sp.
Phoenix dactylifera
  reclinata
  roebelenii
  rupicola
  sylvestris
  sp.
  sp.
Pigafetta filaris
Pinanga javana
  kuhlii
  malaiana
  sp. aff. densiflora
  sp.
  sp.
  sp.
Polyandrococos caudescens
Pritchardia eriostachya

kaalae
martioides
pacifica
thurstonii
Ptychosperma elegans
  macarthurii
  microcarpum
  propinquum
  robustum
  salomonense
  sanderianum
  sp.
  wendlandianum
Raphia vinifera
Reinhardtia gracilis var. rostrata
Rhapis excelsa
  sp.
Rhopaloblaste sp.
Roystonea borinquena
  elata
  hispaniolandia
  oleracea
Roystonea regia
Sabal sp. aff. bermudana

causiarum
etonia
jamaicensis
mexicana
minor
palmetto
parviflora
princeps
sp. aff. rosei
sp.
sp.
sp.
uresana
Salacca wallichiana
  zalacca
Serenoa repens
Thrinax morrisii
Veitchia joannis
  merrillii
  montgomeryana
  winin
Verschaffeltia splendida
Washingtonia robusta
Zombia antillarum

Mt Coot-tha Botanic Gardens, Brisbane

Acoelorrhaphe wrightii
Acrocomia aculeata
Aiphanes caryotifolia
Archontophoenix alexandrae var.
  beatricae
  cunninghamiana
  sp. Mt Lewis
Areca aliceae
  catechu
  concinna
  ipot
  triandra
Arecastrum romanzoffianum
Arenga australasica
  caudata
  engleri
  microcarpa
  pinnata
  tremula
  undulatifolia
Arikuryroba schizophylla
Astrocaryum mexicanum
Bentinckia nicobarica
Brahea armata
  edulis
  edulis x brandeegei
Butia capitata var. capitata
  capitata var. odorata
  eriospatha
Calamus mindorensis
  moti
  muelleri
  ornatus
  usitatus var. palawanensis
  reyesianus
Carpentaria acuminata
Caryota cumingii
  mitis
  rumphiana
  urens
Chamaedorea brachypoda

concolor
costaricana
elatior
elegans
erumpens
geonomiformis
glaucifolia
karwinskyana
metallica
microspadix
oblongata
seifrizii
spp.
Chamaerops humilis
Chrysalidocarpus lucubensis
  lutescens
Clinostigma orthorrhynchum
Coccothrinax argentea
  dussiana
  miraguama
Cocos nucifera
Copernicia baileyana
  macroglossa
Corypha elata
Crysophila warscewiczii
Cyrtostachys renda*
Dictyosperma album
Drymophloeus sp.
Elaeis guineensis
Euterpe edulis
  globosa
  sp.
Gaussia attenuata
Gronophyllum ramsayi
Hedyscepe canterburyana
Heterospathe elata
  negrosensis
  sensis
  silvyanensis
Howea belmoreana
  forsteriana

Hydiastele wendlandiana
Hyophorbe lagenicaulis
  verschaffeltii
Hyphaene sp.
Jubaea chilensis x Butia capitata
Laccospadix australasica
Latania lantaroides
  loddigesii
  verschaffeltii
Licuala grandis
  ramsayi
  spinosa
Linospadix minor
  monostachya
Livistona australis
  chinensis
  decipiens
  drudei
  eastonii
  humilis
  loriphylla
  mariae
  merrillii
  muelleri
  rigida
  rotundifolia var. luzonensis
  saribus
  sp.
Metroxylon salomonense*
Microcoelum weddellianum
Nannorrhops stocksii
Neodypsis decaryi
Neoveitchia storckii*
Nephrosperma vanhoutteana
Normanbya normanbyi
Oncosperma tigillarium*
Opsiandra maya
Orania appendiculata
Orbignya cohune
Phoenicophorium borsigianum*
Phoenix canariensis

reclinata
roebelenii
rupicola
sylvestris
Pigafetta filaris*
Pinanga barnesii
  elmeri
  geonomiformis
  insignis
  kuhlii
  malaiana
  merrillii
  noe
  sp.
Pritchardia gaudichaudii
  hillebrandii
  kahukuensis
  remota
  thurstonii
  woodfordii
Pseudophoenix sargentii
Ptychosperma macarthurii
  propinquum
  robusta
  salomonense
Reinhardtia gracilis var. rostrata
Rhapis excelsa
  excelsa var. minor
  humilis
Rhopalostylis baueri
  cheesemanii
Roystonea elata
  oleracea
  regia
Sabal bermudana
  havanensis (?)
  mauritiiformis
  mexicana
  minor
  uresana
Salacca zalacca

Serenoa repens
Thrinax morrisii
  radiata
Trachycarpus fortunei

martianus
wagnerianus
Trithrinax acanthocoma
  campestris

Veitchia hendersonii
  joannis
  merrillii
Verschaffeltia splendida*

Washingtonia filifera
  robusta
Wissmannia carinensis

Perth Municipal Gardens

Lake Monger Reserve
Phoenix canariensis
  reclinata
Washingtonia filifera
  robusta
Hyde Park
Arecastrum romanzoffianum
Caryota urens
Chamaerops humilis
Phoenix canariensis
  reclinata
Washingtonia filifera
  robusta
Stirling Gardens
Arecastrum romanzoffianum
Chamaerops humilis
Howea fosteriana
Phoenix canariensis
  reclinata

roebelenii
Supreme Court Gardens
Arecastrum romanzoffianum
Caryota rumphiana/urens
Howea fosteriana
Livistona chinensis
Phoenix canariensis
  dactylifera
Washingtonia filifera
  robusta
Queens Gardens
Achontophoenix cunninghamiana
Arecastrum romanzoffianum
Butia capitata
Caryota urens
Chamaerops humilis
Howea forsteriana
Livistona australis
  chinensis

Phoenix canariensis
  dactylifera
  roebelenii
Washingtonia filifera
  robusta
Esplanade
Arecastrum romanzoffianum
Butia capitata
Phoenix canariensis
  reclinata
  roebelenii
Washingtonia filifera
  robusta
Conservatory
Chamaedorea elegans
  erumpens
Chrysalidocarpus lutescens
Cocos nucifera
Howea fosteriana

Linospadix monstachya
Phoenix reclinata
  roebelenii
Rhapis excelsa
Harold Boas Gardens
Caryota rumphiana/urens
Chamaerops humilis
Phoenix roebelenii
Washingtonia filifera
  robusta
Harper Square (Barrack St Jetty)
Arecastrum romanzoffianum
Chamaerops humilis
Phoenix canariensis
  reclinata
Washingtonia filifera
  robusta

Rockhampton Botanic Gardens

Aiphanes caryotifolia
Arecastrum romanzoffianum
Arenga pinnata
  engleri
Borassus flabellifer
Butia eriospatha
Carpentaria acuminata
Caryota mitis
  urens
  rumphiana
Chamaedorea erumpens
Chamaerops humilis
Chrysalidocarpus lucubensis

lutescens
Coccothrinax miraguama
Cocos nucifera
Dictyosperma album
  album var. rubrum
Elaeis guineensis
Hyophorbe verschaffeltii
Latania loddigesii
Licuala ramsayi
Livistona chinensis
  decipiens
  mariae
  rotundifolia

saribus
Orbignya cohune
Phoenix canariensis
  dactylifera
  reclinata
  roebelenii
  rupicola
  sylvestris
Pinanga kuhlii
Ptychosperma elegans
  macarthurii
Rhapis excelsa
  humilis

Roystonea oleracea
  regia
Sabal causiarum
  domingensis
  minor
  palmetto
Thrinax parviflora
Trachycarpus martianus
Wallichia caryotoides
Washingtonia filifera
  robusta

Royal Botanic Gardens, Hobart

Butia capitata
  capitata var. pulposa

Chamaerops humilis
Phoenix canariensis
  dactylifera

Washingtonia filifera
  robusta

Royal Botanic Gardens, Melbourne

Archontophoenix alexandrae
  cunninghamiana
Areca catechu*
Arecastrum romanzoffianum
Brahea armata
  dulcis*
Butia capitata
Calamus muelleri
Caryota mitis*
  urens*
Chamaedorea elegans
  ernesti-augusti

microspadix
Chamaerops humilis
  humilis var. elatior
Chrysalidocarpus lutescens
Coccothrinax crinita*
Elaeis guineensis*
Hedyscepe canterburyana
Howea belmoreana
  forsteriana
Hydriastele microspadix*
Jubaea chilensis
Laccospadix australasica

Latania verschaffeltii*
Licuala spinosa*
Linospadix monstachya
Livistona australis
  chinensis
  decipiens*
  mariae
  saribus*
Phoenix canariensis
  dactylifera
  loureirii
  pusilla

  reclinata
  rupicola
Rhopalostylis baueri
  sapida
Roystonea regia*
Sabal bermudana
Thrinax radiata*
Trachycarpus fortunei
Veitchia joannis*
Washingtonia filifera
  robusta

Royal Botanic Gardens, Sydney

Acoelorrhaphe wrightii
Acrocomia aculeata
Actinokentia divaricata
Aiphanes caryotifolia
Allagoptera arenaria
Archontophoenix alexandrae
  cunninghamiana
  sp.
Arecastrum romanzoffianum
Arenga australasica
  engleri
  *microcarpa**
  pinnata
  tremula
Basselinia eriostachys
Brahea aculeata
  armata
  *bella**
  brandegeei
  *clara**
Butia   bonnetii
  capitata
  eriospatha
*Calamus caryotoides**
  muelleri
  *moti**
  viminalis
Caryota mitis
  *ochlandra**
  *rumphiana**
  rumphiana var. *albertii*
  urens
  *sp.**
Chamaedorea concolor
  costaricana
  elegans
  ernesti-augusti

geonomiformis
glaucifolia
klotzschiana
metallica
microspadix
*oblongata**
seifrizii
tepejilote
*sp.**
Chamaerops humilis
Chambeyronia macrocarpa
Chrysalidocarpus lucubensis
  lutescens
*Coccothrinax acuminata**
  argentata
  *crinita**
*Copernicia prunifera**
*Cyphophoenix elegans**
  *nucele**
*Cyphosperma balansae**
Dictyosperma album
*Gaussia attenuata**
Hedyscepe canterburyana
Howea belmoreana
  forsterana
Hyophorbe lagenicaulis
Hyphaene thebaica
Jubaea chilensis
*Jubaeopsis caffra**
Kentiopsis oliviformis
Laccospadix australasica
Linospadix cf. *aequisegmentosa*
  cf. *microcarya*
  minor
  monostachya
  *palmerana**
Lepidorrhachis mooreana

*Licuala grandis**
  ramsayi
  *spinosa**
*Livistona alfredii**
  australis
  sp. aff. *australis**
  *benthamii**
  chinensis
  decipiens
  *drudei**
  mariae
  *muelleri**
  *rigida**
  *rotundifolia**
  *sp.**
  *sp.**
Microcoelum weddellianum
Normanbya normanbyi
Opsiandra maya
*Orania appendiculata**
Parajubaea cocoides
Phoenix canariensis
  dactylifera
  *loureirii**
  pusilla
  reclinata
  roebelenii
  rupicola
  sylvestris
*Pinanga kuhlii**
  sp. (Philippines)*
  sp. (Philippines)*
Pritchardia maideniana
  martii
*Ptychosperma ambiguum**
  elegans
  macarthurii

*Ravenea robustior**
Reinhardtia gracilis var. *gracilior*
Rhapis excelsa
  humilis
  *sp.**
Rhapidophyllum hystrix
Rhopalostylis baueri
  *cheesemanii**
  sapida
*Roystonea oleracea**
  regia
Sabal bermudana
  causiarum
  domingensis
  havanensis (?)
  longipedunculata (?)
  mauritiiformis
  *megacarpa**
  mexicana
  minor
  palmetto
  princeps
  uresana
Serenoa repens
*Thrinax parviflora**
Trachycarpus fortunei
  martianus
  takil
Trithrinax acanthocoma
  brasiliensis
  *campestris**
Veitchia joannis
  montgomeryana
Wallichia densiflora
Washingtonia filifera
  robusta

Waite Institute Arboretum, Adelaide

Jubaea chilensis
Livistona australis
  chinensis
Phoenix canariensis
  reclinata
  sylvestris

theophrastii
Sabal domingensis
  texana
Trachycarpus fortunei
Washingtonia filifera
  robusta

Bibliography

Anderson, A. B. (1978), 'The Names and Uses of Palms Among a Tribe of Yanomama Indians' *Principes* 22, 30-41.

Backer, C.A. & Bakhuizen van den Brink (1968) *Flora of Java: Arecaceae*, Vol 3, 165-99.

Bailey, F. M. (1899-1902), *The Queensland Flora*, Parts 1-6 H. J. Diddams & Coy, Brisbane.

Bailey, F. M. (1909), *A Comprehensive Catalogue of Queensland Plants*, Government Printer, Queensland.

Bailey, L. H. (1935) 'The King Palms of Australia – *Archontophoenix' Gentes Herbarium* 3, 391-409.

Bailey, L. H. (1939) '*Howea* in cultivation – the Sentry Palms', *Gentes Herbarium* 4, 189-98.

Bailey, L. H. (1939) 'The species of *Rhapis* in cultivation – the Lady Palms', *Gentes Herbarium* 4, 199-208.

Balick, M. J. (1976), 'The Palm Heart as a New Commercial Crop from Tropical America' *Principes* 20, 24-8.

Beccari, O. and J.F. Rock (1921), A Monographic Study of the Genus *Pritchardia*, Memoirs of the Bernice Bishop Museum 8.

Beccari, O. ('931), Asiatic Palms – Corypheae, revised and edited by V. Martelli, Annals of Royal Botanic Gardens, Calcutta 13.

Bentham, G. and F. Mueller (1863-78), *Flora Australiensis*, Parts 1-7, Lovell Reeve & Coy, London.

Blatter, E. (1926), *The Palms of British India and Ceylon*, Oxford University Press, London.

Brown, W. H. (1921), *Minor Products of Philippine Forests*, Vol 1, Manila Bureau of Printing.

Burbidge, N.T. (1963), *Dictionary of Australian Plant Genera*, Angus & Robertson, Sydney.

Corner, E. J. H. (1966), *The Natural History of Palms*, Weidenfield & Nicholson, London.

Cribb, A. B. & J. W. (1974), *Wild Food in Australia*, Collins, Sydney.

Cribb, A. B. & J. W. (1981), *Useful Wild Plants in Australia*, Collins, Sydney.

DeLeon, N. J. (1961), 'Viability of Palm Seeds', *American Horticultural Magazine* 40, 131-2.

Dransfield, J. (1972), 'The Genus *Borassodendron* (Palmae) in Malesia', *Reinwardtia*, 8, 351-63.

Dransfield, J. (1972), 'Notes on *Caryota no* and other Malesian *Caryota* species', *Principes*, 18, 87-93.

Dransfield, J. (1974) 'New Light on *Areca langloisiana'*, *Principes*, 18, 51-7.

Dransfield, J. (1976), 'Palms in the Everyday Life of West Indonesia', *Principes*, 20, 39-47.

Dransfield, J. (1976), 'A note on the Habitat of *Pigafetta filaris* in North Celebes', *Principes*, 20, 48.

Dransfield, J. (1976), 'Terminal Flowering in *Daemonorops' Principes*, 20, 29-32.

Dransfield, J. (1977), A Dwarf *Livistona* from Borneo, *Kew Bulletin* 31, 759-62.

Dransfield, J. (1977), A Note on the Genus *Cornera* – (Palmae: Lepidocaryoideae), *The Malaysian Forester* 40, 200-202.

Dransfield, J. (1978), The Genus *Maxburretia* (Palmae) *Gentes Herbarium* 11, 187-99.

Dransfield, J. (1979), A Manual of the Rattans of the Malay Peninsula, Malayan Forest Records No 29, Ministry Primary Industries, Malaysia.

Dransfield, J. (1980), 'A Monograph of *Ceratolobus* (Palmae)', *Kew Bulletin* 34, 1-33.

Dransfield, J. (1980), '*Retispatha*, a New Genus of Palmae (Lepidocaryoideae) from Borneo', *Kew Bulletin* 34, 529-36.

Dransfield, J. (1980), '*Pogonotium* (Palmae, Lepidocaryoideae), a New Genus Related to *Daemonorops'*, *Kew Bulletin* 34, 761-8.

Dransfield, J. (1980), 'Systematic Notes on *Pinanga* (Palmae) in Borneo', *Kew Bulletin* 34, 769-88.

Dransfield, J. (1980), 'Systematic Notes on Some Bornean Palms', *Botanical Journal of the Linnaean Society* 81, 4-42.

Dransfield, J. (1981), 'A Synopsis of the genus *Korthalsia* (Palmae: Lepidocaryoideae)' *Kew Bulletin* 36, 163-94.

Dunlop, C. R., P. K. Latz & J. R. Maconochie (1975), 'A Botanical Survey of Elcho Island', *Report of the Herbaria of the Northern Territory*, Alice Springs and Darwin, Australia.

Essig, F. B. (1977), The Palm Flora of New Guinea, Botany Bulletin No 9, Division of Botany, Lae, Papua New Guinea.

Essig, F. B. (1978), 'A Revision of the Genus *Ptychosperma* Labill'. *Allertonia*, 1(7), 415-78.

Essig, F. B. (1980), 'The genus *Orania* Zipp (Arecaceae) in New Guinea', *Lyonia* 1, 211-33.

Essig, F. B. (1982), 'A Synopsis of the Genus *Gulubia'* *Principes*, 26, 159-73.

Fenner, L. T. (1981). *Palm Leaf Beetle*, Agnote Division of Agriculture & Stock, Darwin.

Glassman, S. F. (1970), 'A Synopsis of the Palm Genus *Syagrus* Mart'. *Fieldiana Botany* 32, 215-40.

Glassman, S. F. (1977), 'Preliminary Taxonomic Studies in the Palm Genus *Orbignya* Mart.' *Phytologia* 36, 89-115.

Glassman, S. F. (1977), 'Preliminary Taxonomic Studies in the Palm Genus *Scheelea* Karsten.' *Phytologia* 37, 219-50.

Glassman, S. F. (1979), 'Re-evaluation of the Genus *Butia* with a Description of a New Species' *Principes* 23, 65-79.

Harmer, J. (1975), *North Australian Plants*, Part 1, Society for Growing Australian Plants, Sydney.

Harries, H. C. (1979), 'The Evolution, Dissemination and Classification of *Cocos nucifera* L.' *Botanical Review* 44, 265-319.

Harries, H. C. (1981), 'Germination and Taxonomy of the Coconut' *Annals of Botany* 48, 873-83.

Hearne, D. A. (1975), *Trees for Darwin and Northern Australia*, Australian Government Publishing Service, Canberra.

Hodel, D. (1982), 'Cultivated Palms in Tahiti and the Jardin Botanique de Papeari' *Principes*, 26, 77-85.

Holmquist, J. de D. and J. Popenoe (1967) 'The Effects of Scarification on the Germination of Seed of *Acrocomia crispa* and *Arenga engleri'*, *Principes* 11, 23-5.

Johnson, D. (1982), 'Commerical Palm Products of Brazil' *Principes,* 26, 141-3.

Jones, D. L. and B. Gray (1977), *Australian Climbing Plants,* A. H. & A. W. Reed, Sydney.

Kimnach, M. (1977) 'The Species of *Trachycarpus'* *Principes,* 21, 155-60.

Kitzke, E. D. and D. Johnson (1975), 'Commercial Palm Products Other than Oils' *Principes* 19, 3-26.

Laing, R. M. and E. W. Blackwell (1957), *Plants of New Zealand,* Whitcombe & Tombs, Auckland.

Langlois, A. C. (1976), *Supplement to Palms of the World,* University Press, Florida.

Li, H. L. (1963), *Woody Flora of Taiwan,* Livingston Publishing Coy, Pennsylvania.

Loomis, W. F. (1961), 'Preparation and Germination of Palm Seeds', *American Horticultural Magazine* 40, 120-30.

McCurrach, J. C. (1960), *Palms of the World,* Harper and Brothers, New York.

Merrill, E. D. (1922) *Enumeration of Philippine Plants –* *Palmae* 1, 142-72 Bureau of Science, Manila.

Mogea, J. P. (1980), 'The Flabellate-leaved Species of *Salacca* (Palmae)' *Reinwardtia* 9, 461-79.

Moore, H. E. Jr. (1963), 'An Annotated Checklist of Cultivated Palms', *Principes* 7, 118-82.

Moore, H. E. Jr. (1971), 'Additions and Corrections to An Annotated Checklist of Cultivated Palms', *Principes* 15, 102-6.

Moore, H. E. Jr. (1973), 'The Major Groups of Palms and Their Distribution' *Gentes Herbarium* 11, 27-141.

Moore, H. E. Jr. and N. W. Uhl (1973), 'The Monocotyledons, Their Evolution and Comparative Biology', *Quarterly Review of Biology* 48, 414-34.

Moore, H. E. Jr. (1978), 'The Genus Hyophorbe (Palmae)' *Gentes Herbarium* 11, 212-45.

Moore, H. E. Jr. (1978), 'New Genera and Species of Palmae from New Caledonia – I' *Gentes Herbarium* 11, 291-309.

Moore, H. E. Jr & J. Dransfield, (1978), 'A New Species of *Wettinia* and notes on the genus', *Notes from the Royal Botanic Garden,* Edinburgh, 36, 259-67.

Moore, H. E. Jr. and L. J. Gueho (1980) '*Acanthophoenix* and *Dictyosperma* (Palmae) in the Mascarene Islands', *Gentes Herbarium* 12, 1-16.

Moore, H. E. Jr. (1980) 'New Genera and Species of Palmae from New Caledonia – 11' *Gentes Herbarium* 12, 17-24.

Moore, H. E. Jr. (1980) 'Four New Species of Palmae from South America' *Gentes Herbarium* 12, 30-8.

Moore, L. B. and E. Edgar (1970) *Flora of New Zealand* Vol II Government Printer, Wellington.

Mullet, J. H. and D. V. Beardsell (1980) 'Seed Propagation of Ornamental Palms', *Seed and Nursery Trader* 17-9.

Mullet, J. H., D. V. Beardsell and H. M. King (1981), 'The Effect of Seed Treatment on the Germination and Early Growth of *Euterpe edulis'* *Scientia Horticulturae* 15, 239-44.

Nagoa, M. A. and W. S. Sakai (1979), 'Effect of Growth Regulators on Seed Germination of *Archontophoenix alexandrae'* *Horticultural Science* 14, 182-3.

Okita, Y. and J. L. Hollenberg (1981), *The Miniature Palms of Japan,* Weatherhill, Tokyo.

Parham, J. W. (1972), *Plants of the Fiji Islands* Government Printer, Suva.

Putz, F. E. (1979), 'Biology and Human use of *Leopoldinia piassaba'* *Principes* 23, 149-56.

Quero, H. J. (1982) *Opsiadra gomez-pompae,* a New Species from Oaxaxa, Mexico, *Principes* 26, 144-9.

Read, R. W. (1975), The Genus *Thrinax* (Palmae: Coryphoideae), Smithsonian Contributions to Botany No 19.

Rees, A. R. (1962), 'High Temperature Pre-treatment and Germination of Seed of the Oil Palm *(Elaeis guineensis)'* *Annals of Botany* 26, 581-96.

Rees, A. R. (1963), 'Germination of Palm Seeds using a Method Developed for the Oil Palm' *Principes* 7, 27-31.

Stevenson, G. B. (1974), *Palms of South Florida,* published by the author.

Stewart, J. L. and D. Brandis (1874), *Forest Flora of North-west and central India,* W. H. Allen & Coy, Lond

Stewart, L. (1982) *Palms for the Home and Garden,* Angus and Robertson, Sydney.

Tisserat, B. (1981), 'Date Palm Tissue Culture', *Advances in Agricultural Technology,* Western Series No 17, U.S. Department of Agricultural Research Service.

Tomlinson, P. B. (1960), 'Essays on the Morphology of Palms: Germination and the Seedling' *Principes* 4, 56-61.

Tomlinson, P. B. (1979) 'Systematics and Ecology of the Palmae' *Annual Review of Ecology & Systematics* 10, 85-107.

Uhl, N. W. (1978), 'Floral Anatomy of the Five Species of *Hyophorbe* (Palmae)' *Gentes Herbarium* 11, 246-67.

Wendland, H. and O. Drude (1875), 'Palmae Australasicae', *Linnaea* 39, Heft II and III.

Whitmore, T. C. (1973), *Palms of Malaya,* Oxford Unversity Press, Kuala Lumpur.

Willis, J. C. (1973), *A Dictionary of the Flowering Plants and Ferns,* 8th Edn, revised by H. K. Airy Shaw, Cambridge University Press.

Willis, J. H. (1962), *A Handbook to Plants in Victoria* Vol I Melbourne University Press, Carlton.

267

Glossary

abaxial On the side of a lateral organ away from the axis; the lower side of a leaf or petiole

abscission Shedding of plant parts such as leaves either through old age or prematurely as a result of stress

acaulescent Without a trunk

accessory roots Lateral roots developing from the base of the trunk as opposed to those arising from the seed root system

aculeate Bearing short, sharp prickles or spines

acuminate Tapering into a long, drawn-out point

acute Bearing a short, sharp point

adaxial On the side of a lateral organ next to the axis: the upper side of a leaf or petiole

adnate Fused together tightly

aerial roots Adventitious roots arising on stems and growing in the air

aff. or affinity A botanical reference used to denote an undescribed species closely related to an already described species

after-ripening The changes that occur in a dormant seed and render it capable of germinating

albumen An old term used for the endosperm of seeds

alternate Organs borne at different levels in a straight line or spiral, e.g. leaves

androecium The male parts of a flower (i.e. the stamens)

annular Prominent ring-scars left on the trunk of certain palms after leaf fall, e.g. *Archontophoenix*

annulate Bearing annular rings on the trunk

anomalous An abnormal or freak form

anther The pollen-bearing part of a stamen

apical dominance The dominance of the apical growing shoot which produces hormones and prevents lateral buds or suckers developing while it is still growing actively, e.g. the growth habit of *Linospadix minor*

apiculate With a short, pointed tip or beak

apocole The cotyledonary sheath of germinating palm seedlings

appendage A small growth attached to an organ

arborescent With a tree-like growth habit

arcuate Arched, as in the fronds of *Howea belmoreana*

aril A fleshy outgrowth of the stalk of the ovary which covers or partially covers the seed e.g. Lepidocaryoid palms.

armed Bearing spines or prickles

asexual reproduction Reproduction by vegetative means without the fusion of sexual cells

attenuated Drawn out

auricle An ear-like appendage at the base of the leaflets of some species, e.g. *Arenga*.

axil Angle formed between a leaf petiole and a trunk

barbed Bearing sharp, backward-sloping hooks as in *Calamus* spp.

berry A simple, fleshy, one-to-many-seeded fruit which doesn't split when ripe

bifid Deeply notched for more than half its length

bilobed Two-lobed

binding Threads joining young leaflet tips together

before the frond has expanded

bipinnate Twice pinnately divided as in fronds of *Caryota* spp.

bisexual Both male and female sexes present

blade The expanded part of a leaf

bole The trunk of a tree or palm

bottom heat A propagation term used to denote the application of artificial heat around a seed or cutting

bract A leaf-like structure which subtends a flower stem or part thereof

bracteole A small, leaf-like structure which subtends a single flower

bulbil In palms a vegetative aerial growth arising from a modified inflorescence and sometimes caused by damage to the growing apex of a stem

bulbous Bulb-shaped or swollen

caducous Falling off prematurely

caespitose Growing in a clump, as in suckering or clumping palms

calcareous An excess of lime in a soil

callus Growth of undifferentiated cells that develop on a wound or in tissue culture

calyx All of the sepals of a flower

cambium The growing tissue lying just beneath the bark (absent in palms)

cane A reed-like plant stem, as in species of *Calamus* and *Chamaedorea*

canopy The cover of foliage

capitate Enlarged and head-like, as in the female inflorescence of *Elaeis* and *Nypa*

carpel Female reproductive organ

catkin A dense, pendulous spike of unisexual flowers

caudex A trunk-like growth axis, as in the trunks of palms

ciliate With a fringe of hairs

cirrus A whip-like organ bearing recurved hooks used as an aid for climbing: it arises as an extension of the leaf rhachis and is present in some species of *Calamus*

clavate Club-shaped

clone A group of vegetatively propagated plants with a common ancestry, e.g. commercial cultivars of the date palm which are all propagated by suckers

colonial A term sometimes used for palms which branch basally by rhizomes, e.g. *Calamus* spp.

coma A term sometimes used for the crown of a palm

compound leaf A leaf with two or more separate leaflets or divisions (both pinnate and palmate leaves are compound)

compressed Flattened laterally

confluent Leaflets remaining united and not separating

congested Crowded close together

contracted Narrowed

cordate Heart-shaped

coriaceus Leathery in texture

costa The rib of a costapalmate leaf

costapalmate Palmate leaves with a well-developed rib which is an extension of the petiole into the blade and is the equivalent of the rhachis

cotyledon The seed leaf of a plant, in palms there is a single cotyledon which may be greatly modified

cross Offspring or hybrid

cross-pollination Transfer of pollen from flower to flower

crown The head of foliage of a palm

crownshaft A series of tightly packed, specialised tubular leaf bases which terminate the trunk of some pinnate-leaved palms

cupule A bowl or cup-shaped calyx developed at the base of the fruit of some palms

cultivar A horticultural variety, e.g. variegated *Rhapis* palms

cymbiform Boat-shaped, sometimes used to describe the spathes of some palms

deciduous Falling off or shedding of any plant part

decumbent Reclining on the ground with the apex ascending, as in the trunk of *Elaeis oleifera*

decurrent Running downward beyond a junction, as in the leaflets of many pinnate palms

deflexed Abruptly turning downwards

dentate Toothed

denticulate Finely toothed

depauperate A weak plant or one imperfectly developed

depressed Flattened at one end, as in the fruit of some palms

determinate With the definite cessation of growth in the main axis, as in monocarpic palms

dichotomous Regular forking into equal branches, as in the branching of the trunks of *Hyphaene* spp. and *Nypa fruticans*

dicotyledons A section of the Angiosperms bearing two seed leaves in the seedling stage

diffuse Of widely spreading and open growth

digitate Spreading like the fingers of a hand from one point

dimorphic Existing in two different forms: the juvenile and seedling leaves of most palms are dimorphic: sucker leaves may be different from leaves on mature stems: species of *Nengella* and *Heterospathe humilis* have simple and pinnate-leaved plants present in the same population

dioecious Bearing male and female flowers on separate plants

dissected Deeply divided into segments

distichous Alternate leaves or leaflets arranged along a stem or rhachis in two opposite rows in the one plane, e.g. *Wallichia disticha*

divided Separated to the base

drupe A fleshy indehiscent fruit with seed(s) enclosed in a stony endocarp

ebracteate Without bracts

ecology The study of the interaction of plants and animals within their natural environment

effuse Very open and spreading, usually referring to the growth habit

elliptic Oval and flat and narrowed to each end which is rounded

elongate Drawn-out in length

emarginate Having a notch at the apex

embryo Dormant plant contained within a seed

endemic Restricted to a particular country, region or area

endocarp A woody layer surrounding a seed in a fleshy fruit

endosperm Tissue rich in nutrients which surrounds the embryo in seeds

ensiform Sword-shaped, as in the leaflets of many pinnate palms

entire Whole, not toothed, or divided in any way

eophyll The first green leaf produced by a palm seedling

epicarp The outermost layer of a fruit

epigeal A term used for roots which grow above ground, e.g. *Catostigma* spp.

equable A term used to describe the endosperm of a seed when it is smooth and uniform

erect Upright

exocarp The outermost layer of the fruit wall

exotic A plant introduced from overseas

exserted Protruding beyond the surrounding parts as in the terminal inflorescence of *Corypha* and *Metroxylon*

extrafoliar Said of an inflorescence arising from the stem below the leaf bases

falcate Sickle-shaped

farinaceous Containing starch, as in the trunks of palms used for sago: also appearing as if dusted or coated with flour

fasciculate Arranged in clusters as in the flowers of some palms: also refers to the arrangement of leaflets of some pinnate palms, e.g. *Calyptrocalyx* spp.

ferruginous Rusty brown colour

fertile bract Bracts on a palm inflorescence which subtend branches and rhachillae (cf. sterile bracts)

fibrose Containing fibres, as on the leaf based and trunks of many palms and the outer covering of some fruit, e.g. coconut

filament The stalk of the stamen supporting the anther

fimbria The fine, hair-like fringes of a scale

fimbriate Fringed with fine hairs

flabellate Fan-shaped

flabellum A term sometimes applied to the united pair of terminal leaflets of a pinnate leaf, e.g. *Hydriastele, Pinanga*

flaccid Soft, limp, lax

flagellum A whip-like organ that bears curved hooks and is used as an aid to climbing: it is a modified inflorescence and arises in a leaf axil, e.g. *Calamus*

flexuose Having a zig-zag form, as in the rhachillae of some palms

floccose Having tufts of woolly hairs, as on the spathes of *Pritchardia*

floriferous Bearing numerous flowers

foetid Having an offensive odour

forked Divided into equal or nearly equal parts

form A botanical division below a species

free Not joined to any other part

frond Leaf of a palm or fern

fruit The seed-bearing organ

fused Joined or growing together

fusiform Spindle-shaped, swollen in the middle and narrowed to each end, as in the trunk of *Hyophorbe verschaffeltii*

geniculate Bent like a knee

genus A taxonomic group of closely related species

germination The active growth of an embryo resulting in the development of a young plant

glabrous Smooth, hairless

glaucous Covered with a bloom giving a bluish lustre

globose Globular, almost spherical

growth split A vertical crack or split that develops in the trunk of fast-growing palms

gynoecium Collectively the female parts of a flower

habitat The environment in which a plant grows

hapaxanthic A term describing clumping palms, individual stems of which die after flowering, c.f. monocarpic, pleonanthic

haustorium In palms this term refers to the apex of the cotyledon which is embedded in the endosperm and on germination of the seed, enlarges, secretes enzymes and transports soluble materials to the developing seedling

hastula A collar-like extension of the petiole in certain palmate palms, e.g. *Pritchardia* spp. and *Sabal* spp.

head A composite cluster of flowers or fruit, e.g. *Elaeis guineensis, Nypa fruticans*

hermaphrodite Bearing both male and female sex organs in the same flower

hilum The scar left on the seed from its point of attachment with the seed stalk

hirsute Covered with long, spreading, coarse hairs or fibres

hoary Covered with short white hairs or wool giving the surface a greyish appearance

hybrid Progeny resulting from the cross-fertilisation of parents either within the same genus (e.g. *Phoenix* spp.) or between different genera (e.g. *Arecastrum* x *Butia*)

imbricate Overlapping as in the scales covering the fruit of such palms as *Calamus* spp. and *Metroxylon* spp.

imparipinnate Pinnate leaves bearing a single terminal leaflet which extends from the end of the rhachis, e.g. *Phoenix* spp.

incurved Curved inwards

indehiscent Not opening on maturity

indeterminate Growing on without termination as in the trunks of most palms

indigenous Native to a country, region or area but not necessarily restricted there

indumentum A collective term describing the hairs or scales found on the surface of an organ

induplicate Leaflets folded longitudinally with the V opened upwards (i.e. the margins upwards)

inflorescence The flowering structure of a plant

infrafoliar Below the foliage – a term used for palms which bear their inflorescences below the leaves, e.g. *Archontophoenix* spp.

infructescence A term used to describe a fruiting inflorescence

interfoliar Between the leaves – a term used for palms which bear their inflorescences between the leaves in the crown, e.g. *Sabal* spp.

internode The part of a stem between two nodes

involute Rolled inwards

jointed Bearing joints or nodes, used in reference to the cane-like stems of *Chamaedorea* spp.

juvenile The young stage of growth before the plant is capable of flowering

lacerate Irregularly cut or torn into narrow segments

laciniate Cut into narrow segments

lamina The expanded part of a leaf

lanceolate Lance-shaped, tapering to each end especially the apex

lateral Arising at the side of the main axis

lax Open and loose

leaf-base Specialised expanded and sheathing part of the petiole where it joins the trunk

leaf-spine A term sometimes used for the spine-like basal leaflets of *Phoenix* leaves: may also be used to refer to spines on leaves

leaflet Strictly a segment of a bipinnate leaf, as in *Caryota* spp. (also pinnule) but generally also used loosely for pinnae

lepidote Dotted with persistent, small, scurfy, peltate scales

liana A large, woody climber

ligule A growth at the junction of leaf sheath and petiole, in palms often incorrectly referring to the hastula: in seedlings of some palm species it is a tubular structure developed around the cotyledonary sheath

linear Long and narrow with parallel sides

littoral Growing in communities near the sea

loricate Covered with scales, as in the fruits of lepidocaryoid palms, e.g. *Calamus*

mangrove A specialised plant growing in brackish or sea water, e.g. *Nypa fruticans*

marcescent Withering while still attached to the plant

maritime Growing near the sea

mealy Covered with fine, flour-like powder

membranous Thin-textured

meristem The apical growing point which is an area of active cell division

mesocarp The middle layer of a fruit

midrib The main vein that runs the full length of a leaflet or segment

monocarpic A term describing plants which flower once and then die. In palms this term is now applied to solitary trunked species while clumping palms are described as hapaxanthic

monocotyledons The section of Angiosperms to which palms belong and characterised by bearing a single seed leaf

monoecious Bearing separate male and female flowers on the same plant

monopodial A term used to describe a growth habit with unlimited apical growth, e.g. all solitary, polycarpic palms

monotypic A genus with a single species

mucronate With a short, sharp point

nerves The fine veins which traverse the leaf blade

node A point on the stem where leaves or bracts arise

obcordate Ovate with the broadest part above the middle

obtuse Blunt or rounded at the apex

ochrea A swollen or membranous appendage at the opening of the leaf-sheath, found in some climbing palms, e.g. *Korthalsia* spp.: in some species ants inhabit this organ

offset A growth arising from the base of a plant

orbicular Nearly circular

oval Rounded but longer than wide

ovary Part of the gynoecium that encloses the ovules

ovate Egg-shaped in a flat plane

ovoid Egg shaped in a solid plane

ovule The structure within the ovary which becomes the seed after fertilisation

palman That region of a palmate leaf lamina where the segments are fused together at their margins

palmate In palms this refers to a circular or semi-circular leaf with the segments radiating from a common point

palmetum A collection of planted palms

palmito Palm hearts harvested and prepared for eating

palmlet A dwarf growing palm, e.g. *Areca ridleyana, Rhopaloblaste singaporensis*

panicle A much-branched racemose inflorescence

paniculate Arranged in a panicle

paripinnate Compound pinnate leaves lacking a terminal leaflet

parthenocarpic Fruit developing without fertilisation and seed formation, such seedless fruit are known in *Bactris gasipaes*

patent Spreading out

pedicel The stalk of a flower

peduncle The main axis of an inflorescence

pellicle The membrane surrounding a palm seed

peltate Circular with the stalk attached in the middle on the underside: leaves of *Licuala* spp. appear as if peltate but are not strictly so: the scales of some palms are peltate

pericarp The hardened ovary wall that surrounds a seed

petiole The stalk of a leaf

petticoat A collective term for the persistent, hanging, dead leaves of some palms, e.g. species of *Copernicia* and *Washingtonia*

pinna A primary segment of a pinnate leaf (see also segment)

pinnate Once divided with the divisions extending to the midrib, usually referring to leaves

pinnule The segment of a compound leaf divided

more than once (also leaflet)

pistil The female reproductive part of a flower

pistillate Female flowers

pistillode A sterile pistil, often found in male flowers

pleonanthic A term describing palms which flower regularly each year after reaching maturity, c.f. hapaxanthic

plicate Folded or pleated longitudinally, as in the leaves of many fan palms

plumose In palm leaves, referring to pinnae orientated in different directions, e.g. *Arecastrum romanzoffianum*, as opposed to leaflets in one flat plane

pneumatophore Specialised upright roots carrying oxygen to the plant, e.g. *Raphia* spp.

pollination The transference of the pollen from the anther to the stigma of a flower

polycarpic Flowering over many years, as opposed to monocarpic

polygamous Having mixed unisexual and bisexual flowers together

praemorse As though bitten off – often used in reference to the leaflet tips of palms such as species of *Hydriastele* and *Ptychosperma*

proliferous Bearing offshoot and other vegetative propagation structures

prophyll The first (or outer) sheathing bract of a palm inflorescence

pubescent Covered with short, downy hairs

pulvinus A cushion-like growth of inflated cells at the base of leaflets, spines or inflorescence branches

punctations A term to describe the presence of small, rounded scales

puncticulations As above but describing very small scales

pyriform Pear-shaped

radical Arranged in a basal rosette

radicle The undeveloped root of the embryo: also the primary root of a seedling

ramenta Elongated, entire scales attached at one end only

recurved Curved backwards

reduplicate Leaflets folded with the V opened downwards (margins downward)

reflexed Bent backwards and downwards

reins Leaf fibres of palms, in particular referring to those that tie the developing fronds together

repent Creeping – may be used to describe palms with a spreading growth habit

revolute With the margins rolled backwards

rhachilla A small rhachis, the secondary and lesser axes of a compound inflorescence

rhachis The main axis of an entire or compound leaf of a palm extending from the petiole to the end of the lamina

rhizome An underground stem which produces growths at intervals, e.g, species of *Calamus* and other climbing palms

rib The section of the petiole of a costapalmate leaf that extends into the blade, e.g, *Sabal palmetto*

ring-scars Annular rings

root spines Thin, spiny projections on the trunk of

some palms (they may actually be primordial aerial roots)

rostrate With a beak, as in the fruit of some palms

ruminate Folded like a stomach lining – used to describe folds of the seed coat of some palms

saccate Pouch or sac-like, as in the spathes of some palms, e.g. *Astrocaryum mexicanum*

scabrous Rough to the touch

scale A dry, flattened, papery body, found on the young fronds and petioles of some palms

scandent Climbing

scarious Thin, dry and membranous, as in the bracts found on the inflorescence of many palms

scurfy Bearing small, flattened, papery scales

secondary thickening The increase in trunk diameter as the result of cambial growth (absent in palms)

secund With all parts directed to one side

seed A mature ovule, consisting of an embryo, endosperm and protective coat

seedcoat The protective covering of a seed, also called testa

seedling A young plant raised from seed

segment A subdivision or part of an organ, in palms the term is generally used for the divisions of a palmate leaf

sepal A segment of the calyx or outer whorl of the perianth

serrate Toothed

sessile Without a stalk

shag A collective term for the persistent, hanging, dead leaves of some palms, e.g. *Washingtonia* spp.

simple Undivided as in the leaves of *Phoenicophorium*

sinker A term for the long shoot of some palm species which emerges from the seed prior to leaf development

sinus A junction: the joint where the segments of a palmate leaf meet

soboliferous Bearing creeping, rooting stems, although sometimes interpreted as bearing suckers and applied to clumping palms (also caespitose)

solitary Describing a palm with a single stem or trunk

spadix A palm inflorescence

spathe A large sheathing bract which encloses the young inflorescence, often very prominent in palms

spathel A small sheathing bract subtending a secondary or lesser rhachilla

spear-leaf The erect, unopened young leaf of a palm

species A taxonomic group of closely related plants, all possessing a common set of characteristics which sets them apart from another species

spicate Arranged like a spike

spike A simple, unbranched inflorescence with sessile flowers: found in palms such as *Howea belmoreana*, *Linospadix* spp. and *Raphia* spp.

spine A sharp, rigid projection

spinous Modified or resembling a spine

spinule A weak spine

stamen A male part of a flower producing pollen, consisting of an anther and a filament

staminate flowers Male flowers

staminode A sterile stamen

stem clasping Enfolding a stem, as in the leaf sheath

of palms

sterile bracts Bracts on the palm inflorescence between the prophyll and the first branch (c.f. fertile bracts)

stigma The expanded area of the style that is receptive to the pollen

stipitate Stalked

stolon A basal stem growing just below the ground surface and rooting at intervals

stoloniferous Spreading by stolons

strain An improved selection within a variety: also cultivar

stratification The technique of burying seed in moist, coarse sand to expose it to periods of low temperature or to soften the seed coat

striate Marked with narrow lines

style Part of the gynoecium connecting the stigma with the ovary

subspecies A taxonomic subgroup within a species used to differentiate geographically isolated variants

subulate Narrow and drawn out to a fine point

succulent Fleshy or juicy

sucker A shoot arising from the roots or trunk below ground level

sulcate Grooved or furrowed

sympodial Used to describe a growth habit that branches from the base e.g. *Calamus* spp, *Chamaedorea microspadix*

taxon A term used to describe any taxonomic group e.g. genus, species

taxonomy The classification of plants or animals

ternate Divided or arranged in threes

terminal The apex or end

terete Slender and cylindrical

testa The outer covering of the seed, the seedcoat

tomentose Densely covered with short, matted soft hairs

tortuose Twisted, with irregular bending, as in the rhachillae of some palm inflorescences

transpiration The loss of water vapour to the atmosphere through openings in the leaves

triad A group of three, in some palms the flowers are arranged in triads

tribe A taxonomic group of related genera within a family or subfamily

trichomes A term used to describe outgrowths of the epidermis such as scales or hairs

truncate Ending abruptly, as if cut off

trunkless Without a trunk, in palms apparently trunkless species usually have a subterranean trunk

tuberculate With knobby or warty projections, as on the fruit of *Pelagodoxa*

tuberous Swollen and fleshy

tufted Growing in small, erect clumps

turgid Swollen or bloated

unarmed Smooth, without spines, hooks or thorns

unisexual Of one sex only

united Joined together, wholly or partially

variety A taxonomic subgroup within a species used

to differentiate variable populations

vegetative Asexual development or propagation

vein The conducting tissue of leaves

venation The pattern formed by veins

ventricose Swollen or inflated as in the trunks of some palms, e.g. *Hyophorbe verschaffeltii*

verrucose Rough and warty

verticillate Arranged in whorls as in the spines on the stems of some *Calamus* species

viable Alive and able to germinate

viviparous Germinating while still attached to the parent plant, e.g. seeds of *Metroxylon upolense*

xerophitic Adapted to growing in dry conditions

Index for Common Names

Figures in bold indicate illustration page numbers including Aboriginal Names for Australia Palms

Index for Botanical Names

Figures in bold indicate illustration page numbers

PHOTOGRAPHIC CREDITS

All photographs in this book were taken by David Jones and Bruce Gray except for the following:

J.H. Willis	Pages 101, 128, 137
A.K. Irvine	Pages 112 (right), 131 (left), 132, 139, 140, 141 (left), 152, 153
Trevor Blake	Pages 117 (bottom), 119, 141 (right)
Clyde Dunlop	Pages 120, 133
Dennis Hundscheidt	Pages 145 (right), 158, 188, 190 (bottom), 195, 200 (left and centre), 204 (right), 205, 214, 217, 223, 226, 227, 238, 251 (bottom)
Chris Goudey	Pages 151, 164, 204 (left), 207 (left), 230, 249 (bottom).

Ivy Loves to Give

FREYA BLACKWOOD

LITTLE HARE
www.littleharebooks.com

Ivy loves to give.

Sometimes her presents
are the wrong size,

don't sit properly,

taste funny,

or feel strange.

But other times,
her presents feel fine,

taste delicious,

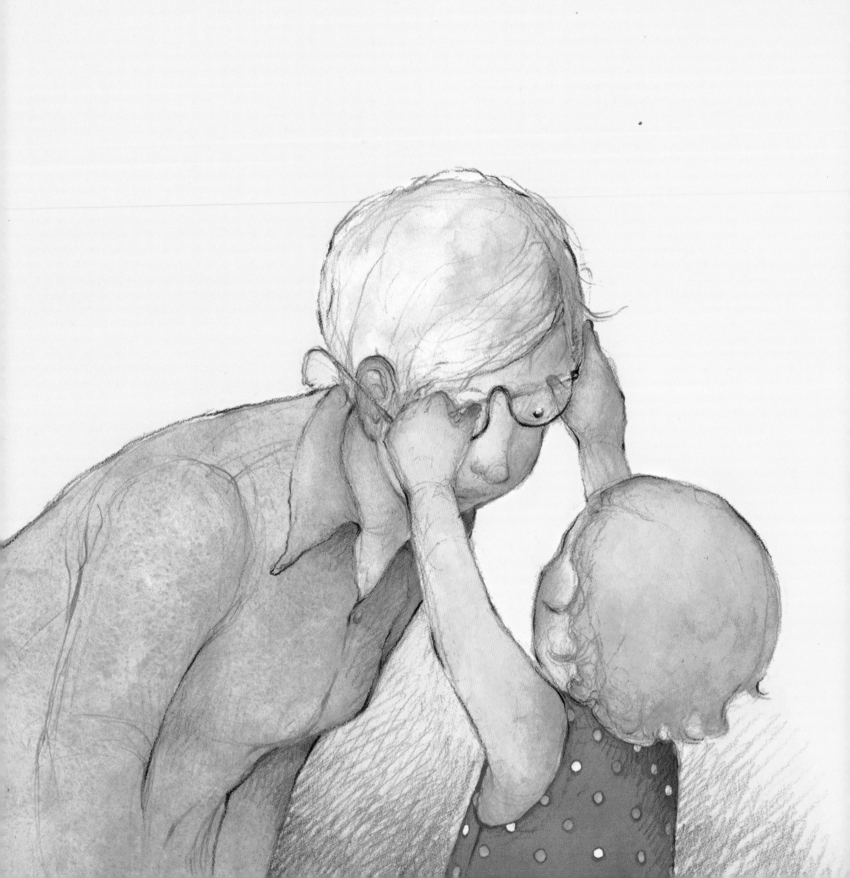

sit perfectly,

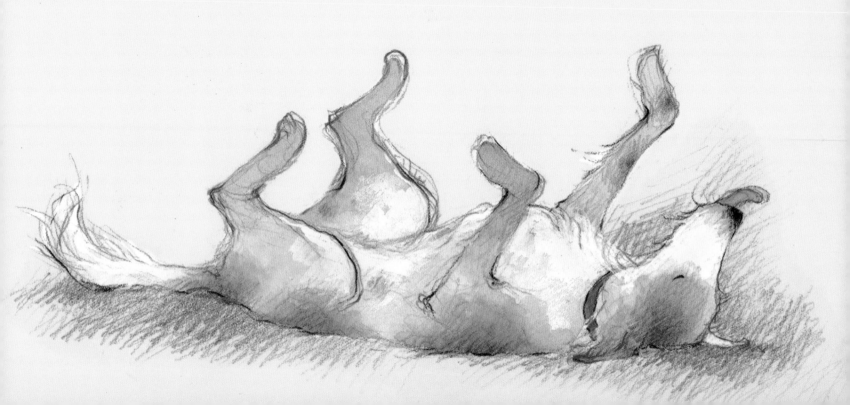

and are exactly the right size.

Ivy loves to give,

but sometimes she
would rather keep.

So when someone gives to Ivy,
Ivy gives the best gift of all.

for Baba

Little Hare Books
8/21 Mary Street, Surry Hills
NSW 2010 AUSTRALIA

www.littleharebooks.com

Copyright © Freya Blackwood 2009

First published 2009

National Library of Australia
Cataloguing-in-Publication entry

Blackwood, Freya.
Ivy loves to give / Freya Blackwood.
9781921541377 (hbk.)
For pre-school children.
Generosity--Juvenile fiction.
A823.4

Designed by Vida and Luke Kelly
Produced by Pica Digital
Printed in China through Phoenix Offset

5 4 3 2 1